NOTHING LIKE A
DAME

EDDIE SHAPIRO

NOTHING LIKE A
DAME

CONVERSATIONS WITH THE GREAT
WOMEN OF MUSICAL THEATER

OXFORD
UNIVERSITY PRESS

OXFORD
UNIVERSITY PRESS

Oxford University Press is a department of the University of Oxford.
It furthers the University's objective of excellence in research,
scholarship, and education by publishing worldwide.

Oxford   New York
Auckland   Cape Town   Dar es Salaam   Hong Kong   Karachi
Kuala Lumpur   Madrid   Melbourne   Mexico City   Nairobi
New Delhi   Shanghai   Taipei   Toronto

With offices in
Argentina   Austria   Brazil   Chile   Czech Republic   France   Greece
Guatemala   Hungary   Italy   Japan   Poland   Portugal   Singapore
South Korea   Switzerland   Thailand   Turkey   Ukraine   Vietnam

Oxford is a registered trade mark of Oxford University Press
in the UK and certain other countries.

Published in the United States of America by
Oxford University Press
198 Madison Avenue, New York, NY 10016

Library of Congress Cataloging-in-Publication Data
Shapiro, Eddie, 1969–
Nothing like a dame: conversations with the great women
of musical theater /Eddie Shapiro.
pages   cm
Includes index.
ISBN 978-0-19-994120-9 (alk. paper); 978-0-19-023119-4 (pbk.)
1. Women singers—Interviews. 2. Actresses—Interviews.
3. Musical theater. I. Title.
ML400.S48   2013
782.1′409252—dc23   2013011267

This book is dedicated to Gertrude, Ethel, Mary, Gwen, Pearl, Dolores, and all the spiritual ancestors of the women in these pages, and to all of the great women of the theater who are still to come.

CONTENTS

FOREWORD

MUSIC HAS BEEN A PART of my life from as far back as I can remember—I grew up listening to jazz and the crooners, but it was *West Side Story* that really thrilled me and was my inspiration for a career in musical theater.

The history of musical theater is full of incredible, indelible female roles. Mama Rose, Mrs. Lovett, Mrs. Anna, Sally Bowles, Charity Hope Valentine, Mame Dennis, Dolly Levi, Velma Kelly, Norma Desmond, Elphaba, Cassie, Reno Sweeney, Nellie Forbush, Millie Dillmount, Marian the librarian, Effie White, Ruth Sherwood, Lorelei Lee, and luckily for me personally, Eva Peron, Grizabella, and Florence Vassey, to name a few.

Every one of these amazing characters has been played (and in many cases, created) by at least one of the incredible women in this book, who share their stories in the pages that follow.

I am so proud that, like them, I have had the opportunity to devote a career to the craft of musicals. I know what these women have gone through to create the magic that they did.

My hat and my tap shoes (Yes, I tap!) are off to each and every one of them.

I hope you enjoy their humor, their passion, and their "memories"—a true insight into this "fine, fine life!" And then come see us in a theater and keep this unique art form alive forever!

INTRODUCTION

I WAS LUCKY ENOUGH to grow up in New York City, with parents who took me to the theater. I was obsessed, especially with the dames. My eleventh birthday was spent seeing Ethel Merman in concert. Once I was introduced to standing room (by my first grade teacher) and was old enough to see over the railing at the back of the theater, I went by myself. I saw everything, and I loved it all. Even the stuff I hated, I loved.

But viewing the shows themselves was never enough. I would memorize cast albums and pore over the liner notes. I would devour books and everything I could that gave me more insight into these magical worlds that would open up to me nightly at 8:00 and on Wednesdays and Saturdays at 2:00. There were so many stories.

As I got older, I would go to cabaret performances of some of Broadway's leading ladies. They would talk about Broadway's Golden Age and their own personal recollections of Rodgers and Hammerstein, Leonard Bernstein, Comden and Green, Jule Styne. I'd listen, enraptured, always wanting more, more, more! And I was always aware, too, that these women were getting older and that these stories wouldn't be with us forever.

I decided I wanted to capture them. And an idea was born.

As that idea evolved I had a few goals. One was that I wanted each of the conversations with Broadway's iconic women to be career encompassing. I had read my share of articles on these women and frequently I'd feel unsatisfied. I wanted these chapters to be bigger than anything I'd read on the subjects, except perhaps books they themselves had written. And in the few cases where they had already written their own stories, I saw an opportunity to ask clarifying questions.

Given the realities of publishing, I knew that big, long chapters would mean a short list of women. As much as I wanted to meet with everyone I could, I had to come up with pretty strict, albeit subjective, criteria for whom to include.

The women in this book all had to have devoted the majority of their careers to the theater: no one who started in theater but moved on (Streisand), no stars from other media who visit Broadway (Minnelli), and no one-hit wonders (Holiday). Each of the women had to have at least one Tony Award and one other nomination or major award.

Then I had to attempt to differentiate between the "stars," those women whose names are likely to be above the title in their next show, and the group of very fine, very wonderful, working actors who might not yet have quite the same level of name recognition, box office command, or robust resumé, much as I may love them.

And finally (and here's where it gets the most subjective), as artists, they had to be unique. Oh, and one other thing: they had to say "yes."

The twenty-two women in this work not only said "yes" but they were also incredibly generous with their time and their stories. We'd talk until we were done. Sometimes that took a few hours, sometimes it took nine or ten. They patiently indulged me until I was satisfied . . . or out of batteries.

I hope that as you read, you'll feel like a fly on the wall, experiencing these chats as they unfolded (which, be warned, wasn't always in logical sequence).

But the goal of this book was not just to celebrate the subjects nor to merely accumulate the twenty-two conversations; it was to put them together, creating a tapestry, an oral history of the last sixty years of the American musical theater and what it means to be a woman in that world. The subjects are each others' role models, mentors, descendants, and co-stars. They are as informed and inspired by each other as we are by them. They are a group whose ephemeral product is the stuff of legend. And they are working women whose job happens to be creating magic.

NOTHING LIKE A DAME

ELAINE STRITCH

November and December 2008

"WHAT'S THIS ALL ABOUT, AGAIN?!" came Elaine Stritch's unmistakable rattle of a voice, part Rosalind Russell, part dry martini, part cheese grater, on the other end of the phone. I was taken aback. After all, we had spoken the day before and the day before that. On the first call, she had told me that she was swamped but really wanted to get this interview out of the way. "Well," I had offered, "there's no great rush. I would rather you do this when you feel relaxed than when you are cramming it in." "Don't you worry about my disposition," came the steely reply. "I'll worry about my disposition." She hated me, I thought, until the second call, during which she called me "dear" and apologized twice for her schedule. So now, on call number three, when it seemed we were back at square one, I didn't know what to say. "Well, it's the interview for my book, *Nothing Like a Dame*," I explained. "You asked me to call today." "And when did you want to do this," came the deliberate reply. "Well, you asked me about today." "To*day*? I can't possibly do today." "That's fine. It's just that when you called me on Friday, you said you wanted to get it done this weekend." "I don't recall saying that to anyone. Gee, Ed, I hate to leave you hanging like this. How about Thanksgiving?" "Thanksgiving Day?" "Yeah, before dinner. You could come for tea." "That would be fine." "But I tell you what, give me a call on Wednesday night after 11:00, just to confirm. And I promise I'll remember." And that is how I ended up having tea with irascible, cantankerous, outspoken, and utterly charming Elaine Stritch at The Carlyle Hotel on Thanksgiving Day.

Elaine Stritch was born outside of Detroit in 1925. She came to New York to study under Erwin Piscator at The New School, where her classmates included Marlon Brando and Bea Arthur (with whom she'd compete for a Tony Award sixty years later. And win.). She made her musical debut in *Angel in the Wings*, singing the absurd "Bongo, Bongo, Bongo (I Don't Want to Leave the Congo)" before her long run as Ethel Merman's understudy in *Call Me Madam*. Since Merman never missed a performance, Stritch never went on, and felt safe simultaneously taking a one-scene part in the hit 1952 revival of *Pal Joey* a block away. "I was close if they needed me," she says, "which they never did." When *Call Me Madam* went out on national tour, though, Stritch, all of twenty-five, was leading the company. *Goldilocks* followed, before Noel Coward wrote the role of Mimi Paragon in *Sail Away* just for Stritch. Mimi, like her inspiration, knew her way around an arched eyebrow and a sarcastic bon mot. Not surprisingly, Stritch was a sensation. It nonetheless took almost a decade for her next Broadway musical, but this one was legendary.

As Joanne in Stephen Sondheim and George Furth's *Company*, Stritch bellowed the searing eleven o'clock number, "The Ladies Who Lunch." To this day, it is considered one of the

In *Goldilocks*, the performance about which Noel Coward remarked, "Any leading lady who doesn't do a double-take when a nine-foot bear asks her to dance is my kind of actress." (Photofest)

all-time greatest interpretations of any musical theater song. Hal Prince's acclaimed 1994 revival of *Show Boat* was another triumph but the best was still to come. In 2001, under the direction of George C. Wolfe, Stritch premiered *Elaine Stritch at Liberty*, an autobiographical one-woman show in which Stritch gossiped, confessed, kvetched, cajoled, and reveled in a musical tour of her life and career. For *At Liberty*, she finally took home a Tony Award, before playing the show for years in New York, London, and on tour. In 2010, she successfully, if improbably, succeeded Angela Lansbury in *A Little Night Music*.

Of all the women in this book, she was the only one I was scared to meet. The phone calls didn't assuage my fears, nor did the Carlyle's waiter who, upon hearing I was there to meet

Stritch laughingly said, "Good luck!" But I needn't have worried. Stritch isn't mean, she's just blunt to a degree that's so unusual it's occasionally unnerving. As Bebe Neuwirth says of her, "She doesn't know how to lie, on or offstage." And she doesn't suffer fools well. But once she trusts, she's delightful. And warm enough to have extended an invitation to Thanksgiving dinner.

A couple of months before she passed in 2014, I heard from a mutual friend that Elaine loved her chapter in this book. I probably shouldn't be invested in that, but I am, and hearing it was awfully gratifying.

In your show, *Elaine Stritch: At Liberty*, you said that you didn't know why you wanted to be an actress. But you did choose to pursue acting over anything else. What gave you the instinct that you'd be any good?

I don't think it's an instinct, I don't think that's the right word. I don't have an answer to that today.

Elaine Stritch

Angel in the Wings, Broadway, 1947
Call Me Madam, Broadway, 1950
Pal Joey, Broadway, 1952
Call Me Madam, National Tour, 1952
On Your Toes, Broadway, 1954
Goldilocks, Broadway, 1958
Sail Away, Broadway and West End, 1961
The King and I, National Tour, 1965
Wonderful Town, City Center, 1967
Mame, National Tour, 1967
Company, Broadway and West End, 1970
Follies in Concert, Lincoln Center, 1985
Show Boat, Broadway, 1994
Elaine Stritch at Liberty, off-Broadway, Broadway, National Tour and West End 2001 (Tony Award)
The Full Monty, Milburn, NJ, 2009
A Little Night Music, Broadway, 2010

Calling?

Those are all two-dollar words. I don't believe in all of that, "calling" and "career." I wasn't thinking about . . . I think if I was really dead-honest, I was . . . everybody else was going away to college and I didn't want to. I don't know the reason why that was, either. I thought I'd rather learn by experience all of the subjects they were going to teach me in college. That's a dumb statement. But I didn't want to go to college. I wanted to be an actress but I still can't tell you why. I think I'm . . . I don't think I'm really a happy camper inside and I think it's an escape for me. I've gotten to like myself a lot better as the years go by, but I'm still not hung up on myself.

You have actually said that it's really hard for you to play yourself. During *Elaine Stritch: At Liberty*, you said that a vacation would be putting on a costume and playing someone else.

At the time I was doing *Elaine Stritch: At Liberty* I wasn't thinking about philosophizing my position and what I would or wouldn't like to do. This was a tremendously courageous thing for me to do, but it was good. Just like I read a good play—I read a Tennessee Williams play, an Edward Albee play—I read what I wrote and what John Lahr wrote and I liked it. I thought, "This is a good part for me." That sounds like a joke but it was a good part for me to play. It was the first time I had an opportunity to put myself on the stage. Because I am a really true-blue actress. When I take on a part I play the part. Of course I bring Elaine Stritch to it, that's why they hire me. But I am interpreting another, I am inside somebody else's skin. So, you know, acting is . . . I don't know what it is. I don't think it's given enough credit in the arts. I think it's a real art form, acting. I don't know. I don't think a lot of people have the talent—my kind of talent—to be an actress. But there are a lot of good ones out there. I am always so thrilled when I go to the theater and see a performance. I just think that's the best. There was a marvelous expression in the *Times* the other day in the review of *Australia*. They talked about all of the epic qualities of the movie but they said a very simple thing about Nicole Kidman, who I think is a very good actress. They said: "she gave a performance." And I thought, "what a wonderful notice." I hope she appreciates it.

I want to go back to your early days, you came to New York for whatever reason you . . .
For whatever reason. Look, it's not as complicated as all that. I was not going steady with someone. My beau had already gone to New York to become an actor. He was a writer named James Lee. He wrote [the play] *Career* and he also wrote for television; he was one of the writers on *Roots*. So what was I gonna do? I didn't want to go to college. I wasn't in love. I mean, I loved Jimmy but I wasn't interested in getting married. I wish it would stop there. I wanted to become an actress. Why? I don't know. I think you deal with that better than I deal with it. I'd like to be able to answer it better. But I do think that I wasn't too hung up on myself and I wanted to be everybody else I could think of.

The reason I used the word "instinct" is because I think sometimes people have a desire or gut feeling that isn't calculated, but they know that something speaks to them.
Something stirring.

Yeah.
I see what you mean. Yes. And I also wanted out of Michigan. I love Michigan but I didn't want to spend all my life there, I wanted to see the world. Another answer I've given to the question, "why did you want to become an actress" is that I wanted higher ceilings. It's as good an answer as any. I once played a game at a party and we all had to give the best answer for "why did you become an actor." Mine was, "to get a good table at 21." Ho ho ho. I think "higher ceilings" would have won at that party but I hadn't thought of that yet. [The actor] Marti Stevens gave the best answer ever. Actually, the question was, "why did you go on the stage" and Marti Stevens said, "to get out of the audience." That's a great answer.

Once you were in New York and at The New School, how did you get work and audition?
I was going to school.

Yes, but you were cast in *Loco* pretty quickly after school. Did that seem like a fluke to you or were your peers also getting work easily? Did it feel like a struggle?
I don't know.

Did you have to work for money?
I waited tables at The New School, but I did it not because I needed the money; I did it for the experience.

The human experience?
Yeah.

Did it work?
Yeah. And I did it to show off to Marlon Brando.

Did that work?
Yeah. I was showing that I wasn't just this rich girl from Michigan. I could be a waitress, too. You see there's a little Joan Crawford/Mildred Pierce in all of us! It was all of those things. . . . I am very honest about things like that today. Then I wasn't.

In what ways are you honest now that you were not then?

Well, I wish I could have laughed and told Marlon Brando that I was trying to influence him. But you don't do that at seventeen. You wait 'til you're in your eighties 'til you get that kind of honesty. I think I could do a lot of things today that I couldn't do then as far as being straightforward and on the level with people. I figured it out that none of us have anything to hide. There's nothing about me that I couldn't tell everybody in the world. There really isn't. And that's a good way to be. I love the expression "secrets are dangerous." I really think they are. "Don't tell anybody, but . . ." is the most boring line in the world. It really is. If you don't want them to tell anybody, don't tell them!

In saying secrets are dangerous, do you mean that the truth frees you?

Absolutely. And I think what has transpired without your knowing it is that you kind of, at last, dig yourself.

After *Loco* came *Angel in the Wings*. You sang in that one.

Singing to me was fun, it was a party. I had always sung. When I go to parties I get up and sing, so why not? Why not sing?

Yeah but how did you have the confidence to decide that you were ready to sing on Broadway?

I was a little bit nervous about it but I knew I could do it. I knew I could do it all or I wouldn't have been there. But I didn't *know* I didn't say "I can do that." I did it. I went through the process. I guess I had guts.

Do you have specific memories about doing *Angel in the Wings*?

Sure. During my first few shows, until I really began to get serious about it—I was serious about it but I was very much thinking about my popularity, who my boyfriend was at the time, what restaurants I went to—I was thinking about theater bringing me this exciting life, all of that that went along with it. So it made you think to yourself, "I've got to be successful so that I can have all of this." And over the period of years . . . we're now sitting here in 2008 and I have about as much interest in going out to dinner or to openings or to social gatherings . . . I can't take it anymore. So there's a satiation point and you just don't want to do those things any more. But at the time I met a lot of fellas in the theater and they were taking me out and dating me. What could be better? That wouldn't have been happening in Birmingham, Michigan. You'd probably be going out with the son of someone your mother and father knew, you know what I mean? Especially, if you weren't in school. I think sometimes if I didn't have any ambition, what would I have done? I don't know.

But even though you were doing it for the trappings, it sounds like you really committed yourself.

Absolutely, but I didn't realize that yet. I only knew the superficial things in life, you know what I mean? I didn't get to know myself well enough to know that it was a need in me. It was not a choice, I *had* to do this. I had to. You know, this is an interesting way of putting it: I don't know which is right yet. . . . I had the experience of singing the Comden and Green song "I Like Myself" for Alec Baldwin the other night at a Tisch [School of the Arts] celebration. "Can it be, I like myself?/You like me so I like myself./Someone as wonderful as you is/can think I'm wonderful/then quite a gal am I./Feeling so unlike myself/always used to dislike myself/but now your love has got me riding high./You like me so so do I." Now, today, that would be called codependency but in those days . . . I think this song is the other way around; you're told today that you've got to like yourself before anybody else can like you. That's the big hotshot news of the week in psychotherapy. This song is the opposite. It's, "if you give me some encouragement and you tell me that you like me or that you love me then I'll like myself. I'll think I'm hot stuff if he likes me." The jury's still out on that, I think. I don't know what to say about that. I forget my point. What was I talking about? Oh, I know—within my work, let's make the audience the other person. If they like me, then I get pretty hung up on myself. They think I'm good. However, I also like to live by the fact that what the audience thinks of me is none of my business. 'Cause I can't think of what they are going to think or I'll be too frightened for words. You can't wait for an audience to approve of you before you think you're good; you have to think you're good before the first clap. If you walk on that stage like "I own this joint and I'm good and I can do this" they are going to come right along with you. But if you go out terrified you're gonna make 'em uneasy. You gotta really fall in love with yourself if you wanna be in show business.

Those are two competing approaches.

Yeah, they are. I think it's confidence and high self-esteem. When I was in the theater I was having a ball. I drank, I was high half the time. I mean, not drunk, but high. I had a drink before I went onstage, I had a drink before I did everything. Like a cigarette. Same thing. It didn't start to bother me until way late in life. It began to be a problem when I was in my fifties. That's a long time of drinking.

In some of the interviews you granted after you stopped, you said that one of the things that you love about sobriety is that you don't miss anything.

Yeah, I used to drink because I thought that was making me not miss anything. That's not true.

You also said that you don't have any regrets.

It's finished. The past had a reason for happening and it's happened. I learned from it, I suffered through it. It doesn't bother me at all, the past.

Are you conscious of things that you wish you had been more present for?

Yes, my marriage [to John Bay], which was a great marriage but I was still drinking when I was married. But much less than when I was not married. I don't have to explain that. I was with someone I loved and I didn't have to have so many martinis to make an evening work 'cause I had John. I think a lot of people have experienced that when they find Mr. Right, if he is indeed Mr. Right. I think they don't need drugs, alcohol, stuff like that.

As you describe it, you needed the alcohol to feel comfortable. Are you saying that with him, you didn't need it to feel comfortable?

Yes, absolutely.

Back to the early days. You were cast as the understudy to Ethel Merman in *Call Me Madam* **at the age of twenty . . .**

I was twenty, I looked forty, I got the job. That's the line from the play [*Elaine Stritch: At Liberty*].

Were you very sophisticated seeming, even then? Like Eve Arden? She seems to have always been an adult. Nothing girlish about her.

I didn't want that to happen, with all due respect to Eve Arden. I didn't want to be just this comedienne. The wonderful thing about *Call Me Madam* and lots of other shows that I've done

Unexpected casting: with Renato Cibelli in *The King and I*. (Photofest)

was that I had the love interest. That was very exciting to me because it made me feel feminine, the way I should feel. Not always the clown.

At that time did you feel that you had broken through with this job?

It was a way I got to do more material. [When I took *Call Me Madam* out on tour] I went from doing one song in *Pal Joey* to eight songs in *Call Me Madam* and playing the lead. But I don't know how I felt about that then, it's too long ago. I was in the theater and I was doing what was offered to me. I was in a smash hit on Broadway and I thought, "My God, to be a leading lady and travel all over the country, that's another step." Forwards, backwards, I didn't give a shit about which way I was going. It was a new experience. I don't have much patience with things. Do you have any idea how hard it is for me to sit here at age eighty-three and talk about this shit? It is so hard! Do you have any idea how many times I've talked about this?

But you . . .

But *what*?

I am sure it's hard for you to perceive yourself this way, but your stories, hard as they may be to tell, are fascinating.

That's great. I am not talking about that. I am not going to argue that I am not interesting. I am not arguing that, Ed. You didn't listen to what I am saying.

I did.

No you didn't. I am just saying that I am just soo . . . *oh*. (sigh). I have talked about it. When you have lived this long in your profession, it's a real trial to go over your life. But I try to keep it interesting because I keep learning about myself. Every single day I learn more about myself. I don't know how I do but I just do. Because I am aware. I'm fully there and fully aware without any drugs or alcohol, as you said before. I'm 100 percent there. That teaches me something. I wouldn't recognize these lessons if I wasn't sober. And I mean sober in every way, you know? Just sober. Take it easy, not running around chasing a tiger's tail, going out all of the time and meeting new people. My dream is to be home and to have my dinner and watch television. That's what I love.

Some of the questions I am asking about your awareness of your own career trajectory are about whether you were calculating or planning your career or if you . . .

I never calculated or planned anything in my whole life except maybe what kind of lipstick to wear to get a guy. Anything that has to do with my career I never planned or negotiated except for money. That was the only thing I ever negotiated. Lately I do my own deals. No, I didn't think that "this is the way I'll do that, and then I'll take this step." I am not quite sure I know what that question was all about.

I think there are some people who very carefully strategize their careers.

No way. Everything was very spur of the moment. I lived in the "now" years ago, long before it became fashionable to do that, psychotherapy-wise. It's very chic now to live in the "now," you know that. The thing to do. It just happens to be the truth that it is [what worked for me]. It makes everything much easier. I've been doing that my whole life. I don't sit around and think about whether I am going to succeed in something tomorrow. I don't allow myself to do that. I certainly didn't do it before it was even thought about to do it, I just naturally did it. There are a lot of things in acting that you naturally know how to do. It's doin' what comes naturally, to borrow a line from Irving Berlin. That's what it is, it's doin' what comes naturally. Imitations, mimicry, pretending I'm somebody else. . . . And now, certainly, I don't want to watch variety shows on television, I want to watch drama. I want to watch movies and good plays. I wish they would do more of that on television.

What about plays that are not so good? What happens when you choose work that doesn't take off? Sometimes a show can have great pedigree, like with *Goldilocks* or *Sail Away* . . .

Sail Away took off for me. I worked for two and a half years in *Sail Away*. That's taking off. It wasn't *South Pacific*.

I understand. But it still only ran 167 performances in New York. That is far less of a run than it should have had considering how good the material was. And *Goldilocks*, with that pedigree . . .

What pedigree did *Goldilocks* have?

Robert Whitehead [producer], Agnes de Mille [choreographer], the Kerrs [Walter Kerr, writer and director, Jean Kerr, writer].

The Kerrs! That was their first shot at this! Good writers, though. Smart people. But that doesn't necessarily make a good musical. Hemingway never did a musical. I don't think he could have done it. I don't think *Goldilocks* had a pedigree at all. It was Walter and Jean Kerr's first time writing a book for a musical; it was Walter Kerr's first time directing a musical; it was my first time in the lead in a musical on Broadway. Everything bad that could happen to you happened to me in *Goldilocks*. I was crazy about Barry Sullivan [the show's original leading man, replaced in Philadelphia by Don Ameche]. He was going to be just sensational. He was sexy and adorable and had a wonderful voice. Didn't they think Rex Harrison was good in *My Fair Lady*? Are they kidding? Just because he didn't have this great booming voice, what the hell did that have to do with anything? They were wrong to get rid of him. And Agnes de Mille made the whole show . . . she robbed the book and put more dancing in because that's her forte. She was a selfish woman. She told me I was a genius on opening night. This show business is so full of shit that it makes me nervous. When I think of how disheartening this business can be . . . well, any business. But when show business gets bad, it really hurts because it's so personal. It's you up there, physically, every single night.

You went into *Goldilocks* after *Pal Joey* and *Call Me Madam*, having worked with people like George Abbott and Jule Styne . . .

I didn't even notice it! I was so happy that they knew how to do it. And this is something that has taken years and years for me to understand because I'm too hard on myself; I was okay in everything that I did with talented people. My problems only started when the people didn't know what to do and didn't tell me how to do it. I need help. I don't care how talented and creative I am. And I *am*. I've got good ideas and I can admit all of this to myself because—it's that thing, "they like me now so so do I," so I can talk about it. Audiences like me. I have a terrible problem of being . . . I didn't think I did well at the Tisch thing the other night; I went up on my lyrics. It's a killer. When someone is as talented as I am . . . when I go wrong, I go wrong. And it takes me days to get over it. It's so, so insulting to myself, to the audience. At least I tell them when I go up. I don't try to fool them. Maybe I'm wrong to do that, I don't know. But I just wasn't relaxed out there and it's time I got relaxed and stopped worrying so much about whether or not I was going to be accepted, It's just ridiculous to be so hard on yourself. And the discovery I made out of that is that a bad experience is worth nothing if you don't learn something from it. If I go into rehearsal for something and I've got a bad director [I think] it's all my fault. And I should know that it's not all my fault if I did not have someone who I was working with, helping me. It takes two.

When you found yourself working on something like *Goldilocks* with a director who wasn't as experienced, were you aware of the difference from working with people like George Abbott?

I didn't think about it then. You only understand yourself in retrospect. At the time, no. As far as I was concerned, the Kerrs were . . . I didn't know it was Walter Kerr's first directorial thing. He was Walter Kerr! He was the critic from the *Tribune* directing me in a musical. As far as I knew, they could do anything because they were my superiors.

So you were not even fazed when you were told you'd be dancing with a seven-foot bear?

No, that was my inner talent standing by me. That's what Coward saw and that's what got me *Sail Away*. It really breaks my heart to hear you say that *Sail Away* was . . . what did you call it?

A disappointment. And I wanted to know if that was heartbreaking.

It was something that was necessary in my career, I'm sure, because I learned so much from it.

Sail Away was the first time you got to go to London with a show.

Yes! And to show you what I didn't know, I had to be talked into going to London. I didn't think I wanted to go to London. Noel Coward . . . only in retrospect did I realize what a genius I was working with. You don't know that at the time. Maybe some people do but I didn't.

Did you realize that he was a legend?

No I did not. He wasn't a legend then, he was just doing his stuff. You don't know that when you are working with someone. How did I know who that was? When I met him I didn't know who he was. I liked him right away and I loved his talent. I heard his records after that. I didn't know anything about Noel Coward. You don't think "now I have to investigate this play-wright."

During that period, there was a very glamorous life that Noel Coward sort of epitomized. Stars would finish their shows and go to El Morocco and the Stork Club and party all night. You have said that there were days you went to the theater for a matinee straight from the party the night before. How did you function?

You're in your twenties, what's the trick? I had enormous energy, always have had. I might have napped in the dressing room. They had to wake me up sometimes on matinee days. But I didn't do that often. That's very dramatic to say that. I did that a few times, not many times.

That whole scene seems so foreign to me: getting out of costume and putting on new makeup and dress clothes and going out to the kinds of places where Walter Winchell would be writing about high society. I have heard so many actors talk about the rigors of eight shows a week . . .

I didn't know the rigors of eight shows a week because they weren't rigors. I loved doing them. When I was young I hadn't gotten my fill of going out and going to famous places. I loved doing that. Everybody did that, it wasn't just me. Gertie Lawrence, Ethel Merman—she was everyplace—and all of the big people in the theater.

Your next show when you came back from London . . .
Was Who's Afraid of Virginia Woolf?

I was actually going to ask about your next musical, but since you mention that show, I am interested in how you play a drunk onstage when you are drinking.

It's an entirely different thing because I didn't think I drank too much. I was playing somebody who drank too much. And I didn't drink [large] quantities of alcohol. I drank all the time but I wasn't drunk. But I think it hurt my career. But I don't want to make this about alcohol. I am sick of talking about it. It's over, in the past. I don't want to talk about booze any-more; I've lost interest in it.

You did several tours after Virginia Woolf.

I did a lot of musicals on tour and in stock. I did the national company of Mame. Then I played Vera for a while and I liked that part much better than Mame. Much better part. I did that for a year. That was just to be active and make money because I didn't get much of a kick playing Mame. It's a lot of costume changes. It doesn't pay off. It's about the costumes, you know?

Let's talk about *Company*. *Company* was . . . it can be hard to know that you're in the middle of something great when you are in the middle of it . . .

Now you are finally talking! Now you understand why I can't tell you how I felt then. I'll tell you how I knew that I was in something extraordinary: we rehearsed on 18th Street and I lived way uptown. I moved into the Chelsea Hotel for the rehearsal period because I just wanted a plain room with clean sheets every night—no tchotchkes, no pictures of family, I wanted to get someplace all by myself so that I could work. That's being on-the-money. I knew what I was doing. I didn't want to make that trip every day, it's a waste of time. That's unusual behavior. I would say that most of my life is unusual behavior. That's why I have a very good biography in me; I did it all a little bit differently. Sometimes it worries me but . . . no it doesn't. You do what you have to do.

What do you mean it worries you?

Sometimes you think you should have done things more like other people. Anyway, I think that's unusual behavior to move into a hotel a few blocks from where you are rehearsing. But if I talk to someone like Miles Davis, he might have done the same thing.

A certain level of focus?

Yes, indeed. But you don't know that about yourself. You can't talk about yourself at age thirty as being an artist. But on a good day I may refer to myself as being an artist today because I worked that way. I take my work so seriously that it's dangerous.

How do you mean dangerous?

Dangerous, it's dangerous.

You're in danger of what happening?

Getting sick because you are so intent about accomplishing; getting comfortable in a part; not knowing how to interpret a song—it hits me so hard and until I get it right, I am a mess. And then when I get it right, I just fly.

Your personal frustration with work that isn't right is documented in the film about the recording of *Company* . . .

Thank God! I don't have to talk about it so much anymore. That's why I think movies must be a lot of fun for a really good actor. Hard work, but it's so good to have the work recorded and see the process.

***Company*, on paper, looks different from any other musical that preceded it. The book is not structured like any other book and . . .**

They are short stories.

In working on it . . .

Never questioned it for a minute. I had no idea what I was talking about, singing "The Ladies Who Lunch," but I just grew into it. I grew into that song. And I looked like I knew what I was talking about. I think that meant that I did know what I was talking about, but I just couldn't explain how it was hitting me. I just could do it.

Inside you knew it before you knew it?

That's right. Very well said. That's exactly right. You know *Company* was a very cold show and that permeated backstage. Everyone was doing their own thing, it wasn't an ensemble piece. It was very interesting and it had to be that way to be good. I felt very lonely in *Company*. The only friends I had were in the audience. One night Donna [McKechnie] asked me to go to the movies and I cried. I couldn't stop crying. Nobody ever asked me to do anything. She's a good broad. I like Donna. Very talented.

You also worked with Michael Bennett on *Company*.

I loved him, I loved everything about him. I loved his talent. He made me want to go to work in the morning and he made me want to do what he wanted me to do. He was so clever and so talented. Oh my God!

Do you remember how he did that?

Of course I don't. How could I know what went on in his head. What kind of question is that?

You worked with many directors prior to him . . .

You never notice it when it's right. It just gets to be fun for a change and not just work, trying to do what somebody wants you to do when it goes against your grain. I never will have a bad director ever again in my life. That's a really wonderful thing to be able to say to myself. Because if it starts to show that he or she doesn't know what he's talking about, I'm out of there. I wouldn't do it to myself. Ever. If that happens, if a director doesn't know what he's doing . . . mmm, mmm, mmm.

Company was also directed by Hal Prince. Was your experience of him equally good?

I love Hal Prince. He makes me want to be in the business I'm in. Every time he walks in the theater, you want to be better, better, better. He gives you a goal. He's a terrific guy.

You stayed with *Company* for two and a half years. How did the experience change for you over time?

I never got tired of doing it. Everyone was applauding so every night. You don't walk away from that very easily. But I got tired. Not of it, just tired. I'm in a show doing the same thing every night for two and a half years, that's a long time.

And at that point, when you decided you needed the break, you were in London. What made you decide to stay there?

I liked it there and I wanted to stay. And then I got work. I did *Small Craft Warnings*, a Tennessee Williams play on the West End and then I did the series [*Two's Company*]. I was working all the time for twelve years straight.

Why did you come back?

I was married to John and he felt that he wanted to come home. He went to London because he didn't have me and I went to London because I didn't have him. Once we found each other, we both went home. That's the way that works most of the time.

Your next musical after *Company* was *Show Boat* and you were back with Hal Prince again . . .

Show Boat was a wonderful experience. To be in a musical of that stature, with the way it was treated, in a full-blown production . . . so much talent involved. And I loved [producer] Garth Drabinsky.

"And one for Mahler." With Hal Prince, recording the original cast album of *Company*. (Photofest)

To me, Parthy was the heart of that production.

That's good. I'm serious. I think a lot of people could play Parthy and not be noticed. I took it very seriously. Hal was nervous about my playing a small part and I really believe it about there being no small parts. Is it a part worth playing? You don't look at how long you're on-stage. It's all kind of boring. Parthy held the family together and from her point of view, ran the showboat. I was given that wonderful song "Why Do I Love You?" that used to be the ingénue's. Hal gave it to me. It was a good idea, it paid off. I loved *Show Boat*. It was a big epic, like doing *A Farewell to Arms* or *Gone with the Wind*.

***Show Boat* was your first show sober. Was that particularly . . .**

I don't like the way you said that. I had a couple of drinks before I went out onstage, but "your first show sober?" I don't think you're not sober with a drink or two in you. It's an unfor-tunate way of putting that.

I didn't mean . . .

No, I know you didn't.

It was your first show after you had stopped drinking.

I did a lot of things before *Show Boat* where I didn't have the drink or two before I went onstage. I did a play by Pete Feibleman, who was the lover that lived with [Lillian] Hellman, *Cakewalk*, up at A.R.T. That is a tough play. It wasn't a good play but it was a wonderful part, to play Hellman. So I did a lot of things before *Show Boat*. I stopped drinking in '87 when I was on the Woody Allen movie, *September*. *Show Boat* was not 'til '93. I can't tell you what I did but I'd love you to look it up and tell me what I did do. [In addition to *Cakewalk*, Stritch did a great deal of television and film work including the series *The Ellen Burstyn Show*; *Cadillac Man*; *Cocoon: The Return*; several episodes of *The Cosby Show*; and her Emmy-winning turn on *Law & Order*.] Whatever I did between then and *Show Boat* I did when I was in AA.

What was it like for you going onstage without alcohol?

That took time but it finally worked out. I wasn't as good as I used to be without the booze, so it took a lot of guts to stay with it. Naturally I wasn't as free. Then it goes full circle and you get better.

When you were doing *Elaine Stritch: At Liberty*, you had to be completely free. How did you ultimately get to that place?

I have no idea. I can't put into words how I do it, you just do. By hard work and rehearsal until you can't see straight anymore. I believe in so much rehearsal it hurts. Discipline and taking care of yourself and working hard and rehearsing hard and having good people around you. I had a wonderful director, George C. Wolfe.

All of that is true for how you get any great performance. I was asking specifically about *Elaine Stritch: At Liberty*, in which you revealed so much personal information that you had to be especially free. How did you manage to get to that level of freedom without the alcohol to help you?

It just took courage. I knew I could do it somewhere, I knew I could do it. The first time I ever went out on the stage without a drink I thought I was gonna die. And I did *not* stop the show, incidentally, with a number that usually does, "The Ladies Who Lunch." It was very polite applause, but not whop-oh. That shows you a lesson; that's how free and easy you have to be onstage to really be good. But you can get that freedom without the help of anything if you stay with it long enough. And if you can't, go back to the drinking. You can't get put in jail for having two drinks before you go out onstage.

No, but as you say, you end up missing pieces along the way.

Oh, absolutely. It's a very difficult subject to talk about.

On the subject of *At Liberty*, what made you decide to do it? What was the impetus.

People were always telling me I ought to do a show. Because I was such an exceptionally good storyteller and a funny gal. Very funny. I made people laugh all the time. It sorta hit me, too, "Why don't you get money for this?" Because I would always end up having the floor at every party I went to. And then you're not very popular with other women because you're getting all the attention. It's not all good stuff. But anyway, I had so many people saying "You ought to do it, you ought to do it!" People used to say, "You have a club act, don't you?" And I'd say, "What night do you have in mind?" Because I didn't know what they were talking about. I never thought of doing that for money. The only thing I ever thought of—and then I was surprised they paid me—was doing a play. Because I knew that you needed everybody else— other characters, director, producer, a theater. That was really organized stuff. But this business of doing a club act—to me a club act was going to a party. You know what I'm saying? But then a director named John Schreiber asked me to do an evening dedicated to Judy Garland at Carnegie Hall. There were going to be a lot of people on the bill. I, at first, didn't want to sing any of the Judy Garland songs. How dare anybody, you know? But I wanted to do the show. So I had a wonderful arrangement written combining "If Love Were All" and "But Not for Me" [later incorporated into *Elaine Stritch: At Liberty*]. Before I could get off the stage I was caught up with talking about Judy. So I told three or four stories about her. The audience went wild. These delicious stories about Garland that were really funny because Judy Garland was a genuinely funny woman. It was a huge hit. So John Schreiber said, "I will give you expenses and get you a co-writer if you start writing right away." And he got me John Lahr. That's what made it start.

I need a Judy Garland story.
I'd have to look 'em up, Honey.

For people like me, it's like sitting at my grandmother's lap and listening to family legend.
I know, I know. Judy Garland, when she came to the opening night party of *Sail Away*, I made up my mind not to drink at all at that party. There were a lot of famous people there. Before I knew it I saw Judy leaving the Noel Coward suite, and she was going home. I thought, "My God, I haven't talked to her, she hasn't told me how she liked the show, and I really want to hear what she thought more than anyone." They had those see-through elevators at the Savoy Hotel. I ran out to the hall and she was just on the elevator and it was starting to disappear. And before her head got out of view from me, she went, "Elaine, about your fucking timing . . ." and then she disappeared. It was absolutely brilliant. She knew what she was doing! Her timing was divine! And music to my ears, of course.

Do you have any stories about working with George Abbott on *Call Me Madam*?
Oh, he was a marvelous director, a wonderful man and an extraordinary human being. I loved him. He did one great thing once with me. When I came down to get notes before opening night, I had a scotch and soda in a coffee mug. Of course I was making it very believable. 'Cause while he was giving the notes I was blowing on the coffee. I was blowing on the scotch. And all of sudden George Abbott said to me, "Can I have a taste of that Elaine? Is that coffee?" And my voice went up two octaves and I said, "Yes." And he said, "Could I have a taste?" And I said, "Sure." I'll tell you what a great guy he was. He took the coffee mug from me and he blew on it and then he took a sip. And then he handed it back to me and said, "Man that's good coffee."

Do you have Richard Rodgers stories?
Oh, I loved him. But he didn't like me. He was an alcoholic, you know, and alcoholics resent other alcoholics. He paid me a great compliment once, though. He said, "I would give her the lead in a show but I just don't think she could handle it. Because when she does a number, it is so good that I never think she can do it again." It's a great compliment but it isn't very conducive to working.

It is a back-handed compliment.
Well he was a back-handed kind of fellow. He is a hard person to talk about.

Did you think it was personal?
Oh no, he liked me very much. But I made him nervous because I drank. That would make any director or producer—but the funny thing with him was that he drank twice as much as I did.

Did he recognize that?

No, he didn't at all.

Both Abbott and Rodgers knew that you were drinking . . .

It never bothered George Abbott because I didn't drink too much. Well, I probably did drink too much, but I was never drunk on the stage in my life.

Was drinking in the theater more commonplace in general?

Absolutely. Everybody had booze in their dressing room. Nobody does anymore. In London, in the theater you have cocktail parties at intermission. It's a big deal having a little sherry or a little of this or that. But too many people have abused the privilege in this country. All of our great actors were huge drinkers. Tallulah Bankhead, John Barrymore, Bela Lugosi. So many. Lots and lots of people.

The people you mention famously got seriously drunk. That was never you, though.

No, absolutely not. Maybe a couple of times my timing was off because I had three instead of two drinks, but nothing to write home about.

I didn't ask you about the *Follies* concert. Who came up with the idea of slowing down "Broadway Baby?"

Me.

And Sondheim didn't mind?

He didn't say a word.

At *Liberty* opened at The Public; did you have any notion that . . .

Don't ask me that question, Eddie, that's a stupid question.

I don't mean beforehand . . .

Every once in a while during rehearsal, I would get an idea, "this is good, this feels good." And when I feel good it's usually good. So I had inklings about it being a big success. Maybe not to the extent it was.

Do you feel like it changed your standing in the community at all?

Absolutely. My peers reacted to that kind of honesty. And it gets laughs! And it's rare. The rarity of the whole truth and nothing but the truth, it's a kind of shock therapy.

Do you read reviews?

Oh yes, I can't wait. Terrified to read them and thrilled to death when they are good. I haven't gotten a lot of bad reviews; I've gotten a few in my life but nothing that upset me terribly.

There are a lot of actors who . . .

I can't believe that they don't read their reviews.

Do you go to the theater today?

Yeah, I go. But I am not going to see *The Little Mermaid* if that's what you mean. I like Jane Krakowski, I think she's good. And I like Kristin Chenoweth. I'm getting very excited about the opening of *Pal Joey* because my good friend Stockard Channing is in it. The theater is not what it was. It's the fabulous invalid. It's having a tough time because of the economy but it will come back. I worry about Maxwell [her nephew, a twenty-nine-year-old actor who just moved to New York]. Nobody who comes here to get into the theater can get an agent. It takes years. You have to go on those cattle calls. This is a tough racket. It really is a tough racket.

You have said there's no sin greater than boredom.
If someone's boring what could be worse than that? To be with a boring person? But the truth of the matter is, if you think somebody's boring, something's usually the matter with you. You've got a problem.

That reminds me of something else I read that you said: You said that you love people and that you learn a tremendous amount from all people.
Oh God yes. Absolutely.

I think that there are a lot of people out there who don't take the time to really notice other people.
Oh, I do too. They think that they can only learn from important people or big successes. Not true. It's like, you learn from failure as well as success. Probably more from failure. As far as people are concerned, all people are interesting to me. But occasionally . . . maybe it's a bad word to use, "boring." I had dinner last night with a couple of people and I thought I was gonna kill myself in the ladies room. I've never been that bored, I don't think, my whole life. I would find myself looking at them and maybe saying [under her breath], "Oh jeez, I gotta go home." I'd be *saying* it! I was playing a game with myself. Anything to keep the evening going. Wow, it was awful. Nice people.

Nice isn't enough.
No, it isn't.

You said before that going home to your TV is your fantasy.
Yeah. And diabetes is great because I can say, "My blood sugar is off, I have to go."

How late did it get before you played that card?
I played it at the beginning. I said I'd have to go in an hour. I stayed an hour and a half so I was a champion, I can't tell you. Very nice people.

Didn't you tend bar at Elaine's at one time?
Oh yeah. When I got out of *Time of the Barracuda*, which is an awful play I did with Laurence Harvey in California. I was sitting in there and Elaine came over. We got to talkin', having a few beers, and I asked if there was an opening. I was very depressed after *Time of the Barracuda*. It was a bad experience and it made me just want to do something like waitressing at The New School. I wanted to . . .

Do something different?
That's not different. There was nothing different about mixing drinks for me. But just doing something simple, that wasn't complicated with all of the assholes in show business which you sometimes get involved with. [They] are killers as far as your talent is concerned, your abilities. It almost did me in, that experience in that play. That's why I got a job at Elaine's

and could mix dry martinis. And it worked for me because I drank very little. I didn't have time. Bartending is a very difficult job. Your timing has to be brilliant.

Why was *Time of the Barracuda* so bad?
It was not a good play, it was working with a person who was not really—what was he not really?—mature. And he was a really good actor. But he wasn't a grown-up actor who could look after me. I was kind of a baby then. I am still in a way. If I am gonna play a lead opposite a guy, I need that guy to take care of me. This is codependency, too, but I wasn't old enough to look after myself. All I brought to the table was talent. Big talent. Therefore I wiped the stage up with him. And that's not a good place to be when you're . . .

When you are a romantic lead?
Yeah. I was so frightened that when I got my first review in San Francisco it was one of the scariest reviews I have ever gotten in my life. I was afraid to go to rehearsal. Because the reviewer said, "Elaine Stritch was directed with her back to the audience practically the entire evening. However, this reviewer would rather look at Elaine Stritch's back than Laurence Harvey's front."

Wow!
I know. And don't think it didn't take its toll. But the play closed anyway. And Kennedy was assassinated the following week. The worst.

Is there a show that was the bottom of the bottom for you? The very worst?
I think *Time of the Barracuda* was it. I have had funny, funny experiences with bad plays. I mean, oh my God. They can be so bad that they're funny. Listen, If you don't think I have a book in me you're crazy.

I thought *Elaine Stritch: At Liberty* was the equivalent of your book but I guess there's so much more.
Of course there is. That's a teaspoon full!

If performing hadn't worked out for you, do you have any notion of what you might have been doing?
Supposition is really boring but I'll give it a shot: Stay home!!

Is there anyone you've never worked with who you wish you had?
If I am supposed to, it'll happen. I reiterate: supposition to me is a long yawn.

I think the word is "boring."
[Laughs] OK, whatever you think is fair.

CAROL CHANNING

June 2008; January 2009

CAROL CHANNING'S RANCHO MIRAGE HOME features an awe-inspiring gallery of her life in the theater. Dozens and dozens of framed photos of Channing with the likes of Sophie Tucker, Ethel Waters, Walt Disney, Marlene Dietrich, John Gielgud, Maurice Chevalier, Lucille Ball, Louis Armstrong, Andy Warhol, Queen Elizabeth, and eight presidents share wall space with some of the many Hirschfeld caricatures the artist did throughout her career. Sitting under one such Hirschfeld, looking no less animated, is the woman herself in a Ralph Lauren jogging suit. Channing is an eager conversationalist, but she's the first to admit that she regularly wanders off track. In talking to her I felt a bit like a child happily trying to catch bubbles; catch a bubble and it instantly pops, leaving a spattering of bubble—related to the bubble, but not quite the thing you tried to catch. So it went.

As we chat, Harry Kullijian, Channing's high school sweetheart, to whom she was married in 2003 after an almost seventy-year estrangement, pops in and out. The two are clearly very much in love. Together they formed a foundation to restore arts education to the public school system. It is their primary focus.

Carol Channing was born in Seattle in 1921 to parents of unexpected heritage. Her mother told an adult Carol that contrary to what her father's birth certificate said, he had actually been born to a white father and black mother. She was therefore a quarter African American, a fact Channing kept private until recently. Her father was a lawyer and a noted Christian Science lecturer who toured the country. Channing idolized him and credits him with her talent for vocal projection. After a short stint at Bennington College, Channing moved to New York and made her Broadway debut as an understudy in Cole Porter's *Let's Face It*, from which she was fired. The 1948 revue *Lend an Ear* marked the first time Channing was featured on Broadway and it remains, to this day, her favorite show. It also got the attention of author Anita Loos, who cast Channing in *Gentlemen Prefer Blondes*, the star-making vehicle in which she introduced "Diamonds Are a Girl's Best Friend" to the world. Given the magnitude of her success in *Blondes* it's surprising that show after show didn't follow. Though Channing was never far from the public eye, performing in nightclubs and on television, she did only three Broadway musicals over the next fifteen years: *Wonderful Town* in which she replaced Rosalind Russell; *Show Girl*, an expanded version of her club act; and the flop, *The Vamp*. But then in 1964, she opened, historically, triumphantly, emphatically, in *Hello, Dolly!* in the role that she'd continue to play in productions all over the world for more than 5,000 performances during the next thirty years. In later years there were plays, tours, and even an Oscar nomination for *Thoroughly Modern Millie*, but Channing was and always will be remembered for Dolly Gallagher Levi.

As the dumb-like-a-fox Lorelei Lee in *Gentlemen Prefer Blondes*. (Photofest)

In 2011, I interviewed the ninety-year-old Channing in front of an audience, at the annual Gay Days at Disneyland. She was sharp, funny, dynamic, and delighted to be there. She had recently fallen, though, and was feeling a little physically fragile. But there she was with Kullijian (who passed away less than three months later), adoring her fans, tirelessly posing for pictures, and, the following day, riding rides at Disneyland. As we boarded the steam train while singing "Put on Your Sunday Clothes," I was amazed by her drive, realizing that if there is an ounce of juice to squeeze from life, you can count on Carol Channing to be squeezing it.

You are spending the majority of your time working, through your foundation, to get the arts put back into California's public school system as part of the required curriculum. How did you get involved in that?

Oh, we got involved when I was twelve, and he [Kullijian] was thirteen. It was right in the middle of the Depression but we got arts in school anyway. There was no money anywhere. He had a small band and I was the vocalist. He booked us for political rallies. I never got off of the school auditorium stage. He was the most beautiful thing I ever did see. He looked biblical. Like Moses on Mount Sinai, eating a fig. He had that wonderful Middle Eastern—oh gosh, he's Armenian. Well anyway, my mother was crazy about him, too. He came from an Armenian-speaking family. They didn't speak English, yet. I was an only child. I was the last of the Channings. But now I have this gorgeous Armenian family. You look a little Armenian.

> **Carol Channing**
>
> *Lend an Ear*, Broadway, 1948
> *Gentlemen Prefer Blondes*, Broadway, 1949
> *Wonderful Town*, Broadway and National Tour, 1953
> *The Vamp*, Broadway, 1955
> *Show Girl*, Broadway, 1961
> *Hello, Dolly!* Broadway and National Tour, 1964 (Tony Award)
> *Lorelei*, Broadway, 1974
> *Hello, Dolly!* Broadway and National Tour, 1978
> *Sugar Babies*, National Tour, 1980
> *Jerry's Girls*, National Tour, 1985
> *Legends*, National Tour, 1986
> *Hello, Dolly!* Broadway and National Tour, 1995

I'm Jewish.

Ah. It's the holy land. There is a look. They don't look like Charlton Heston, but he did a great job. He did a great job, so the heck with it. He understood it spiritually and mentally. They are the chosen people, I absolutely feel that. There are holy land people. All they have to do is acknowledge that it's not them doing it. It's just that they are chosen. I know this. We exist. No doctor could create ears that hear or teeth that chew or eyes that see. No doctor could create us. They tried with Frankenstein in the movie. It didn't work.

So you guys meet onstage at your public school, and now here you are championing arts in public schools.

Yes. Harry insists, when he's in a good mood, late at night, he will say that it was my family that opened him up to the arts. And he's the biggest art lover I ever met. Harry formed this orchestra, and he would book us for anything we could get in San Francisco. Political rallies, union meetings—even though we were non-union. We had gas for the car, and people didn't even have cars in those days. My mother was feeding families at the back door. It was just terrible, the Depression. I got paid with a three-scoop ice cream cone. I'll never forget it. It was so wonderful. He knew where to go. Three scoops, and it had walnuts and whipped cream and a cherry on top. I sang "When Irish Eyes Are Smiling" and things like that. Things that were popular at the time. These beautiful Armenians were all over the house. Gee, they were beautiful. I didn't understand the language, but I thought it was the most exotic house in San Francisco. Harry insists that my family was one of the more prominent, and I guess it was. My father was a lawyer. So aside from being a Christian Science leader, he lobbied for the Christian Scientists. He would come home and open the front door, and he was in love with Milton, Keats, Shelley, Elizabeth Barrett Browning, Shakespeare. "Good night sweet prince, may flights of angels guide thee to thy rest," he would recite—I thought every father would recite poetry all over the house, but they didn't. I found out when a girlfriend asked me to stay over. I don't know what age I was, because Christian Scientists don't believe in ages. You know, you can hit the prime of life at any age. That's true. Even the AMA says so. I obviously haven't reached it yet. You can see that. I feel it's just ahead of me.

The way you speak of appreciating Harry's Armenian family I am reminded that throughout your whole career, you have always been so embracing of different cultures and ways of life. You say "yes" to all influences. You sing in different languages. Why do you think that is?

I don't know. It just fascinates me. The moment a Russian walks in the room, I grab him. As far back as I can remember I used to listen to the sound of everybody's voice. The most fascinating were the ones that had a foreign accent. That's my talent.

Is there anything that pisses you off?
I'm trying to think. Tomatoes.
[Harry interrupts] I can answer that. People who don't try to achieve their best. When you spoke to the job corps . . .

Ohhh! Thank you. There is a wonderful organization called Job Corps. They asked me to come and speak to them. These are all dropouts. There is a 30 percent dropout rate. Maybe more. They're bored to tears because they don't have the arts. None of them. Job Corps has students every color of the rainbow. Pretty tough looking, some of them, boys and girls who have dropped out of high school. They are asked what they might want to do. And they answer, "I want to design things," or, "I want to be a chef" and Job Corps teaches and trains them and then tries to get them jobs. They start at the bottom and work their way up. I said, "Harry, what do I say to them? I don't know what to say." And he said, "Tell them about what your family did for me." I was madly in love with him. It was my first love. But . . . But . . . where was I, Harry?

[Harry] His question was, "what's the thing, that makes you most angry. In your life." When arts were taken out of school this has deprived these kids of a full life . . .

Yes! Not that we want to make artists—Van Cliburn will be Van Cliburn no matter what happens to him, whether they have arts in the school or not. He's got a calling. There are people with the calling. Gene Shalit asked me, "When did you first want to lay your life down to the theater?" And he said it with me—"seven years old." And I said, "How did you know?" And he said, "They all answer the same thing. Seven years old." Something happens to our metabolism at seven. If you have any feeling at all, at seven you say, "I want that, I want to go for that." You see, once you are exposed to the arts—you don't have to be an artist. Not all of us are. Some of us are mathematicians or engineers or things that have nothing to do with the arts. But once you're exposed to the arts the whole world looks like a work of art. It really does. A piece of machinery looks like a work of art, an air-conditioning system looks like a work of art. All right, so they're more mechanical . . . My father—I didn't finish about my father—I told the students, "All I can do is tell you about my experience. My father would come home from legislature, and he'd open the door and say, "Achievement. There's nothing like it. It's the greatest feeling in the world, it's the greatest sensation. It's the greatest high." I thought, "Gee this must be better than sex, better than drugs, better than anything you can imagine. Better than a cup of coffee or something. This must be the most wonderful thing in the world!" And he said, "Don't talk about what you're going to do, Tootsie Puss. Don't talk about what your ambition is, don't let anybody know. Otherwise you let it off in talk and half the energy is gone. Get it done!" I was fortunate; my mother took Harry and me to museums that were free for children. Now they're nine dollars apiece for children. Not all children can afford nine dollars. These are public school children we're worried about. I'm skipping back and forth. You've got to put it back into order for me in print.

You talk about achievement being the greatest high. It reminds me of something I've always thought about you every time I've seen you perform. I've seen many, many people perform but I've never seen anyone love it quite like you do.

It's good to know that, because I get terribly frightened. This could be the audience that just doesn't get it. They just don't get what you're talking about. Helen Hayes when asked the question, "Do you get nervous before you go on?" said, "It's so painful. The nervousness that maybe they won't get it or maybe I won't make my points clear." Now I realize that I've been long enough in the theater, sixty-five years on the legitimate stage—that it's God-given. It's a blessing that you get so nervous before you go on. As soon as you get the first bit out and they start to go with you and understand you . . . the brain focuses and I am smarter than at any other time in my life. Al Pacino came to me and said, "Wait a minute, you're the long-run girl of all time. Tell me, how do you keep it fresh? I can do it in a movie . . ." I think he's fabulous in a movie! I mean he's one of our greatest. He's the grea—well, not THE—there's Henry Fonda, there are all kinds, but he's up there. He says, "How do you keep it fresh over a span of thirty years? That's some kind of a record." Apparently, even Sarah Bernhardt didn't do that. "Thirty years of the *same* show. How do you do it?" You put someone who is your understanding heart in the audience, in your imagination. Noel Coward told me to do this during a little review called *Lend an Ear*. I did nine different parts. He came backstage after the matinee in New York and he said, "Listen." He got down on his knees, this craggy, wonderful thing. Gee, I guess he was about seventy-five at the time [he was forty-nine], and he said, "Love, put me in your audience when you feel you're losing them. We all do that. In your imagination, put me—that's how you find who your friends are. I love what you're doing on that stage." I was one of twenty unknowns. And he said, "Every character you do, you get to the bottom of the character. When you feel that you are losing your audience, put me in your audience, tell it to me and you'll see it will work." And I said, "I can do that?" and he said, "Yes!" And I felt his love. I felt it. The next thing I knew I met somebody so exciting—she's the doyenne of society in San Francisco. Chaaaaarming! I went to lunch with her. I thought, "I'm gonna put her in the matinee audience. I am just entranced with her, I love her to pieces." I put her in the audience and it didn't work. Nothing worked. And I suddenly realized that I was crazy about her but she wasn't crazy about me. It has to be a two-way thing.

Does it ever not work?

No. Never. It works every single time. It gives you that . . . we were just looking at Dean Martin. I was on his show. Gosh what an artist he was. I don't think he ever drank at all. He was pretending to be drunk all the time. Happily drunk. Totally relaxed and totally focused. I couldn't relax like that. I couldn't do it. But he did.

Were you watching yourself on his show?

I wasn't very good. I just wasn't.

You said having that person always works . . .

It gives me the Dean Martin relaxation. He was an artist at that. Walk out there and relax. You have to lie to them for a minute. You are not relaxed but you have to relax into them and talk to your understanding heart. They know you are glad to see them. They know that's what they've paid their money to see and they know that you are not pretending. They are like an X-ray machine. They know if you are just saying the line or if you really mean it. I put Harry in the audience now.

I bet he's actually there quite a bit.
No, he's usually backstage.

Your last husband was in the audience at every show. Did that help?
Not a bit. [Charles Lowe was infamous for sitting up front at every Channing performance and starting the standing ovations.] It was just the most dreadful thing. I have wires that [the producer] Mr. Merrick sent him. But I have nothing to say against him. I mean what good is that going to do Charles or me.

Wires?
He forbade him to come to the theater. He knew he was ruining the whole thing. He said, "Ms. Channing is too great an artist to have somebody pretending, leading the applause before she's even finished saying the line."

Did you ever ask him to stop?
There was no stopping him.

You mentioned David Merrick . . .
I adored him. Nobody else did. Everybody was mad at him.

In his book, Jerry Herman said that both Gower Champion and David Merrick were monsters to him during the out-of-town run of *Hello, Dolly!* in Detroit. Even though you didn't personally have a bad experience with any of them, did that affect the environment for you?
I was focused on the character of Dolly. I had to find her. I was totally focused and consumed with that. Anyway there was nothing wrong because Mr. Merrick said, "You listen to her and do exactly what she wants."

So you weren't aware of tension?
I didn't think of the environment. I was focused on Dolly. My job is to change character with every show. You'd never recognize Lorelei Lee next to Dolly. It's not the same person. It's just the opposite. Dolly was running everybody's life. Well, so was Lorelei but she didn't let anyone know. But the thing is . . . you hire a great actor like Jimmy Stewart to just be Jimmy Stewart. And they are fabulous. People like Gary Cooper. They are whoever they are playing. That's who they are. My job is like a revue artist. You jump from character to character and you don't recognize me from one character to another. That's my talent. But it's different from being John Wayne. Except I just heard him sing on *The Dean Martin Show* and he was marvelous! Almost as good as Dean! He was a great singer! Isn't that something? But he never used it because they liked him the way that it was. Dumb businessmen.

I wonder if John Wayne chose not to sing because he had chosen this tough guy image for himself and that's what he was selling throughout his career. That's what he knew was marketable.

No. We don't think "what's marketable and what's not." No. Never. No actor does. That's phony. You've got to get *this* character that you are playing now, across to somebody who will understand what you are trying to do. And believe me that I am Dolly, that I am Lorelei. The most wonderful character was Ruth Sherwood in *Wonderful Town*. While you are doing that character there isn't any other character. That's all you were born with.

You've seen other people play Dolly, after you . . .
I saw Pearl Bailey and I thought she was wonderful as Pearl Bailey. And why not? Why shouldn't Dolly be Pearl Bailey. You know who did a good job in the movie? Shirley Booth [*The Matchmaker*]! She was soft and sweet and entirely different. A whole other Dolly. She was just heaven. But look, I have no perspective on myself. So if I sound phony . . . I can't see myself doing it. I only see Dolly. I just have my eyes on Dolly and Thornton Wilder.

You have to have known the response to your performance.
Oh yes. It's quite a feeling. At the end of the "Dolly" number, it used to hit me right where I carried my son. It would go right to my waist, to my tummy. It knocked me over backwards the first time. I had to get used to standing there and standing straight.

Jerry Herman said that the night *Dolly* opened on Broadway, he knew that his life had changed forever. Did you have that same sense?
No. There are critics who can look straight at you and say, "That's not what I think *Dolly* should have been." So you always have that to face. Betty White tells me she was there opening night and she knew she was witnessing history. We didn't know. I was focused on Dolly's salvation.

Somewhere during the run, though, you must have realized that this wasn't your average show.
Yes, we knew that we were a hit.

In more than thirty years of playing Dolly around the world, how did the experience of playing her change for you?
What do you mean?

Over the years, was it different?
It could have been but I don't—Oh, I would check with critics. Christiansen was with the *Chicago Tribune*, I would check with Elliot Norton in Boston. These are the great critics. And critics can be great. Claudia Cassidy was the meanest, rottenest critic in the whole United States and she said, "In *Wonderful Town*, Rosalind Russell played the leading character for intelligence, Carol Channing played her for genius." My God! She came to New York to see *Dolly* before she died [in 1996]. But before she died I called her and thanked her for raising the level of the theater across the United States. I said, "Miss Cassidy, I want you to know that I keep touring." If you are fortunate enough to have a show run, to have it be enough of a hit, the whole world hears about it. You can tour with it. That's the privilege that you get and it's a privilege to work in the theater but you've got to recreate the *Mona Lisa* every night.

You wrote in your book that Alfred Lunt and Lynn Fontanne told you that you must tour, that you had to take your hits to the provinces.

That rare moment when Channing preferred brunette: *Wonderful Town* in 1953. (Photofest)

Yes! Lynn Fontanne! "Love, you must take your show to the provinces. If you're enough of a hit, you can bring it to them and they consider you a houseguest. There was a flop show that Noel wrote. We thought it was impossible for Noel to write a flop, but he did. And this was the most terrible show. Just didn't work. But they all went, 'Oh! Lynne and Alfred, they're friends of ours we have to go!'" It's funny how the audience changes the show. I remember noticing with *Gentlemen Prefer Blondes* in Detroit, Lorelei was seen as a tough little prostitute. But in Dallas, she is sweet. She's just as sweet as she can be. As long as you are sweet you can do anything you want.

That's fascinating.
It *is* fascinating. They change the show! The audience does it! What can you do? You go along with them.

That's what I mean about you being open to what's coming from the audience. I can't imagine Ethel Merman changing her show based on the audience.
Oh she was great!

She was great, but I can't imagine her changing her show.
[Imitating Merman] "Well what the hell's the matter with 'em! It's so quiet! They sit there!" There's a prejudice against a New York accent outside of New York. It scares them. It sounds like a gangster to them.

You've referred to the songs "Diamonds Are a Girl's Best Friend" and "Hello, Dolly" as your battle hymns. What's it like for you to perform them?

Oh! "What's the meaning of this? What do I have to convey?" I was there when Leo Robin wrote the lyrics [to "Diamonds"], you see. He wrote them on me. Like "Little Rock." He said I think Lorelei comes through strongest when you're grateful. It's like the poor little match girl on Thanksgiving. Maybe they'll throw me a bone. It's her innocence that makes her palatable. You can't play her tough. Did you know the movie [studio] sent Marilyn Monroe to see the show every night for a month? Third row center!

What was it like to play for her for a month?

Well, I know somebody right now that we're working with said [about Channing's performance in *Thoroughly Modern Millie*], "Oh, you're doing Marilyn Monroe!" "Are you kidding, she stole it from me! What's the matter with you? I'm older than Marilyn Monroe. Way older." She had no idea. But there's an innate innocence. If you don't smother the audience with that, she's unpalatable. And it's funny. Lorelei just misspelled everything. She became a "Christian Science." Not a "Scientist." "A Science." So she realized where diamonds came from. From above.

What was it like having to perform for Marilyn?

Oh, it was too funny. The orchestra never saw anything that beautiful. Milt Rosenstock is prone to women. He's the conductor. Even he couldn't stop looking at her. They kept saying to Bus Davis—I don't know, are you going to print this in a gay magazine?

It's actually for a book.

Right, it's a book! OK! Anyway, I don't want to offend anybody because they've been too great. I'm too grateful. I'm too grateful. I'm their queen. This generation doesn't know that. You know it.

Oh yeah, I do.

I was made the queen [at a gay event in San Francisco]. You know an empress is only for three years but a queen is forever! A [drag queen] named Baby Ruth gave it to me! (laughs) Tallulah Bankhead and Judith Anderson couldn't touch him. Could not touch him! He was the empress and it was his last night. He was going to walk over the Golden Gate Bridge and throw himself off. He crawled up the side of the proscenium arch and said, "It's the end of me, I don't want to live any more." He went on and on. Dear Tallulah should take lessons from that guy. He was terrific. What did you ask me?

I asked about Marilyn.

Well, so Bus Davis, the greatest musical accompanist in the Broadway theater. He sat there playing the piano and they kept saying, "Bus!" All of the orchestra was getting weaker and weaker and Milt was just looking at Marilyn Monroe. Just looking. They couldn't believe it. And Bus Davis . . . they kept saying, "Bus you've got to see this!" And he saved me, he just kept playing the piano and the drummer kept playing. And they said, "Bus, look! Get up and see this beauty. You've never seen anything like it." So finally he stood up and he looked and he said, "Ask her does she have a brother."

With *Gentlemen Prefer Blondes* and then again with *Hello, Dolly!* you had tremendous success onstage but then were not given the opportunity to recreate your two signature performances on film.

Marilyn was so dear and it was the cutest movie. It just wasn't funny!

And the *Dolly* movie? Anything you want to say about Barbra Streisand?

The year that she did *Funny Girl*, she was fabulous! We used to be good friends. We would eat dinner between shows at Sardi's with Bea Lillie, who was doing *High Spirits*. But we were friends. And we'd say, "You're gonna get the Tony Award." "No *you're* gonna get it." I got the award.

You wrote in your book that every time you have been on the Fox lot and have seen the remnants of the *Dolly* set, it gives you pleasure remembering that the film was a flop.

They still can't afford to take it down. Isn't that a shame? What a pity.

I asked before what it feels like when you are singing your battle hymns. I am also . . .

Are they getting the point of this? That's all. Do they hear it? I've got to stop on certain audiences. There are some audiences that aren't very quick. And there are some that are benefit audiences which are *death!* All benefit audiences are . . .

That's today. You've got a benefit audience today.

Oh, no, really?

The Actors Fund.

Oh, well the Actors Fund is different. All the actors know how we have Mondays for Actors Funds and we can go see each other. All of them sat there at *Gypsy*. We're all sitting there and Ethel comes out and she's singing [imitates and pounds her chest], "For Me! For Me! For Me! For Me!" Gosh, the woman's [Mama Rose] insane! And the orchestra can't keep up with her because the woman's crazy. "For me! This time for me!" She wrecks the orchestra because they couldn't—she was so crazy. Then slowly, "For meeeee." She was totally insane. We all sat there watching, thinking [in a sweet voice], "Oh!!! That's Mommy!" In Oklahoma they sit there thinking, "What kind of a mother is that? We never heard of a mother like that." When Angela [Lansbury] brought it over, she said, "We have to take some of the viciousness out of her." It's funny with Ethel. It's funny! Jesus! Wow! The woman really was insane and then when she finishes the number, it's funny because she doesn't know she's insane. "Yeah! Curtain up!"

I know that you have the original Dolly headdress in your closet. How many costume pieces have you stolen?

Well, you see, they tell you that you *can not* touch your clothes. That was the one dress that I was able to get to the window. . . . I told my Tiv, Tiv Davenport, he dressed me for most of my life—oh he was wonderful, really marvelous. On matinee days he would put my fish—fish is a good choice to eat before a show, it's not too heavy—and he would put the fish in the wig oven. It would be all cooked and perfect by the end of the matinee. The company objected after a while because every time I went by them I smelled of swordfish or salmon. But I only got that one dress out. I still fit into it.

You are legendary for your stamina and your lack of absenteeism. You never missed a show.

I missed half a show once. Food poisoning. It was the hotel food. They had to drag me off in an ambulance. It was a whole show. For the sake of the truth, I have to tell you. I just kept throwing up and throwing up. I missed a whole show. The understudy sure remembers. She was awfully good.

Recording the original cast album of *Hello, Dolly!* It's easy to see why Channing was Al Hirschfeld's favorite subject. (Photofest)

How do you conserve your energy?

No actor ever feels fatigue or pain on the stage. Never. Ethel Barrymore, in *The Corn Is Green*, that was her last show on Broadway. I saw it again and again. She said, "Can we keep this show going because it's the only time that I don't feel this terribly painful arthritis." It riddled her from head to toe like it did Lionel. He was in a wheelchair. I did the show in a wheelchair for two weeks in London.

And you performed *Dolly* with cancer.

Oh yes. Ovarian cancer. But I didn't feel it as long as I was onstage. Nobody does. My arm was broken, blood and gore all over the stage. I fell off the stage. I broke this arm once, this one twice. I went to the hospital and this officious nurse said, "Cause of accident?"—Do you remember the Ann Miller story?

The Ann Miller story when she fell off the stage and a nail went into her wig?

The nail went into her wig? (Laughs hysterically)

You haven't heard that story?

No! I haven't!

Yeah, she was rehearsing and fell right off the stage into the orchestra pit. Later they found a six-inch nail in her wig. But she never felt it because the wig was so thick.

(Laughs uproariously) Wig!!!!!! Well let me tell you one that Bobby Fryer told me, the producer of *Mame*. She took over as Mame and she was awfully good. So was Angela, of course. But Bobby said she made out the insurance papers: "Name: Ann Miller. Occupation: Star." Clearly she's occupied with being a star. "Cause of accident: Big yellow prop moon." Now these papers go to the insurance people. They don't go to Broadway shows. Can you imagine? What could that mean to insurance workers. "Big yellow prop moon?" Isn't that brilliant. And you mustn't repeat it in front of her.

Well I can't because she's no longer with us.

That's true. She's no longer with us. Yes! You know the one about, "Mother I've forgotten my telephone book?"

No.

She calls her mother from the road and asks her, "Would you send my telephone book to me?" Her mother sends her all five of the Los Angeles telephone books. Huge! I mean the postage!

You got to work with her a couple of times, didn't you?

When I did *Sugar Babies* [on tour] Annie Miller came to Boston on weekends to teach me her routines. She said, "I want you to do the steps right because they are good steps." Imagine doing that for me. She helped me. I loved that girl! We actors think more of one another than the audience ever will. Ethel Merman, there are things she told me that I'll never tell anyone. And I didn't. Things she wrestles with but I have, too. It's nobody else's business!

You were on *The Love Boat* with both Ann Miller and Ethel Merman.

That's when I became good friends with Ethel. But I can't tell you the filthy thing she called me.

You put it in your book.

Did I?

Yes, she couldn't remember your character's name, Sylvia, so she said "Come here Sybil. No, Sarah . . ."

"Get your ass over here you dumb cunt." And I would *do* it! That's what made me mad at myself. She asked the producer if we could travel to the set together. Oh, I idolized her. I never saw anybody like that. The thrill of her voice. The toughest broad that ever walked the boards. And tender, if you knew her. She asked me, "What do you do with a son who doesn't know you love him just because you are doing eight shows a week and you gotta do all kinds of publicity to keep the show running? How do you let a son know you love him?" I said, "You sure asked the wrong mother, Ethel, because you're talking to the worst mother in the world. But Mary Martin thinks she's the worst mother in the world." I lost my son completely.

You are not in touch?

No. [Note: This changed in 2011 at Kullijian's instigation.]

I am sorry to hear that.

Yes, I'm sorry too. I don't know what's the matter. He just didn't understand that I . . . he wanted his mother, of course. I don't blame him. I had a mother. And Ethel thought she was the worst mother in the world. Her son, Bobby Levitt, used to come backstage and visit me. Two shows a night, he'd sit there. Chan [Channing Lowe, Carol's son] was the same way. He loved Hermione Gingold. She had done the wicked witch in *Cinderella* and Chan went crazy about her. Bobby the same way. The Crosby boys were the same, too. They'd come in my dressing room in Las Vegas every night before the show. They'd come in because I was bleached and had the eyelashes like their mother. To them, that's Mommy. You get them a sweet little old lady baby sitter, they're scared to death. They never saw a mother like that.

What was your worst experience onstage?

The Vamp. Nobody knew what they were doing. But it was produced by amateurs all the way around. And they didn't care. They were crooks.

You had another disappointment with *Legends*, touring with Mary Martin.

We decided not to bring it into New York. We knew it didn't work. But working with Mary . . . we loved each other. We worked very closely together. I knew her very well before, so we were already close. I was used to her. I knew what she was like. I knew her faults and her virtues.

So was there joy in performing with her even though the show didn't work?

The show is no joy. It never is. It's work. If you start enjoying it yourself no one else does. It's like the old adage: if you start listening to your own voice you can bet that no one else is. Same with acting. Anything. Start watching your own performance and no one else is.

You were, nominated for an Oscar and you won a Golden Globe for *Thoroughly Modern Millie* but you have said that you didn't like your work in it? Why?

The movie? I don't remember that. No! I was crazy about it because Julie was so wonderful.

But you have said that you didn't like your work in it.

Well nobody does. That's human. If you like yourself on the screen you're insane. You really are. You get caught up in which side you look good from. You can't do that. You keep your mind on what you're saying and the character you're playing. Otherwise nobody cares about you.

What do you remember about working with Julie Andrews?

She was wonderful. Boy, she was a great star. She respected me and I will never forget her for that. It was my first day and George Roy Hill, the director, decided to start with a close-up on me. Julie came in on her first day off. She had her jeans on, no makeup, and she knew that I was called for just my scenes for a close-up. She walked in and I said, "Julie! I wouldn't have done these scenes the same to your stand-in. It's not you I am talking to. It's you I have to talk to." She said, "I knew that, that's why I'm here." And she came in and held both my hands. George Roy Hill kept saying, "Give me energy, give me Muzzy, give me performance pitch, but relax." And she said to me, "Just tell it to me." And she held my hands throughout the whole thing. I just kept my eye on Julie and I kept talking to her and I thought, "I am Muzzy. I don't have to pretend." Later I asked the people who voted on the Golden Globes, "Why did you vote for me? It's not a tragedy. It's not one of those Ethel Barrymore roles or something like that." And they said, "It was that scene with Julie." I could cry. When I think of Julie I cry. How could anybody be so understanding? And to this day we are like that. She will forever be my angel.

You're wearing your own hair right now and it looks lovely, but for a long time you wouldn't be caught dead without a wig. When did that become your signature look?

Well, I noticed that when Ginger Rogers took over for me in *Dolly*, she wore her makeup all the time offstage. I looked very washed out without it. So probably that's it.

So you decided then?

I didn't decide, I looked in the mirror! "Oh my gosh! You gotta get your eyelashes on."

You told me that your book [*Just Lucky I Guess*] didn't include as much as you would have liked to have had in there.

I never reread it, it bothered me so. I didn't get to finish it. I had a deadline. But I recently ran into the original manuscript that I wrote and I was shocked. There was so much in it that wasn't in the book, So much. And it was dynamite. The secret to how to reach an audience! But, of course, not everybody wants to know. I read the last page of the book that they didn't publish. It was about my cousin, Dickie. My mother and father raised my cousin Richard until he was twelve years old. Now they [Richard and his wife, Sylvia] have saved me from a marriage in which everything was taken from me. Everything. All of the money. It was all stolen along the way. And it was all done before the marriage. I signed legal things and I didn't know what I was signing. He [Charles Lowe] got paid for everything I ever did instead of me, so I had nothing. But my cousin Dickie was able to look after me just the way my parents looked after him. My life seems to be made up of divine moves that saved me.

Now that you are reflecting on the book, do you want to do a sequel?

I have to follow it up. I thought Harry was dead of course. I am so grateful for whatever being has guided me all of my life.

Who knows why things happen, but you put out so much positive energy . . .

Do you think so? I am glad to hear it, because being married to a crook, to a con man who was very good at his job . . . He moved in on Gracie Allen and George Burns, he was an excellent con man. He was Aimee Semple McPherson's business manager—so you can imagine—and she never caught on.

So you are saying that being married to him, it surprises you that you are positive?

Yeah. He was so negative. I don't know how it happened. I hate to say it's God because I am not a preacher but . . . I don't know what it is. Charles used me as a tool. But it doesn't matter. If you love and appreciate and are grateful for the positive force, that helps you.

You are one of the most imitated people in show business.

Yeah, because you see it's easy to imitate. I am imitating the character that I have in mind, so it's easy for other people to imitate. I have seen Debbie Reynolds imitate me but she was doing Lorelei. It wasn't Carol Channing. It's easy for someone to imitate someone who is not doing herself.

Do you recognize yourself when you see yourself being impersonated.

Never. Not at all. It's funny. At one time there were seven boys impersonating me in Las Vegas. I went with George Burns. I didn't recognize myself at all but I do enjoy what they do, it's terribly funny. It's just not me. One of them had two elastic like ropes that came down to his hands and he kept leaning forward and forward as if he was going to fall into the orchestra pit. Everybody applauded him because apparently I do that. You keep leaning forward and you don't realize that eventually you are going to fall into the pit.

Haven't you actually done that?

Oh, yes, many times. We had a runway in *Hello, Dolly!* and finally Mr. Merrick got so mad that I kept falling, he had them put little John Mineo in front of me and Mr. Merrick said, "Now look, if he falls off that runway, don't go that way!" But John couldn't see either so finally they put Christmas tree lights around the thing. And we could see. So Johnny, that saved his life.

You've also been caricatured. And, of course, the greatest caricature artist of all time, Al Hirschfeld, said you were his favorite subject.

Well, Zero Mostel and me. That's a dubious compliment.

Well, you two share . . .

An exaggeration of some kind that's totally unacceptable as a human being.

Unacceptable?

Would you like to look like Zero Mostel?

CHITA RIVERA

March and May 2009; April and August 2012

IN 2012, CHITA RIVERA OPENED in a Broadway revival of *The Mystery of Edwin Drood*. Not only a triumph on its own, that production elongated a staggering record: Chita Rivera has performed in at least one major Broadway musical in each of the seven decades between the 1950s and today. But longevity isn't all that makes Rivera great. Her athletic dancing, of course, initially propelled her forward, but she's an equally adept actor and singer with that unique quality that makes her simply . . . Chita, a category unto herself.

Rivera's career began in 1951 when she was cast in the chorus of the national tour of *Call Me Madam* starring Elaine Stritch. Rivera followed the path of the Broadway gypsy, going from show to show to show in a career trajectory that doesn't seem to happen any more. She was Broadway's resident spitfire, enlivening every production she graced.

Sometimes she was lucky and found herself performing in landmarks like *West Side Story* and *Bye Bye Birdie*, where her creations of Anita and Rosie, respectively, made her a star. Other times she was in less stellar material like *1491* or *Zenda*, both of which closed on the road. But no matter the quality of any given show, season after season, Rivera was always performing with gusto.

Another landmark, *Chicago*, came in 1975. In it, Rivera, alongside her idol, Gwen Verdon, gave life to the legendary Bob Fosse choreography that epitomized his style. It was her first Broadway show with John Kander and Fred Ebb, who would go on to write three others just for her. Two of those shows, *The Rink* and *Kiss of the Spider Woman*, brought her Tony Awards while the third, *The Visit*, continues its winding (and, for Rivera, maddeningly long) journey toward Broadway. In the meantime, she memorably tangoed with Antonio Banderas in *Nine* (kicking her then seventy-year-old leg onto his shoulder) and starred in her autobiographical show, *Chita Rivera: The Dancer's Life*, with the mission of teaching and inspiring a new generation with the joy and satisfaction of a life devoted to the theater.

There's not a dancer in this book who doesn't speak of Rivera with reverence. That's not merely a tribute to what she's done but to who she is. Rivera is a life force who remains staunchly committed to putting forth positivity. To this day, she waves off mention of the grueling years of pain and therapy she endured after her legs were crushed in a horrible car accident that doctors said would end her career. She won't dwell on the negative. That doesn't mean that she doesn't have her opinions or enjoy a bit of dish when her feet are up in her dressing room, but on the record, Chita Rivera is determined to remain constructive. It's not because she's a goody-two-shoes, but because she loves and respects the theater so much. "Why," she asks? "What good can [complaining] possibly do?" It's that very philosophy that

Chita Rivera: The Dancer's Life, Rivera's answer to a memoir. (Paul Kolnik)

Chita Rivera

Call Me Madam, National Tour, 1952
Guys and Dolls, Broadway, 1953
Can-Can (Ensemble), Broadway, 1953
Shoestring Revue, off-Broadway, 1955
Seventh Heaven, Broadway, 1955
Mr. Wonderful, Broadway, 1956
West Side Story, Broadway and West End, 1957
Bye Bye Birdie, Broadway, West End, National Tour, 1960
Zenda, San Francisco and Los Angeles, 1963
Bajour, Broadway, 1964
Sweet Charity, National Tour, 1967
1491, Los Angeles and San Francisco, 1969
Zorba, National Tour, 1969
Jacques Brel Is Alive and Well and Living in Paris, National Tour, 1972
Kiss Me Kate, National Tour, 1974
Chicago (as Velma), Broadway and National Tour, 1975
Bring Back Birdie, Broadway, 1981
Merlin, Broadway, 1983
The Rink, Broadway, 1984 (Tony Award)
Jerry's Girls, Broadway, 1985
Can-Can (as La Mome Pistache), National Tour, 1988
Kiss of the Spider Woman, Broadway and West End, 1993 (Tony Award)
Chicago (as Roxie), Las Vegas, Toronto, West End, 2000
Anything Goes, Millburn, NJ, 2000
The Visit, Chicago and Washington, D.C., 2001, 2008
Nine, Broadway, 2003
Chita Rivera: The Dancer's Life, Broadway and National Tour, 2005
The Mystery of Edwin Drood, Broadway, 2012

may explain why she's still in rehearsal halls, still kicking. Literally.

What's it like going back to a revival of a show you did? Is it weird for you watching other people playing your roles?

Oh you want so badly to like it. You *really* want to like it. It's not weird at all. Time marches on. You just hope you see everything you want to see. You hope that they are properly cast and having a good time. You want to support the kids. You don't want to see anybody arrogant. You want to see them working hard, doing their thing.

Without Jerome Robbins there, you wonder . . .

But the great thing about Jerry Robbins, and you almost wish that all the great choreographers had done this—you can't change his choreography. It's got to be Robbins. You don't want people making variations on Jerome Robbins's choreography at all. He was a director/choreographer. You have to act. Be a person. You have to be truthful through the choreography. It's not just technical steps. Choreography comes out of emotion. It's dialogue without words.

Do you think that understanding exists the way it should today?

There's not as much choreography today.

There's a lot of acrobatics. All tricks but no heart.

I haven't seen a lot of stuff lately so I don't really know. But I do know that I've seen a lot of acrobatics.

It's fun to watch . . .

Oh, it's entertaining. I am happy for them. But it doesn't move me. Where's the story? Where does it come from? Why? Why?

In *The Dancer's Life* you featured an amazing choreographer crash course. It felt like you were saying, "Know these people! Understand them!" But it was presented in a non-threatening way.

You don't want to put your hand in somebody's face. You want to educate. You just want to give them the basket of goodies and make it appealing enough for them to think, "I want to do that!" That's how it happened with me. So that when you go to these auditions, you're thrilled because you are going to learn something different. It's our job to make it appealing for the kids, to make them want to learn it. It extends their careers. Knowledge is great. Makes the body stronger. I have a choreographer friend who is doing very well. I heard his choreography is very difficult. It's very good but almost impossible to do. I asked him point blank at dinner, "Are you doing the right thing? Are you hurting any bodies out there? Does it make sense to do all of that?" I put my li'l two cents in there.

If somebody arrived in New York today with the kind of talent you had when you got here, do you think it'd be possible for them to have a career?

I hope so. I would love for somebody to just jump out at me. I look. I haven't seen too many that really make me go, "Yeah!"

Let's go back to the beginning. You were born in Washington, D.C., one of five kids. You fell into dancing accidentally as you described it in your show. You were so energetic you were breaking the furniture and your parents had to do something with you.

Oh, I was always in trouble and always crazy, but I was always obedient. I was a good kid. I mean, sneaking out of houses and stealing this or that, running wild in the streets, but obeying my mother.

So when you were with a ballet master you were able to take in the discipline?

Totally! I was too scared of grownups screaming at me. I didn't want to do anything wrong. Mr. Obukhoff—the only picture of a ballet teacher in my house is of Mr. Anatole Obukhoff— who did everything but beat us up. He taught us how to dance and how to be strong, thick-skinned, obedient.

A lot of people complained about Jerome Robbins being a bully. Even Sondheim said about him, "He could be a really, really mean, awful man, but I would work with him any-time." Helen Gallagher said, "He would strip you naked, pull the flesh right off of your bones, and then rebuild you. It wasn't fun to be around. He was mean." But you have been quoted saying that you wouldn't have been what you were without him being that way. Before I ask you about that, do you think the discipline of your ballet training prepared you for him?

Totally. I was ready for somebody like that. That's exactly right. That's why it's good to have it. You can either take it or you can't and if you can't take it you are not going to make it any further than the door. You are doing something that's not normal. You are throwing your body around and you need a technique in order for it not to break. It's hard. You don't really realize until later on in life.

You look back and realize, "what was I doing?"

Now I know why I've got this new hip! But it's like war wounds. It's medals. It's great. It's a sign of working hard. It's a Michael Kidd hip or a Jack Cole thing in the neck.

You relished it.

Absolutely. I was always happy when I pleased my superiors. I always wanted to do well. Yeah. But that was the time, too. You truly respected the older generation.

You also said that Jerome Robbins taught you how to act.

Without a doubt. I had no idea. I remember sitting on the steps of the Mark Hellinger, we were on a break or something, and we talked about my character in colors and textures. "How do you see her?" he said. I can see the image in my head right now, sitting on these metal steps. I had never thought about a life within my life. I was getting to know me, my mind, my imagination. When you open up, that forms the foundation for you, it gives you strength.

At that point you had a few shows under your belt.

I did, I did. Chris Hewitt was a great director for *Shoestring* [Ben Bagley's *Shoestring Revue*]. That was just before *West Side*. But I never took it as seriously. I was never asked to go inside myself. Jerry Friedman, who was Jerry Robbins's assistant director, I give him all the credit for "A Boy Like That . . ." We were doing it in the rehearsal hall and I sang it and he said, "That's great Chita. Now, don't you have two brothers?" And I said, "You think you're cool? You really think I don't know what you're getting at?" And he said, "Okay. Then let's just start again." That's all he did. I started to sing and my mind flashed right to my brothers. I am looking at you and I remember it just like it happened five minutes ago. As I sang I started to choke up. And he said, "Keep going, keep going." I started to cry. "Keep going, keep going." And as I was doing that I was backing up out of the room. I am backing away, still singing, "A boy like that, he killed your brother!"

Your body wanted to resist it.

Totally. It was a brilliant breakthrough for me.

Don't you think it takes a certain kind of talent to take in and understand those moments?

You have to open up. You have to trust. You have to want it so badly that . . . you don't know everything. I have been around all of these years and I still don't know because every single day brings you something different. You can learn from a baby walking around. You have to keep open.

That is the key. If you characterize a director as a bully, you may shut yourself down and you won't get that stuff.

He taught things that we swore we couldn't do. I'd say, "I can't."

You mean physically?

Yeah. And even acting-wise. The taunting scene, he wouldn't let me do it more than once a day because it was too traumatic for me. We would go down to the Alvin Theatre and rehearse it on the Alvin stage. We had these chairs lined up and he had me sitting in the middle. He said, "Let's just read. If you want to get up, get up. Whatever you feel like doing, just do it." Nobody had ever said anything like that to us before. We had to *think*! We had to act and express something. We had to be true. We started and I headed for the door and somebody got me. Then another one got up. And he said, "Keep going." It was so horrific that one day I kicked my ex-husband [cast member Tony Mordente] right in his you-know-what. I didn't mean to. But every night was different. It was so difficult to be called "a Spic." I didn't realize that it was going to bother me so much. It was just words. But one day, in the middle, it hit me they called me *that*! It was written so brilliantly.

One of the other things you said about *West Side* in *The Dancer's Life* that shocked me was that Peter Gennaro choreographed "America" and "Dance at the Gym."

That's right.

Isn't it sort of odd that those numbers ended up in *Jerome Robbins' Broadway*?

Well, it was his show. He was smart enough to hire somebody who knew those kinds of rhythms better than he. Peter originally choreographed it ["America"] like it was in the movie—the boys and girls together. We showed Jerry the number and we were excused and when we came back it was only the girls. So what Jerry did was he took what he saw and sat down with Peter and he helped shape it and rethink it. That's working together. That's theater at its best. It's hard. You don't act by yourself.

On opening night, at the curtain call, the audience was silent?

Yeah. And then they went nuts. Silence is very loud. It was a deafening moment. That's good stuff. They were moved.

Can you share any recollections of Leonard Bernstein?

He was a genius. He was sweet and kind and fun and easy. It was at a time when dancers weren't supposed to sing and singers couldn't dance, and he blew me away with what he made me do. I never would have thought I could do it. And no one conducted like him, no one. He was standing on a chair in the pit, conducting "Quintet" and he got so excited that he pounded and went straight through the chair. That's the kind of energy and exuberance he had. Just total passion. Maybe one of the easiest people in the world to be around.

What about Arthur Laurents?

Arthur was wonderful with me. I don't know what went on behind closed doors. People that write books and things, they want the dirt. I don't give the dirt. And I never will. It's like family. It's all private time, it's all part of the process.

When they took *West Side* to London, they held the entire production, waiting for you to give birth. That's extraordinary.

It was kind of amazing that they would wait, but I was having a baby so I didn't give it a lot of thought. I had other concerns. Lisa was four weeks old [when we left for London] if you can believe that. I popped her out, lost that weight, and just went on. And I was in perfect shape. I didn't look pregnant from the back; all front. She just dropped out like a basketball. And then we headed over there. The opening night was something you can't really explain. It was extraordinary. They really got it. I always felt that they got it more than the Americans.

Why do you suppose it was?

Because, the Americans thought it was right there in their backyards, which it was.

Too close for comfort?

Too close for comfort! It took a while. We lost the Tony. And now, they're going, "It's brilliant! It's classic!" It's the same show that was up against *The Music Man*, which was a very nice, American, wholesome. . . . I tell kids today, "Whatever you're doing, really believe in it. Don't let the reviewers make you feel anything less than what you know in your gut." And we knew.

Your career started with *Call Me Madam*. What was it like to go on calls in the '50s?

Fabulous. Fabulous, she says now. How you forget those crying nights. I remember my girlfriend Mary Alice and I were living in a hotel together. We auditioned for a Jack Cole show, *Carnival in Flanders*. They only needed one girl and we both went. They said they'd call us and I remember the phone ringing. We had these little twin beds. That's what I get for going to the East Side. We

As Anita in the legendary *West Side Story*. (Photofest)

both dove for the phone. I got it. "Hello? It's for you." She got it. She should have. I remember lining up. I remember being short and not tall and blonde and blue-eyed. I remember lying about my height. I don't know what it's like today, but there were 500 people at an audition, easily.

Were all of your friends other gypsies?

Only. I lived it. Ate it. Breathed it. Went to places like Sid and Al's on 46th Street, or Downey's. We all went there. All my friends were dancers. We didn't even hang out with singers. We used to make fun of the singers. But this piano player said to me one night, "Why don't you come over to my studio. I want to talk to you." Are you kidding? So I went to him maybe six, seven times. I can't remember. And I am in the bar one night and I was on my way out when they locked the door on me. They said, "We know you've been studying. We know you can sing. You're gonna sing." You could have shot me then. I got so scared. We didn't do that! We belted on the stage, but I never heard myself alone. That was my first time.

Until you discovered you could sing, you probably never would have gone up for any role that wasn't in the dancing ensemble.

Never. Never. I would have been like Lee Theodore who was this brilliant dancer. I tried to get her to audition for something with me and she said, "Dancers dance. Singers sing. I don't go where I have to sing." But I was curious and I thought, "Let me just check it out." I don't know why. My little angel just pushed me in that direction.

Your story about booking the *Call Me Madam* tour is right out of a movie [Rivera only went to the audition to accompany a friend and ended up booking the show herself]. Do you have specific recollections of what that transition was like for you—"Oh, OK, I'm doing a musical?"

It was extremely exciting. I was a very young girl and I was going to join a ballet company. But then I was offered this show. One of four soloists and it was Jerome Robbins directing. It was too wonderful and a beginning of another life.

Do you have particular recollections of Elaine Stritch from that time?

I used to watch her all the time in the wings. That's what I did in all the shows I ever did; I stood in the wings, and that's how I learned. I thought she was amazing and beautiful, and strong. Since then she has said to me, "I taught you everything you know."

Did she scare you at all?

No, she didn't scare me. She was so kind and I was smart enough to accept her kindness. She was sort of like one of my ballet teachers. Fear is always there with your teachers, but I was never so frightened that I did not accept something that obviously was going to help me.

You never had an acting class?

No, and I've only had about six singing classes and it's beginning to sound like that.

But you learned what you know watching?

Absolutely. Because I was around when the great ones were around. The Elaine Stritches, the Gwen Verdons, the Mermans. All of those. So I guess in my own way, I was shrewd, I was smart!

I think it takes a certain personality at that age to have the instinct to stand there and watch instead of running around backstage.

Yes, absolutely. And I was a clown, I loved to have fun. But it was all new to me and I really wanted to learn, without knowing that I wanted to learn. It was something that I needed to do. And I enjoyed it.

After *Call Me Madam*, you came back to New York and you got *Guys and Dolls*. As a learning experience you can't get any better than being in that company, and having that kind of choreography. Is that how it felt at the time?

Totally! Totally! I remember one time I was so nervous, I had to go over to Sky Masterson in the Latin Club, sit on his lap in this sexy little devil [outfit], grab his cigarette and stick it in my mouth, puff on it, and throw it out. Well, I was so nervous, the first time I went on, I grabbed his nose!

When you go into a hit like that, you have the opportunity to do a long run and you can really learn.

I believe you really learn what theater is truly about if you stay in there. Every night is different. It's a challenge to make it fresh every night. If you just keep jumping from one thing to another. . . . I always say we record the cast album too soon.

Because it takes time to really get the role?

You haven't gotten the role yet, you just started it. It takes time to find all those wonderful things that the writer has conceived. You can't get it in three or four weeks.

Is there an example of a cast album you wish you could have had . . .

All of them. I do love *Chicago*. But I'd like to be richer in *Spider Woman*.

Did you ever have to work a survival job?

No, I was lucky. But in those days there were a lot of shows, a lot of shows! Later, [there was a period] when I didn't have a lot of work, when the work changed in New York and the shows suddenly became small shows . . . but there was also summer stock.

So when that happened, were you doing a lot of . . .

Summer stock. I did *Born Yesterday*. I did *Flower Drum Song*.

Did you ever take anything that you didn't want to take?

No, because I never thought anything would be something that I couldn't make work.

And there was never anything that was like, "I really don't want to play that role, but here we go"?

No, no. Isn't that great? I remember I did *1491* with John Cullum at Pacific Light Opera in LA and San Francisco. It was dreadful, but we didn't know it was going to be a catastrophe.

Did you know at the time though? When you're in something that's not working?

No. I never believe it. Because you always have that tryout time, you always have faith in your director, and choreographer. . . . Either that or you're stupid. Do you think I might have just been stupid?

I can't opine. But with big out-of-town flops like *1491* or *Zenda* . . .

Zenda . . . to be on the stage with Alfred Drake? Who wouldn't want to go to work every night? I don't care what the reviews are.

But when you're doing it, does it feel like, "Oh God, they're going to hate me!"

A couple of times in *1491* but not *Zenda*. I loved *Zenda*. I thought *Zenda* was terrific, but who knows, I don't know what the situation was with the producers, and all that sort of stuff . . .

Well, you've also done your share of disappointing shows here in New York. *Bring Back Birdie* is a show that you told me should have made it.

But you see, the cast was not right with that. Donald O'Conner was wonderful and de-lightful and all that, but if you're going to bring something back, and the guy that originally did it is alive and breathing [Dick Van Dyke], you do everything you can to get that guy! How do you replace that? Also, we didn't go out of town, and I feel you should always go out of town. It could have been really terrific but too many things went wrong and we didn't have time to fix it. That's when you need the road. The original was a wonderful show. And it appealed to so many people. It should have worked. It was a huge disappointment. As I said in *The Dancer's Life*, the flowers I got opening night were just as fresh on closing night.

A couple of years later brought another disappointment, *Merlin*.

That's another one! I think they made a huge mistake! How in God's name, could you not . . . [Doug Henning] was not an actor, but this man created . . . the stage was not about his acting or anyone's acting; it was about magic! I always thought there was an audience for this show. Once every year at Radio City; for children. I thought the costumes were fabulous; that the magic was fabulous. I mean, he can't act, he can't sing, but. . . . The critics were also pissed at the fact that we didn't allow them to come in . . .

The longest preview period ever at that time . . .

It needed it! They were just pissed. I swear to you, I never felt good about the critics with that show.

Do you ever?

They were disgusting to Liza in *The Rink*. Just totally unnecessary.

What do you think that was about?

I think people expect Liza to be a certain way and Liza is a wonderful actress. But she's this mold: the hair, the eyes . . . they won't let her get out of it. It's too late now; she's in it to stay.

So not seeing her in sequins in *The Rink*, you think . . .

Absolutely. Absolutely. It wasn't the best time of her life, either. And I also think that people have a hard time, not seeing Liza, instead of Angel, or whomever she might be playing. We had Halston—it's almost embarrassing—design two red glitter gowns for our curtain call.

The fact that she was having struggles and ended up having to leave the show to get treatment was well documented. There was no anger on your part, that the show closed because of her struggles?

No, she was not well! You don't get angry with someone who's not well. No, you sympathize and you care about someone. Not in that case. I can get angry. But not in that case. It was clear. It couldn't go on.

When you won the Tony for *The Rink*, Liza was beyond happy for you.

That's exactly right. And that's honest. That's not put on. I know people somewhere in their living rooms were saying, "Oh, look at her acting." That's bull crap.

You idolized Gwen Verdon from the very beginning of your career. During *Can-Can* were you watching her and learning as you were doing with Elaine Stritch?

I still do! With George Hearn in *The Visit*, I watched him very carefully. I still think that you can learn from every single thing you do if you you're paying attention. [When I did *Mr. Wonderful*] I was such a little snot. The first act was the show, the plot, but the second act was this club act. I was sitting backstage thinking, "What are we doing? This is the theater!" Actors think they know it all. Wrong. The more I sat there the more I realized I was watching the greatest entertainer I had ever seen in my entire damned life [Sammy Davis Jr.] and there was a world to learn from this man. A world! And every single night he was singing, dancing, playing the drums, playing the trumpet, satisfying the audience. You look in the mirror and you say, "Can *you* do that? No!" I learned a huge lesson with *Mr. Wonderful*.

Can you talk about getting cast in *Bye Bye Birdie?*

I got a call to come in and to hear the score. Tom Poston called and said, "I just went and read for this show that is so awful, so terrible. It's the worst thing I've ever seen." And I'm thinking, "Oh no, my God, this is horrible, these are my friends." So, I called my agent, Dick, and I said, "We're going to go in, and we'll listen, and I'll say, 'Wow, that's really great,' and you'll say, 'We'll talk later' and we'll get the heck out of there." We get there and [director] Gower Champion is there, [author] Michael Stewart, [composer] Charles Strouse, all the guys. They start playing it and we get through the whole first act, and I flipped! I loved it. Totally, totally flipped. I stand up and I say, "I have to do this! I have to be a part of this!" And Dick is saying, "Uh, wait a minute . . ." Poor guy didn't know whether I was serious or not. I also remember thinking "Spanish Rose" kind of made me nervous. It was really typecasting me. You have to really trust your director and composers. Fortunately, we had brilliant people.

You got to go to London with *Birdie*. By that time you were a star in London so was the experience different?

Well, I was different. When we went with *West Side*, our eyes were as big as our heads! We were in England! This time it was, "Will I be what they thought I was?" You feel a little more responsible. It was a time when we were doing phenomenal musicals. You know, two years ago, I was walking down the street, and I saw this billboard and it says "*Bye Bye Birdie.*" I go a little further and I see this poster of a fearless blonde with a short sequined dress, straddling a chair, and it's "*Chicago.*" And then all of a sudden this big bus goes by me, and on the side of the bus it says "*West Side Story*!" And I say to myself, "Shouldn't I be someplace at 8:00 tonight?" I was at the right place at the right time. It was a good wonderful era. The golden age.

There are very few people from the golden age still working in the theater, though. You are.

I think that's my life path. I tell the kids, "Just be ready. If you want to do it and stay, make sure that you're ready." But I think I can give credit to the proper training I had. And a lot is luck, too. Parts came along at the right time.

West Side Story and *Bye Bye Birdie*, were two huge hits, but you didn't get to make the movies.

Yeah. But with *West Side*, I was in Philadelphia with *Birdie*. I would have cut my throat if *Birdie* hadn't been a hit. [Actually] I didn't really feel like that. I was always happy with what I was doing. When the movie thing didn't happen, I was in *Birdie*, having a great time with Dick Van Dyke and Kay Medford. I'm the kind of person . . . I'll figure myself out maybe before I die, but I'm the kind of person that really lives in the moment.

Thank God the movie *Sweet Charity* exists, because you have a film of you dancing!

That's nice, I love that. I'm sorry they never filmed Gwen doing that. But then she went on to do other things, and we're still talking about her today. I never thought, "I want a career in the theater."

Film, you mean?

No, theater in general. I never said I wanted a career. I just wanted to dance. But if all the gods put me in plays, that's where I'm supposed to be. I always say there's a huge tapestry that we're all born with and it's plain except for one red spot and that's your heart. Your life experiences are the things that make this painting your life. So you get colors and circles and jagged things and sad, dark places and bright lights and golds and things. That's what our life is. You can't control that, you can only be ready for it and do the very best you can. You can't yearn for the movie of *West Side*, or the movie of *Birdie*. Even though it upset me a little with *Birdie*, I was in London having a glorious time; with my husband, my baby, my new friends. Tell me what's bad about that? I wish I was in Hollywood? I wish I was dancing on a table? I was dancing on a table in London! Someone from the film asked if I would allow them to film one of my performances so that they could use it as reference. That got me! How rude is that? But Janet Leigh was the sweetest thing ever. She was a doll!

In 1970 you went to California and you did *Zorba* with John Raitt. That was your first experience with Kander and Ebb.

Yeah. I would not be standing here if not for them. They're my angels that have led me, taught me, given to me, shared with me, loved me. I was out on the road and John came and was teaching me "Life Is" in the pit of the theater. That's so theatrical. Everyone thinks it's all so glamorous but we were down in the hole in the pit. And I remember being pretty nervous because that was a hell of a score. I loved that show!

Your relationship with Kander and Ebb continued when you got to do *Chicago* in 1975. You're up there with Gwen Verdon, who, as we discussed, you had idolized. And now you're standing next to her.

It was a magical moment, one of the many I had with her. You can't beat that. A movie can't do that for me. And you do it every night! You get a chance to get into their aura, into their self; and you invite yourself, you exchange, and that's when the painting suddenly comes together. Gwen and I could be gold and red. But when we worked together, we became . . .

A fireburst?

Right! That's the goodness of life. You know Freddy and John wrote a song [for *Flora, the Red Menace*], "It's a quiet thing. Happiness comes in on tiptoe. . . . " That's a great song because the best things in life are quiet. Sometimes you can miss them if you don't live in the moment. I'm always so afraid I'm going to miss something. It all becomes a part of you. Gwen is a very big part of me. I have these memories in my head.

When you were doing *Chicago* in Vegas, you told me that you felt really comforted by feeling her presence, by feeling her ghost there with you.

Absolutely. And when I first did the part of Charity on the road, I realized I'm being asked to literally step into the greatest pair of shoes. And then I thought, "You know what? Take everything she's done, and bring your own shoes. Don't forget your own shoes. Why fix something that isn't broken?" So you use that because it's been already proven, and then you add yourself to it. That's why I have respect for the person that originates the part. They're the very first person that breathes life into something. And then you take that life, and you add what you have.

"He had it comin'" chant the merry murderesses in *Chicago*'s "Cell Block Tango." (Photofest)

Fred Ebb said that Bob Fosse was a bully to him during *Chicago*. Did that tension infiltrate your work?

Actually, we did have a situation, where he treated Freddy not very nicely, and Freddy, John, and I were pretty upset. I said, "Well, if you guys go, I'll go. We'll all go together." Of course we didn't.

While you were rehearsing *Chicago*, Bob Fosse had a heart attack, putting the show on hold. But that window of time gave you a club act! You got . . .

Another life. I mean it was just amazing thanks to Freddy and John. I had just moved from California, I had rented furniture, I put Lisa in professional children's school. Freddy, John, and Ron Field, said, "Let's do an act for you." We did it on a stage the size of this table in a gay bar. You do what you have to do when you have to. And who comes through this place? Gregory Peck, Liza and Jack Haley Jr., Fred Astaire, Gene Kelly. Everybody came right through that little dance hall where boys would dance with boys [to get to the cabaret in back].

The revival of *Chicago*. You did it in Vegas, you did it in Toronto, and London.

And that's funny, because I said I would never do it.

What made you change your mind?

Well, London. I like me some London. And then they asked me to do Vegas, and I thought, "Open a brand new theater? Excuse me? The scale is weighing. Go!" Everything is what you make of it. Everything. Living is how you accept whatever is before you.

What was the experience of doing the show again like for you . . .

Well, I had to accept and adjust. You have to go with it and you will continue to learn and be a part of it. It didn't feel anything like what I knew *Chicago* was about. I was doing Gwen's part, which made it a little easier for me to accept. But it felt empty compared to the feeling I had [originally]. It was like doing something in Technicolor and then doing it in black and white. It was slimmer and leaner and it was different. That's what was good about it, too. But you do wish audiences could have seen the huge spotlights come up and the spotlight down in that shaft of black and they could have seen the finger and then the arm and then the feather and then the entire body.

Your next Kander and Ebb show after the original *Chicago* was *The Rink* in 1984, which was also your first Tony win.

I don't anticipate a lot of stuff. I don't expect a lot of stuff. I can hope, but I don't expect. But I remember my mother had just died, and she was a great, great, great, wonderful, eloquent human being. When my name was announced, my mother stood up through me and I felt the earth. I had this beautiful posture, and I'm only like 5'4" . . .

You're 5'3".

See! I lied [about it] from the beginning and I'll die lying! I cannot believe to this day [that I forgot to thank Liza]. Every night I apologized during the curtain call. I was in such shock, and there's this huge clock, counting down thirty seconds, it really made me crazy. So, at the end of my curtain call, I would stop the applause, and say, "I would like to thank Liza."

Your next show was *Jerry's Girls*, the following season.

I'd been madly in love with Jerry. I think he's the people's composer. You leave a Jerry Herman show and you can hum just about all of the melody. He's the kindest, sweetest guy. There was a dress in there that Dorothy Collins had worn in *Follies*. Gorgeous dress. It weighed ninety-five pounds. It was absolutely fabulous, but I put it on and dropped to my knees. So I'm downstairs in my dressing room and I called Jerry down. I loved and adored [costume designer] Florence Klotz, but she was a little tyrant. I was so scared of her and Jerry was too. We were like two kids, peeking out the door, checking to see if she was gonna come down, because I was complaining about this gorgeous dress that I didn't want to wear. I didn't want to tell her. So finally, I said to Jerry, "Your name is Jerry Herman! The show is called *Jerry's Girls*! Why are we scared of Florence Klotz?" But it was wonderful! I was able to do a number like a guy, it was just a great experience.

And then, of course, during the run you had your accident and a grueling recovery.

But I lived!

You did more than live; you danced.

Hello! I remember, someone saying to me, "You'll be fine. You'll be different, but you'll be fine." And I thought, "I won't be different! Of course I won't be different. With the training, nothing is impossible." You just do it. This fabulous dancer called me crying, "Chita, oh my God, how horrible, it's just terrible . . ." and I had to say, "Wait, calm down. . . ." Me calming her down, and I'm the one with my leg up. I'm alive! And I'm going to go back to do whatever it is that I'm supposed to be doing. I don't know what it's going to be. You never know. You have to think of it that way. You have a choice. You think the older you get everything is going to be smooth and nice, because you've worked hard? No, it just gets harder.

Your recovery . . .

Well, I had an excellent doctor, and I had all the trust in the world in him. I believe it was only a year later that I did *Can-Can.* As you go along, you start to recover. You feel more and more sure of yourself. It just felt like me. There was no problem at all. I had a good doctor and good genes. And I'm a good patient. I follow what the doctor tells me. But also, it's a lot of luck.

I think it has everything to do with faith and believing that there is a future.

Oh, absolutely, absolutely. I thought, "I've got to fix this," and that's what you do.

And then, when you healed, you were doing *Can-Can* again . . .

If you line up in a kick line with the Rockettes, it's a whole other understanding of movement, so it was really exciting to be with them. I mean they're serious.

And given that you had been a Fosse dancer, and Fosse's all about precision, to be surrounded by the Rockettes who are nothing if not precise . . .

That's why being in the chorus of a show is so important. It's a shame when kids don't have that experience, and they become stars before they become part of a company, because the chorus line teaches you the unison.

After *Can-Can* your return to the Broadway stage was so triumphant; *Kiss of the Spider Woman.*

Oh, yeah. How about that for luck, huh?

Do you think it's luck?

It's everything. Being in the right place at the right time. They did that up in Purchase. If I had been hired for the Purchase thing, who knows, maybe I wouldn't have done Broadway. You don't know. So whatever that word "luck" is—and I think we should really define it a little better—you have to be at the right place at the right time. If we call that luck, then luck and being ready is what it's all about.

Luck, destiny . . .

You never know what that is until you take your last breath. You really don't know. That's why I feel so sad when people give up. And it's so easy to do that, just give up, having no hope for the next day. People who take their lives and all of that. It's just—you just never ever know.

Hal Prince said about the Toronto run that you were "stuck performing a dud song, never once complaining, never once the diva." Was that your feeling about it?

Well, I knew it wasn't right, but you pray that the great people that you're working with see it. And I was surrounded by geniuses, and they saw it and fortunately fixed it. Rob Marshall! Actually, Graciela [director/ choreographer Graciela Daniele] brought Rob to the piece because she couldn't stay.

Given the degree to which you are so conscious about nurturing young talent, was it gratifying watching Rob Marshall take the lead?

It is one of the most gratifying feelings you could have. He was in the chorus of *The Rink,* and now he's directing the Caribbean pirate things [the fourth *Pirates of the Caribbean* film] and *Chicago* and—it's just—you kind of fly on their wings also. You're all flying together. It's a beautiful thing to see that he's successful. And Graciela was in the chorus of *Chicago.* So you're just surrounded by beautiful memories and possibilities and all that sort of thing. I called Jerry Robbins first to find out if he could come and help us, and he could not. Then I thought, "why not my soul mate, Graciela, my sister?" She said, "I have two days, and I'll bring up Rob." Well, if you hang out with the good people, if you rub elbows with the right people who you can trust, then whatever it is they say . . . She brought up Rob, and I believed he could do it, and sure enough he did. You feel safe.

You have also told me that you're fascinated with death. So given that you were the embodiment of death in that show, was that an interesting exploration?

Yeah. I just let it happen. I remember something I saw so clearly when one of the boys was escaping and shot down on the fence: I said to Hal, "I would love to fly up" since I flew in the show, "and just hold onto him, as death." That would be a fabulous image. One hopes that when you die, it'll be a beautiful, painless, death. That's what one prays for, and a beautiful life afterwards, and so it was my opportunity to put some of those feelings into that character and make her not so frightening.

The concept that when we die we are received. If we could all be received—

That's exactly right. When you die you're received. So that's what I tried to do, and Brent Carver was just a beautiful guy to assist in his imagination and his fantasy. He was so brilliant. I remember somebody saying in an interview that we did together, "How do you feel at your age being someone's fantasy," and Brent was totally insulted by that. He totally took charge. I didn't have to even answer. I never forgot it.

Part of what was so triumphant about that performance is that every time Aurora showed up, you owned the stage in a way that was just—it was almost like all of your years on the stage were coming together for this ownership.

I've said that if *Spider Woman* had come maybe ten, fifteen years earlier, I might not have been really ready for it. But it came at the perfect time in my life. I was ready to accept the subject matter: death and movie star, particularly the movie star thing of it. I would never have thought of myself as an elegant, really beautifully clothed movie star and somebody's fantasy. But it came at the perfect time. I was ready to receive it. I was ready to interpret it. I was just—it was like going in and having the perfect pair of shoes, perfect. That doesn't happen too often.

Even in a great career, it only happens a couple of times, if ever. That perfect match.

Yeah. That's very true. And when I think about—and I do, I'm very grateful. Think about how many times it's happened to me. It came around at a phenomenal time with *Spider Woman*, *Chicago*, *West Side*, *Bye Bye Birdie*. That's pretty exceptional.

During *Spider Woman* your fame took on a whole new level. You were suddenly an icon. Did you experience it that way?

Well, everything was so perfect. Every creative department just fit. It was like a perfect puzzle. And so everything was elevated. We all felt a bit like royalty because we were extremely proud of what we were doing, really proud. So we were riding on a great wave that was carrying us. Whatever it is I do, I want it to be 200 percent, and it to be something in which I can seriously respect myself and everybody connected with it. That's the thing you pray for. I always say I don't want to do something that is beneath what I believe in. Because you also carry the dreams of young kids that may look at you and say, "because of you I want to do that."

At this stage of your career also, you inspire on a whole other level. You prove that one can have a sixty-year career in the musical theater. That's astonishing.

Yeah, it is, it is. A lot has to do with timing. When I came along there were great, great shows. I'm trying to fight for real musicals. That's why I wanted *The Visit* to go because nobody creates great musicals like we do. And we need some new, smart, creative musicals. It's great to do the revivals. It's fabulous to do them, but only revivals? No.

Well, it's an interesting segue because your next Broadway show after *Spider Woman* . . .
Was a revival.

What made you decide to do *Nine*?
I listen to the voices in my head. I listen to what people say, and I stand by my decisions. And so even years and years ago when I was doing *Zenda*, *1491*, if anybody said it was terrible, I didn't believe it. When we closed, "okay, it was just supposed to close," or, "isn't that a shame we didn't go to New York but okay, next." You've got to believe that they're really good.

How else can you perform it? How can you commit to it on the stage if you don't believe it?
Oh, you can. You can make it true for yourself. You just fake it. You add your person to it, which hopefully elevates it a bit.

So *Nine* comes along, and what did you think when you decided it was for you?
I love telling the story. I was out in California doing something at The Mark Taper Forum and [Director] David Leveaux was staying in Hollywood. He wanted to talk to me about *Nine*, and I thought, "I don't want to do that." I saw the [original] show. I loved Raul Julia, I loved what Tommy Tune did with the show, I thought it was wonderful. But I came from a time where I did my own roles. It's just what you're used to. You know what I mean? David Leveaux and I had an amazing lunch, and I loved everything he said about the show. If I look at you, and I believe in you, I'll go with it. I'm pretty good at picking people out. So I looked at David and I said, "You know what? I have this image of myself in *Nine*. I see Antonio as this huge, huge bird with long, long wings, and a long body, and this beautiful feathered tail, and I see me on the back of the tail dressed fabulously and just on the tail for the ride, as I soar with Antonio." That was my image, and we both laughed. But that really was my image. I wanted to be on Antonio's trip.

And you were?
Yep, I was.

You had your leg up on Antonio Banderas's shoulder every night; how was that for you?
How would that have been for you?

That's why I'm asking the question.
Eat your heart out. You just take advantage of those moments. And they're fabulous. You don't want moments to go by. I don't want my life to go by. I want to be present in all those great moments, in every moment. To get that tango with Antonio—I describe it in my show, and there he is blindfolded, which is a very sexy sight. I describe it as being a leather blindfold. It wasn't leather at all.

You're allowed.

Oh, sure I am. Practically everybody in that audience was saying, "I wish I was her."

Your next endeavor was so, so fascinating. You told your own story in *The Dancer's Life*. What was the impetus for doing it to begin with?

Well, I've been asked many times, "When are you going to write your book?" I haven't really ever wanted to write a book. I always wanted to say it, do it, describe it, share it myself. I sat with a writer, Patrick Pacheco, hour after hour, day after day, and we just talked over dinner, over drinks, and he wrote all of my stories and all of my thoughts and the years in the business, and then we gave those papers to Terrence McNally.

So it was as if you were writing your book, as if you were dictating your memoirs.

Yeah. And Terrence knew me so well. I knew that the words would come out right. And Graciela is like my sister. I wish I could tell you exactly how long it took us to pull all this together, and I wish I could tell you how many sheets of paper, but we gave it to Terrence, Terrence put it together—he and Gracie—and that was that.

So once you found it on paper, and you went to through that creation process, was the experience of living it onstage nightly what you thought it was going to be?

Oh, it was fab. I didn't have any preconceived ideas. I just wanted to be able to tell stories and share choreographers and enjoy the dances. When [composers] Lynn Ahrens and Stephen Flaherty played the special material for me, I was gone. It was just perfect. I absolutely knew that it was right. And I loved the whole formula of the piece. I just thought it was terrific. It exposed me the way I wanted to be exposed.

Looking back on it now with some perspective, did it do what you wanted to do?

Yeah, absolutely. I wouldn't want it to have been done any other way.

As I mentioned before, the piece of the show that is both so theatrical and also just seared in my memory is the choreographic lesson with the dancers in silhouette.

Amazing. My purpose is to share and to teach. To educate the young dancers that want that. And so many kids today don't know who Jack Cole is, don't know anybody but Bob Fosse. And I think that show was a lesson. I consider that show a gift from me to any dancer or any performer that wanted to be in the theater. This woman can do it. It can be done. And it can last a nice, long time. And I think Terrence and Gracie allowed me to do that.

It's beautiful, not only to have that career and that life and those opportunities, but the desire to teach and pass on the inspiration.

Yeah, yeah. It is beautiful. That's why I really—I'm blessed, Eddie, and I know it. I truly am grateful for it, and I won't do anything, I hope, consciously to mess it up. I always said to Lisa, "Lisa, if you see me with a skirt too short or too much lipstick or too much makeup, would you kindly tell me?"

That also speaks to your rule about never ever being destructive and never saying anything that you think can be harmful.

No. If people can just understand that caring, sharing, and loving or healing—life would be so much simpler. You just break hearts when you put something dark out there, when you put out something evil or mean. It's destructive. It's not worth it. I just believe what goes around comes around, and I have too many examples of sharing and loving and laughing getting you so much more than being destructive.

At the beginning and the end of *The Dancer's Life* you reference winning the Kennedy Center Honors. How do you digest getting that kind of recognition and honor for your work? What's it like to be a legend?

The word is kind of funky to me.

It's been tossed your way enough times that you must have considered it.

It just goes in one ear and out the other. But I think when you do what you feel you have to do, and you've been blessed enough to have a gift for it or way to express it . . . but you hit your head, like, "I should have had a V8." You go, "Oh my God. I did that? I forgot. Look at all these people. Look at Brian Stokes Mitchell coming all the way down here to D.C. to talk. Look at all these fabulous dancers dancing to music that I know so well." I'm sitting with my daughter behind me, the president a little further down, I'm in the Kennedy Center. It's like I'm slapping myself saying, "how the heck did I get here? I can't believe this has happened to me." I had these diamond earrings on. They were not mine. I got so excited that I jumped up, applauding, and an earring flew off. I caught it in midair. I could not believe it. I was bombarded with all of the—I'm crying, I'm sending such love to all those kids who were so happy to be there. It was really quite something. And to have gone into one of the rooms in the White House from which I could see the monument from the window? If it were a movie, I could have seen these four kids—because my older sister was too old—but say five kids, running around the monument with my mother and father, and there I was standing in the White House. That caught me right in my stomach. And then when I went for the Medal of Freedom I'm sitting there with all of these amazing people. I see the Marine on the other side, and I'm thinking any minute now he's going to come over and go, "Miss Rivera, I'm sorry we've made a mistake. Would you come with me, please?" How the heck did I get there? Well, I got there because I was chosen. I worked hard. I have no qualms with saying I worked my butt off, but I loved every minute of it and still do. And I keep telling the kids, if you work hard enough and long enough, something is going to happen, something. I am doing it to communicate and to really entertain, to make people happy, to educate, to open eyes, to excite, give a little bit of my passion. That's why we love Liza; expecting nothing other than that you love her back, she gives it all. When you see someone who really wants to give you their heart . . . [as a performer] there's nothing like being there with people who care. It's the biggest greatest party you can have.

You once told me that you wished you could have accepted the Kennedy Center Honor in the gypsy robe.

Totally. You just brought tears to my eyes. Completely, completely. I would have worn—you know what that would have done for the kids? How amazing could that be? That's what it's all about. It's about all of us. *The Dancer's Life* was about all of us, not just me. Just told through me, but it was for every dancer that's ever given their time and wanted to dance.

What you're talking about is community. It's about recognizing that it's all about collaboration and community.

Right. We don't do anything alone. We never do anything alone. Even an imagination comes from other places and seeing other things. Different things put together in a different way. You do it with the world.

Here we are in 2012 and you're about to go into another Broadway show, *The Mystery of Edwin Drood*. What made you say "yes" to this one?

I've got to keep moving. I've got to keep doing.

But you've been moving. You've been performing your act all over the place.

I have, but it was a choice of whether or not I was going to do another completely different show. And this came around. Just like *Bye Bye Birdie* came, and I didn't think it was going to work. That was a good-enough example for me to keep in mind for the rest of my life because you never know. So even though I had no desire, I said, "Okay, let me have lunch with [director] Scott Ellis" who was in *The Rink*, and [author] Rupert Holmes." And it felt good. And I said yes. It was as simple as that. I simply want to keep active. I remember hearing about this show, and I remember Graciela getting some fabulous reviews [for the original production]. Anything Graciela decides to do, I always think it's got to be interesting.

What about *The Visit*? You have been working for years to get that show to Broadway. Is that chapter closed?

I had just put *The Visit* someplace in my head where it wasn't going to hurt my heart anymore. There are a lot of things that take years to get going.

Is it heartbreaking to be that invested?

Yeah. Oh yeah, it hurts. It really hurts. It throws you into some strange places. I have been lucky because it hasn't happened to me very often. *The Rink* didn't run. *Bring Back Birdie* didn't run very long. Everybody tells you, "It's really great" but you cannot believe all of it. You really believe what you feel from the inside. You hope that it is going to be brilliant. Closed. Nothing. You are disappointed. And then people keep coming at you, "It was fabulous!" I have to numb myself to it because you hear all of these conversations—they want it in LA, they want it in Canada, but nothing is being done. So what you do is you save yourself and put it someplace way back here. You just want to know the truth but that's not the way the business is.

You are implying that the economics and business have something to do with quality and frequently they do not.

That's what you have to say to yourself. You do what you do. You believe in what you believe. You've been around long enough, you know what the business is like, so you have to say to yourself, "Were you proud of that piece?" Yes, I was seriously proud of it. But then the ego kicks in and you're thinking, "I want the world to see this! Especially since THAT piece of shit is on Broadway." I describe *The Visit* as this thing over in the corner and every time I look it's over there waving at me. You are going on with your life and it jumps out and says, "HI! I'm back again. But not 100 percent."

It teases you. Tuning out the chatter throughout your entire career must be something you've had to deal with.

That's the only way you save yourself. That's the only way.

People can be so rhapsodic about you and about your contributions. As I said, you are called a legend. I'm wondering if that makes sense to you when you hear it?

Well, I'm honored. Hey. I'll take all the love I can get. Keep it coming. Just keep it coming. You just want to make sure that you do justice to everything that is before you, and you respect everything.

I guess where the question comes from . . . I'm really bad at taking compliments and if I had to magnify that by about 400,000 times to the way it comes at you, I don't know how I would process it.

You know what? Sometimes you feel it's kind of overdone a little bit. You can control how long you want to stand in front of somebody that's gushing. You're your own measuring cup, you know? But you accept it, because people want to do that. You're satisfying them. They want to thank you.

You were quoted once as saying, "Each time out it's harder because people expect more from you." Do you still feel that way?

Oh, sure. And it's doubly kind of strange when you're doing something that somebody else has done. They have that automatic comparison in their brain. I do feel that. But you know what? If you go out there as you are, and you give everything that you've got, there's nothing more you can do. As you get older, you hope that you take some gratification in knowing that, knowing that you have done the best you can. But I still want to knock their socks off.

DONNA MCKECHNIE

May 2008

"YOU VACUUMED!" EXCLAIMED DONNA MCKECHNIE with an admonishing laugh. She had told me not to clean for her, but in all the years I've been conducting interviews, never had a subject come to my home before. Of course, I vacuumed. I had to do something and I couldn't buy her any food since McKechnie's diet is a careful one. In the early '80s, she suffered agonizing, debilitating rheumatoid arthritis. She was told she would never walk again, let alone dance. McKechnie rejected the prognosis and through a combination of diet and therapy (both physical and psycho-), slowly restored her health. But I wasn't about to buy food for a woman whose very mobility is influenced by her diet. So the least I could do was clean. I needn't have worried about taking care of her. McKechnie sailed in to my home looking self-assured and radiant with a black iced coffee and a sandwich. Although she arrived directly from dance class (something she attends five times a week), McKechnie was freshly made up and stylishly springy, conveying warmth, confidence and an easy grace. "I used to live right there!" she said, pointing out my window to a building directly across the way. "In a ground floor sublet." Not surprising, as McKechnie has lived everywhere in the fifty years since she came to New York to dance at the advanced age of fifteen. In the grand tradition of the Broadway gypsy, McKechnie has had a new apartment almost every time she had a new show. And there were lots of them. She saves everything, which doesn't make moving easy. But at the time of our meeting, she and her sister were preparing for a massive garage sale, just to purge. "I have too much," she confessed. "I got rid of a hundred books and my shelves still looked completely full!" This, too, was no surprise. Because even though McKechnie makes much of never having graduated from high school, she is clearly quite well read, intelligent, and very intuitive.

Donna McKechnie was born in Pontiac, Michigan, in 1942. Like the character of Sheila in *A Chorus Line*, as a child she saw *The Red Shoes* and knew instantly that she had to dance. Like *A Chorus Line*'s Maggie, her parents were not particularly well matched and her father wasn't particularly supportive of her performing. Her mother was, though, making sacrifices so that McKechnie could attend ballet class starting from the age of five. Her move to New York paid off almost instantaneously when McKechnie was cast in the original company of the smash hit musical *How to Succeed in Business Without Really Trying*, where she encountered lifelong idols Bob Fosse and Gwen Verdon. Subsequent shows included tours of *A Funny Thing Happened on the Way to the Forum* and *Call Me Madam*, the short-lived *The Education of H*Y*M*A*N K*A*P*L*A*N*, and then her breakout in *Promises, Promises* in which her Act 1 closer, "Turkey Lurkey Time," stopped the show cold. After taking *Promises* to London, she came back to Broadway in another smash, *Company*.

As the title character in the national tour of *Sweet Charity*, Bob Fosse's final production. (Photofest)

Promises and *Company* were both choreographed by Michael Bennett, who had danced with McKechnie on the television series *Hullabaloo* during the mid-'60s. It was he who conceived of one of Broadway's greatest masterpieces, *A Chorus Line*. The legendary workshopping sessions, of which McKechnie was a part, had him gathering dancers to tell the stories that ultimately became the basis for the show. McKechnie's portrayal of Cassie won her a Tony Award and made her a star. At the height of *A Chorus Line*'s popularity, McKechnie and Bennett were married. The marriage ended quickly and with it, their collaboration. But McKechnie continued playing Cassie around the world for years, including a triumphant return to the

Broadway production in 1986. Immediately after, she headlined the national tour of *Sweet Charity*, directed by Bob Fosse and coached by Gwen Verdon in what would be Fosse's final production. Her subsequent shows have played Broadway (*State Fair*), the West End (*Can-Can*), off-Broadway (*Cut the Ribbons, Annie Warbucks*), regional theatre (*Gypsy, Ten Cents a Dance, The Glass Menagerie*, and two separate, acclaimed productions of *Follies*), and most notably, tours of her autobiographical shows, *Inside the Music* and *My Musical Comedy Life.*

In 2007, McKechnie published her autobiography, *Time Steps*. The book is striking in its honesty. What *Time Steps* doesn't capture, however, is the pure, unadulterated joy McKechnie gets from performing. It has to be seen to be truly understood.

A few weeks after the conversation that follows, I saw McKechnie in a late-night turn to promote *Time Steps* at New York's venerable gay bar, Splash. On a stage barely big enough for McKechnie, her keyboardist, and her water bottle, she belted out "Turkey Lurkey Time" and *A Chorus Line's* "The Music and the Mirror," among others. Even in such a confined space, she was unmistakably a dancer. A pop of the head, a hip undulation, and a reach of her arms were enough to send the crowd into a state of prolonged hysteria, none of it gratuitous. Even with the limitations of space, McKechnie, at sixty-six years old, sold those moves, which were created for her instrument, like no one else. Afterward, dripping with sweat, she asked me if I thought it was "okay," but her incandescent smile made it clear that she knew that she was more than okay. She was untouchable.

Donna McKechnie

How to Succeed in Business without Really Trying, Broadway, 1961

A Funny Thing Happened on the Way to the Forum, National Tour, 1963

The Education of H*Y*M*A*N K*A*P*L*A*N, Broadway, 1968

Call Me Madam, National Tour, 1968

Promises, Promises, Broadway and West End, 1968

Company, Broadway, Los Angeles, West End, 1970, 1972

On the Town, Broadway, 1971

A Chorus Line, off-Broadway, Broadway, National Tour, Japan, West End, 1975, 1986 (Tony Award)

Sweet Charity, National Tour, 1987

Can-Can, West End, 1988

Cut the Ribbons, off-Broadway, 1992

Annie Warbucks, off-Broadway, 1993

Fiorello! Encores! 1994

State Fair, Broadway and National Tour, 1996

Follies, Millburn, N.J., 1998

Babes in Arms, Encores! 1999

In your book you were very candid about the life of a gypsy in New York.

Well, I was a dancer growing up in New York, independent and on her own. You don't have any money. You never have any money. I didn't. Because even though you're working on Broadway—I started on Broadway when we were making $165 a week. I loved the fact that I could support myself, but it all went to lessons. Thank goodness I had that wherewithal. Subletting was the only way to do it. And you had roommates. I wasn't alone. We just went from sublet to sublet and survived.

I think that people who aren't in the business have the perception that that kind of lifestyle exists when you're twenty or twenty-two. But the reality is that even after you've "made it," you're still going from job to job and sublet to sublet.

Well, that's how I was able to live in New York. It's what you do. But I really liked that lifestyle. I really enjoyed it. And I still do. But it really makes a difference to have your own home, and I'm lucky to have that now.

You grew up outside of Detroit and you came to New York at the mature age of fifteen.

Yeah. I do master classes all over the country and I use my story as a cautionary tale. I suffered many years from tearing myself away from my family that young. I did something really good for myself in a way, but I wasn't mature enough to take responsibility for it. I took a lot of baggage that I didn't need. I had a lot of emotional pain and guilt.

I imagine that for students hearing you, it's hard to really accept your story as a cautionary tale. Because while what you say was true for you, it's also true that you were working almost immediately after you got here.

That was lucky. I say to them, "Don't be so quick to come to New York. It will be here. But in the meantime, there are a lot of great teachers all over the country. Make sure that when you do come here, you know how to sing and act."

In your case, your parents really didn't want you to go, but you knew you had to be here?

Well, I didn't so much need to be in New York as much as I had an opportunity. Someone offered me a job. I don't think I would've done it without that. I had the opportunity to work and get a paycheck, and I thought it would be my way out.

That sounds so much like Sheila in *A Chorus Line* [who says she started dancing to get out of her childhood home]. It's been said that Cassie is based on you, but really, all three women who sing "At the Ballet," Bebe, Sheila, and Maggie, are also all somewhat based on you.

And Judy Turner.

It's interesting, the boxes people want you to be in.

Cassie is actually the most fictionalized of the characters but people don't want to believe it. It was all manufactured. But I got really tired of trying to explain it that way. So I started saying, "Yeah, it's the truth, yeah, yeah, yeah." That musical has so much significance for so many people, I'm not going to take away from something that moves them.

Going back to your earlier years, you ended up in theater sort of by accident. You were trained as a ballet dancer.

I was one of those little ballerina girls. Kind of precious. Musical theater was not considered art. I don't know where I got that idea. I got my Equity card at the Cass Theater in Detroit. Betty White came in and did Anna in *The King and I*. I did *Bittersweet* with Jeanette MacDonald. I thought it was great fun, but it was almost like a guilty pleasure. When I came to New York, musical theater wasn't as artistic in my mind. But, [in 1961] when I started working on *How to Succeed . . .* with those giants, I knew right away that it really was great. And I was very lucky. Even as a silly teenager, I knew that I was into something wonderful and I could learn something. That's when I turned around and went, "I have to really learn how to do this well, because this is great work."

It's amazing that you knew that. You were in the presence of Bob Fosse and Gwen Verdon and [producer] Cy Feuer and [composer] Frank Loesser and [director/librettist] Abe Burrows but still, I wonder how many seventeen-year-olds would have the presence of mind to know that they're at the heart of something incredible.

I knew it. I loved the professionalism. I loved being with people like myself. It was a family that I took to. Although I'm sure I got on everyone's nerves.

Why do you say that?

I just know I did. I was silly in some ways, I was so naïve. I had my initiation in the ladies dressing room—the girls dressing room, we called it. That was back when we had eight singing ladies and eight dancing ladies, and we all shared this one great big dressing room. I was really put to the test. I would be Chatty Cathy. I remember Mara Landi saying, "Would you shut the fuck up?" It terrified me. But I was growing up. I was learning from everybody and taking it all in. I was trying to be part of it. Phil Friedman was our great stage manager, and he helped me. I had to learn discipline. I had it as a dancer. But that was the first show where I truly got it and understood collaboration. I learned that everybody works together. We all have these crazy personalities, but you keep it in check. I loved being part of that world. [*How to Succeed . . .*] turned me around, and I'm glad it was a hit. Because I was able to study acting and voice. With all my silliness, I do respect myself for being able to do the right thing and study.

In what ways were you silly?

I was the girl who couldn't say "no." I would make a date with two people and then I would try to get someone to get rid of one of them. One friend who sat next to me [in the dressing room], Silver Saundors, she would say, "What have you done today?" She was a big sister who would sit me down and tell me the ways of the world and how to behave. There was a lot of affection there but I think I got on her nerves.

That's what any seventeen-year-old would have been doing. But you were never silly onstage?

No no no. But I do remember Phil would come to me and say, "What are you doing to your shoes?" Because I was a really strong dancer and I used to go through shoes faster than anyone. They had to keep replacing the soles.

How did you end up getting the show?

I was picked to do the show by Cy Feuer. I didn't even go to a dance call. That never happened again. I thought that was the way you got in: you meet a nice producer, and he'd say, "Why don't you be in our show?" What did I know? The whole style of the show was an adjustment for me, but ballet gave me a great reference. Usually dancers with a classical background can make those transitions. . . . I shouldn't say that because I can only speak for myself. But I think that classical training teaches you something so solid that you can take on other styles of dance. You have to learn how to turn everything in but the basic fundamental things that keep you strong so you don't have injuries, you get those from ballet training. I see dancers who don't have it. They have that great jazzy energy but they don't have the ballet training so they don't know that, for example, when they put their arms up their shoulders go up too. They're not aware of how their muscles work and how everything has to stay open and up. They have their moves but they're limited. If you have classical basic training you can adapt more easily.

After *How to Succeed . . .* , you went on tour as Philia in *A Funny Thing Happened on the Way to the Forum* and then in 1968 you did *Call Me Madam* with Ethel Merman.

Oh yeah, she was someone I admired. You know, I didn't know at the time, but Ethel Jr., her daughter, had just committed suicide like three months earlier. Merman was in grief. She never toured, but Merman took this circuit, I think, to work, to escape her grief. It was great. Every night she had people on their feet. She was really strict, standoffish. She'd go from the stage to the dressing room and not socialize. But when I was leaving to go do *Promises, Promises,* on my last night, she paid me this high compliment by trying to break me up onstage, which is something you would never see her do any other night. Someone explained to me that they used to do that in vaudeville; when someone would leave the fold to go onto another show that's what you would do.

What was she doing?

Making funny sounds in her throat while we were speaking in our scene. Crossing her eyes. I didn't know what was wrong. I thought she was having a stroke. I got it, eventually. A little late. She was saying to me, "job well done." The first day I met her, I was rehearsing. The director was so happy that I was a dancer because he could do "The Ocarina" number with the principal dancing instead of what it had been, with the chorus dancing around her. So I was learning that number and another number that I had and that's when I met her. She came to the pavilion that we had outside of the theater. I see her sit down at the table with the director and I'm up there performing. I'm showing off a little because I'm so excited to be in the show with her. And I finish and she says, "Who did she fuck to get two dance numbers?"

Was that terrifying?

I just thought I'd better watch out. [After that] I was having a grand time, springing from show to show, and I thought that it always happens that way. It's not that I took it for granted. If I was out of work for a few weeks I would get desperate. I didn't have a sense that that was the nature of it.

It's even harder to be a gypsy and go from show to show now.

I think it is. And that's how we learned. We would go from audition to audition. You'd go from [director/choreographer] Joe Layton to [director/choreographer] Michael Kidd. It was a way to learn different styles. You know, when I first came to New York, I did a show with Peggy Cass and she gave me some good advice. She said, "You've got to work with everybody you can, every choreographer. Learn their style, and they will keep hiring you." She knew how to survive in this business. Thank God for Michael Bennett in my life. He really liked my style and he really liked the way his work looked on my body. Choreographers will find dancers who can take their work and interpret it. They gather their instruments.

How would you define his style?

Michael never had a real style. He worked with character and story. He had a lot of long lines and a lot of reaching as opposed to keeping energy right under you but he didn't have a specific style.

Well, there certainly is a through-line from "Tick-Tock" [in *Company*] to "Music and the Mirror," don't you think?

Right, but when you see his shows the dancing comes from the story and the characters and the psychology. I like to see that. I see it in new choreographers too, and it's gratifying. I was talking to Mercedes Ellington [choreographer and granddaughter of Duke Ellington] about how, with AIDS, we lost a whole generation. In our business, you train people to pass it on. And those people either become dance captains or choreographers or artists. It's a living, breathing art form. We missed a whole bridging of a generation when we lost our choreographers, directors, and dancers who had come up from show to show to show. You can never know, but I think it really hurt a whole generation. I said to Mercedes that you notice it when you go to the schools. The young dancers don't know how to fill space. They don't know about momentum. They miss fundamentals like using their plié. Everything is up, up, up, not down, down, down. We learned the ability to fill space and to travel, to build strength. I'm not seeing it now. I think it's because of losing so many people who pass these techniques down.

There were many more auditions back then, weren't there?

Well, shows didn't run for years and years. You could run a season and be a hit. A couple of years was a long run. You can't make the money back now unless you run longer.

Let's go back to *Promises, Promises*, your first show with Michael Bennett choreographing for you. Would you say that show changed your career?

Yeah, that was like a dream. Thank God I had my dancing. Before I was stricken with arthritis and was told I couldn't dance anymore, there were so many years I was trying to get out of that dancer mold. I thought it was keeping me from achieving, from getting singing and acting roles. *Promises* was the first show that a producer outside of Cy Feuer hired me to be an actress and a singer and not a dancer. When we were in Boston, they had to cut half an hour out of the show. I played a secretary who is having an affair with one of the guys and the secondary roles were getting cut. We had these cute little silly scenes, and we sang a song called "Marriage Is for Single Girls" that was cut. Two of the secretaries were fired, and I definitely would have been let go if Michael hadn't come up with the dance. Originally, the three secretaries were not dancers. The number "Turkey Lurkey Time" was going to be built around them and this drunken Christmas party. It was horrible. It was Michael's stab at trying to find a reality in his staging and it really backfired. He went, "Oh my God, I can fix this" and he made this really big production number. And that's how I was able to keep the role which now had only one line, but it had a great number. So I stopped resenting dancing that year.

Did you have the perception that you were transitioning and that you were getting a new kind of recognition?

Yes, I felt that there was recognition value. It was an important step.

And obviously it was an important step in terms of your dancing relationship with Michael. You had danced with him on *Hullabaloo* and you had worked together. But at this point, did you feel that you were becoming his primary muse?

I never perceived it that way. We had an affinity. We had the same language, I guess. And he appreciated it. I was excited to work with him, but it never took the characterization of "muse," in my mind, anyway. But then when Hal Prince interviewed me for *Company*, that was a landmark for me because I thought I was going to audition but I wasn't. He was showing me the sets and introducing me to people. I was cast without an audition. He wanted Michael to do the show and Michael wasn't interested. I think that bringing me in was a way to get Michael. I don't think that's the only reason, but I think that's the main reason.

That's outstanding on a number of levels. Kathy [McKechnie's *Company* role] wasn't a dance role yet and in *Promises*, all you did was dance. Yet he had the faith in you as a performer to cast you and use you as bait for Michael?

Actually, he saw a performance of a show that was really good but didn't have much of a run [*The Education of H*Y*M*A*N K*A*P*L*A*N*]. I did have a number and a song in that. I tell this to students all the time—you never know who's in the audience. Hal Prince remembered me years later. Now, in *Company*, that's when I felt something really thrilling was happening. I mean, I loved *Promises*. I thought it was first-rate, very smart. Michael's work was tremendous. But *Company* was a big step. It was the first adult musical. It was ensemble and you were there and part of this whole world of contemporary New York City. And Stephen Sondheim. I remember the first day, at the reading, his pages just overflowed. That was a really important show and I knew it. It was special. You don't always know how it's going to be accepted, but if you're an artist you appreciate the artistic endeavor. You really do feel it. It moves you. I had never seen anything like it. I had never been in anything like it and I had done enough to know that this show was indeed really cutting edge for that time.

And again, you were with giants: Sondheim, Hal Prince, George Furth, and a perfect cast.
I loved everybody. I still maintain friendships from those days and from that show. It was a phenomenal experience. Very, very lucky.

And you were in one of two relationships that came out of the reunion of that show [a 1993 benefit concert for Broadway Cares, reuniting the entire original cast]. You and George Coe and Beth Howland and Charles Kimbrough.
That's right. They were in love for years, but married to other people. Out of respect for their status, they didn't act on it. But they were soul mates. And I adored George. I tortured him because I would never leave New York City. But he was dear. He was a wonderful person.

And you became very friendly with Elaine Stritch during *Company*.
Oh yeah. I loved her. It was like with Merman. You can really learn from people like that. I just love her work and she is so courageous and free. I thought she was a real character. She would make me laugh. In my book I talk about a story that was hilarious to me. She had a nervous breakdown on opening night in Boston. I was onstage, in the Plexiglas, and I'm watching her in reflection. I can't move, but I can see her reflection. And she's doing all these things—putting her fingers in her mouth and on her face. Afterwards. I went to her and said, "What were you doing?" and she said, "I was looking for the words!"

In her show, she speaks at length and quite candidly about her alcohol abuse. That was still going on during *Company*.
But she was consistent. She never was out. But she did ruin a couple of dates of mine, though.

How?
We went for food next door to the theater and she comes in and she's been tippling a bit and she sits on the table and says, "So you finally got a date!" Normally, it might've made me laugh but it didn't make me laugh that night and she couldn't remember it. But she loved her work so much and she was the most consistent. She was there more than anyone.

Today much is made of absenteeism. Do you think there's a sense of entitlement in today's actors that didn't used to exist?
I don't understand it. Maybe it's because long runs can get boring. When I heard that there were people in a show who had gone outside to watch someone in the theater next door, I would go white. Why aren't they involved in their own show? That signals that there's something lacking there. I don't know what it is. I can't fathom it. I'm from that era—and it was drummed into me but it didn't take long for me to appreciate—that the art of our work is that you re-create an opening night every night of the week. It goes right to the hard-earned money of the audience. Even when tickets were only ten dollars apiece, it's still their hard-earned

Company's "Tick Tock," McKechnie's daring dance solo, performed during an onstage couple's copulation. (Photofest)

money. For me, the great challenge was to re-create that experience every night. Because it's an opening night for that audience. That's the part that I love, and that's the part that goes when people are less passionate about their work. There are nights that you go in and you don't want to do it. But your job is to psych yourself into doing it.

I hadn't even been thinking about the hard-earned money part, and that's a great point. But to me, it's about the integrity of the show. When you go see a show that's been running for a long time, a lot of the time you're actually seeing a different show than when it opened. Things slide. People sit back a little, paint peels off the set, the producers don't fix things and it becomes a different show.

It's maintenance. When *A Chorus Line* became such a big hit, there had been no precedent really set for how to maintain. When I came back to the show [in 1986] I saw they weren't really doing Michael's choreography. They were doing sort of a half-assed version of it. And I couldn't really blame the dancers. It's just that over time, things got diffused. I would go, "Wait a minute, that's not the move." Then we had a little resurgence. We cleaned it up.

At your instigation?

Yeah. It was not my intention to come in and shake things up. But when I saw it . . . It was great for the company because they were getting sharp instruction and clear, specific choreography with the back-story and Michael's real work. They had an opening night that they had never had before, because the show was re-reviewed when I came back in. It was great all around for them. There hadn't been maintenance in place to take care of the show. I'm not pointing fingers, but if stage management gets bored or it becomes a job for them . . . Over time, when people move on to other shows, if a stage manager comes in who wasn't there during rehearsals there is natural diffusion. A new stage manager will get the bible or the book but they won't have the benefit of the rehearsal process.

Back to *Company*. In 1971 you got to go to London with this one, too.

Yes and then I went the next year to do [the film] *The Little Prince*, so without planning I was going almost every year to do something. I was lucky because later it got really dicey for Americans to go over.

Well, you ended up at the heart of the scandal involving that when you went over to replace Elizabeth Seal and open *A Chorus Line* over there. There were protests about the fact that an American was taking work away from a British actor. The way you described it in your book, it was very upsetting.

Oh, you have no idea. It's like walking into . . . it was shocking.

I read somewhere that Vanessa Redgrave was instrumental in organizing protests against you. Have you seen her since then?

I did, I saw her a couple of years after that, in London at the BAFTA Awards. I went with the minister of cultural affairs and I sat at this beautiful table at the big supper after the event. And I look up and there she is sitting across from me. I'm thinking, "This is great! Now that we've come past this and recovered, more or less, I can really address it. She's going to recognize me and we are finally going to have that conversation." So, she caught my eye, and I started to get up to talk to her and she got up, too. She rose to meet my eye, and she said, "Excuse me, do you know where the ladies room is?" I thought she recognized me! But I lost it and said, "I think it's over there."

And you never addressed it again?

No, because I realize that it wasn't personal, although it felt that way at the time. She paid nonworking actors a pound each to show up at British Equity and vote me out of the country. At least that's the story I was told. I don't know for sure if it was true. So there I was on the front page of *The Guardian* and *The Times* in a picture that they got from years before. The same picture, smiling every day, with a different headline. The Jimmy Carter inauguration was on the fourth page! I thought, "This makes no sense!" I had to stay closed in a hotel room. Sometimes I think about it and I wonder what I could have done differently. You think about your past and what you could've done to change it. I really don't know.

To make matters worse, as you tell it in your book, you didn't even want to go.

Right, I had a perfectly good job here in New York.

Let's talk about that job. *A Chorus Line* **in New York. Can you describe what it was like to find yourself at the heart of something so insane, to find yourself on the cover of** *Newsweek***?**

I was oblivious to it. I was going down on the subway every day. I had no money. We worked so hard. I called us hothouse tomatoes because we were sort of insulated. There were other things going on in my life. It was right when my father died. I was working hard, just keeping it together and working. I didn't even really look at that *Newsweek* cover until I unearthed it from a box of magazines five years later. I remember sitting there and going, "Wow," but that was five years later. At the time I was just trying to survive. There were a lot of uncomfortable feelings at the theater. We moved to Broadway, and nobody wanted to do publicity, so I started to do a lot of the publicity, because I had been in enough shows before to know that this is part of the job. I started to get a lot of publicity, not just because of the role I was playing but because I was doing a lot of the publicity.

And that caused discomfort backstage?

Oh yeah. It's not even rational. There's competition in our business. Now I would fight to the death for any of these people. I mean, I am so bonded with this original company. You are truly like brothers and sisters and I really love them even though there were instances back then when I wanted to throttle them. It really is just like dealing with a sibling. I love them so much. I have such respect and admiration for every one of those people. We all went through so much together. But anyway, that's a very difficult transition. Michael was going through something and he was kind of creating car crashes. It was a tactic of his that I really hated—seeing him manipulate people to get reactions for the work. That's because Jerome Robbins was his idol and Jerome Robbins did that kind of stuff.

Sammy Williams [*A Chorus Line***'s Paul] has spoken about Michael manipulating him that way and making him cry backstage.**

Terrible, terrible. I myself was removed but I would get wind of it. He would always be on top of [Robert] LuPone, giving him a hard time. Bobby used to think that Michael wanted the role. And, of course, Michael was Zach. He was all of us. He was Cassie, he was Maggie, Michael was up there.

It was interesting for me to read in your book how enthusiastic you were about playing Cassie with companies other than the original cast.

That was the most thrilling thing. To play it in all different parts of the world, that was really exciting. To see how the art translates in all these different cultures.

I had a preconceived notion that that would have been difficult. Having been part of that original, bonded group, directed by Michael, and then finding yourself out onstage with none of them.

Oh, it was better. The other companies were friendly. They liked me.

The original company didn't like you at the time?

People were going through a really weird time. I'm not saying it was directed at me, but it wasn't always comfortable backstage and it wasn't always fun. It was difficult. And it starts at the top. If feelings are hurt, you cannot work that closely and have everybody collaborate well. It was a big adjustment to go from a little off-Broadway show to a major hit all over the world. I probably wasn't in a place emotionally to appreciate it. I was just so happy to be on Broadway and have a job in a show that I loved and had such a personal connection with. When you get a Tony, it's a great honor because it's your peers. That's the greatest honor any actor can get. But still, it wasn't the end-all for me.

When actors win awards, they don't like to think of themselves as having beaten the others in their category, but you did beat Chita Rivera and Gwen Verdon.

But I didn't view it that way. How could I? It was the show. I knew that caused Fosse pain. In 1986, when he called me to do *Charity*, I think that was really hard for him. Because I heard that *Chicago* being overwhelmed by *A Chorus Line* was very painful and very upsetting to Bob. So I had to earn my stripes, you know what I mean? I worked really hard at that.

Were you thrilled being nominated with Chita and Gwen?

Michael took me to Joe Allen's [Restaurant] and I was trying to figure out what he was talking about. He was doing all this strategizing [about the Tonys]. He was "Michael the Producer," trying to get as many awards as he could for his baby. I didn't want to be a part of it. The real benefit, and I'm not just saying this, was that it was so important for me to put all that work and love into something and be able to do it on a Broadway stage.

You do see that you are different in that way though, right? A lot of actors care very much about this kind of thing.

Well, it's a great honor to be acknowledged by your peers. I know that. But this was for all of us. It was the show and I was so proud of it. I'm not trying to minimize it but it's not where I was living. It's great when it happens. It just took me five years to notice emotionally. I was fighting for my life. Plus I was being wined and dined left and right. I had to keep my head on straight. And how many jobs has my Tony gotten me? I know that it opens doors for me. I know that when I do my one-woman shows that's an important selling point. But in terms of jobs you're either right for something or you're not.

Earlier you described Cassie as somewhat fictional . . .

Well, she was based on me, but we had to create a story and a relationship.

Right. But then you ended up living the story that was created. So much of what Cassie says to Zach became true of the relationship between you and Michael. You and Michael hadn't had a relationship yet, but then you did. And then you broke up and stopped speaking, like Cassie and Zach. In your book you talk about coming back and seeing him again at the reunion performance [when *A Chorus Line* became Broadway's longest running musical, in 1983] and it was all business between you, just like when Cassie comes back for the audition and it's all business.

I was following his lead. I thought, "We're not ever going to speak about anything personal. It's too uncomfortable for him. And I can go to that place. I can rise above it. But it's a shame." During the reunion, he was walking around joined at the hip with me, not letting go and I thought, "This is so bizarre." He was taking me everywhere but not speaking to me in a personal way. The behavior was very personal but the words weren't. It was business.

Until I read your book, I had a perception of your relationship with Michael as somewhat analogous to that of Gwen Verdon and Bob Fosse. I thought that even after you split, you were still very connected. Certainly in your performance at the 1988 Tony Awards in the tribute to him or in your presence at his memorial, there was nothing that suggested that you hadn't had an ongoing close relationship. It was a revelation reading in your book that you hadn't spoken for years.

Well, we loved each other. We loved each other. And the work. While, at that time in our lives, we both had problems with trust and the emotional intimacy that we needed desperately, there was love and respect and the work. So that was where the real intimacy was. You don't lose it. We love someone, it doesn't go away really. There was no bitterness. There were a lot of hurt feelings for both of us, but there was no bitterness.

It's interesting that you say "for both of you," because, while I'm sure that he went through a tough time, as you describe it in your book, he hurt you, without being able to communicate about it. That has to have been difficult.

Dancing "The Music and the Mirror" in *A Chorus Line*, choreography created for her body. (Photofest)

Yes, but I had seen that maneuver before. I had seen him do it. That was the only way he had to deal with things. He had to cut it off, shut the door. I've seen other people do that, too, and it's a shame, but that's the way it is. That's who he was.

That is very generous.

Look, there are a lot of situations when I think about it, and I could say, "You little shit." But that doesn't matter in the bigger picture. And that has a lot to do with me growing up and coming to terms with my own part of it. If someone's not going to sit me down and explain it to me, I'd better find a way to comprehend it for myself. My business is my part. That's an easy call for me. To see the love and appreciation, that's easy for me to see. I owe him so much and there've been only a few people in my life who really see me. That was something that I really appreciated him for. I was auditioning here and there and people always liked my work, but he went out of his way to create for me. That's really something to be proud of and to love. In every [one-woman] show I do, now, I make it a point to say his name. It's a way of paying homage. You don't want people to forget these people. It's my way of keeping him alive and keeping the work alive. It gives me a good feeling to do it. He deserves it. I really appreciate him. You don't have to love everything about somebody. There are things that I don't love about him but I knew him for too many years and I knew the trouble in his background. When you know someone that well, you can forgive a lot easier.

It shows great maturity and a big heart. There are horrible stories in your book. You talk, for example, about the fact that Michael was paying for you to live at the Essex House and then one day you came home and were locked out. To be able to move past that kind of thing is huge.

If you live long enough you realize that we're human beings and we are complicated. We have frailties. Some people cannot help their behavior. They can't help it. If you look at it that way . . . you can't be like, "They're doing this to me, I'm the victim." That gets you nowhere. It's like when I get depressed or I'm not working; I can go for weeks without getting any calls. I look in the mirror and I go, "You picked it." That helps me. You make the choice.

You talk in your book about how, when you were doing *A Chorus Line* in Los Angeles, Fred Astaire came to the show and invited you back to his house afterwards . . .

It was so great! When we went to Los Angeles, there was this big party in Beverly Hills. And every movie star . . . I remember sitting down with Jack Lemmon who had heard that I was going to be married so he brought a sixpence for me for good luck. I still have that. It was so personal. James Stewart took me around by the hand and introduced me at every single table. Roz Russell, Merle Oberon, all the great stars.

I cannot imagine cast members from a show of today getting to meet Hollywood royalty. It was a different age. Why doesn't that happen now?

It was different. This show touched a nerve. It touched a chord in everyone, and it was served up in such a beautiful package. Early on, before any of the trouble we had, when the show was up and running, Michael said to me, "Don't ever try to compete with the show." I didn't get it then the way I do now. He also said, "This may never happen again. It stands alone, and I might have done you a disservice."

Most of that cast didn't continue doing regular work as performers. Do you think the cast was done a disservice by being in a show that was so much bigger than them?

That was one of the reasons I left. I thought Cassie was an albatross around my neck, like when I used to resent my dancing. I had to go through the fires of hell [her recovery from arthritis] in order to come back. My going back into the show and reclaiming Cassie, I thought, "Here the show is, giving it back to me again. After all of the stress, having my body implode as it did, the show brings me back." I reclaimed it and it reclaimed me. It looms over me, but now instead of resenting it I embrace it.

This will sound gratuitous so forgive me; I've seen many, many Cassies. Nobody can touch it like you.

It was designed for my personality and designed for the way I dance. Michael left so much of the interpretation to me. It's all acting based. The structure was there, but I would free associate. Now sometimes when I watch others do it, there's no dance. There are steps, but it's all the same level. No beginning, middle, or end. When I train people to do it, I never give anyone arms. I tell people to explore. For example, "In this section explore these feelings." The dance here is about the insecurity of "can I dance again?" That's why Michael has all of the sharp angular moves that stop. You're checking yourself in the mirror; it's that narcissistic thing. Explore your own way of looking in the mirror, looking at your hand. I call it "the non-dancing parts." It can be taught but it can't be taught the way that I did it. It has to be someone's own interpretation. The person is more important than the steps. Michael always believed that. It doesn't always have to be the same, but I think that's always been a problem when people have trained people to do that number. They try to make it "Your arms go here, 11 o'clock." It's a shame, because they're not giving them a chance to emerge and find their own lives and their own expression physically. You know, when you tell a dancer to do something, they do it. If you tell an actor to do something, if they can't justify it, they say, "Why?" When I did a play, right after *A Chorus Line*, that was an eye opener for me. It was like, "You can actually confront a director and say, 'Why?' That's great!" That's when you really start taking a hold of something. You try to find a way to make it work but you don't just arbitrarily move because someone told you to.

How did you feel when the show closed in 1990?

I remember sitting there. I don't think I had ever seen the show before, not from beginning to end. That was the first time. I had never sat in the audience and seen it. I thought, "What a great show" and I was keeping my emotions at bay. But it hit me at the end during the finale as the lights faded on the kick line. I just couldn't control myself. It was such a dramatic effect. For all those years, friends would come backstage and say, "That ending just kills me." And of course I'm up there doing it, trying to get my leg at the right level so I wasn't into the emotion of it. But sitting there seeing it, seeing what a great show it was, as the lights faded my thoughts went to, "It's closing. It's the last time we're going to see Michael Bennett's work onstage." I just lost it. I am so happy that the show was revived because the part of me that felt the death, it was like feeling Michael's death again because that was him. To see it up there on the boards again on Broadway was very exciting.

In your book you talk about bumping into Gwen Verdon after Michael's memorial in Shubert Alley. What did she say to you?

We literally bumped into each other. I said, "Gwen, we're so worried about you! How are you?" Because she had just lost Bob. She says, "I'm fine and I'm so sorry. We keep them alive inside." She didn't mention Bobby or Michael by name. She just said, "We keep them alive inside." I know she paid me a great compliment. It meant so much to me. Remember it had been twenty-five years since she was the dance captain in *How to Succeed* . . . And now, I had just been working with her every day on *Sweet Charity*. To be with her every single day in that close proximity, to be able to spend that kind of privileged time, really working with an artist on that level, that's gold to me. If you look at a whole life, certain things pop out as highlights. You actually reminded me of a few of them. And this is one of them. Way up there.

One of the things you detail in the book is how when Gwen taught you the show, she didn't just teach you moves, she showed you what each of the different Charitys did. "This was my version. This was Debbie Allen's version. This was Juliet Prowse's version. Which would you like to learn?"

I was like, "Is she being serious? Uh—yours!" But you know, she could be a dragon. She was so serious about the work and I realized later that it's painful. She was giving me the goods. It's not as dramatic as passing the torch but there's something about giving up your soul. When I teach Cassie to anyone, I have to really work hard so I can make sure that this person finds her own voice and her own connection. But while I'm doing that I'm going through all of the agonies of birth again and giving it over. It's like I'm giving them my heart and soul as Gwen was with me. We never took breaks. I think I lost forty pounds in two weeks.

Let's talk about your book. You have said that the primary reason you wrote it was to share your story with people who may also be suffering from arthritis.

When I came back to *A Chorus Line* [in 1986], I had come so far. I had put this behind me through diet and therapy and found my legs, as it were, again. And for me, the show, in a whole kind of mystical way comes back and I reclaim myself through the show again. But then, the bigger, more important story, more important than my feelings, than revealing personal things—which I think is nobody's business—was a desire to tell this story of the psychology of this young girl coming to New York, without having the kind of encouragement and confidence. You know, I had to read it again and I had to take all of the anger out. I was surprised that there was a residue of unfinished business. I thought I had completed that. I found out through the writing that I hadn't. Not enough. I had, sort of, in theory, intellectually, but not emotionally. And it came back to haunt me and it showed me that it was very important to write the book. It made me aware of dealing with things that it's too easy to run away from or distract myself with something else. I had to tell the story accurately. I was forced to deal with it. [Director] Lonny Price asked me if it was fun and I said, "Fun? No." But it was important.

Cathartic?

It was helpful. But cathartic? No. But there was a great feeling of accomplishment. It was important to me. Once it's out there and it's done and you reread it, you go, "Oh, I left an important thing out!" But I gave up on that. I realized that will just drive me crazy. Really, I just wanted people to read it and think, "If she can do it, I can do it."

ANGELA LANSBURY

May 2009; July 2012

"HOO-HOO," CALLS ANGELA LANSBURY, her head poking out of her apartment's door to greet me as I step off the elevator. Already I am feeling like I need to be pinched. I have been "hoo-hooed" by Angela Lansbury.

I actually walked in to our first meeting feeling a bit stunned to be there. Lansbury was, after all, an eighty-four-year-old woman performing eight times a week in *Blithe Spirit*. Moreover, it was spring, which meant that we were in the heat of Broadway's busiest season. She was attending galas, luncheons, and award ceremonies almost daily and dealing with the on-slaught of press that comes with the Tony nomination she had received (an award she'd go on to win weeks later). I wouldn't have expected her to make time for me and I was both appreciative and a little amazed that she did.

Stepping into her home, I was struck by the simplicity Lansbury had chosen for herself. Hers is a lovely but unfussy apartment, not especially spacious or showy. A small terrace allows her to indulge her love of gardening with a few flowering plants. With the exception of one 8 × 10 photograph of Lansbury as *Sweeney Todd*'s amoral slattern, Mrs. Lovett, unceremoniously tucked into a corner in the dining room, there was not a single visible trace of a life in show business. None of her four Tony Awards or six Golden Globes were on display; no other pictures of her in some of her great roles; no hint of her Kennedy Center Honor; no posters from her films or television work which netted her three Oscar nominations and eighteen Emmy nods; no souvenirs from her thirteen-year stint as J. B. Fletcher on *Murder She Wrote*. Hers was the Manhattan apartment of a busy working woman with books and newspapers by the couch and an open laptop off to the side. The past, it seemed, was the past, and Lansbury has no need to surround herself with its remnants.

Angela Lansbury was born in London in 1925 and, like most of the women in this book, trained as an actor from an early age. Unlike all of the others women in this book, however, she had no dreams of the musical theater and didn't especially aspire to it. Her career began in film, and she appeared in more than forty movies before she made it to Broadway in 1957 (*Hotel Paradiso*, opposite Bert Lahr, an experience she loved). But it wasn't until 1964 that Lansbury had the opportunity to do a musical. That show, *Anyone Can Whistle*, was one of Broadway's most legendary flops, lasting only nine performances. But it gave Lansbury her first taste of her own strength as a musical performer and it introduced her to Stephen Sondheim with whom she would do three more shows.

Only two years later came Lansbury's triumphant, Tony Award–winning turn as the title character in Jerry Herman's *Mame*. After more than two decades as a supporting player, Lansbury, at forty, was finally a star. Her subsequent shows included another Jerry Herman vehicle,

Backstage at *Mame*, showing a side we seldom associate with Lansbury. (Photofest)

Dear World, the ill-fated *Prettybelle*, Broadway's first revival of *Gypsy*, and a three-week stint in *The King and I* to give that production some star power during Yul Brynner's vacation. Then in 1979, came *Sweeney Todd*, in which Lansbury as Mrs. Lovett served up human meat pies to a Stephen Sondheim score. The *New York Times* said of her performance, which would earn Lansbury her fourth Tony, "Her songs . . . are awesomely difficult and she does them awesomely well."

Lansbury's subsequent shows, a play called *A Little Family Business* and a revival of *Mame*, were both disappointments that led her back to Hollywood where, in 1984, she began her amazing run in *Murder She Wrote*. Despite the ongoing feeling that the show limited her, Lansbury stayed, becoming the executive producer and, with her husband, Peter Shaw, created a mainstay with which they could employ their relatives and friends. "It was," she told me, "an annuity for me and my family. Everyone in my family worked on the show." It took twenty-three years for Lansbury to make it back to Broadway.

When she did, in the 2007 Terrence McNally play, *Deuce*, she claimed it would be her final stage outing. It wasn't. *Blithe Spirit* came in 2009 and then, later that same year, a revival of Sondheim's *A Little Night Music*. 2012 brought a revival of Gore Vidal's *The Best Man* and in 2013, an Australian tour of *Driving Miss Daisy*.

We sit down on her white, overstuffed couch, but not before Lansbury insists on popping into the kitchen to bring me a beverage I insist I don't need. But she is gracious to a fault. She is, in fact, the only woman in this book who called me after the interview to thank me. It's that kind of gesture that makes Lansbury one of the few celebrities who manage to actually be the person that millions of people hope she is.

> **Angela Lansbury**
>
> *Anyone Can Whistle*, Broadway, 1964
> *Mame*, Broadway, 1966 (Tony Award)
> *Dear World*, Broadway, 1969 (Tony Award)
> *Prettybelle*, Boston, 1971
> *Gypsy*, West End, National Tour, Broadway, 1973 (Tony Award)
> *The King and I*, Broadway, 1978
> *Sweeney Todd*, Broadway and National Tour, 1979 (Tony Award)
> *Mame*, Broadway, 1983
> *A Little Night Music*, Broadway, 2010

You are nominated for a Tony this year. Is the experience of being a nominee very different from when you were nominated for *Mame* and *Dear World*?

Oh yes. The business has changed totally. Totally different. Broadway is not the Broadway of the '60s and '70s. Why should it be? My goodness, I am aware of the differences. It all has to do with the fact that, because of the Internet, everything is immediately available. Before, you had to read the papers, the columns, to know what was going on. Now everything is right out there. YouTube. You name it, it's there. Not only is what you're doing now there, but everything you've done in the past comes bubbling up out of the drain.

How do you feel about that?

It's okay on the one hand. On the other hand it's a little daunting, I think. What we did then doesn't belong in today's world. It's old-fashioned and rather studied and strange, you know?

But at the same time it's given people the opportunity to see things like your performance of "Thoroughly Modern Millie" on the 1968 Oscars, things we thought were lost for all time.

I guess so. People have come up to me and said, "Wow! You were doing splits!" In those days I learned how to do those things. All of that was part of being a leading musical comedy actress in the 1960s. And that's what I managed to do, thank God.

You didn't start your musical career until much later in your life. You were already thirty-eight and had three Oscar nominations under your belt. As legend has it, out of the blue, you got a letter from Arthur Laurents [writer and director], asking if you'd be interested in doing a musical.

Well, that was it. That was the beginning. Arthur wrote me this letter. I can see it in my mind's eye as clear as anything. It was a lovely dark blue color, very chic and very unusual in those days. I knew who he was. I knew he had written the books to *West Side Story* and *Gypsy*, but I didn't know him personally. He took it upon himself to write me a personal note. So I auditioned for him and Stephen Sondheim and I managed to persuade them that I could do it [*Anyone Can Whistle*].

One of the things you said about it at the time was, "I thought it was nuts, crackers. But there was something about it that appealed to me." What was it about the role of Cora Hooper that spoke to you?

Cora Hoover Hooper was such an outrageous character and you have to understand that, really and truly from the get-go, I have been interested in character; what that person is like underneath those layers. This [role] said to me, "there's some gold that could be mined here." I heard the score and I realized that this was going to challenge me as a singer and a performer. And the scenes for Cora as the Mayoress were really very funny. Tough and caustic. Although I don't think I was as tough or nasty as Arthur would have liked me to be. I know that for a fact. He used to say, "Angie, here's a woman who's ready to say, 'set the dogs on them!'" That's what he really wanted and I had problems with that. We were too close to the civil rights movement and I didn't want to go there, as the expression goes. And I didn't. But it didn't matter. She was still funny and dreadful and outrageous.

***Anyone Can Whistle* was legendary in the musical theater world. It was reputedly a hellish out-of-town tryout. You said at one point that it was the only time you ever screamed at Stephen Sondheim.**

I did! Not only did I scream at him, I was at the top of the stairs screaming down two stories. I screamed, "I don't know what you want! What do you want me to do?"

But through all of that, it was still your first musical. Do you remember experiencing joy in that?

Oh yes. Doing "Me and My Town" was a blast. It really was. It was fantastic. I had been a great admirer of Kay Thompson and the Williams Brothers and that was what we were doing. She had coached me at MGM in the old days. To have an opportunity to do something like that was incredible, a dream come true.

The show only lasted on Broadway for nine performances . . .

Only nine performances and about three million people saw those nine performances. I've never met anyone of a certain age who hasn't [claimed to have] seen that performance. You weren't born, but those who were in New York not only saw it, they saw every single performance. That was the kind of wonderful old wives' tale built up around the show.

I saw the concert version at Carnegie Hall in 1995 and a big part of the excitement that night was that you were narrating. How was it for you watching that?

It was kind of sweet/sad in a way. I think I thought, "God, I could still have done *that*." I'm always challenged by things. I don't know what it is. I always think I could have done it. But Madeline Kahn who played it, she was great.

Watching the show so many years later, did it seem different to you as a piece?

Yes. It seemed a little bit childish and old-fashioned, you know. There were a couple of great, great songs in it. "With So Little to Be Sure Of" and "Anyone Can Whistle." Those were glorious songs.

That show was your first experience of Stephen Sondheim who was himself very young. Do you have specific memories of him at that time?

Even at that early age, I was very awed by him. I always thought, and I do to this day, that he's been a teacher of how to sing songs. Not necessarily how to get the content across but certainly how to sing them.

Do you mean technically?

No. Well, yes, to a certain extent I do. I think to sing his music you have to have a certain technique. It's all about lyrics, it's all about enunciation, it's all about being understood.

Doesn't that really come from the head and heart?

Well, it doesn't, no. Not necessarily. You can be thinking that you are putting it across but the audience is not getting it because of the way you are singing it. The word does not reach them. With him, that's of prime importance.

It's interesting that he was so adept at teaching even that early in his career.

He was always an old soul in a curious way.

What about Arthur Laurents?

To be perfectly honest, and Arthur, I think, understands this and would agree with me, we didn't get along. I found him difficult as a director. I had never run into anybody like him before. He was also fighting with his own book and trying to make it all work. Of course I think an author believes in his work but you've got to still make it play. We were on the road and trying to make things work better. The audience wasn't liking what they were seeing. They were almost throwing tomatoes at the stage. They were very verbal and noisy, screaming and shouting. That's tough to swallow for the author.

I had read that and it's hard for me to imagine. No one actually screams at the stage any more.

Yes, that's interesting. People were outraged. People got really upset at *Sweeney Todd*, too, but that's different I guess. They didn't like the blood. And now you can show them buckets of blood and they don't mind, as we saw [with the 2005 revival that literally incorporated buckets of blood].

I am interested in your having seen several of your other roles played by other women. Is watching someone else tread in your shoes hard for you? Or is it fun? What's that like?

You just watch. I watched Ann Miller play Mame. She was the only one I saw do it. I thought, "Well, it's a whole different show." She pulled out a few stops and she did it her way and it worked. That show works no matter who's playing it. Audiences love it.

Did you see the film version of *Sweeney Todd*?

Yes I did. That was interesting to me. Johnny Depp is a fascinating performer. I enjoyed watching him. I understood what he was doing and I was impressed with his ability to sing it. He did quite well. He really did. He didn't sing it like a big baritone, no, but he certainly gave it a quality that was quite interesting, I must say. Helena Bonham Carter, I happen to know, was thwarted in her desire to be funny because her husband [director Tim Burton] wouldn't allow her to be. She wanted to bring that sense of musical comedy. But she's so interesting to watch. I am always interested in people's faces and certainly her look is very stunning and interesting. It wasn't Mrs. Lovett but whoever she was . . .

After *Anyone Can Whistle*, you went back to LA but it wasn't too long before *Mame* came into the picture. It was announced that Mary Martin wasn't going to do the show as had been planned and you went after it with great gusto.

I met with [book writers] Jerome Lawrence and Robert Lee in Malibu for brunch one day and Jerry [Herman] was there. We talked about the possibility and at that time I knew that Jerry was really on my team although there were other ladies who were being considered by the producers who, of course, were looking for a money name. I, at that point, certainly was not. I came in to New York to audition. I auditioned once, I auditioned twice, I auditioned three times, and I finally got it.

For him to know you could sing it, apparently Jerry Herman was one of the three million who saw *Anyone Can Whistle*.

Oh yeah. Talk to him, he'll tell you.

But you hadn't seen Rosalind Russell's performance so you didn't know the part except by reputation, yet you knew it was for you?

Well I read the book *Auntie Mame*. That was very helpful to me. But I didn't want to follow in the footsteps of Russell and I didn't want to play it with cigarette holders and all of that stuff. I wanted to go a different route. I knew the movie had been made and the stage version done very successfully. This was the musical. And I knew it was going to be an opportunity to wear some fabulous clothes. I knew that this would be a huge challenge but I had Jerry Herman on my side. He was extraordinary in his willingness to help me in every possible way.

You made four cross-country trips to audition and Jerry taught you the songs in advance and played for you at the audition. Ultimately it was yours but I am curious about your utter confidence that you could tackle the lead in a splashy musical, and in Jerry Herman's confidence in you. After all, the vocal demands were so different from anything in *Anyone Can Whistle*.

I did work over the year to do everything I could do to build my voice for *Mame*. There were several people who helped me learn how to sing the right way. I never knew how to do exercises and I don't to this day. I just stand up and sing. I don't know how to sing except in the role. I am not a stand-up singer. I can't do it. But when it came to *Mame* and the songs that I got to sing, they were natural for me. They sat perfectly within my range. They were just super to sing.

As you were rehearsing that show, did it feel very different from your previous musical theater experience—knowing that this time it was working? And also knowing that it was all resting on your shoulders?

That was the thing. I had a director, Gene Saks, who was extraordinary. I was working with the great Bea Arthur [Lansbury tears up]. We both launched into that show together. We weren't really ready. I was a bit overweight—not too bad. We really went to town with [choreographer] Onna White to get ourselves in shape. The combination of Gene and Bea and Onna and me and everybody in that company, it was like it was blessed from the start. When we finally did get to Philadelphia, it was extraordinary, really, because it was quite evident that we had a huge hit on our hands. The only problem was that I didn't really know how to take the stage. I had the producers, Jimmy Carr and Bobby Fryer, come to me and say, "Angie, you can do this. You've got to believe that you alone are quite enough on that stage. You just take it, it's yours." I had to learn within those few days on the road that it was okay to do that. It's a funny thing to discover that you can stand there and demand the attention of the audience and give them everything you've got and share with them the great moments that are there in the role. It took me awhile to really do that but that was the time when I did it. I didn't know how to do that in *Anyone Can Whistle*.

Mame had twenty-eight costumes which you had to change in and out of in a flash, and then you had to walk onstage as if you had been wearing them for hours.

That's right. It was a hairy experience because at that time I had rather long hair and to get the hats on and to keep redressing the hair—Ronnie DeMann was the hairdresser and he had a fit trying to keep me looking chic and smart and svelte and all of that thirties nonsense we were going for. And finally I said, "This is ridiculous. Bea Lillie had no hair at all. She cut it all off. I'm going to cut it all off, OK?" So we cut it all off. That was the look that made Mame. It was great. Thank God we did it.

One of the things you said about Mame at the time was, "I always suspected I could reach everybody but I never did until now."

Because I was playing a universally accepted character. A woman who only brought fun and hope and gaiety to an audience, who could stop the show and sing a song. She was something for everyone, to coin a phrase. That was a quality I enjoyed being able to project tremendously. That's why *Mame* was such a very important show to me. You have to understand that up to that point I had had a career that was technically interesting and diverse and full of acting opportunities but I had never had a chance to touch a universal audience, really. Men, women, children, dogs, cats, the whole shebang. I include dogs because dogs are very important in my life. You wouldn't think so because I don't have one in here in the room with me right now but I have known a lot of dogs. They know when a person is—what is that wonderful word? Simpatico. I think that Mame was really simpatico.

From Mame forward, almost everything you did, except maybe the film Nanny McPhee, had an inherent warmth that you had not had the opportunity to play prior to Mame. Your previous roles were almost all somewhat cold and hard.

I never thought of it that way prior to *Mame*. I didn't realize that I had the ability to get that across. But it's been that way ever since. It doesn't matter what I'm playing. Except *Nanny McPhee*.

What was the difference in performing Jerry Herman right after Stephen Sondheim?

Well! Huge difference. [Jerry was] writing extremely up, melodious songs with kind of simple, up lyrics. Certainly, in the case of "My Best Girl" or a song like that, it came out of the situation. Mame was broke and found herself with this little lad who became like her son. The lyrics certainly quantify everything that she felt at that point in her life. Jerry is a master of that kind of lyric. He did it with such care. To sing that was so lovely. And "If He Walked into My Life" was a history of her relationship with this lad. It was a very telling and emotionally packed song. Stephen has written some emotionally packed songs but not in the same way. It's a different approach. I am not clever enough to be able to give you a for instance, but you are smart enough to know what I mean.

There's also the musical difference. Sondheim doesn't necessarily go where you think he might whereas Herman is a master . . .

At going exactly where you expect him to, yes.

So would you say they are both challenging in different ways?

Well, let's talk about, in my case, the three roles that I've played written by Sondheim [Lansbury subsequently performed a fourth, in *A Little Night Music*] against the three roles I've played of Jerry Herman's. Jerry writes about people and relationships, happiness, and joy. Steve writes about life and also about very, very acute inner feelings which are not immediately evident in the lyric. They are far more intellectualized than Jerry Herman's. But Jerry Herman is capable of writing an incredibly astute and carefully crafted lyric. He really, really is. I really give it to him in that respect. And he also writes magnificent melodies. Some of the songs and lyrics in *La Cage aux Folles* are really quite glorious.

Or *Mack & Mabel*.

Mack & Mabel! Yeah! They are representative of him at his absolute top form. Even more than *Mame*. With *Mame*, it was all in the script by Lawrence and Lee. He didn't have to kill himself to write that, but he did when it came to *Mack & Mabel*. "I Won't Send Roses" is absolute perfection. *Mame* was the most glamorous time of my life certainly. I had never experienced something like that.

I don't think people know what it means now to be the toast of Broadway. There is no Stork Club or El Morocco; there is no Walter Winchell.

I know. We used to dress up to go out after the show. We'd go dancing.

Actors and dancers today complain about the exhaustion of doing eight shows a week. How is it that you were having such a party life and carrying a huge show?

We were living on adrenaline. We created our own energy. We went without sleep. How we ever managed to sing our way through the shows, I'll never know. It was very short-lived. I went to Los Angeles and San Francisco with the show and I had huge successes in both places. And I finally closed my performance in *Mame* in Los Angeles. That was the last time I played it. Well, it wasn't the last time because as you know in '72 I took out that first tour which was a big success. We played in tents in the round.

Bizarre.

It was bizarre. I don't know how we did it. I can't even picture it in my mind's eye now.

The costume changes alone would seem to be a choreographic nightmare.

It was. It really, really was, yes. It's amazing what we do. Your energy will guide you and you do it.

When you chose to leave the show in LA, you said to a columnist, "When at last you are there, a star, with all of these people loving you, let me tell you something: you don't give it up in a hurry. And I hate the thought of anyone else going out and playing me." One of those other women who wanted to play you was Judy Garland. Apparently she came to see you a few times and you arranged for her to watch from backstage?

That was the saddest thing I ever had to take part in because I knew the producers wouldn't take a chance on putting her in. She was a little waif of a person by that time. She was going through hell, you know. We knew each other from MGM days and she just adored the show. And she needed the work. That was the bottom line. She wasn't right for it. She could have sung the hell out of it, but that was about it. She could have done it I suppose but they never would have underwritten her [insurance] in it.

Do you think she was any less right for the role than Ann Miller?
Ann Miller had chutzpah!

Before we move on from *Mame*, I need to ask you about the movie.
I pretended not to care [about not getting the role] but I really did care. I knew it wouldn't work. I knew it couldn't be the same. It would be *Auntie Mame* again, not *Mame*. And I admired Lucille Ball tremendously. She had also come backstage several times to see me, so I knew she had her eye on it. I can never forgive Warner Brothers for not letting me do it because I think it could have been a huge movie.

Why did you pretend not to care? Did you think you were taking the high road?
When you say "the high road," what does that mean?

The classier approach.
Probably. I always tried to be very classy.

You said she came back several times. Knowing that someone is eyeing you, was it hard to be gracious?
I don't think I was savvy enough to be aware that that's what she really had in mind. I thought that she might want to replace me in the theater; I didn't realize that it was aimed at the movie.

Ignorance was probably bliss.
Yes! I felt so sure of myself, as you do if you're queen. You just don't think that far ahead.

As the Countess Aueliea in *Dear World*, a mere two years after Lansbury glammed it up in *Mame*. (Photofest)

Immediately after *Mame* was *Dear World*. And you had another disastrous out-of-town experience pre-Broadway.

So much happened on the road with *Dear World*. The original production, directed by Peter Glenville, was a gem of a musical. Absolutely a gem in Boston. And the audience hated it. Why? Because they were given to believe [from advertising] that they were going to see Angela Lansbury doing another version of *Mame* and here I come out as this old lady, wildly eccentric. It's [a musicalization of] *The Madwoman of Chaillot* and they just weren't prepared for that and didn't want to know. It was a bitter disappointment to me, it really, really was. I loved most of the score. The only song that I didn't particularly like, and Jerry knows this, was the title song, "Dear World."

He claims it's a song he wishes he never wrote.

Yes, exactly. Well there you go. The producer, Alexander Cohen, was intent on making it a success. So he proceeded to bring in people: new writers, directors. He fired Peter Glenville and we ended up with Joe Layton. He had a lot of dance experience, of course, and he added a lot of dance. The original choreographer had been Donald Saddler, who I adore. He [Layton] fiddled and changed it and goosed the whole thing. He made it busy. The audiences weren't that interested and they weren't that interested in me looking and behaving as I did onstage.

It was a very bold choice for you.

I was so sure I could do it. Katharine Hepburn was going to do the movie. She was kind of a heroine of mine. And I thought, "this is rather more along the lines of what I eventually want to do. I've done the glamour gal, now I am gonna show them that I can do the character" and all that. I think I sang it very well—better than I had sung anywhere. I am very glad I did it.

With a show like that, even though you know it's not working but there are elements that are strong, when the audiences aren't appreciating it . . .

They did, finally. They did. The critics were pretty darn good to me and to the show. They weren't great reviews but they gave it its due and they gave me my due. Which encourages one, always. Artists in the theater, we're always trying to prove that we can make it work. We don't just lie back and say, "Oh this is no good" and go through the motions. You never give up on trying to sell the audience on the material. That's natural with most performers. We *have* to. If you are going to go out there every night at eight o'clock, you have got to be prepared to sell the material, the character, the songs, every aspect of the show. You have to assume that you can bring them around and win them over.

No matter what the critics might have said.

No matter what the critics might have said. And obviously if there's an audience there, why are they coming? Not because of the bad review but to see this show and to see you in this show. You have got to give them your best.

Were you reading the reviews?

Yes. I have always read reviews. I don't particularly believe them but I do read them.

Do they ever inform you?

No.

Is it difficult to read them without becoming self-conscious?

I can't say that I was ever diverted from my task by a review.

Right after *Dear World* you did *Prettybelle* and had another disaster in Boston.

Yes, another disaster. With Gower Champion, Bob Merrill, and Jule Styne [director/chore-ographer, book writer/lyricist, and composer, respectively].

All huge personalities. Do you have specific memories of them?

Oh, yes. Jule Styne's enthusiasm for his own music and his own talents was tremendous. And it was certainly earned. Jule always had a tune in his pocket. He was really prolific, he al-ways had it. He had it for all of his shows. His enthusiasm was just outrageous—nothing was out of the question, nothing was impossible. He was a tremendous help when he could be. He didn't always solve the problem that you might have but he would always be there trying.

An optimist?

An optimist! You bet! And bigger than life. One of the old school. It's fun to work with those people for me. He wrote the music for *Gypsy* for god's sake!

What about Gower Champion?

He got me doing things dance-wise that I had never done before. It was exciting and kind of wonderful. People who saw the show thought it was one of the best things I ever did in mu-sical theater.

What do you think was wrong with *Prettybelle*?

I think the subject matter was very difficult to swallow. It was built around this woman who was really out of her head, who was married to a very corrupt, dreadful, southern police chief who was beating up on the blacks. And it was about the friendship with this young black boy. Forget it, we couldn't sell it. The audience didn't want to know. We also had a terrible song called "No Tell Motel." That tells you something.

It was another courageous choice on your part. You had learned from *Dear World* that audiences were looking to see you as Mame and yet you took on an alcoholic prostitute. It was almost as if you were saying, "I know you're all looking for the glamour girl, sorry."

"Not this time!" I had to force them to accept me in these other roles. The production was doomed to close out of town and I was in such a state of worry and concern about my kids [both of whom were in Los Angeles and had gotten involved with drugs] that when we closed I took a plane straight from Boston to Ireland to set up a place for us to go to. The kids and Peter [her husband] came over soon after. I borrowed a sweater from one of the stagehands because I didn't have any warm clothes. I went right to Ireland.

You were willing to walk away from your work to tend to your family.

How could it be otherwise? If you have a family, family is all. It's always for them.

Carol Channing said to me that she considered herself the worst mother in the world and that every woman in her position in theater has that constant struggle.

It's absolutely true.

But you managed to prioritize your family and still have a career.

I tried to but I couldn't always succeed. You're the victim of tours and rehearsal schedules and school. It's impossible to put it all together. It is just sad for people in the business who have children, trying to have a career and be good mothers.

But when push came to shove, you left the career and took the family to Ireland. Family was paramount.

It had to be at that moment. We had a succession of terrible events including our house burning down in Malibu and losing every vestige of evidence of a life. That's what happens in a fire. And the children were in a very bad way so there was really no question. We just went. It was a very impulsive move on both Peter's and my part. It was the only way I could see saving their lives at that time.

Once you were there, you did periodically have the struggle of having to leave to go perform and make money. The tour of *Mame* that you weren't terribly interested in doing.

I didn't want to do it. I didn't want to leave Ireland because I was so happy. Life was good. But from a business point of view it was an important move. And quite frankly, we needed the money. We were not able to carry on without working. My husband had retired from his job in '72.

That brings up a question I often think about with regard to the women in this book. After you have a reputation and you're a star, you can be in a somewhat delicate position. Stardom doesn't necessarily mean wealth and you still have bills to pay. But you can't just take a job for the money because a lot of eyes are on you. Was it limiting?

Very. And let's face it, I have never been an easy person to cast. Not in movies, no. Not in television. Not in the theater for that matter. I was always somewhat of an odd quantity. A quantity of talent, yes, that was proven, but a little off center. I really didn't fit into the average groove as a leading lady or as a secondary figure in a setup. Yes, I *could* play anything given the opportunity. I'm not saying I could have played it well but I could have taken a crack at it if I needed to work. I would have. But I wasn't an easy person to cast. Ever. And I am not to this day.

Before you went out on the *Mame* tour, you did *Bedknobs and Broomsticks*. What was that like?

That was different. But I got to work with Donald McKayle, the great choreographer. He really devised some lovely stuff in that movie. I think it's a divine movie. Kids love it and I am so glad I did it, I really am. My best number was cut, though. A very funny number with a broomstick. But the music was running too long. Later they wanted to reinstate it but they couldn't find it! Gone forever.

Now that you were an anointed musical theater star, you were finally *the star* of a movie.

Indeed. It was the only time, and it was written for kids.

Then, while you were in Ireland, you were offered *Gypsy* and you turned it down. Why?

I just didn't think I could pull that off. I didn't think I could follow Merman. The original recording of Merman doing *Gypsy* was so stunning. I thought, "I can't do this, I don't know how to do this." Which was ridiculous, of course.

I don't think you can be faulted for being daunted.

I was daunted. I didn't think I had the lung power.

What made you change your mind?

Persuasion. Very tender and wonderful persuasion on the part of Barry Brown and Fritz Holt, who were going to produce it in London with Arthur Laurents directing and with Stephen Sondheim and Jule Styne right there with me, so I would have them to help me make it work.

Did you have apprehensions about Arthur Laurents after *Anyone Can Whistle*?

I was very unsure about Arthur directing, I can tell you that. We didn't have the happiest experience with *Whistle*. We didn't. He'd be the first person to agree with me. But when it came to *Gypsy*, he believed in me being able to do it, oddly enough. So did Steve. This was a big idea, to redo *Gypsy*, for goodness sakes. So I really had their backing and that made a big difference to me. Without their help, without their being there, without their encouragement, I don't think I could have done it.

There are two quotes regarding *Gypsy* that I want to read to you. You said at the time, "I can't beat Merman at the singing game and she can't beat me at the acting game, so no contest." She said, in typical Merman way, "I have no hard feelings, why should I? I could have done the role if I wanted to. I am just glad I created the role so others can copy it."

That's funny!

Did she see you in it?

I believe she saw it. I don't know for sure. When I won the Tony Award I gave her credit. She wrote me a note thanking me. I thought that was very touching.

Very classy.

Very classy. Right. I thought it was pretty damned nice.

After London you got to tour it for a while and then take it to Broadway. Was it a disappointment that it only played 170 performances in New York?

Did I only do 170? I didn't realize that. Memory is mud, I guess. We had toured it. We started in Canada and crossed the country. So it was a long haul.

And you won yet another Tony. Number three in less than ten years. You must have been getting very good at the acceptance speeches. Very proficient.

You're never proficient, my dear. It's always an absolute surprise. But it's absolutely lovely.

Did that one feel any different?

No, it's never different. The preparation, going to the event, you know who you're up against. And you just *don't know* who is going to win until they shout out your name. And then you do and it's incredible. Your stomach falls out.

Your next Broadway role after *Gypsy* was *The King and I*.

Oh, yes, that was a real side trip, an opportunity to play a famous lovely role. Also to sing a score which was totally different from anything I had ever done before. And working on it very briefly, really, with just a couple of weeks of rehearsal. But working with Richard Rodgers. He came to rehearsals. He sat there and helped me and taught me every line of those songs. I was so struck by his kindness. It was a singular experience and I loved it.

You said that Anna was a restrained role and that restrained roles are very trying. Did that make playing her a different kind of challenge?

Absolutely, she was very contained, very proper. Maybe I was trying to beat Deborah Kerr at her own game. She was my contemporary at MGM all of those years.

But you actually sang it. She was dubbed.

I sang it! That's right!

During her short stint in *The King and I*, who knew that Lansbury would be serving human meat pies in the same theater only months later. (Photofest)

And less than a year later came *Sweeney Todd*.

That came out of the blue. It appealed to me because as a child we would terrify each other talking about Sweeney Todd. I thought, "Well, that's interesting. It's a London story. What have they got in mind?" So of course I had to come and hear the score. I was in Ireland when they approached me. I think my first inkling was a cable that came to me from Hal Prince. It said, "Stephen Sondheim and I are planning a production of *Sweeney Todd* and we'd be very interested in knowing if you'd be interested in considering playing the role of Mrs. Lovett." I remember that I wrote back, in my very careful way, "What is the name of the show?" They told me, "*Sweeney Todd, the Demon Barber of Fleet Street*" and I said, "Then who is Mrs. Lovett?" They proceeded to tell me and I said, "Uh-huh." I came to New York, very skeptical. I went and listened to the score with Stephen. He played me "The Worst Pies in London" and I thought it was so damned funny. It just killed me. He did it all. He kept slapping the piano for the dough. He kept getting the lyrics all mixed up. I was immediately terribly interested. How could I not be? And I was also interested because Hugh Wheeler, who I knew from the movie *Something for Everyone*, was going to be the book writer. Hugh was such an inventive and clever writer. He understood the British and cockney humor. I knew his dialogue would be tremendously good and it was. He and Stephen together came up with some marvelous, original, and terrific nonsense with "A Little Priest."

Is it true that you had to push for the comedy because initially it wasn't there?

Absolutely true. I just kept weaving it into the cloth of the piece. The score was so huge and sonorous in places, we had to lighten it. It gave me the opportunity to make Mrs. Lovett an engaging and palatable character, even though what she was doing was despicable and terrible.

She was only interested in Mr. Todd. She just wanted him to love and cherish her and she wanted to love and cherish him. And she would do anything to bring that about. If it meant murdering people and chopping them up, she was quite willing to do it. I know quite a few women like that, don't you?

I have seen many Mrs. Lovetts and no one matched what you brought to the role. It's all so specific. Do you think it's because you're the only person who's played it who actually had the cockney roots?

I think that has a lot to do with it. The cockney mentality is quite something unto itself. I knew a lot of cockney people in my time. I did use a woman I had known as a kid, when I was ten or eleven. She worked for us. Her name was Beattie and she was from the East End of London. She had this kind of sluttish aspect and an unbelievable accent that you could cut with a knife. She was such a lovable, engaging, fat woman that we just adored her, my sister and I. The characters I have portrayed are often rooted in my memory of people I have known or have had dealings with. Sometimes I do it without even being aware that that's who I'm using for a muse. Luckily that is something which comes easily to me. I just pluck from places I've observed or seen. Beattie is a lot of Mrs. Lovett, I'll tell you that.

You are describing the art of acting: being able to load up your tool box with everything you observe.

That's absolutely true. That's what allows me to be the absolute plain person that I am, only a sponge. I am not a sophisticated person at all. I mean, I can be. I know about sophistication and I know when it's expected. I can do that when I have to. But basically, I'm not. I'm just malleable clay. The only thing I know how to do is to act and to keep house. I do that quite well. And if I'm not acting that's what I'll do. Or make a garden or something.

During rehearsals you apparently weren't getting a lot of direction from Hal Prince. Considering that Mrs. Lovett was so out there, how did you deal with getting so little feedback?

Some directors will climb in and say, "Angie, in this instance, I think you fight him on that" or something like that. "I think you should be more argumentative." Hal doesn't do that, that's not the kind of director he is. One wasn't looking for it. But I must say that in the early days I felt a little, "Gee, we're doing this by ourselves. Is this going to be all right?" But if it wasn't all right I know that Hal would have told us. He lets you alone.

So you weren't looking for help finding the character?

Oh God no. Just validation. And Hal is a great audience. He'll sit there and laugh. At the start of rehearsals he made the most wonderful speech in which he really delineated who everybody represented and what was going on in London at that time. We talked about the beehive. I never quite understood what that meant. He described the social climate of England at that time, the corruption that went on between the judges and police. People were victims. All of the people the audience were going to be seeing, except for the Judge and the Beadle, were victims and very poor, needing support and not getting it.

Was it true that you initially didn't think your costume was dirty enough?

The designer, Franny Lee, didn't think it was dirty enough at the first preview, so we all went down to the basement and she took a plate of Bolognese and dumped it on me. So I had to go out and sing with this terrible smell. Sour! Cheese and stuff permeating my nostrils. It was just dreadful. But that's the way Franny was. She did *Saturday Night Live.*

And in that setting, you wore the costume for five minutes and you were done with it. Not in this one.

You talk about yourself as an actor who sings. But *Sweeney* was vocally so demanding. And you mentioned earlier that you never took a singing lesson. How did you get through it?

It was there. It was in my voice. I simply had to keep singing and keep practicing. When you have to do something and you've got the voice, and I did, I had the voice in those days, I could do it and I did it. And I am fortunate enough to have very strong vocal equipment. I think I got it from my grandfather. He was a great orator. He used to speak morning, noon, and night with no microphones. I think I inherited that. I never lost my voice.

What was the audience response to the show like?

Once the audience had been told by the critics that it was okay, then they went for it. Then they sat back and allowed themselves to go with the flow, whereas during previews, they were appalled by the premise and what we were doing: people tipping out of chairs and landing in a heap on the floor. Although we never showed that as they did in subsequent productions and in the movie. Oooh, that was really tough to take, I thought. Seeing those bodies schlumped in the corner waiting for the saw to come in. We were a very purified version compared to everything that was done subsequently. Once they got into the spirit of what we were trying to get across, the audience just went with it. People became addicted to it. I knew a woman who lived in Washington, D.C., a kind of straight-laced, very rich American lady. She came to see it eight times in Washington! Now what was it that appealed to her so strongly? Why would this woman come back eight times?

Are there shows that you've ever gone to see that many times?

No! Never.

I can see someone wanting to see you eight times, wanting to study your work. You are so revered in the theater community. You are looking at me quizzically. Do you not feel revered?

Yes, I do. I do. But I don't quite know why.

So when things happen like when you receive the Kennedy Center Honor, you're not . . .

Of course I am. I am stopped in my tracks. I don't know what it stems from. I don't really know.

You once said about your overall career, "I never really made it in movies." I read that and I thought, "She doesn't feel that her career was quite what she wanted it to be." And I can see, looking back, how you could think that.

You can, can't you? I mean you can understand the fact that I came to a dead halt. And I've never wanted to give the impression that I was badly done by Hollywood. I have had my moments, I tell you, where I felt that they didn't believe in me enough to prove that I could work as well in motion pictures as I have in theater. I could have reached a much bigger audience, but I did find one through Jessica Fletcher. But that was a very one-note lady. What was interesting about Hollywood, and I don't mean to be mealy-mouthed about it, but I never got an Emmy in all the years. What does that tell you? It says that the people who voted in Hollywood never watched *Murder She Wrote*. It was a worldwide success and it got Golden Globes. I got about three of them, actually, but never an Emmy. Every other actress who did a series of any length got at least one Emmy. It became a joke! What I am saying is that a prophet is without honor in their own town and that was the case with me in Hollywood. I couldn't get arrested, I couldn't get a role. I wasn't considered for parts. I didn't exist as far as movies were concerned, except in the early days when unique and marvelous directors gave me great roles—not great starring roles, but great roles, which suited me down to the ground in those days. That's another conversation, we mustn't get into that. You and I could talk all day and all night and I have to take a nap soon.

So in your whole vast and varied career, in which you were able to show such tremendous range, while each of the assignments might have been satisfying, the totality of the career . . .
Yeah, I'd stop and start and stop and start all the time.

In 1983, after *Sweeney Todd*, you had the opportunity to bring *Mame* back to Broadway.
That was one of the most mismanaged productions I was ever part of. Mitch Leigh, who produced it, would not run any print advertising. He only wanted television. It opened in July in Philadelphia and the people there thought it was a summer tour or tent show. It was a first-class revival of the original *Mame* starring Angela Lansbury. Nobody came. And then the Gershwin Theatre. Full production, very expensive, all new costumes and no advertising. Nobody knew we were there! We only ran for three weeks. It was one of the biggest flops of my life. I couldn't believe it. It was a rotten experience, it really was. That soured me for a while. And then I did one more play which did not succeed, *A Little Family Business*. I thought that was a fine play, but the critics didn't. We suffered the consequences but I'm glad I did it. After that I made up my mind that I didn't want to tour; Peter and I decided to go back to Los Angeles. Maybe it was time for me to do some television. The rest is *Murder She Wrote* history.

During *Murder She Wrote* you were able to give work to so many of the people you had worked with in the theater.
That's right! We really took care of them. They had the right hotels and trailers and all of that. I give credit to my husband. He was a great believer in that. He had been an agent and he knew how to take care of people. We had the best actors to play all of those parts. It was such fun. It really was. It was a dream.

Your TV work led to a TV musical, *Mrs. Santa Claus*.
What can I say? It's a seasonal story about a lady who never saw the light of day. Who was behind this great man? Mrs. Santa Claus, a character that Jerry Herman was able to take and run with. When I read it I thought, "this is kind of basic stuff but the songs are charming and it'll be a seasonal favorite." And it was for a number of years.

Jerry Herman's health was an issue at that point, wasn't it? Is it true that you did it for him?
I was certainly not going to say no. Although I was a little bit unsure about it. She was slightly a cardboard character. How could it be otherwise? I don't mean to denigrate the work of the author or his idea, but when you start off with a premise that's as basic as "who's the woman behind the guy . . ." The screenwriter wrote a very basic story. We knew it wouldn't be the world's greatest movie, just something charming and enchanting that people would enjoy.

It was very exciting from an audience perspective that you were doing a new Jerry Herman piece. It was a holiday bon-bon.
That's what I hoped it would be. We had Rob Marshall doing the choreography. He was very, very nice. I am thrilled for him that he's had the success he's had.

I didn't ask about Mrs. Potts in *Beauty and the Beast*, but she also figures into your musical career. Did that one take you by surprise?

Absolutely. That one came out of the blue. I'll never forget when I first got that tape of them singing the song and then they came on the phone, they being Howard Ashman and Alan Menken. Howard was very sick, even at that time. I had listened to their recording and it was kind of a rock rhythm. I said, "this isn't quite my style" and they said, "we don't mind, you do it the way you'd like to do it if you were playing this tea pot." So I made a demo for them, sent it, and they said, "That's it!" That's how that came about. And now children know my voice. It's so funny.

Was there ever a dream role for you?

Um, no. I have never truthfully felt, "Oh, God, if only I could have gotten my hands on that." Although I'll tell you a role I'd love to have played was Eliza in *My Fair Lady*. There was a moment when I was considered as a possibility. I was barely considered. That would have been fascinating.

If you could go back and play any of your roles over again, would you and would you do it differently?

I don't think I could go back to any of the roles I've played. I have great difficulty now singing any of the music that I have sung. I just can't do it. It upsets me. I can say in all honesty that it reminds me of parts of my life that I can't go back upon. Not being somebody who ever sang mechanically, every time I sang it was always acting that moment. And sometimes those moments were attached to desperately difficult times in my own life. For me to pick up and sing those songs now—which I'm not saying I couldn't do although I couldn't do them as well; I would do them differently. But I am constantly asked to go to Feinstein's or here or there and I say, "I am not a stand-up singer. I don't know how to do that. That's not my speed." But I really have quite a repertoire of songs.

In 2009, you took on another Sondheim musical, *A Little Night Music*.

Well I didn't consider that a musical. It *is* a musical but it is a play first and foremost. I was so well acquainted with the material. At one point in my career I was sought to play Desiree in the original but I was doing *Gypsy* at the time.

Did you have memories of having seen Hermione Gingold in the role?

Absolutely, yes. But thank God it didn't register with me to the extent that it colored my own interpretation of the role. From an actress's point of view it's a full meal of possibilities.

Did you enjoy working with Trevor Nunn?

I was very, very happy to have had the opportunity. He was tremendously encouraging and he trusted me and let me do my thing. I never really like to talk about how we arrive at a performance because it's rather a holy thing among actors. At least it is for me. People ask, "How do you do that?" I can't really tell them. I don't want to tell them. That's the thing that is my particular ability, shall we say. When you try to break something down you take away the entire mystique. It's nobody's business how you arrive at a character.

Have you decided that you are never going to stop?

Yes I have. I truly have. If I can keep body and soul intact, I don't see why I shouldn't go on, you know? There are all sorts of possibilities. It's really amazing what's out there, even at my advanced age.

LESLIE UGGAMS

April and May 2009

LESLIE UGGAMS CAN COOK. CHRISTMAS DINNER at her house is a massive feast of comfort food paired with excellent wines. Don't expect to spend time with the hostess, though; she's in the kitchen and doesn't want your help. The Columbus Circle apartment where all this cooking occurs is only a few subway stops from the Apollo Theater where Uggams first started singing onstage, at age nine, opening for the likes of Louis Armstrong and Ella Fitzgerald. But even by then she was an experienced actor, having appeared at six on the series *Beulah* as Ethel Waters's niece. By fifteen, she was appearing weekly on the TV show *Sing Along with Mitch*. She was the first African American female singer to appear weekly on a national prime time television series. So by the time Uggams made her Broadway debut at twenty-four, she was a seasoned pro.

That debut came in the 1967 Jule Styne, Comden and Green, Arthur Laurents show, *Hallelujah, Baby!*, which, despite running under a year, won Tony Awards for Best Musical and for Uggams as Best Actress.

Uggams's subsequent career found her in almost every possible medium. She had her own TV series, *The Leslie Uggams Show*, in 1969 and later won great acclaim for her work in the landmark miniseries *Roots*; recorded a dozen albums; appeared in films; won an Emmy; played Vegas repeatedly; and even hosted *The Muppet Show*. She returned to Broadway throughout in the shows *Her First Roman*, *Blues in the Night*, *Jerry's Girls*, *Anything Goes* [an unexpected replacement for Patti LuPone], *Thoroughly Modern Millie*, *King Hedley II*, and *On Golden Pond*.

What's unusual about Uggams, however, is that unlike many stars of her caliber she works regularly in regional theaters all over the country—not because she needs the work, but because she wants it. Also unusual is the degree to which her amazing voice has not diminished one iota as she's aged. In *Stormy Weather*, the 2009 Lena Horne biography she hopes to bring to Broadway, Uggams sang thirteen full-throated Horne songs with the same power and luster she demonstrated at the beginning of her career.

But perhaps what's most remarkable about Uggams is her outlook. Unlike so many performers, she is seemingly without bitterness or rancor about anything. She's no Pollyanna, but she also doesn't hold a grudge. Moments of conflict she's experienced are just that—moments. The most negativity you'll typically get from her will be an arched eyebrow. Maybe two. Which might explain how, even after sixty years in the business, Leslie Uggams is still an ebullient, delightful, force of nature.

Reveling in the fabulousness and fur of Muzzy Van Hossmere in *Thoroughly Modern Millie*. (Joan Marcus)

How would you compare the musical theater scene today to how it was forty years ago?
Well, today you see a lot of people who were in television coming to Broadway . . .

You were!
Even though I was from television, I had a background playing the Apollo four and five shows a day . . .

Twenty-nine shows a week, you said at one point.
Exactly. So theater was a piece of cake after playing the Apollo. I learned early as a kid you had to pace yourself and take care of that singing voice. I lost my voice a few times as a kid and still had to go out there on that stage. So theater wasn't as frightening for me as for a lot of people who come from television and think, "Oh my goodness! Eight shows!" If your name is there you need to be there. People are not interested in discovering the understudy most of the time. It's a deep commitment. It's hard. People don't realize how hard it is when you do a musical. You really have no life. God forbid somebody has a cold, they can't come near you. Really, no life.

Ethel Merman used to say you eat alone a lot.
Exactly. You have to rest, pace yourself. It's quite a commitment. But I love the theater. I love the theater because people are right there and they let you know that they love it. Or that they don't love it.

On your very first show, you were working with legends.
When I did *Hallelujah, Baby!*, looking back I realize, "Oh my God, I was working with Comden and Green, Jule Styne, Arthur Laurents." I didn't realize how legendary, legendary. Jule Styne taught me the songs. I didn't have a rehearsal pianist doing it. Jule Styne was my

rehearsal pianist. He was just wonderful and wild and crazy. He would get up and demonstrate how he wanted the songs to go and stuff like that. It's really amazing that for my first Broadway show I started at the top.

What do you remember about Comden and Green?

They were wild and crazy and you put them together with Jule Styne and you've got three huge egos in the room. Sometimes they would be fighting with each other like mad.

By that time they had done eight shows together.

Oh yeah, it was part of who they were. Betty was the calming force, Adolph was wild. Jule was typically down to earth but

> **Leslie Uggams**
>
> *Hallelujah, Baby!* Broadway, 1967 (Tony Award)
> *Her First Roman,* Broadway, 1968
> *Blues in the Night,* Broadway, 1982
> *Jerry's Girls,* National Tour and Broadway, 1984
> *Anything Goes,* National Tour and Broadway, 1988
> *Call Me Madam,* Milburn, N.J., 1996
> *Thunder Knocking on the Door,* off-Broadway, 2002
> *Thoroughly Modern Millie,* Broadway, 2003
> *Stormy Weather,* Philadelphia and Pasadena, 2007, 2009
> *Pipe Dream,* Encores! 2012

crazy and loved the women. He had not been married very long to his wife. She was a lovely, lovely woman. It was electrifying every day. Electrifying.

And then you throw Arthur Laurents into the mix.

Arthur was Arthur. Arthur was and is the kind of person who tells you exactly how he feels. If you are one of those people who can't take criticism or gets their feelings hurt, too bad. I survived. And I figured, if I could survive that I can survive anything. Everything else is no big deal. I was criticized by a master. Recently when they were talking about touring *Gypsy* with Bernadette [Peters], Arthur said, "You know, you could take over the tour." I feel honored that he thought I'd be a good Mama Rose.

What do you remember about rehearsing *Hallelujah, Baby!*?

I was so green! I thought that on the first day of rehearsal I had to know the whole script so I had memorized it already. I am at the first reading and everybody is sitting there with their script, looking at it, and everybody slowly turned and looked at me. [During previews] whenever there were line changes, they could give me something and I'd be like, "we can put it in tonight." People finally came to me and said, "Would you please stop learning so quickly! You're not the only one in the scene."

You won a Tony for your first show.

Well, first of all, I had no clue what the Tony Awards were. I had no clue what being nominated meant which was really lovely because I didn't get caught up in it. I was oblivious. I didn't realize until it was time to be there. Of course now when you are nominated for a Tony there are all of these things that you do, the talk shows, the luncheons, every minute you are aware, but we didn't have all that back then. It didn't hit me until that day and I was sitting in my seat and I thought, "Gee, I'd like to win this." And they called my name. You know, I was tied [with Patricia Routledge] and they said her name first. It was really a lovely moment. But it wasn't the kind of pressure that there is now. You didn't walk the red carpet and do all of these interviews.

Your show had closed by the time of the awards, right?

That was the weird thing. David Merrick was originally supposed to produce it and then he dropped out, so we wound up with producers who really didn't know theater. They didn't know that even if business goes down a little bit, you keep the show going, so they closed the show. And then we won all of those Tonys and we were closed. That's one thing that I have also learned over the years: we have wonderful producers who have been doing this a long time. I'd like to work with those people. They know what to do. It's not enough to have a wonderful show; you've got to make sure that people come in to see the wonderful show. A lot of times you have people that have a lot of money and they want to put money into a show, but they don't realize what you have to do. I found that out doing another show that will remain nameless. They had nooooo clue. We should have been running and running and running but they didn't know how to go about that. They thought, "We have Leslie, people will come." Well, no. There are so many other shows out there, you have to get them to come. You have to fight for your show. That's one thing I know about Broadway. Unfortunately with that first show, we had people that were more business-people. They didn't cut their teeth in the theater. Great producers know how to keep a show going.

Do you think great showman producers still exist?

David Merrick was as big a star as the people in his shows. He would do all kinds of wild and crazy things to get attention but it worked! He was the publicist as well as the producer. People wanted to go see some of his shows because they were David Merrick shows. Now everyone has their own department. The other thing is that now you can do workshops of a show for ten years before it even gets to New York. They were not workshopping *Hallelujah, Baby!* for ten years. That's amazing to me. I had never done a workshop and someone asked me to do one on the life of Lena Horne. I thought a workshop was where you sat down with your scripts and read it and people came and that was it. Now, doing a workshop, you might as well be doing the show! I was doing *Thoroughly Modern Millie* at the time and I said, "I can't do all of that! I am doing a show on Broadway right now." This business has come a loooong way. And it costs a lot of money to do those workshops.

Let's go back to the very beginning. You were born in Washington Heights. Your parents both flirted with performing. Your mother was a Cotton Club dancer . . .

For a second. She was in it for a second. She was no great dancer. And my father was with the [Hal Johnson] choir. He always told the story, they rehearsed for two years, never got a gig and he went on to a life of being a civilian. After he left they started doing all of the movies. So it wasn't meant to be. But my Aunt Eloise was in the business. She was in *Porgy and Bess* everywhere and she and my cousin were on Broadway in *Blackbirds of 1928*. She had done theater and stuff like that. She was really the show business professional in my family.

But she's not the one who got you involved.

No. A friend of the family got me involved. She thought I had talent. My parents thought I was cute but they weren't show business parents. I was taking tap and singing and acting at school. It kept me busy and off the street. This friend played piano at the school, the Wally Wanger School. And she would give me little vocal lessons and songs to sing. At that time television was new and producers would go around to the different schools looking for kids to do stuff. I was one of the kids who would get chosen. In fact, Maurice Hines and I were the token black kids on Milton Berle whenever he had kids on the show. It was great. I got to do great shows. [At school] there was a line of kids and the people who came to choose would just look at you and point. "That one, that one."

Just based on your looks?

Just based on your looks. It had nothing to do with singing. I never really did any singing on the Milton Berle show. It was always a background thing. Or if the kids sang we all sang together. But for some reason, Milton Berle's mother, who always came to his shows, turned to my mother one day and said, "Your kid has talent!" I was about eight. My mother said to her, "How can you tell?" She saw something in me. Television was wonderful because as a kid you could learn and you could make mistakes and not be banished from the world of show business. I always loved music and taking lessons. My mother said I started singing when I was three. I was not shy, I was . . . hammy. If anybody asked me to sing, I'd sing in a minute. I have a sister, older than I am, with a beautiful voice. She was always shy. Not me. I was always ready.

Even before you started singing, you were on TV in *Beulah*, playing Ethel Waters's niece. Do you have any recollections of her?

She was always very nice to me. I remember hearing the grown-ups talk about her reputation and that she could be tough to work with. But she loved my mother and me and was very, very helpful with my career. She gave my mother the name of the lady who made my clothes when I played the Apollo. She took a shine to me. She liked us so much that whenever she would perform these private soiree kind of things, she would invite my mother and me and we would go and watch her sing. I was just so fascinated by her.

You ended up at the Professional Children's School even though your parents weren't stage parents.

That was because I couldn't go to public school because I was out too much doing television and the Board of Education wouldn't allow that. [The Professional Children's School] was incredible. It was for kids who were either working professionally or whose parents were stars. Us little kids were always around the high school kids. Everybody knew each other. We would put on shows at hospitals and school bazaars and things like that.

You went to school with Mary Martin's daughter and you got to see a lot of Mary Martin shows.

Yes! That was wonderful! I got to see musicals with great musical stars and I was always amazed. I got to see *King and I* with Gertrude Lawrence and stuff like that.

Were you getting a sense that that was something you wanted to do?

You know, I didn't get a sense of that because there weren't a lot of black stars. Everybody was Caucasian. Even though I was working a lot at the Apollo and in Baltimore, Washington, D.C., and Philadelphia, I still wasn't thinking, "this is what I want to be." I was thinking more in practical terms. My father believed in education and I was thinking of being a psychologist or something like that. There just weren't a lot of role models unless you wanted a record deal. I wasn't really a rock 'n' roll kind of person. I had a very legit voice. And there weren't a lot of Dorothy Dandridges or Lena Hornes. And even they were really limited in the roles they played in the movies. I was good and I could do it but where was it going to lead? I wasn't sure. I knew I had the talent but I didn't know whether it was gonna be what I would like it to be. But I was studying with wonderful teachers and just kind of doing it. What put it into focus was Mitch Miller. *Sing Along with Mitch.* Because then I became a television star. I was the first black female singing every week on national television. That opened up a lot of doors. Then I got opportunities. Vegas, those kinds of things. Then I knew: Ah-ha!

Performing in Vegas in that period, there are famous stories about people like Dinah Washington and Eartha Kitt being denied the front door . . .
By the time I got to Vegas, no. I didn't have any of those problems. There was one hotel, the Desert Inn, that did not allow blacks. Eddie Fisher was playing there doing a midnight show. All of the performers from the strip went down there and naturally I was invited and I must say that the people that were running it were not the businesspeople yet. It was the mafia. But they made sure that they welcomed me. So there I was. That was something.

I read somewhere that you weren't aware that Mitch Miller met with opposition to you from the network.
Yeah, he had to fight to keep me on the show. My career has been fascinating. It's never been planned. Some people have a plan. Mine always came from around the corner somewhere. I was on a quiz show trying to get money for college and they asked me what I liked to sing. I sang "Whole World in His Hands." People started writing in [asking that I sing] and therefore some weeks I didn't even get to answer the question. All of a sudden life changed. One night Mitch heard me sing "The Lord's Prayer." I went and did some demos for him and he signed me to Columbia. I was not aware of this idea for a show he had been trying to sell but NBC put us on and we became a huge hit. I wasn't supposed to be a regular, but the mail was so much that I became a regular. And then the South wouldn't take the show because I was on it, I found out later on. And the networks said to Mitch, "You know . . ." And he said, "No . . ." They kept trying to come up with all of these different scenarios. Like to have me sing a solo with no one else so that they could cut me out like they did with Lena. Or having me not touch the other performers. All of these things and Mitch kept saying, "No, no, no. As long as there's a show, she's on it." I will always be forever grateful. And then my life changed. And because of that I ended up doing *The Boyfriend* because they were interested in shows with television people in them.

And *The Boyfriend*, of all shows! Playing a British 1920s Polly . . .
Hello! I was the only black person. And the audience went wild. We did all kinds of business.

Did you think about it at the time or was it just "here we go?"
My father always told me, "Whatever you do, you can do it." Therefore my whole life has been, "Oh, I want to do that. I can do that." I looked around and thought, "Interesting. Look at all these Caucasian people." But I had a role to learn. It was a two-week run and a two-week rehearsal. I didn't know about learning the script and choreography. All of a sudden I was like, "Oh my God! Look at all these lines I have to say!" It was a good lesson for me. I said, "Ooooo-kaaaaay. This is serious business and you have to know your stuff." I had no clue. I had never done a full show. And the audience loved it. That kind of filtered back to New York and that's how I wound up auditioning for *Hallelujah, Baby!*

So you were too caught up in learning the show to pay attention to the fact that you were breaking racial boundaries?
Yes! A friend of mine said once that I am the kind of person that walks into the room and I'm like, "Aren't you lucky that I'm here?" Fearless! Fearless. My husband and I went to Martin

Luther King's funeral and we didn't know there was still a law about black and white being married, even then.

Didn't you know other people who filled you in on this stuff?

You grew up hearing stories about people like Lena Horne having to pretend she wasn't married, or Pearl Bailey and her husband, but I guess I am just fearless. This is how I live my life and if you have something to say to me, you say it to me. I am a fabulous black woman. I wouldn't want to be anything else but what I am. If that's a problem you need to get over yourself. That's how I always lived my life. Every now and then things would happen to kick me upside my head. When I was working in the Catskills, I was looking for our room with my mother and we asked someone who worked there and he said, "Are you the maid?" [That was a reminder that] there are still those stupid people who see a black person and they have to be a servant. But I never felt inferior. I was raised to believe, "You can be somebody. You just go and you do it." I remember I was doing some terrible movie and we were down in the South. We were having a luncheon break and a guy in a plaid shirt and cap says to me, "You know, I always loved you. And you're a niggress!" He thought he was complimenting me!

You got unanimous raves in *Hallelujah, Baby!* Were you aware of that as it was happening?

A lot of it. When you come out the stage door and see all of the people waiting to get autographs you realize that something spectacular has happened. It was wonderful because I loved the show and I loved the character. And at the time, there was a lot going on. I was a newlywed! And my parents finally got it. There was prestige, class. It made the family very, very proud. It was a wonderful part to be playing. The show said a lot about the history of America, Sort of like a musical *Roots*. It was great. And then I went and did my second show, *Her First Roman*, and got slapped down a few pegs.

That was an interesting one. You were working with Richard Kiley, who was just coming off *Man of La Mancha*, and you were playing Cleopatra, of all things.

I really didn't want to do the show. I had just finished doing *Hallelujah, Baby!* and I wanted a break. I wasn't sure about the show. They had to really sell me on it. But I really wanted to work with Richard. I've since learned to follow my gut instinct and not let people talk me into things. Of course, the show was trouble.

Did you know all along? Did you know in rehearsals?

It just didn't feel right. I wasn't being bowled over. And again, we had producers that really didn't know theater well. They didn't know what needed work. We had trouble.

So what's it like performing in a show when you know it's not working?

Terrible! The thing that kept us going was Richard's great sense of humor. We would just laugh. We would look at each other and go, "Okay . . . " That's all you could do. There was a problem with my wig where it was so heavy I couldn't keep my head up. Things with the music and people sneaking around during the night, writing other material . . .

Bock and Harnick put songs in, right?

Yes, but nobody had told [songwriter] Ervin Drake. It was crazy, crazy, crazy. I am out there singing a song and I can hear, "Stop!!!!" Ervin Drake in the balcony.

Uggams in *Hallelujah, Baby!*, the record holder for shortest run (when including previews) of any musical to win the Best Musical Tony Award. (Photofest)

During a show?

Yes! He had no clue. Richard lost his voice in Philly and the understudy didn't know the part. He went out there with the book and couldn't read it. And he was way too old to be the understudy to begin with. They fired the original director and they got this young guy who had done an off-the-wall comedy. One minute he wanted me to have an English accent, the next he didn't. It was crazy. I knew we were in deeeep trouble. And of course we came to New York and . . .

Closed seventeen performances later. Were you relieved?
Oh yeah. Richard and I both.

After *Her First Roman* closed you headed west?
Well, not because I was done with New York. My husband is from Australia and the weather was not to his liking. So we went someplace warmer and I was away from theater for awhile.

Going to California didn't scare you in terms of your career?
No, I wasn't worried about what I would do. The goal was to do a television series.

You achieved that pretty fast with *The Leslie Uggams Show*.
Yeah. That was also very political. Took over for the Smothers Brothers. It was a fabulous ten weeks but they never meant for us to stay on TV. Again, pioneer. John Amos [who went on to play her father in *Roots*] was one of my writers. Black cameraman. We accomplished a few things in those ten weeks.

By political, you mean that they never intended to keep you? I read that they were re-hearsing *Hee Haw* all the while, but they chose you as the immediate replacement so that the choice to fire the Smothers Brothers couldn't be criticized.
Yeah. I was working on ideas for a situation comedy and out of the blue my agent was knocking on the door saying, "You've got your own television show replacing *The Smothers Brothers Comedy Hour*." We had just moved into our house. We didn't even have all the lights hooked up.

Then you did a lot of nightclub work. You did say at one point during that time, "I have no intention of going through a phase when you lean on a mirror and sing."
And I wound up in a movie leaning on a mirror and singing. And that came because I had known Liza [Minnelli] and she recommended me to her father [Vincente Minnelli] who was shooting a movie called *Two Weeks in Another Town*. I got the part and there I am, out in Hollywood, and they put me in this tight, orange, beaded gown, on a stool, and there I am leaning against a mirror singing. And I went, "Wait a minute! This is not what I had planned. How did this happen!" But it was a wonderful experience. Vincente Minnelli was fabulous. Kirk Douglas couldn't have been sweeter. And Cyd Charisse. I got to know them. They were lovely to my mother. And during that number, Kirk is sitting right at my feet, looking up at me while I sing "Don't Blame Me."

It's fascinating to me that your next stage role was Maria in *West Side Story*.
Mess Side Story! That was purely . . . they offered a lot . . . of . . . money. A guy who had a lot of money wanted to do this tour and he made an offer that I couldn't refuse. That was the worst situation. It was so bad. I would have to say to the guys, "Could you butch it up a little?" Tony was lighter on his feet than I was. That was where I learned not to do anything just for the money.

That was the only time you did something just for the money?
That was it. You can dangle the money but I have to like the project and not be embar-rassed going out there.

I have always wondered about that. When a woman has been in the business for a long time, there can be lean years. Even though you are a star, the roles aren't always there and you have to pay rent. Other than *West Side*, you never did work that you felt you had to?

I was never crazy about nightclubs and Vegas but I did them because you did make a lot of money. And it was hard. It's *dry* in Vegas and you really have to worry about your throat. Every singer will tell you that. There are some people who have that nightclub thing down. But for me? People there are distracted by alcohol and waiters and, back then, cigarettes. You are trying to create a moment. I never liked doing that but I did it. That was part of the deal. And when you were asked to headline in Vegas, you did it.

West Side Story's Maria was one of several roles that I don't think most people would expect to find on your resumé. Sally Bowles in *Cabaret*. The Witch in *Into the Woods*. Sally Adams in *Call Me Madam*. Maria Callas in *Master Class*. *Side by Side by Sondheim*.

I was gooood in *Cabaret*, too.

Did you like performing regionally?

What I like about touring and regional theater is that it gives you the opportunity to do roles that Broadway is never going to ask you to do. I got a chance to stretch. They worked very well. I would *never* get those opportunities on Broadway. And I think, "Yeah! I want to do that role."

Living out of a hotel didn't bother you?

Well, I'd always rather be home. And the packing and unpacking is the worst. I don't care if I am only doing a one-nighter, I always over-pack. It drives my husband crazy. And I say, "Well, you never know! I might need this!" You try to have a system and it never works. But what I did learn is that when I am on the road, I don't stay in hotels anymore. Room service gets to be a pain. I get an apartment, I love to cook, I am more relaxed.

Before your next trip to Broadway, you got to do a TV special with Ethel Merman. *Christmas Eve on Sesame Street.*

Oh God! She's a hoot! You know what I remember most about Ethel? Those eyelashes!

More than Carol Channing's?

Yeah! They had so much gunk on them. I was sitting next to her and I was like [mouth hanging open]. I was fascinated. By the time I worked with her she had mellowed. She had become a calmer, down several notches, person. It wasn't crazy. But I remember sitting and thinking, "I am doing a show with Ethel Merman!" It was wonderful. And that thing: "Hi sweetheart, how ya' doin'? C'mon over here!" that was really her. That was her. I have never, never had a bad situation with any other actor I have worked with. I get along with everybody. Life is too short. Even with Carol [Channing]. Because Carol is used to being *the* light of everything. But we got along great. There were times she could be annoyed with the audience. She'd do a number and come off and say, "Well, they loved *you*." But we always laughed together. She always trusted me on the stage. She had allergies so she couldn't eat normal food and the stuff she had to eat was like, "Oh, Lordy, Lordy, Lordy." But I adored her. And I learned so much. I believe that when you work with people like that you study them and you learn.

What did you learn from her?

The way she brings her audience in to her. People would come over and over to see her. They just adored her. If you watch her in *Hello, Dolly!*, she just brings the people in. They lean forward in their seats. That's a great quality in the theater. She was eccentric but she was wonderful. I loved and adored her. Sometimes we had our knocking of the heads but it was never anything crazy. I have great respect for her.

She's truly unique.

Yeah. And bigger than life. That's what makes a star a lot of the time. That's what made Ethel a star. If you think of the ladies of the theater of the time, each of them was unique. They were characters as well, no matter what they were in, you were always aware of them. Then there are stars that try to get into the character more than bringing themselves. But no matter what they were in, you couldn't say that's not Ethel or Carol.

We are focused on your musical work but in telling your story, we can't ignore _Roots_ in 1977. You said, "This will change opportunities for African American performers." Now looking back, do you think that's what happened?

The men from _Roots_ did better than the women. It was rough. A lot of things didn't come our way. It just didn't happen, which was very surprising because we changed history. I just thought that I would get more opportunity as an actress. Even now, I was in LA for the thirtieth anniversary of _Roots_ on the Emmy Awards and I was backstage and one of the producers of _Law & Order_ says, "Leslie Uggams!!! I love you! I drive my car, and I play 'My Own Morning,'" and I said, "Oh, that's great." But have I been cast on _Law & Order_? No!

You're the only actor in New York who hasn't.

Only one.

In 1982 you came back to New York with _Blues in the Night_.

My husband had been trying to get me out of California for eight years. I was on the road doing concerts and stuff like that. I was living in paradise: the house, the pool—why would I want to leave? But [director] Sheldon Epps called me and said, "You know, you haven't done a musical in awhile." And the show was an interesting idea, so I said, "Yeah." Now, unbeknownst to me, the theater that we were doing the show in [the Rialto] was a theater that had shown porn! And that was before they cleaned up the streets. Every night I'd go [stepping over people passed out on the street], "Excuse me, excuse me, excuse me." The ladies of the night used to hang in the neighborhood. But the audience went absolutely crazy for that show. They loved it, loved it. Then the reviews came out and the critics were not crazy about it. But it was good to get back. And that was a different kind of character for me to play, so it was a good experience.

During that time in the early '80s you became one of the actors producer Alexander Cohen called on quite a bit. You performed for many years on his Tony Award shows and _Night of 100 Stars_.

So much fun, so much fun. I still say that Alex is the best person that ever did the Tonys because he knew how to be theatrical and how to get an audience. We were all doing something, we weren't just coming out and presenting. We were like his little theater company and people tuned in to watch it. I miss that.

Did you have a favorite moment from any of those or from _Night of 100 Stars_?

Well, my head exploded at _Night of 100 Stars_. I mean there were so many different stars there. Rock Hudson, Lucille Ball, Sidney Poitier, Robert DeNiro . . . I remember Melba Moore and I had autograph books and we were going around getting everybody's autograph. It was extraordinary. It was just an incredible night and it was like a party backstage. Everybody was hanging with everybody. Incredible. We'd come in for rehearsal and everybody would be there in the audience, and we'd all cheer each other on—Liza, Chita, Carol Channing, all of us.

When you put that many stars in a room, do those things ever get bitchy? You have people who have had long-term slights or grudges . . .

You know, that's interesting. I've been in a lot of dressing rooms with a lot of divas, and it's always been laughing and giggling and putting each other on and talking about something stupid. Everybody that I've ever worked with has been embracing.

I don't think you can have that kind of show today because so many of today's stars come from reality shows or are created by the tabloids. Everybody's actually nobody—

[Back then] everybody studied their craft. Everybody. Everybody paid their dues to be in the theater. When I finally got accepted into the theater with *Hallelujah, Baby!* it was extraordinary because I had studied all my life and hoped that maybe someday this would happen to me. But I had studied acting, dancing, singing. It wasn't just that I came from television. That opened the door for me to get a chance, but I had studied. I wasn't just someone that won a contest on TV and was shoved out the door.

Your next big show was *Jerry's Girls*. That was supposed to be a little tour.

Eight weeks. Jerry Herman called and he said, "Would you like to do . . . it's going to be Carol Channing and Andrea McArdle." "When do we start?" I mean Carol, Mary

Uggams flanked by Chita Rivera and Dorothy Loudon in a publicity shot for *Jerry's Girls*. (Photofest)

Martin, and Ethel Merman were the queens of theater! Why would I not have wanted to be in something involving Carol? Plus Andrea? We were such a smash from the first show and never looked back. Eight weeks became forty-eight weeks. An all-female cast. I had a great time. I became the Equity deputy. Honey, I was on that telephone constantly. In Louisville, we were supposed to play the new, beautiful theater, and then they had a problem so they put us in this old theater that hadn't been cleaned since 1702. We were wheezing and honking! Oh, it was a nightmare. When we were in San Antonio Carol threw this wonderful birthday party for my son. It had this Mexican theme, piñatas and everything. She adored him.

Touring in *Jerry's Girls* was your first professional connection with Jerry Herman, but now you are closely associated with him.

Jerry and I had known each other off and on in social things. And he would sit down at the piano and we'd sing and we'd say, "We've got to work together!" Through this opportunity, we became extremely close. We had a great time. He wanted me because he knew I could bring soulfulness to his music. Even recently, when I was doing *Dolly*, he gave me some of the songs he had written for Ethel Merman and was so complimentary. Because Ethel was fabulous, but, you know, starts loud, ends loud, middle loud. Loud.

Jerry's Girls came to New York without Andrea and Carol. Why?

Carol didn't want to come into New York. I don't know the exact reason why. So Jerry put in Chita Rivera and Dorothy Loudon and it became a different kind of show. They started fiddling with it and it wasn't as successful as the tour had been. But we had fun. Wonderful, crazy Dorothy Loudon always made me laugh. She was a tortured soul. She was going through some things. Some days her personality would take a left turn. So it was, "which Dorothy is it going to be today?"

Did that ever affect what was going on onstage?

No, it really didn't. She was amazing. She did her show. Unfortunately she hurt her foot, and then Chita was in a car accident and [we closed]. But I loved having that experience working with them.

You toured the show for so long and you were getting such a great reception everywhere, and then you open in New York and the reviews were incredibly harsh.

[*New York Times* critic Frank Rich] went after me ["Miss Uggams, whose voice increasingly swings from a whisper to a harsh belt without humane warning . . . "]. I don't know why he went after me. But I also know that the fact that Jerry Herman won [the Tony] for *La Cage Aux Folles* [the year before] and he [Rich] was a big Sondheim fan and friend . . . he found a way to go after me. I think that had a lot to do with it. Funny thing   I've seen him many times since, and he'll tell me how fabulous I am, and—well, really, what's so different? I was stunned. But it didn't stop the applause that I was getting. I'm confident enough with myself to know that when I walk out on the stage I'm going to bring it. The show should have done much better than it did.

It would have if Chita hadn't been sideswiped by a cab. With Dorothy's broken foot, you were the last woman standing. What did that feel like?

They started talking names to the point where Pia Zadora was mentioned. I thought, "What drugs are you on? Party's over. Give it up."

What was working with Chita like for you?

Oh, we had a great time. She is just as crazy as I am and we were always laughing. I love Chita because Chita is a competitor, you know? I like working with people like that because you have to raise your game. There's no slacking. Same with James Earl Jones.

When the show closed, you went back to California, but not for very long because Lincoln Center called.

To do the National Tour of *Anything Goes*. They decided to build the ship bigger and better than the ship on Broadway. The next thing you know we were touring and then we find out that the set is too big for [the theaters on] a big part of the national tour. So what do they do? They [cancel our dates and] put us in the National Theater in D.C. [with no advance notice] at the time where everybody is on vacation. We sit there and we die. We just died there. The ship is sinking and it's sinking us with it. Lincoln Center had never done a tour before. We were about to close when I get the call that Patti LuPone's leaving Broadway and they ask me if I would take it over. I loved it. I had the amazing Howard McGillin and wonderful Nancy Opel [as co-stars]. But there was a strange atmosphere backstage.

In what way?

Well, it was a very divided kind of group. Factions. There was the Patti group and then there was the other group. It was kind of toxic when I got there. But then I came in and we had a ball. People loved the show. You could just see them smiling in their seats and they would just jump up and have a great time. Even at the end, you'd see them dancing up the aisle.

After *Anything Goes* you moved back to New York but you stayed away from the New York stage for awhile.

I was doing a lot of concert work, which I really enjoy doing.

The next time a Broadway musical that you were interested in came your way, you weren't available for it?

Thoroughly Modern Millie. Yeah. They asked me three times. First, it wasn't written yet, so we didn't really know what it was, so I said "no" when they wanted me originally. Then the second time they asked me I couldn't do it because I was doing *Thunder Knocking at the Door*. The producers said it was going to run and then two days later, they closed it. Third time, I said, "Okay!" And boy, I loved doing that show. I loved the company. I loved going to the theater every day. I was in that show for almost a year and a half and it did not feel that way. Oh, and I was dressed to the nines! The music was fabulous! I loved Sutton [Foster] and Christian [Borle]. It had a great cast. It was just an absolute ball.

Not every established, Tony Award–winning star is willing to be a replacement.

To me that's just silly. I mean sure you'd like to be the first but I like to work. I can sit home, looking at the old posters, waiting for somebody to say, "Okay, this is your vehicle." But I like to work and I was kicking myself because I didn't do it originally.

Do you have a specific memory of working with Sutton Foster?

She is so real. She has enormous talent but she's still down to earth. There's a sweetness about her. And then she gets out on that stage and just wows me. I loved to watch her. I'll tell you what's amazing to me; when I was a kid working the Apollo, I'd stand in the wings and watch what the [headliners] did to see why they had that magic. Today a lot of these kids, they're in their dressing rooms [during the show]. Some of them are understudies and they're in their dressing rooms! Why aren't you watching these people? They are fabulous for a reason; try and learn some of that fabulousness! But they're off doing other things. You should be in the wings watching! And then half the time they're not even in the show. One day in *Millie* instead of this huge party [scene onstage], we had a small soiree of five people. Where is everybody? Well, this one had a personal day. . . . What's a personal day? That's another thing; I don't understand the personal day thing. Personal day to me is your day off.

So that all felt very different from when you were doing *Hallelujah, Baby!*? What do you think changed? How do you think that happened?

I don't know. I just find that a lot of times people are happy to be in a show for a certain amount of time, and then the next thing you know they can't wait to audition for a new thing that they heard about. Do they stay for a year? I don't know. I come from that same school that Chita comes from. I don't want my understudy going on. She's going to have to kill me [to go on] because I'm going to be out there! And the audience wants to see you. I don't care if the understudy turns out to be the greatest thing ever. So therefore, it's my responsibility to keep myself healthy, to not hang out, not overexpose my voice but to be there Tuesday through Sunday and that's me. I take it very seriously and I think most of the people in the business that are legends take it very seriously and they're there every night. Musicals are hard because it takes a lot of discipline. You have no life with other people.

Have you gone on when you're sick?

I won't not go on unless I'm really sick. In *Hallelujah, Baby!* I had the flu and I did my show with buckets on each side of the stage. I threw up on both sides. During *Millie* [something got in my eye] it was very irritated and all kinds of goo was coming out. The doctor put things in to stop the pain and I did the show that night even though I couldn't see in that eye. My understudy was going on in the other role, so I could not miss. I did the show like this [one eye shut]. I was weeping and avoiding the glare of the lights. People were saying, "Oh, my God, I can't believe that you are here!" I said, "Well, who else is going to be here?" I'm not going to abandon the show.

You set an example.

I just know that when I worked with Carol Channing, I had great respect for her because she was a great lady of the theater. She never missed. Sometimes I feel that the new generation doesn't realize that the people that they're working with demand a certain respect. I grew up in this business knowing who went before me. You ask [younger] people, and they don't know who anybody is if they're not the same age as them. That is so wrong, so wrong. How committed are you to your craft? I was always committed to my craft. Chita and all the wonderful people that I look up to are committed to their craft. And I mean here's Chita, up there in age, and she can do a kick better than some of these young people can.

And you yourself were talking about watching Sutton Foster from the wings. You still think there's something to be learned?

Absolutely, absolutely. I would wait for her to sing "Gimme, Gimme." Just amazing. And I'm looking for the other people that should have been there standing in the wings with me and they weren't. If I can't be in the wings you can be darn sure that I have my sound up on the monitor to hear everything that's going on. And I always have my script. I look at my script every single day. I always discover something new. And I look at the lines because after awhile sometimes you might paraphrase a line. So I always read my script top to bottom every day and I always make notes during rehearsal. I always go back to my notes. I'm always working. I come to the theater early. I like to be there. I don't wait 'til close to half hour. That just freaks me out. And I always have my music, whether I'm in a straight play or a musical, I have my music. It chills me out. I have a little cup of tea and I have a water and I have my script. And then I'll sit there and start doing makeup, getting myself together, looking at my script, checking out my notes.

You did several straight plays after *Millie*, **and you got another Tony nomination, but you've been spending years involved with different incarnations of** *Stormy Weather*, **Lena Horne's life story.**

I'm so excited about it. Other than *Master Class* it's the hardest work that I've ever done. I'm never off the stage. And there are these incredible songs that I get to sing. I think this is so necessary. [People don't realize that] Lena was involved in things other than being beautiful and in the movies. She was involved in civil rights. She was a trailblazer.

Does your life as a performer look like you wanted it to look?

My life as a performer is much more than I ever thought could possibly happen. If I had planned it, I wouldn't have planned it this way. I mean a lot of things came from left field. I really realize that I love theater more and more. I couldn't have planned my life better than what happened, you know? I got two great kids and a fabulous husband who puts up with me. It's a wonderful ride and I'm still hoping to keep my E-ticket or whatever they do now at Disneyland and keep going.

I just have one last question. What happened during the concert in D.C.? [during a live televised performance on the National Mall, Uggams infamously flubbed virtually all of the lyrics to Rodgers and Hammerstein's "June Is Bustin' Out All Over"].

I learned a lesson from that, too. I will never do a song that I don't know without rehearsal time. They [asked me to sing it the night before and they] said, "don't worry about it, it's going to be on cue cards." . . . So what happened? It's a live show and it rained the night before. They had me walking through the aisle while I am singing—big mistake. The cue card guy is walking ahead of me with the cards. He hit a thing of mud, he slipped and he was gone. I can't find him. The camera's still going, I have no idea what the hell I'm singing but I got to keep going. You can't stop the show. So whatever came out of my mouth is what came out of my mouth. I came off the stage and nobody said anything to me. They didn't dare say anything to me and I thought, "What the hell, I made up a new language!" I just remembered "Because it's June!"

Every time I see it, I am amazed by your commitment to your made-up words. And then you hit the stage and plant it: "Because it's June!" It is art.

Isn't that what it's all about? The show must go on But you know what? Because it wound up on YouTube, I got fans that I never had before. That screw-up is legendary.

JUDY KAYE

November 2012; March 2013

"DO YOU WANT TO SEE MY EGO WALL?" asks Judy Kaye with a laugh. "It's where I go to feel better when I'm out of work." The wall, an interior hallway in Kaye's sunny New Jersey apartment overlooking the Hudson and the Manhattan skyline, is sizable and covered with framed photos of both Kaye and her husband, the actor David Green, in their varying roles. But as an ego wall, it's surprisingly modest. Sure, there's a slew of photos of Kaye but they aren't of her accepting either of her two Tony Awards (for *The Phantom of the Opera* and *Nice Work if You Can Get It*) or of her and the celebrities she's worked with like Rock Hudson or John Travolta. They include flops, like *Oh, Brother!* and *The Moony Shapiro Songbook*, and there are more pictures from small regional theaters and concerts than from her big Broadway hits like *Mamma Mia!* and *Ragtime*. This isn't so much an ego wall as the framed scrapbook of an actor who's been working in the business for more than forty years.

It began in Phoenix where Kaye was born and "came out singing and dancing." She started getting principal roles almost immediately out of college (Lucy in the Los Angeles production of *You're a Good Man, Charlie Brown*; Rizzo in the first national tour of *Grease*) but the show that shot her out of a cannon was the one in which she was the understudy, a job she took mostly for the opportunity to work with legendary director Harold Prince. But the leading lady of *On the Twentieth Century*, Madeline Kahn, was unhappy in the show and left a mere five weeks after opening night. Kaye assumed the role of Lily Garland, the tempestuous movie star with a stratospheric soprano, and was heralded for both her performance and for saving the show.

Over the subsequent thirty-five years Kaye has seen her career peak and dip several times, but she never stopped working. She's not the easiest to cast because, unlike some of her peers, she defies type. She's played daffy, severe, impoverished, wealthy, soprano, alto, diva, and den mother. If her roles have anything in common, it's strength.

Kaye herself shares that strength. She is easygoing and warm but not especially interested in artifice or small talk. She's a pragmatist who doesn't hold back. "I'm never the first choice," she told me without bitterness. "I'm who they call when they can't make a deal with someone else." But if those calls led to the two Tonys, two Ovation Awards, and the Drama Desk Award, which are all arm's reach from where we sit, being the go-to second choice seems to have paid dividends.

Battling Demon Rum in *Nice Work if You Can Get It*. (Joan Marcus)

You started your training as a kid. How were your parents with all of this stuff?

They didn't want me to leave school to join the circus. They wanted me to have an education. And they were right to do so. My mother was very shy and not of the theater at all. My father grew up in New York. He was used to going to the theater and I think there was a part of him that would have loved to have done that.

So he had some context.

Oh, yeah. He was a singing waiter in the Catskills when he was a kid with his brother, my Uncle Harry. My mother was sometimes fearful that rejection would do me in. And my dad would be terribly offended by bad reviews, but they always rooted for me. I got involved in high school theater in Arizona. A man named Harvey Smith, who was the choral director at Central High in Phoenix, really taught me about singing. I never really learned anything new afterward that he hadn't already said to me at some point. He was wonderful with young voices. Nowadays you see so many kids just pushing and pushing. This *American Idol* singing. In those days, I was really imbued with the knowledge that I had to protect myself, to make sound in a healthy way so I could hopefully do this for a very long time as opposed to having a brief, fabulous blaze of a career that went down in flames. You can't scream and yell forever.

Belting like that wasn't really happening on Broadway.

No, it wasn't. And I'm trying to think if microphones had started even being used on the stage. I mean when I did *Twentieth Century* we did not have body mics. I didn't encounter that until some theater in the round where if you didn't wear a mic, they were never going to hear you. It's a luxury now to hear what the human voice actually sounds like.

Judy Kaye

You're a Good Man, Charlie Brown, Los Angeles, 1968
Grease, National Tour and Broadway, 1973 and 1977
On the Twentieth Century, Broadway and National Tour, 1978
The Moony Shapiro Songbook, Broadway, 1981
Oh, Brother! Broadway, 1981
Love, off-Broadway, 1984
The Phantom of the Opera, Broadway, 1988 (Tony Award)
The Pajama Game, New York City Opera, 1989
Brigadoon, New York City Opera, 1996
Ragtime, Los Angeles and Broadway, 1997 and 1998
Mama Mia! Broadway, 2001
Candide, New York City Opera, 2005
Sweeney Todd, Broadway and National Tour, 2006 and 2007
Face the Music, Encores! 2007
Paradise Found, London, 2010
Bells Are Ringing, Encores! 2010
Tales of the City, San Francisco, 2011
Nice Work If You Can Get It, Broadway, 2012 (Tony Award)
Little Me, Encores! 2014
Cinderella, Broadway, 2014

Barbra Streisand was probably the only person singing that way at that time.

Streisand was at the height of the young part of her career and every Jew in the world was so proud of her. So there I was in Phoenix, and I could sort of emulate that. People would say, "Sing like Streisand, sing like Streisand!" I finally said, "No, no." Something in me said I better not do this any more. I love the sound, and it's okay in the privacy of my bedroom to pretend, but I'm going to stop this now.

Do you have a recollection of recognizing that you were talented?

I just did it because I loved it. And I was always fascinated with how to create sound and how to make sound better. I just started devising exercises for myself and it turned out they were exactly the right thing to do. My instinct naturally was just sort of right on the money.

You chose to go to UCLA. Why?

Well, if we'd all had our heads screwed on completely about this, I probably would have gone to New York. I had grandparents and family in LA and a support group. It did not occur to me to go that far away from home. I was in the opera workshop at UCLA and learned very early on that I'm just not made for opera as it was being done in those days. I just couldn't do it. I had a wonderful coach named Maestro Carta. One day he said [with a heavy Italian accent], "Judy, Judy, you are so sad. Judy, you don't want to do this, do you? No, this doesn't make you happy, Judy. Go. Go do what makes you happy."

Do you know why it wasn't satisfying you?

It's very rigid. The music is beautiful but characters in opera scenes weren't real to me, and we were being given a vocabulary of style of how we were to comport ourselves as opera singers. You sit this way, and you do this with the fan. Eventually I wound up doing some opera. Not a lot, but some.

You got your Equity card very quickly.

Yeah. The summer after my freshman year, I got hired for a season at the Melodyland Theater in Anaheim, California. It's a church now. A round church. If you go out to Disneyland, you'll see it. A bunch of us in the theater department wanted to audition, so I drove us out, and they divided the theater into quarters: soprano, alto, tenor, and bass. We all had to sit there and watch each other audition, and I saw all the mannerisms—inappropriate auditions in all quarters. I saw middle-aged women with deep dyed black hair in their one good dress and their pearls singing sixteen bars of something. I thought, "My God, this is a disease. Is this what I am getting myself into? Am I going to be that age and still doing this?" I didn't get hired that day because they were looking for one soprano and she had to be tall and blonde. Soon thereafter, my then boyfriend's father got me an audition and I was hired to do the season. I learned that summer that I didn't like being in the ensemble. I wasn't made for it. First of all, the producers treated the ensemble people like shit. They were nasty to them. In those days, they didn't really have to take care of them at all. I was making $105 a week. And they were bringing in movie stars. Kathryn Grayson was doing *Camelot*. And the rest of us were just treated miserably. I wanted to be treated like Kathryn or like Betsy Palmer who took me under her wing. I did *South Pacific* with her.

Did having that ensemble experience teach you some important lessons other than just that you didn't like it?

It taught me to have a great deal of respect for people that do that and do that well because I'm not good enough to do that. I couldn't do it. Nor could I be an understudy again. I did that once, and it worked out. That is a hard, hard job. Hard on your heart. Emotionally wrenching. You have to make this deal with yourself that (a) I'm never going on. It's never going to happen; and (b) if you go on, you're going to be so ready. But it's a hard balancing act.

Well, I would think that even if you do get to go on, you still can't really do your show. You've got to, at least to some degree, do someone else's.

It was interesting. We were coming into New York from Boston [during *On the Twentieth Century*], and there had been a huge snowstorm. They couldn't get the sets into the theater properly on time, so we did a run-through on chairs. Madeline didn't come to that rehearsal and Hal asked me if I would do the run. So I did it, and the way he would deal with me was to simply ignore me. But finally I said, "Hal, I'm here. I'm a fact. Please give me notes." So he grudgingly gave me notes, and one of them was to find another template. If Madeline was Carole Lombard, I was a Jean Harlow. Something a little tougher. That was helpful.

And it makes sense because to layer her on top of you, it's going to be a hybrid that doesn't work.

That happened to me when I did the road company of *Grease* in '73. They really tried to direct me into Adrienne Barbeau's performance. She's got a very specific face. She's got very high cheekbones and she always looks like she's got a little Mona Lisa smile. So she would do that after every line, and they wanted me to do that. It wasn't coming out that way on me. You can't direct someone that way. And these were smart people! Eventually I just said, "I'm exhausted. I'm going to do it my way." And then they came back and said, "That's what we need."

Back to the Los Angeles days. So you'd gotten your card at the Melodyland . . .

Then that next winter I was back in school, my sophomore year, and I was buying the trades. I would mark each moment, like the first time I bought *Variety*, getting my union card. . . . And when I got my first unemployment I called my parents. I was so proud because I had actually made enough to have unemployment. My mother started to cry and put the phone down. "My daughter's on welfare!" There was an open call for *Charlie Brown*. Hundreds and hundreds of people. I got hired. I thought I was going to get fired, though. Patsy Birch [choreographer Patricia Birch] saved me. She's been my angel forever and it started on that show. She was the choreographer on *Grease*, she introduced me to Hal . . .

In what way did she save you?

She saw me struggling, and she wanted me to learn how to act. I'd had all this bad acting teaching in college. I'd been totally misinformed. Everything that I did naturally I was told was all wrong. One of my teachers creamed me. She said, "You're not an actor and you never will be." Totally "Morales-ed" me [referencing the character of Diana Morales in *A Chorus Line*]. Patsy taught me how to listen. Nobody ever mentioned that. If they had, it wasn't couched in a way that made any sense to me. So between Pat Birch and the audiences eight times a week, I think I finally got it beaten into me.

What do you remember about doing the show?

It was a huge thing to be in the show. Every star in the world came to see that thing. A knock at the door, and you didn't know who was going to be there. Opening night, a knock at the door, it's Groucho Marx. He sticks his head in, and he says—because I was playing Lucy—"I pity the man who marries you." Slam. Knock at the door: Gregory Peck and his family. I met Fred Astaire and Gene Kelly! Unbelievable. I never took it for granted. Ever. Still don't. I was just amazed.

After *Charlie Brown*, you did multiple regional productions of *Jesus Christ Superstar*, and multiple productions of *Fiddler on the Roof*.

First time I did *Fiddler* was while I was doing *Charlie Brown*. I got a leave of absence for five weeks to go to Honolulu. They loved it over there, much like they loved it in Asia, because family and tradition are very important. They got it. Boy, they got it. And then I did it everywhere. I was up for the movie of *Fiddler*. I was told I was too beautiful. I couldn't get cast in the revivals here, either. I was told I was somewhere between Yente and Golde.

You did a production of *Hair*, and then you got *Grease* on the road with some pretty auspicious company: Jerry Zaks, John Travolta, Marilu Henner . . .

She and I roomed together a lot on the road. We had a lot of fun. We grew up together. Michael Lembeck, Jeff Conaway, Walter Charles, Barry Bostwick: such a talented group of people. I was the Equity deputy. The first and only time I was ever a deputy. Everybody would take advantage of us a little bit because we were all young. That's when I found my inner Emma Goldman [whom Kaye later played in *Ragtime*], you know? Better I should do that on the stage than in life.

Grease the musical is a lot raunchier than the film version. What was it like playing that show all over the country at a time when that material was still considered pretty risqué?

We didn't do the Southern route. They had another company do that and the cleanup was pretty substantial. They changed the line "You hauled your ass all the way to the beach . . . ?" to "You hauled your cookies all the way to the beach . . . !"

You made your Broadway debut in the show. Did that feel special?

It didn't feel as special to me as other shows which started in New York. It felt sort of like another stop on the road. But it was great fun being in New York. We were there the night of the blackout. We did the show with flashlights and then went out and drank ourselves silly.

After Grease, somehow Hal Prince convinced you to take the small role of Agnes in On the Twentieth Century.

I had auditioned for him the first time in Los Angeles when he was putting together a road company of *Company*, and I gave what I think to this day was one of the top three worst auditions I've ever done. The next time I'd auditioned for him was for the revival of *Candide*. I didn't get it, but then he wanted me to replace twice. He offered it to me, but I rejected it twice for various reasons. By then I had a house in LA and the pay was going to be terrible. I was about to say "yes" the last time he offered it but there was a musicians' strike and then the show closed. At this audition, I knew it went well but I knew they were going to call me to be an understudy. I also knew in my bones that I really didn't want to do that because I was sure that that was going to be the end of my career. I thought, "If I'm good at understudying, that's what I'll become," and I knew that my ego could not deal with that. I turned it down and went back to LA. But I realized that this was a chance to get to do a Broadway musical from its inception with incredible people. [So I took it]. I showed up the first day with a tape recorder and a camera. I have a tape of that first day, Betty Comden and Adolph Green singing the score. I was a tourist! I didn't know enough to sort of keep to my place. At the end of the day, I asked, "Does anybody want to go have something to eat?" and the next thing I knew I was sitting at Sardi's with John Cullum and Madeline Kahn. What was I doing there? I had no idea. And I did not know how to extricate myself so there I was, a fly on the wall, listening to the misgivings. Already she [Kahn] was scared.

Is that what happened? She was scared of it?

They kept talking about the "Hal Prince machine." She was nervous about when he was going to make her freeze the show. He is results oriented, that's true. He didn't like people being on-book, he didn't want to watch the process. That was hard for her because she was all about the process. When she was on, like opening night, she was *on* and she was fabulous. But then she said that Cy Coleman said she didn't have to sing the high notes after opening. She started cutting back, cutting back. And I wanted to slap her silly because I thought, "This is such an opportunity for you, Girlfriend. You should be having the time of your life." She was just living in total fear.

Was she never happy in it?

Well, I remember I was with Kevin Kline and George Lee Andrews, and we walked into her dressing room in Boston and she said, "I have to keep reminding myself that it's only a job." No, no, it's not just a job! Shut up! You didn't ever know if she was not going to show up and I would be needed, so I had to be on top of it. I think we always have to be on top of it.

Well, sometimes an understudy will be covering for Ethel Merman or Carol Channing and know that while they have to be prepared, they will never have to go on. And sometimes . . .

That's why I was not made for that job. I find when I'm working in a company—and this has only happened a couple of times in my life—and somebody needs to have a lot of hand-holding, it sucks all the air out of the room. It wastes time. Everybody's time, and I'm offended by it. So while I want to be supportive, and I try to be . . . I don't have the patience to be diplomatic about this. There's no time for that. There's just no time.

And especially in a musical of that size and with so many personalities in the room. Cy Coleman, Comden and Green, Imogene Coca . . .

I don't think Imogene and Madeline got along. I'm not sure what was going on there, but I don't think that Madeline paid the kind of respect that Imogene thought she deserved. I think she felt she was—"dissed" isn't the right word, but I know that she did not feel appreciated. She wasn't crazy about the part she was playing.

Really?

She wasn't crazy about her song, she wasn't—she had a lot of issues. But I think at the bottom of all of it was that Madeline was not collegial with her, was not—no communication there. Madeline was in her bubble. The only person who penetrated that bubble at all was John. John is such the salt of the earth. He would support his leading lady. And he told me that he had gone to Madeline and said that he saw me rehearsing and said, "Don't ever let her go on." It's a compliment.

How was it working with Cy Coleman and Comden and Green?

Well, I'm crazy in love with those guys and in awe of their talent. That's why I can't believe Cy would have ever told Madeline she didn't have to sing the high notes. Somehow she must have misconstrued something that was said. He was a stickler for getting the music right and he had a right to do that. He gave strict notes. My personality is that I love being directed. I don't care if I'm given a line reading. I invite that. It's going to be different when it comes out of my mouth. If I'm not giving you what you want, tell me so I can do that. And they appreciated that.

And Hal Prince?

He's not an actor's director. You won't be sitting around doing theater games with Hal Prince. I'm happy about that. Having said that, if he doesn't like something, he'll let you know. And if you say, "Did you like that?" he'll say, "I didn't tell you not to do it so yeah, I liked it."

You went on the first time with very little notice. Were you panicked, or did you feel ready?

I was so grateful that I was the age that I was. I was twenty-nine and I had enough experience under my belt to be able to put this in some kind of perspective that made sense for me. So no, I never had any panic. I knew I was right where I was supposed to be, I really did.

Were you worried about audience expectations?

No. I had been sitting up in my dressing room every night listening to her give away the show. Just give it away. She was neither sharing the stage nor taking it. And I would listen and think, "Why is she doing that? Why is she squandering this opportunity?" And hostility started to build in me. I started to get extremely angry about it. So when I finally had the opportunity to do it, I thought, "Dammit, I'm going to have a good time with it. I don't know if I'll ever come this way again." I thought I would wind up doing matinees, and then maybe she would feel okay about doing the show as written. But she wouldn't rehearse and that was a problem.

That must have been difficult for the company.

Well, I can't speak for everybody else, but there was anxiety. We weren't sure we were going to make it. People were walking out in droves.

During previews?

No, after we opened, too. They were walking out because there was nothing happening on the stage. It wasn't the Madeline Kahn they knew and had fallen in love with on the screen. She wasn't showing up. The producers thought we were going to die. After all those glowing reviews.

So how did that turn around?

They had a pretty good advance. She actually came to the show after I went in for her and brought a bottle of champagne. Very nice. Really, really dear. I think she wanted more of a dialogue than I was capable of, because I was embarrassed at what had happened, and I couldn't change it. And I didn't want to make her feel bad.

You did a run for two years and took the show on the road with Rock Hudson.

What a wonderful man. He was completely supportive of me. He would take himself out of his own comfort zone in order to help me. When we were in Chicago, they wanted us on a TV show there. He didn't want to do it but they didn't want me without him, so he went on the show just so that I would have the opportunity. I have pictures of me in a bathing suit at Rock Hudson's house. I looked fit. I looked as good as I could possibly look. But people were telling me I weighed too much.

Has that been a battle for you?

It drives me crazy. And Mr. Blackwell said I was an idiot for not dyeing my hair blond because when I left the stage door, nobody knew it was me. He thought I should bleach my hair. I thought it was a stupid idea.

Did it matter to you that no one knew you at the stage door?

Nobody ever knows who I am. They still don't know who I am. I had an agent at William Morris used to call me "my underground star."

That has its perks.

It has its perks. I would not like Johnny's [Travolta] life. When I was asked [by prospective agents and managers at the time of *Twentieth Century*], "What do you want?" they wanted me to say, "I want to be a big, fat star. I want to make loads of money." All I could ever say was, "I want to be a working actor. I want to make my life doing this," and that's exactly what's happened. So I cannot complain about any of it.

After *On the Twentieth Century*, you were a newly minted star. Did you feel that?

Things weren't really coming together. Part of it was my inability to come up with ideas. All these people kept coming to me and saying, "Give me an idea, and I'll write it for you," and

I could not come up with an idea. Jerry Herman wanted to write something for me. It was on me to find something and I couldn't do it. I let a lot of time go by. There should have been something right in the wings. Actually, what was in the wings was *Evita*. I wanted to audition. Hal would not allow it. So I go out on the road [in *Twentieth Century*] and Patti LuPone gets the job. We're in San Francisco closing the tour and I get a call asking if I would be interested in doing *Evita* in LA. But by that time, I had been offered a television series with Sally Struthers. Ruthie [Mitchell, Hal Prince's assistant] came up to me backstage and said, "So what do you think?" And just then Hal walked up, and said, "Did she say yes?" I said, "Hal, you told me I was completely wrong." He said, "Well, maybe I was wrong. I thought you were wrong for *this* show, too." He wanted to protect the tour. The tour wouldn't have happened without me. So I didn't do *Evita* and I did the pilot for the series but it cooled down my career. I was not allowed to take a job for a year because I had made a commitment to this television pilot, which never took off. What was a very hot career went right into the toilet. You have to follow things up. I felt my career was very hot and then very cold. And it was. It's like when I won a Tony Award for *Phantom of the Opera*. I couldn't get an audition after I won that Tony Award for quite a long time. I wanted to be seen for *110 in the Shade* at Lincoln Center. They would not see me.

You once said to me, "I'm never the first one they call." Have you given a lot of thought to why you think that is?

I don't know. I think they very often go for people who they think are going to be huge draws. I'm not a drama queen. In fact, I've been told, "If you'd only develop some really good neuroses, you would be a much bigger star."

But then you'd be the person who sucks the air out of the room.

I don't want to suck the air out of the room. Listen, I went through times when I got a little desperate. I mean I called up my agent at one point after *Phantom*. It just amazed me that I couldn't get seen for *110*. I wasn't trying to be seen for an ingénue, I was trying to be seen for the daughter who is now old. I said, "You know what? I'm never going to be better than I am right now. This is it. I'm at the height of my powers. Right at this second. Why can't you get me in?" He had no answer. The other night I did a gala for Encores! And Kelli [O'Hara] is now "the girl" and deservedly so. It's been a long time since I was "the girl," and I was "the girl" very briefly. The articles were always being written—and still are—"What's the matter? Why can't she—what's happened to musical theater? In another age, they'd be writing shows for this person and now they're not." Thank God they're not writing that about Kelli. They're coming up with things for her to do, but she's the girl of the moment and I watched Rebecca Luker in the wings watching her. I got Rebecca Luker her first agent. She was in the first *Sweeney Todd* that I did at the Michigan Opera Theater and I introduced her to my then agent. And now I'm at an age where I get it and I see how it works. But it was very, very hard on me. Because inside you—the whole aging process is bizarre anyway because you never stop being that person that you were at the happiest moment in your life. You don't. So I was watching, and I was thinking, "What's going through Rebecca's mind because she's watching a girl who ten years ago would have been her." And Rebecca's had a wonderful career. She ain't down yet either. But there's a lesson in this whole thing; we have to keep reinventing ourselves. We have to look in the mirror and see who we really are at any given time. It's very hard, but it's what actors have to do. We find out how we are perceived. And learn how to market that new animal. I was watching and I noted it. I had sympathy for it and I felt that I was really glad that I was on the other end of it now. It's hard on the heart.

How do you arrive at that? Time?

I don't know. I think time and some people may never get it.

Those are the people who become increasingly needy. The attention that they got at one time, they're not getting now.

It's like me watching that lady at Melodyland Theater in the black dress with the pearls. "Is this a kind of a disease? Is this a profession? Is this a calling? What is it? Or am I kidding myself? Should I go home and become a mommy? No, unless I find out if I can actually make a living doing this, I'll probably make somebody else's life really miserable." The other expression that seems to calm me is "ride the horse in the direction it's going." It's the way it's going. Don't fight it. You can't.

The reality of the business is that you can be totally down and then totally up.

It's astonishing. And I keep having reminders of that. *Tales of the City*—I didn't know that there was ever going to be a role like that that I'd be right for. And I don't even know if I'm doing it again. I just hope that they give me another shot at it because I just loved it so much.

The lesson is that you never know when a role might come along.

Well, I mean I—it's hard on everybody around you, and I guess I must love that aspect of it, that your life can change on a phone call. In what other business can that happen?

Back to the chronology. *The Moony Shapiro Songbook* was next and you pinned a lot on that. You moved back to New York.

Jonathan Lynn, our director, had a nervous breakdown or something after that. And we had a choreographer who was going off snorting everything he could. I couldn't be around that. That's another suck the air out of the room. Just a waste of time and waste of opportunities in my opinion.

Nowadays, with all of the Internet chatter, I think it's easier to know before opening night if a show is going to hit, but then . . .

You didn't know. I'd drag my sweet parents to so many opening nights [of flops]. There were several of them in a row. We were at the party and they brought out the papers . . . *Moony Shapiro, Oh, Brother!, What About Love?*

***Oh, Brother!* had such a great score.**

Great score! Great part for me. Great parts for everybody. A wonderful, wonderful cast. We wanted to be together forever. We were having such a good time. We deserved so much better. It was so sad. *Moony Shapiro*, too. Actually, before that ever happened, I used to get calls at all hours from Hal Prince. He had this idea or that idea. One of them was for *Rosa*. He had Flossy Klotz [costume designer Florence Klotz] dress me up in a schmata and age me up to see what happened. That one didn't work out, but another phone call was about a show that he had seen in London, and he wanted to bring to the US. In London it was just called *Songbook*. He wanted to produce what became *The Moony Shapiro Songbook*. It was very wonderful. The problem for us was that down the block was *A Day in Hollywood/A Night in the Ukraine*, which was more of a revue than we were. And we were just sort of lumped together. The show was fascinating. And it was a fabulous group. We had Jeff Goldblum and Gary Beach. We really deserved a run.

And it closed on opening night. How do you even process that?

I don't know. I'm not sure I ever have. You just go on. It's a really hard process. You put your heart and soul into something, and yet there has to be just that little bit of reserve, that little piece of you that stays out of there that watches it and allows you to get up the next morning when it doesn't work. If you can't do that, then you need to find another line of work.

After those two you did a lot of regional theater.

I did a lot of stock. I always do. I hadn't done any real regional theater. Actually, my introduction to regional theater was *Souvenir* because Arizona Theater Company wanted to do it after we closed way too quickly on Broadway. With that one I was really licking my wounds. That one I had a personal and emotional investment in and still do.

Why do you think that one was so different?

I was above the title. They were selling me, and if I can't sell a show . . .

So what does that mean going forward? Where do you fit in?

I don't know where I fit exactly. People ask me to play sort of outsized women, and some of them are just one note. It's always the same: loud and high with nothing underneath. No character, nothing. And I don't want to do that any more. I'm done. I think this character that I'm playing [in *Nice Work If You Can Get It*] is—she redeems herself because she really is a romantic under all of that. But that's it. I'm saying it now. Will I stick to it? Because when someone backs the truck up with some more cash and a good show, will I want to do it? I don't know. I want to play people of substance. I want to play characters with dimension that change, that grow. I'm looking at myself going forward, age-wise, and seeing what lies ahead.

Is it scary?

Yes and no. There's a lot of other stuff I love in this world, things that I enjoy doing, so if I had to stop, I would. I don't want to do things that I don't want to do. I've always been that way, but I'm feeling stronger and stronger about that.

Have you had to do things that you don't want to do?

I haven't had to, but I've said "yes." There was a revue years ago called *1971*. Why did I do it? I don't know why I did it. It was just horseshit. It was terrible. I thought it was going to be better than it was. It was something to do, and it was going to be a job. We've all been part of those. Luckily they've been few and far between.

Let's go back to the '80s. How did *Phantom of the Opera* come your way?

Hal called me. He said, "You need to come in. Andrew [Lloyd Webber] needs to know that you can hit the high B natural."

So he had already decided that he wanted you?

Yeah. I got to the audition, and I hit the note, and Hal turned around and said to Andrew, "She can hit the note." And then he came down to the edge of the stage, and he said, "Would you like to do it?" and I said, "Absolutely!" I was back with Hal, which made me very happy. It's a very warm relationship. I actually had a little moment of indecision. The same thing happened with *Mamma Mia!* I was in London, and I hadn't signed the contract yet. I said, "Can I go see it?"

This is *Phantom* or *Mamma Mia!*?

Both of them. I went to see it, and with *Mamma Mia!* I didn't want to do it after I saw it. *Phantom* I did. But I saw something in it as I was watching. I went to Hal, and I said, "Hal, there's a lot of comic opportunity here. If you really want me to do this, I think you need to know that I want to find that, and you may have to throw a net over me to pull me back from the brink." And so he would do that on occasion, but he was always worried that I wasn't going to be frightened enough of the Phantom. At one point I said to him, "If I play more fear of the Phantom, they're going to be calling the acting police. I can't go any further with this." And he bought it. But my understanding is that he's never allowed any of the Carlottas after me to be quite as comic. He let me play it pretty much the way I felt it wanted to be. I couldn't have done it any other way. I couldn't have taken the job if I was going to just be parroting [the London production]. I couldn't do it.

What was your experience of Andrew Lloyd Webber?

I had one. This sort of explains my life a little bit. On Sarah Brightman's last night, there was champagne on the stage after the show and I, for some idiotic reason, went over to Andrew and said, "How's *Aspects of Love* coming? " He said, "Oh, it's going very well. We are having a bit of trouble finding the girl. She's got to go from fifteen to fifty-five." I said, "Well, I did *I Do! I Do!*, and I went from seventeen to eighty." And he looked at me, and he said, "Oh, yes, yes, of course, but she does have to be a great beauty." I think that says it all.

How was the experience of being in such a monster hit? I don't think Broadway had seen a sell-out of those proportions since *A Chorus Line*.

It was wild. Ultimately I sort of started feeling like I was working for General Motors, and the show would come down the line. I would place my comic movements on there and keep it moving. What kept the humanity in it for me was Hal, Hal, Hal, Hal. He's family. And being part of it was fun, but when it was time to leave, I was very clear in my mind that it was time to go.

What made it time to leave?

Well, I was offered a couple of things. One of them was an opera of *Desire Under the Elms*, which was very, very difficult. Ed Thomas had written, as he does, a very difficult score. And I just felt like I needed to do it. It was a stretch. And then I got a call to do *The Pajama Game* up at City Opera soon thereafter. Hal wanted me to stick around longer. He wasn't happy. But it had been a year. I never regretted leaving. And I did it in LA a couple of times, so I got a taste of it again, and it was fun. But I was just really clear that it was time and that I had done all I could do with the part. At a certain point it becomes a job, and that's when it's time to go.

What was the experience of being in a show of that size with costumes that big and moving parts that could crush you?

It's quite something, and it's amazing how you start to take it for granted. But really it is very dangerous. I could not put some of my costumes on in my dressing room. I had to put them on at stage level because they were so heavy. They really did a number on my back. It was physically arduous. But it's wonderful to be part of the *Phantom* family.

You won the Tony for it.

Well, it felt like my time, I guess. It was wonderful to share it with everybody and to be able to call my parents and—it was not like this last time [for *Nice Work If You Can Get It*]. This last time was right after losing my dad, so it was wonderful but very poignant and sad to me in a way. I really wanted him to see this show. It would have been a real high for him. He loved the old songs. He and I would sing together in his hospital room. It was really fun sharing that that first Tony night with my husband. I partied 'til all hours.

Was it fun to be all glammed up for the awards?
Yes. Actually getting glammed up for *Mamma Mia!* was even more fun because by that time, they were doing more of the Oscar-y thing. I went to Harry Winston and got the jewels.

It's amazing how it's changed, isn't it? And now there's so much media when you are nominated.
Not altogether wonderful. It gets tiring. But it's finite. And in my opinion, it's an opportunity to sell the show. I rarely say no to press stuff for the show. I don't employ my own press people. I know that it's worked very well for others but to make that financial commitment and that time commitment, I guess I don't want it that bad.

After *Phantom* you had a big break before your next show in New York, *Ragtime*.
Nothing between them? Is that true? Now I'm depressed. A lot of stuff came and went. I would call my agent and he'd say, "Now, Judy." I should have left him then. Maybe that was my fault. I don't know what it was, but that really got me down. You're reminding me of that period, and I was in a very bad place. I've had this conversation with various women who are now reaching that age and the phone isn't ringing. Every one of them gets very scared. We talk about it, and I say this is where reinvention comes in. The hard part of this business is figuring out how you are perceived.

And it changes.
It changes constantly. And new people come up in the casting area and don't know who you are, especially in television and film. You make your deal with it eventually, but I went through a really bad time there. That's the only time I can honestly say that professionally I've been through a very dark place. I was looking at want ads. I was going to get my real estate license. I was going to do anything else.

So what kept you in it?
Something would happen out of town. I would get a request to do something. And I was keeping busy with stuff that has not been hugely remunerative, but it's soul filling and I love it, love it, love it. So there's been that good stuff. But I wasn't kidding when I said to my agent, "I'm the best I'm ever going to be." It starts going downhill. I was listening to one of my recordings that I did from that time, and I used to sing like that? Wow! I can't do that anymore.

But, of course, you ultimately got older and became right for shows like *Ragtime*.
[Producer] Garth Drabinsky called me for that. He wouldn't have a casting person call. He would call you. I read it and cried. The totality of it is just so special. So I went up and did a staged workshop [in Toronto], and then when they were putting the production together for Toronto [pre-Broadway], he called me and offered it to me. Then he called back and said, "My creative team has overridden me. They want to go a different way. I feel terrible about this. I want to send you something." So he sent me a sizable check to thank me. Then many months later, he calls again. "We're doing LA. If you're available, we'd really like you to do it." On opening night in LA, I'm taken aside by [producer] Marty Bell who says, "We made a mistake. We would

As Emma Goldman, sowing the seeds of anarchy in *Ragtime*. (Photofest)

really like you to open New York." So I played it for like eight months in LA and then Broadway. I loved the piece so much, and I think it's very important. It should still be running. It should always be running. I think it was manhandled because people didn't like Garth. I think the *New York Times* took out their dislike of him on the show. It should be running in that theater today.

When you're doing a historical character like that, was your research focused on E. L. Doctorow's novel, or on history books?

A whole lot of Doctorow. I read Emma Goldman's autobiographies, but it's Doctorow. I loved the novel, and I really loved what I read of Emma Goldman's stuff. It's quite something. What a mind. And then [writer] Terrence McNally and especially with [lyricist and composer] Lynn Ahrens and Stephen Flaherty. I think they're just so special. I had a really hard time doing that show because I'm pretty emotional. I was a mess all the time. I could not watch what would come before any of my scenes. In the workshop I was just a sobbing mess all the time.

Do you have any recollections of working with Audra McDonald?

Oh, Audra and I became buds. Whenever we see each other, it's old home week. I watched her sort of get small. She would sing so gloriously and fill out that character so passionately and still somehow make herself small and vulnerable. But I did the workshop and LA with LaChanze. They wrote it for her. She was not available to do New York because she'd gotten a series, which didn't happen. I think she made a major error turning that down. She was wonderful in the part.

Your next show was *Mamma Mia!* which you said you initially didn't want to do. What changed your mind?

I had girlfriends who called me and said, "Are you crazy? This is a musical about women of a certain age. You've got to do this!" One of the reasons I was going to turn it down is that

With Karen Mason, Louise Pitre, and a whole lot of spandex in *Mamma Mia!* (Photofest)

the girl in London playing that role was about 300 pounds and the perception of me is that I'm fat. I told you this has just been going on forever. So I thought, "Is that what I'm going to do? Play fat ladies? That will make me feel bad." So I said to them, "I'm going to do this my way or I'm not going to do it." And they said, "You have total leeway." Once I said yes, I wound up having just a blast. I stayed with it two years. I've never been in better physical shape in my life. I was working so hard. I was glad to be part of it. They had to kick me out to get rid of me, although my body was not going to hold up.

They had to kick you out?
Oh, yeah. Two years, and you're gone. They wouldn't allow any of us to stay.

Why's that?
I don't know. Maybe they didn't want to give us any more raises. They could get people cheaper, which, at the end of the day, is always what it's about.

You said you shouldn't have been Tony nominated for that. Why did you say that?
It was very nice to be nominated, but I didn't see it as a character portrayal that was worthy. It just didn't feel like that there was that much going on.

You were nominated again for your next show, the play, *Souvenir*, and then you were next on Broadway replacing Patti LuPone in *Sweeney Todd*.
The first time I did Mrs. Lovett was Michigan Opera Theater with the big orchestra, and it was so wonderful. I wasn't sure I wanted to do this cut-down production. I really had trouble with it. I was one of the people who didn't get it. [When I saw it] somebody asked me at intermission, "Don't you want to do this?" and my total visceral reaction was, "No, I don't." And of course what happened was they came to me and offered a pile of cash, and I had nothing going

on, and I loved the character so much, I thought, "Well, maybe I need to do this." So I did. And that first moment when I got up with my triangle was the most scared I'd ever been on a Broadway stage. On any stage! Because I'm not comfortable playing instruments in front of people and accompanying people. I thought, "I'm going to fuck up somebody else's performance. I'm going to just ruin this thing." But then after about a week I started having fun. And then they offered me the tour. Anyway, I wound up having a marvelous time doing it. But I couldn't do what Patti did. I couldn't do it that way.

Meaning?

The direction was different. Again, I said, "I'm going to have to find my own way into this thing." Because I'd done it operatically. I had to find a way to take those emotions and what I found before—I didn't want to throw those things away. I think they're valuable. I'm glad I stuck to my guns because I think I found some really valuable stuff, and I think it worked really well. Especially since we were playing monstrously huge houses in some places.

Do you feel differently about the production now?

I do. If I saw it again, I don't know if I'd still feel that way. I absolutely appreciated the work that went into it, and from whence it came, but it was a production that was born out of necessity to begin with. Do I think it supplants the other? Absolutely not. When people say, "Oh, I like it so much better," that irks me. But I got to the point where I could enjoy it. Once you get into the why and the wherefore, it takes on a new meaning for you.

Did you communicate with Patti at all about it?

We never really talked too much about it, no. She was very lovely when I replaced her for those five weeks. [But] she wouldn't let me play her tuba.

Really?

It wasn't her tuba. It was a tuba they got for her to play. I was not even allowed to touch the fucking tuba. I asked them to find me a tuba of the same size and they could not so I had to play a tuba that was much too big for me. I almost hurt myself a couple of times with it because it was really unwieldy.

She had a name for the tuba. She had a ritual with the tuba.

I'm so glad, so fucking glad. Eventually that was the tuba I used on the road.

Did you have any experiences with Stephen Sondheim during the run?

He came to see me on Broadway and he was lovely and very complimentary. I've had lots of moments with him over the years, some of them very intimate, and some weird ones, too. He wanted me to do *Merrily* for him a couple of different times and I couldn't. He got very upset with me, and he finally said to my husband, "She hates it, doesn't she?" [He took it personally.] But it's the funny relationship I have with him. Whenever he's sitting in on an audition that I'm in, I fuck up really badly. It's really silly. I guess he makes me nervous even now. Probably the worst audition experience I ever had was for the Witch in *Into the Woods*. All that was on the page was a rap. There was no music. I didn't know how to get into it and I was getting no help from [director] James Lapine. I basically threw up my hands in the middle of the audition and said something like, "I'm just not good enough. I can't do it." Eventually I got offered to replace Joanna Gleason as The Baker's Wife, which made much more sense to me. But I couldn't do it. I had another job to go to. Stephen gives great notes, though. He would be a great director. I always learn a lot from him. But in person, he gets all tied into knots unless he's giving notes. And on the phone, he's quite relaxed. But you get him one on one and he doesn't do that well. My first meeting with him was at a party at Hal's house. He sat down at the piano and sang "I feel you, Joanna"—the first time anybody had ever heard it. He had just written it. And Patti [LuPone] was there. She was still going with Kevin Kline. I went into the bathroom and just started bawling that I was even there. I went up to Stephen, and I said, "You . . ."—and he just looked at me, and he said, "I know, I know." Oh, God.

After *Sweeney* you did *Tales of the City*. I wish I could capture in print how your face lights up any time I mention it.

That somehow came out of the ether to me. I had done *Souvenir* at ACT and they called me when they couldn't reach a deal with Betty Buckley. I'm really easy to work with. I'm a team player. Maybe that's the other reason why the whole stardom thing just eluded me; I don't think I could carry it off anyway. I like being in a company of actors. I love being with people making art, trying to tell a story. That's what's fun to me. Anyway, they asked me, and I just backed into this wonderful, wonderful job that I didn't know I was going to have. I segued right from the tour straight up there. I did not go home and change my luggage or anything. I just had a really magical summer in San Francisco. Everybody I know who saw it feels like it should continue but it's in limbo right now. It needs a good lead producer. Those people are hard to find. I think the folks who are producing *Nice Work* are terrific. I don't know how they're doing it, but they managed to get the nut down.

How did you end up in *Nice Work*?

Again, they couldn't make a deal with someone else. . . . The script had been sent to me years and years ago and all the references [to my character], all the jokes were fat jokes and I wanted no part of it. I was very glad to be unavailable. Then all of a sudden it comes back, and this time it's funnier. I had the time free, and I wasn't going to do *Scandalous*. I had done *Saving Aimee* [the original title for *Scandalous*], the very early version right after *Tales*, and I was very clear that I did not want to do that role anymore because there was nothing there on the page for the character. Just one note. And this came along. I started thinking about ways to humanize her and not be just a battle ax. I've been very happy doing it, very happy. So when I've made pronouncements about "I'm not going to do this, this, this or this again . . ."—it's funny how things just come around. Obviously it was meant to be that I was supposed to do it at some point.

When you started rehearsals for this, things were getting increasingly worse with your dad. How do you go through a rehearsal process and opening while there's so much personal life happening?

I don't know. I just did it, and I couldn't leave. I couldn't get there. I didn't ever get to see him alive again after [I started *Nice Work*]. So this time will always be very mixed for me, very conflicted.

Does it help that what you're doing up there is playful?

Yeah, work is much more than just a vocation, an avocation. It really is a salvation in many ways, and you can really heal yourself, at least for the moment, at least in my work. I knew it was important to me, but I never realized how important it was. But still, having said that, because it's that important, I really don't want to do bad stuff. I just don't. Life is pretty short. I need to take a really close look at my decision making going forward.

But, of course, you can't ever know what you'll gain, even from a bad experience. You were on the worst tour of your life and you met your husband.

That is absolutely true, and that's probably been the great lesson of what I like to call my career. You just don't know. The good stuff really doesn't happen to you unless you really let go. You cannot control it. Whenever someone's interviewing me and says, "What do you plan to do next?" or, "Why did you take that role?"—actors are always asked that question—"Why did you take that job?" Because that was the job that was offered to me. I needed to make a living.

Do you ever think of your place in the history of musical theater?

I will always be an underground celebrity, if you will. I'm shocked when anybody ever wants anything from me because truly nobody knows who the fuck I am unless you're really, really a theater junkie, and then I think I'm still like a sidebar. In all tomes about the musical theater thus far, I am never mentioned. And I've got two Tony Awards.

And yet, here I sit.

Yeah, I know. Makes a lie of the whole fucking thing. But I got what I wanted. I've been a working actor. It's a good life.

BETTY BUCKLEY

June 2010; July 2012

BETTY BUCKLEY IS A POWERHOUSE. Anyone who's seen her onstage or heard her clarion voice can attest to her formidable strength. It was immediately apparent upon meeting her, too. But as soon as we sat down to chat, other colors poured forth almost instantly. She was soft-spoken, giggling, reminiscing, confessing, and even tearing up as she told her story with candor, self-deprecation, wit, and a very open emotional and psychological channel. In the same way she interprets a song, she allowed herself to be totally honest and extraordinarily vulnerable.

That balance of strength and vulnerability is actually Buckley's hallmark. Every role she's played onstage has been a fascinating mix of steely conviction and underlying fragility—Grizabella, Norma Desmond, Mama Rose, Margaret White, Edwin Drood; those qualities manifest in Buckley's unique voice, which can belt to the rafters and flicker like a candle flame in the same stanza, and are coupled with her supreme gift for interpretation. She is singular and indelible.

Betty Lynn Buckley was born in Fort Worth, Texas, to parents who could not have been more in conflict about her talent and desire to perform. Her mother, a former singer/dancer, delighted in providing her daughter with lessons and taking her to talent shows and later pageants (where Buckley was crowned Miss Fort Worth) while her father, an Air Force lieutenant colonel, was adamantly opposed. They fought frequently about it, and Buckley was left with great insecurity about her choice to perform. "I've been in analysis for years and have had to work really hard on myself to give myself permission to do what I do," she says. But the inner turmoil she experienced didn't affect her resumé. Buckley booked her first show, *1776*, on the first day she arrived in New York in 1969. *Promises Promises* (in London) and *Pippin* (back in New York) followed in short order and, by the end of the '70s, she was in Hollywood, memorably appearing in the film *Carrie*, as the gym teacher Ms. Collins, and then co-starring as Abby Bradford on the hit series *Eight Is Enough*.

In 1982, Andrew Lloyd Webber's monster hit *Cats* brought her back to Broadway; gave her her signature song, "Memory"; won her a Tony Award; and cemented her place in the musical theater pantheon. She worked steadily and memorably onstage for the next fifteen years (*The Mystery of Edwin Drood, Song and Dance, Sunset Boulevard, Gypsy, Triumph of Love*—for which she received a second Tony nomination—and the legendary *Carrie*) until 2002 when Buckley began pursuing her other passion, horses. In 2003 she co-starred in the song cycle *Elegies* at Lincoln Center and in 2010 off-Broadway in the play *White's Lies*. She has continued to tour internationally as a concert artist in halls and cabarets around the country. She has starred in

As Norma Desmond in *Sunset Boulevard*. Buckley's Norma downplayed the gorgon and emphasized the vulnerability to great effect. (Photofest)

episodic television, mini-series, and films, and has recorded fifteen albums and counting, netting two Grammy nominations. She also teaches song interpretation and acting workshops. Her consummate work for which she has been repeatedly celebrated has afforded her an eclectic career that crosses all genres.

You were born in Texas. How did the stage bug hit?

My mother had been a singer/dancer and her sister, my aunt Mary Ruth, was a dance teacher and had danced at the original Billy Rose Theater, Casa Manana. When my dad married my mom she had to give up her singing and dancing. He had a moral thing about show business. He really disapproved of it. He thought it was a trivial pursuit. He also likened actress/singer-type people to prostitutes or ladies of the evening, because the only actress/singers he had been exposed to were the dance hall girls in Lemon, South Dakota.

> **Betty Buckley**
>
> *1776*, Broadway, 1969, 1971
> *Promises, Promises*, West End, 1969
> *Pippin*, Broadway, 1973
> *I'm Getting My Act Together and Taking It on the Road*, off-Broadway, 1980, and Los Angeles, 1981
> *Cats*, Broadway, 1982 (Tony Award)
> *The Mystery of Edwin Drood*, off-Broadway and Broadway, 1985
> *Song and Dance*, Broadway, 1986
> *Carrie*, Broadway, 1988
> *Stardust*, Washington, D.C., 1989
> *Sunset Boulevard*, West End, 1994 and Broadway, 1995
> *Andrew Lloyd Webber's Music of the Night*, National Tour, 1996
> *Triumph of Love*, Broadway, 1997
> *Gypsy*, Millburn, N.J., 1998
> *Elegies*, off-Broadway, 2003
> *Dear World*, West End, 2013

That sounds like it's from another century!

Yes, exactly. When she was pregnant with me, she actually moved back to Big Spring to have me so I could have Texan citizenship. She wanted me to be a Texan! She had a very extensive record collection of all the great lady singers and Broadway shows and she was thrilled when I manifested a love for music and songs. She told me that I sang "Jesus Loves Me" in church when I was two. And when I was a kid I was always in the church choir, the junior choir, and the all-city chorus. The choir teacher was always putting me in the back row saying, "Blend in, Betty Lynn, blend in." I didn't know that my voice wasn't blending in. I was really self-conscious about it. My mom took me to my first piece of musical theater when I was eleven, *Pajama Game*, with the original Fosse choreography, and I had this epiphany. I didn't know the word epiphany then, but it was a very transcendent moment. I remember it very clearly. I remember where I was sitting in the theater, on the aisle. I remember the row. An energy force rose up through the top of my head and looked back at me and said, "This is it! This is what you are gonna be doing for the rest of your life." I didn't know what "it" was, but I later realized that it was the musical theater. I came home from school, and I said to my mom, "I want to learn 'Steam Heat.'" And she was really excited because she loved show business. I would always sing with these recordings she had . . .

You mentioned that the recordings were girl singers. Are you talking about Rosemary Clooney and Peggy Lee or Mary Martin and Ethel Merman?

Nancy Wilson, Della Reese, Ella Fitzgerald, Sarah Vaughn, and Judy Garland, at Carnegie Hall. I could sing, note by note, the whole Carnegie Hall concert. I taught myself how to sing with these great lady singers. I also loved Michael Jackson and I loved The Beatles. I loved all the '60s music: Led Zeppelin, Jefferson Airplane, Janis Joplin. And I loved jazz. I spent all my babysitting money on jazz and jazz instrumentalists and Brazilian music—Antonio Carlos Jobim and Brazil 66. So anyway, these two guys, Ed Holleman and Larry Howard—one had directed *Pajama Game* and the other was the lead dancer—opened a dance school in Fort Worth. My mom called them and said, "My daughter wants to learn 'Steam Heat.'" I had studied dance from the time I was three—tap/ballet/jazz, with my aunt who was a dance teacher.

How'd you get away with that given your father?

Well, because it was my aunt. From the time I was three I had dance lessons. So I knew I could do "Steam Heat." My mom hired them to give me a private lesson. They said, "Can you sing?" And I said, "Yes." So I sang and they said, "No, no, sing it as loud as you can!" So I sang it and everyone jumped back. I knew I had this big voice, but, prior to this moment, I didn't know that it had a purpose. So, they taught me "Steam Heat." My mother had this little suit made for me with the black bowtie and the Fosse derby hat and she had this local pianist record the track. I got into the talent show. I was just this little teeny kid with this really big voice singing "Steam Heat" with all the original hat tricks and Fosse choreography. They put my number right before the senior girls can-can line, which was the 11 o'clock number position. From that moment, I became an 11 o'clock number specialist. It really is what I do. Give me that and I can bring it home. Anyway, so I finished "Steam Heat," and the whole audience was astonished. And then the house went nuts. I ran offstage and the principal said, "Go back, go back," and he said I said, "Boy, we're havin' fun tonight!" They gave me this huge ovation and from that moment I was notorious. Everybody knew who I was. They called me "little bitty Betty Buckley, with the humongous voice."

So you stopped being afraid of having to blend and having to . . .

Yeah, I realized "I can sing!" So my mom then became a stage mother. If she was in the room right now, she'd be saying, "I was not a stage mother, Betty Lynn! You know I wasn't!" She was, in fact, a stage mother. She entered me in every talent show you can imagine. My father would get angry, and he and my mother would have these huge fights. She would sneak me out of the house for my dance classes. When I went to college my dad wouldn't let me major in theater so I majored in journalism. He told me it was okay for a woman to be a journalist (my mom was a journalist), but really my career should be a compliment to my husband-to-be's career. It was the '60s. For some reason my father approved of beauty pageants, which I thought were ridiculous. As a young budding feminist and later a charter subscriber to *Ms. Magazine*, I saw such a double standard in our community.

But you were Miss Fort Worth . . .

I was recruited because I was the girl singer in town that year.

So you saw it as a performance opportunity?

No, my mother saw it as some great fun thing. I was raised to be this really, do-good, straight-A student, little all-American girl. Just do what people tell you to do and keep smiling. But it was okay. My mother was not as extreme as Mama Rose. She's a very lovely, strong, Southern, Texas gal, and she has a mind of her own. And she taught me great things. And the thing is, by nature, I'm very laid back. Without her impetus, I doubt that I would have had the motivation or the drive to do what I have done, and I'm grateful for all of that. Very grateful. Anyway, I didn't win Miss Texas. But the producer of the Miss America Pageant saw me, and the following year invited to be a guest entertainer at the pageant, and I was on the telecast. It was a really big deal.

You had your first audition in New York on the day that you got here from Texas!

It was January 1969. I called my agent, Rodger Hess, who had signed me to this big agency when I was a junior at TCU [Texas Christian University] after I had appeared on the Miss America Pageant. When I got to town he said, "You have an audition in fifteen minutes. Take your music and go." It was at the American Theater Laboratory, and I was the last girl to audition on the last day of auditions for 1776. After I sang, they said, "Who are you?" I said, "Betty Lynn Buckley." "When did you get to town?" "Today." "Today?!?! It's like a movie! It's like a movie!" So they kept me there for two hours and they taught me "He Plays the Violin" and had me read. The thing was, they'd been in rehearsal, and they had another girl who was a classic soprano [playing Martha Jefferson], but that section of the show wasn't working. So they decided to let her go, but they didn't know what they wanted. Then I walked in and I was different. So they hired me. I got it that day and I was in rehearsal and costume fittings the next day. I was such a naïve kid. I was very sheltered and had no skills for anything. I didn't know how to take care of myself, I didn't know how to cook, I didn't know how to . . . nothing. Nothing and I was completely naïve. These guys [in the cast] Howard Da Silva, William Daniels, Paul Hecht, they really took me under their wings and taught me everything. Da Silva befriended me. He was a fantastic actor. I loved him. These wonderful actors would tell me, "This is what you do well, and this is what you need to learn. This is where you should go study." I did everything they told me to do. They were incredible. Such a wonderful experience! In the beginning of 1776, I had inherited the other girl's costume. I had this brown wig, and I was doing my own makeup. I shared a dressing room with Virginia Vestoff, and I watched her to see how she did her make up. I loved everything about her! I thought, "Ooh, she's an *actress*! I need to study her." She was like, "Why are you staring at me? Get away from me kid!" I was so silly.

You were hungry.

I was trying to learn. I thought, "Oh, my wig is brown, I have to wear darker makeup." Why did I think that? I don't know. I had this pale, pale skin. So I go to the pharmacy and I buy this really dark makeup, and this really red lipstick and this really blue eye shadow. It was our first big dress rehearsal in New Haven. When Martha appears on the second floor at the window and opens these shutters, she's supposed to be like a breath of fresh air. That was the description. I looked like a cigar store Indian. I had this brown makeup, and red, purple lipstick. I'll never forget it as long as I live. I thought I was doing the right thing, but Howard Da Silva and William Daniels, could barely control their laughter. And the audience at this invited dress literally gasped. I was thinking, "Something's wrong but I don't know what it is!" I came down and out on the stage, and no one knew that I needed help opening the door. It had a spring latch and when you opened it, it slammed back. I tried to manage but my costume wasn't cooperating. Patricia Zipprodt, the amazing costume designer, made the clothes exactly like they were made in the 1700s. I had these three-foot paniers on each side and I got one of my paniers caught in the door. So I pulled and pulled on my skirt and lurched free, stumbling down these two little steps onto the raked stage. I tumbled forward and William Daniels caught me. I was pretty sure I was going to be fired. But the producer, Stuart Ostrow was so kind. He came back and said, "We are not going to fire you. We're hiring a makeup artist and we are going to remake your wig and costume just for you." We were four weeks in New Haven, then we were in Washington for four weeks, then we came to New York, previewed and opened and it was huge. I did it for seven months and then I auditioned for [the London company of] *Promises, Promises*, and I got the female lead in that.

You were in a huge, Tony Award–winning hit. How'd you have the instinct to move on to something else?

Because I loved *Promises, Promises*. Burt Bacharach and Hal David scored my life in college, and they were really important to me. And the idea of going to London was thrilling to me. I blew the audition. I learned "Knowing When to Leave" overnight and it's way too difficult to learn that fast. I just didn't do it well. Then I had this inspiration, my inner voice saying "you need to take off your costume and run over to the Shubert where *Promises, Promises* was playing and talk to the stage manager Charlie Blackwell." So I did. I convinced my sweet dresser to unlace that dress, which took forever.

During the show?

Yeah, I just had to sing the violin song, and then I had the whole rest of the show off until the bows. So, I assured my dresser I'd be back in time and I raced over, and it happened to be the intermission at *Promises*. I asked to speak with Charlie, and when he came to the stage door I burst into tears. I said, "Mr. Blackwell, My name is Betty Lynn Buckley and I blew my audition, but I can do this, I can really do this." He was so kind and so generous, and he agreed to coach me. He worked with me for about an hour before the Saturday matinee. And I asked him, "Can I come to the call back?"

Chutzpah!

I did have chutzpah. But, I only had that when I had that inner conviction. In my youth, I had a really loud inner voice that would instruct me quite clearly and say, "Do this, now!" And this voice said . . . and I don't mean to say I "hear voices," but I do, at least this one. It's just this inner instruction, this inner being, and it said, "go, take your costume off, put on your jeans and go talk to the stage manager."

I think we all hear those things but most of us dismiss them.

Yeah, but the hard part is to hear the difference between that clarity of your true inner voice and the clutter of your mind. I tell my students, there are many voices in your head. My father's voice would say, "Get off that stage, who do you think you are?" As recently as *Cats*, not so long ago in the scheme of things, I had this inner voice that clearly came from my father. "Get off the stage! No one cares!" Attack voices, which I was subject to all my life until I really worked on myself through analysis and meditation.

And yet you had the inner conviction to disregard those voices.

In certain moments, yes. That dauntless voice came from my mother. My mother's experience was, "Always ask for what you want Betty Lynn, and when people say 'no,' don't take no for an answer." And, "always think positively and things will work out. If you think you can do something, do it! Don't hesitate, just do it!" Again, that's why I'm really grateful for her motivation and her drive, because I didn't initially have the courage of my own convictions. So anyway, Charlie got me the audition and I went back and sang, and I read the scene. They thanked me and I left. Charlie came bursting through the side doors in the alleyway of the theater and he picked me up, swung me around and said, "Go back, go back, they're calling [producer] David Merrick!" So, I went back into the theater and repeated the audition. Then Hal David, Burt Bacharach, and Neil Simon all came down the aisle and shook my hand. I was euphoric. It was one of the happiest days of my life, because I had followed through and made it work. I got the part. I was in London for a year. I was twenty-two and the leading lady. Tony Roberts was the leading man. I got to work with Michael Bennett. I was nominated for an Evening Standard Award, and I got to sit next to Laurence Olivier at that event. It was so fabulous. David Merrick and his girlfriend, Etan, whom he later married, would take me all around London. Donna McKechnie did the show for the first six weeks. I watched her do the Turkey Lurkey number from the wings every night. I just thought she was the most beautiful, fabulous dancer I'd ever seen in my life. Amazing!

With Michael Rupert and Shane Nickerson in *Pippin*. (Photofest)

After a year of doing that in London, you came back here and you got *Pippin*.

It didn't happen quite that fast. I came back to New York, and I went back into 1776. I did the show for another year and then I did an off-Broadway thing called *The Ballad of Johnny Pot*, with David Carradine and later John Bennett Perry. We all thought we were doing *Hair*; we were so excited. It wasn't *Hair*. Then I did another off-Broadway show called *What's a Nice Country Like You Doing in a State Like This?* I married a wonderful man and my best friend, Peter Flood. And then I got *Pippin*. I wanted to audition for it and my agent, Eric Shepherd, told me there was no role for me. I went to see it and there was the role of Catherine, which Jill Clayburgh originated. So I called my agent and he said, "They didn't want to see you." And I said, "What do you mean they didn't want to see me?" The producer was my friend, Stuart Ostrow, the producer of 1776. I so wanted to audition for Bob Fosse. My teachers had brought me up on Bob Fosse, and when I first moved to New York, I found out where Gwen Verdon had her dance boots made, 'cause I had to have dance boots just like Gwen Verdon's. I still have them. And I used to wear black velvet ribbons tied around my neck like she did. She was one of my heroes. Anyway, six months later Jill was leaving the show and I ran into Merlin Jones who was the property master in 1776 and *Pippin* and later, *Cats*—a wonderful man. He said, "Betty, are you coming in?" And I said, "No, they don't want to see me." And he said, "Well, we'll see about that." A few days later I got this letter from Michael Shurtleff, the casting director, and he says, "Miss Buckley, we've been looking for you but your agent told us that you were out of the business and had gone back to Texas. Mr. Ostrow sends his love and Mr. Fosse looks forward to meeting you at such and such time, next week for an audition." So I called Eric and he said, "Betty, I also represent Jill Clayburgh and I didn't want her to have any competition because I can get $100 more per week for her than for you." She had already done a film. I said, "How could you do that, Eric?" He said, "Oh grow up, don't be so naïve." So I said. "You grow up! You're fired." And then I got the show. Fosse came back and put me into the show himself.

After having grown up idolizing him, how did you even compose yourself?

Well, I had trained for this moment. I was in *Pippin* for a really, really long time, and during that time I studied at an acting school that really focused on emotional work. Really getting to your true feelings. I studied there for four years, and then I studied with the great Stella Adler. I took her script analysis classes several times. I took her scene study, too, but I was too scared to put my work before her. I always sat in the back so she wouldn't see me. I just took copious notes and watched and learned. She was the most amazing teacher. Some time later I also became a member of the Actors Studio.

Right around then you got your first film, *Carrie*.

I had auditioned for Brian De Palma for *Phantom of the Paradise* and I really had a chip on my shoulder because in those days, Hollywood people kind of looked down on theater performers, and they especially dismissed musical theater performers. I met with Brian De Palma, and I think he liked the fact that I seemed unimpressed. He came to see me in *Pippin*, and he hired me, but not for the movie. He hired me to do the voices for all of these minor roles. So I did a bunch of teenage girls and an older woman in *Phantom of the Paradise*. And then he had me do voices for another movie. After about the third of those movies I figured it out: he was going out and hiring these kids that couldn't act on location because they didn't cost any money, and then he'd come back and hire me to create a voice for the character on the screen. Finally I said, "You know what, Brian? I won't do this for you any more. There are all these young actors, like me, who are paying a whole bunch of money to go to acting school, and any one of these parts would be a major debut for us. You need to hire real actors." And so, a few months later, he called me and took me to dinner, and he gave me this book, *Carrie*, which he said was to be his next film. And he said he wanted me to play the gym teacher. A few months later he sent me the script. It was a fabulous movie debut. He combined the parts of the gym teacher and the principal into one role. When I read the script I wept. It was such a gift. So I left *Pippin* and did the film, *Carrie*.

Somewhere in there didn't Stephen Schwartz contact you about *The Baker's Wife*?

Yes, he called me and he said the he'd written a new musical and—this is the quote— "with you in mind," but I'd have to audition because the director didn't know my work. They had me audition for the show over and over again. They taught me the score, but the director did not want me. I didn't get the part, but I got *Carrie*.

But he wrote the show's big hit, "Meadowlark" with you in mind?

So he said. But I was so upset that I didn't get that show. It was the first time, to my knowledge anyway, that someone had actually written something with me in mind, and I could not let it go. I kept telling the story to my therapist over and over again. "How could this be? I didn't get a show that was written for me?" And she said, "Just claim the song as your own. Just put it in your repertoire and get on with your life." So I did. I formed my band over twenty years ago. We started doing these shows at The Bottom Line every year. We did interpretations of classic Broadway, songs from shows I'd done, standards and contemporary music. These incredible jazz musicians and I created what I think are paintings of some great songs.

We talked about how therapy helped you become the interpreter that you are. What made you seek out therapy at such a young age to begin with?

I was tortured. I wasn't comfortable inside myself.

But there you were, on Broadway, actually doing the thing you were destined for, yet you still weren't comfortable living it?

Not at all. It took years of arduous work. When the imprint goes that deep, when the psyche has been so distraught as a child over the essential things that you are, the conflict runs very deep and can take a lifetime to overcome. My father repeatedly attacked the two things that I am most essentially—a person with a talent to sing, and a female.

You have to stay committed to working on it.

That's the most interesting thing about being an actor: the commitment to the craft. I've been a teacher now for over forty years. I tell my students that you need to take into account what your gifts are and what you need to work on about yourself. It takes a lot of discipline and a lot of hard work. To be a great actor is a lifetime commitment. I think I'm getting better as I get older. It becomes more and more effortless. It's a wonderful thing to grow older and to feel sure of your skills and to have them keep mellowing and become richer and deeper and lighter. It's a very sweet experience.

After you did *Carrie*, you did the TV series *Eight Is Enough* and that kept you in Hollywood till 1981 when you first heard about *Cats*.

They auditioned for six months on both coasts to handpick the cast. I went in and sang "Memory" and I didn't get called back. They told Joanna, my agent, "She radiates health and well-being and we're looking for someone who radiates death and dying." I told Joanna, "They'll be back." I just had this feeling about it. It was my turn. I knew who my colleagues were in the business, the girl singers who could act. There were only a handful of us. It was on Page Six [in the *New York Post*] that Cher wanted to do it, and that all these different people were going after the part, so I was reading about the process. Six months later they called me in again. It was a wild audition. Trevor Nunn made me sing "Memory" three times, and each time he would come up on the stage at the Winter Garden and he would say, "More suicidal, more suicidal." I'd sing it again, but by the third time I just felt like my whole insides were turned inside out. He came back up, and he still looked like he wasn't sure. And I said, "Mr. Nunn, can I talk to you? You don't know me. Apparently you think that maybe I am not exactly physically right for this part, but I'm a good actress. If you want me to lose weight I'll lose weight. If you want me to look smaller, I'll look smaller. If you are able to convey to me the vision you want, I can do it. Certainly after six months you've seen a lot of people who can play this part as well as I can but let me tell you this: nobody can do it better. And it's my turn!" [laughs] I thought, "Uh-oh, what did I just do?" Anyway, this is the kind of outspoken stuff I used to get in trouble for. But this time I got the part. It doesn't always work like that, though. Sometimes I've gone in and I've told people that I can really do something and that I really want to do something and they look at me like I'm nuts. I guess it just depends on what the moment is and whether or not it really is your part.

For *Promises, Pippin*, and *Cats*, you had some convincing to do. It may have been your turn but you had to fight!

Well, that's not really fighting, just to tell a director that it's your turn.

Yes it is.

Ok, and it *was* my turn. Because of all my colleagues that are singer/actresses—I know who they are, and hopefully they include me in their fraternity as well. They all had had, at that point, their defining show that had allowed them to establish "this is what she does." I had done several big shows, but I had yet to have that defining role that gave me the opportunity to put all of the things I do into that one moment, and I knew that I was ready for that.

What do you remember about the rehearsal process?

In *Cats*, the job expectation was, "Stop the show! We know the show can be stopped with this song. Elaine Paige stopped the show in London." When I had stopped a show previously, it was by chance. I didn't have a formula for how to stop a show and not in the context of being a cat! Anyway, I was not stopping the show during previews. They panicked. So they started calling special rehearsals for me. In one of hour of rehearsal, Andrew Lloyd Webber just played "Memory" over and over and over again while I sang. He said to me, "Placido Domingo saw the show last night and he said, 'Tell the girl to just sing the song.'" And I thought, "But I AM just singing the song. What are you talking about?" Trevor Nunn called a special rehearsal for me and he told me the whole story of Shakespeare's *The Winter's Tale*. I'm hanging on every word and I had no idea how *The Winter's Tale* applies to "Memory." I'm trying, I'm trying so hard and it's still not working. I called my friend, James Lapine, and asked him to see the show. So he kindly came to a preview, and afterward he said, "You're doing everything fine, but I don't know what you feel about it all." And I said, "What I feel? I feel *The Winter's Tale*! I feel what Trevor wants, what Andrew wants, what [choreographer] Gillian Lynne wants! What do you mean what I feel?" I had this great voice teacher named Paul Gavert with whom I had studied for thirteen years. I called Paul from my dressing room at our lunch break. I went to his studio and he put a pillow on the floor and said, "Hit this pillow." And I said, "Oh Paul, a kinetic exercise is not going to work right now." And he said,

"Hit that pillow." So I got down on my knees and started hitting the pillow and hitting the pillow, and I was not really into it. Finally I am hitting it, and all this rage and pain is coming out, and I am sobbing and all of a sudden I hear this little kid's voice inside me saying, "I'm here too! I'm here too! I'm here too!" and I realized, "Shoot! Of course, the one person I haven't consulted about how she wants to sing this song is this kid in me who does all the work." So I started asking my inner self, "What do you want to do? How do you want to sing this song?" This kid compelled me into the streets of New York, and I started following homeless people. Grizabella is the creation of Trevor Nunn inspired by a four-line fragment of poetry by T. S. Eliot. Trevor had told me, "Grizabella is the pariah of the tribe. She's the Glamour Cat but now, as she is older, the tribe of cats want nothing to do with her. They worship that which is young and beautiful." I think Trevor created Grizabella to reflect his concern about the problem of homelessness, which we were just starting to be aware of as a culture. Finally, the first time it came together, which was like two or three performances before our opening night—thank God! I walked out, and I remember being in the center of myself. I did all of the choreography, but it was not out of that neediness. It was out of the desire of the heart to connect, to really touch, to share. It came from the dignity I had witnessed in the streets. Then finally I sang "Memory," and it became a cry of the heart. I went out that night, and I sang it staying completely inside myself and taking the direction of my voice teacher to always take the audience into you. Paul always said, "Never go out after the audience. Allow them to come to you." So I did it, and I finished the song, and it was like that moment when I was in the seventh grade; that breathless, stunned silence, and then everyone went insane. I thought, "I guess that was it." Trevor came back and said, "That's what I was talking about, that's what I was talking about!" I learned big ol' lessons. I learned how to take a song and deconstruct it, to take it apart, and put it back together. And after I did "Memory," which I think is the jewel in my collection of music, I knew how to work on music, I knew how to do a lot of things that I didn't know how to do before.

You never get tired of the song?

No, I love it. So beautiful! Trevor actually wrote the lyric of "Memory." It's a beautiful piece of poetry with gorgeous music. Grizabella is one of my great teachers. It took me so long to find her. I feel like she's one of my life companions or a soul mate. She's not me; she's herself, and I get to lend my soul to her, to bring life to her song. It's a beautiful, beautiful piece and it keeps evolving for me every time I do it.

And you can always access it?

Yeah. As soon as I hear the first chords I go there. And then I just observe and follow the experience as a witness. And it keeps changing because I keep changing.

You won a Tony. What do you remember?

That week before, I got to thank so many people that crossed my path by chance, or by divine coincidence—all of these people that had opened doors for me or given me opportunities. It was very moving. I think mainly that night I was terrified that I wouldn't win and that I would embarrass everybody and let the team down. I was really worried that I'd say the wrong thing or I'd forget to thank someone—which I did. I thanked my mother and my brother Norman, and I forgot my other two brothers' names in the moment. I said, "And my other brothers." And to this day, my twin brothers, Pat and Mike, are like, "We're just the other brothers." They'll never let me live it down!

Grizabella: "If you touch me, you'll understand what happiness is." (John Napier)

Your mom was there with you?

She was there, yes, and my brother Norman. My dad wouldn't come—wouldn't even come for *1776*—a play about the Declaration of Independence, and he wouldn't come for *Cats*.

Why? At that point you had established not only that you were doing this but that you were successful at it.

A couple of years before when I was doing *Eight Is Enough* in Los Angeles, I invited him out to see a property I was considering buying. He was a very smart guy, and he was very pleased that I was asking his opinion. I was doing *I'm Getting My Act Together* while shooting *Eight Is Enough* in the day. He came to see *Act*. He acknowledged that day that he felt my passion for my work and said he had always been concerned that I would waste my intelligence in what he thought was a superficial business. He complimented my performance and said that he felt that I was doing my best to serve people.

Thank God you got that and his disapproval wasn't the legacy.

Yes we shared that moment. I called it détente.

Your next show was *The Mystery of Edwin Drood*.

That was the most fun job I've ever had. It was an incredible group of people: [director] Wilford Leach, [choreographer] Graciela Daniele, [producer] Joe Papp, [author] Rupert Holmes, [actors] George Rose, Cleo Laine, Patti Cohenour, Howard McGillin . . . Amazing, amazing group! It was a great show. So much fun!

Do you have any personal recollections of George Rose?

George became my mentor in the show because I'd never played a boy before. He had an extensive library of the history of theater, so he brought me several books about male impersonators in the British Music Hall. He was such an elegant man of the theater, a lovely, funny man and so good to me. He mentored me as did the wonderful actor Joe Grifasi, who coached me on how to walk like a boy and how to light my cigar, how to smoke onstage. I loved Patti Cohenour. She sings so beautifully, and during our duet I would try to match her tone perfectly. I think the cast album we did is one of the best cast albums in the history of musical theater. There was this exit when they vote my character, Alice Nutting, out of the show and I put my traveling clothes on and storm out. It was supposed to get a laugh but rarely did. I had a little Shih Tzu, Bridget, who was six months old. I used to bring her to work with me, and one day when we were rehearsing for the Broadway transfer, I came running in late from the dinner break with Bridget because I didn't have time to run her upstairs to the dressing room. Wilford asked if she would walk across stage with me. I had been teaching her obedience training, and she was really into it. Wilford said, "Let's put her into your exit!" So the costume designer made her a little feathered hat and a leash and a collar to match my traveling outfit, and we put her in the show. This section of the show, which had never worked, suddenly got this huge laugh every night. So she became part of the show. When I was out sick they sent a car for her and she did a handful of shows without me! When I was in *Sunset Boulevard*, my fabulous dresser Jim Nadeaux made her these little sunglasses and a little, tiny turban, and a little leopard skin coat, and she went on with me in my last performance in New York.

Your next Broadway show, immediately after *Edwin Drood*, was *Song and Dance*. Usually when you step into a show, you are asked to recreate much of the performance of your predecessor, but in *Song and Dance*, since you were the only one onstage, were you given more license to find your own way?

No, actually. It was really nuts. My hair was cut really short—this kind of punk haircut, and they said, "You have to have bobby pins in your hair, and then pull them out" because that was what Bernadette Peters, with her beautiful curly hair, had done previously. I said, "Look at my hair! I have punk hair!" We finally worked it out. It was fun. I like the music a lot. I learned it really fast, and that was really terrifying.

Before *Song and Dance* you did the first *Into the Woods* workshop.

They cast me when they just had Act 1. I was mixing my first album, so I told them ahead of time that there were times that I wouldn't be there. They had to work their schedule with my schedule and that really annoyed the director, my friend, James Lapine. It appeared to him that I was constantly late, which I wasn't. We had prearranged it all in the schedule. This was my first Sondheim show, and I was so excited. I couldn't wait to sing a soaring Sondheim monologue song. At that point, the Witch had "The Rap" song. One day in rehearsal Sondheim came in and said, "I wrote this for you. " It was "Stay with Me." I was thrilled! It was a major dream come true! And then in rehearsal, Lapine said, " In the second act the Witch will maybe have another rap song." I said, "Rap song?" I wanted to really sing. And he said, "Yes, rap song!" He was annoyed. I just kept rubbing him the wrong way. He also felt that the Witch's relationship with Rapunzel was a lesbian relationship, and I said, "No, it's an abusive mother." He kept saying "lesbian," and I kept saying, "abusive mother." So our interpretations were completely different, too. Anyway, while I was in *Song and Dance*, they did the show in San Diego, and I wasn't available. He called me from San Diego and said, "You were right. She's an abusive mother. You've got to be my Witch." So when they came back from San Diego, I did the pre-

Broadway workshop. I was playing the Witch as a really, really, scary character. Or at least I was trying to. I also collaborated with the designer on the idea of the costume designs. I had a very clear image of her, which they ended up using, by the way. They also kept all my staging with Rapunzel. We did the workshop, and my sections with Rapunzel were as scary as I could make them. Our negotiation reached a stalemate. I passed, and my career took a definite turn.

In what way?

I don't think it helped too much in the theatrical community when I didn't come to terms on *Into the Woods*. To this day, there's a perception in some circles that I'm a difficult person. I know I'm a team player. I've heard all the rumors, and I've heard all the gossip. People have different ideas about "difficult." To be sure I've been outspoken. I care a lot about the work, and I think sometimes that intensity has struck people the wrong way. I've mellowed through the years. Now I try to quickly get the vibe of where everybody's going with something and see where I can fit in. Texas women are bold, brash, and outspoken. I have had to learn to soften that through the years. Personally, I think any intelligent, talented woman in a very patriarchal business and society, has to attend to some version of this phenomenon one way or another.

Your next show took chutzpah, because when they offered you *Carrie*, you knew it was in trouble.

They offered me *Carrie* at the beginning. [Lyricist] Dean Pitchford was my first Pippin on Broadway and years later when he wrote *Fame* with Michael Gore, I was Dean's date to the Oscars the night he and Michael won. And [librettist] Larry Cohen wrote the script for *Carrie*, the film. They offered it to me and we negotiated for three months, and we couldn't come to terms. So they rescinded the offer and cast Barbara Cook for the RSC [Royal Shakespeare Company] version in Britain. They spent millions of dollars on that production. It got the worst reviews in theatrical history. They wanted me to step in for New York because Barbara Cook was leaving so they sent me a video, and I saw the show as it had been done. Barbara Cook's a stunningly beautiful singer. I'm really an athletic actress, so I felt there was something I could bring to it. When we started rehearsal in New York I met Linzi Hateley, the seventeen-year-old playing Carrie, and we had this really nice rapport. I said, "Listen, I'm a coach. Trust me. I will help you be so 'kick ass' in this part!" And she did. So I asked to work on the mother/daughter sequences with just the rehearsal pianist, the director, and us. Linzi and I did some really spontaneous theater game exercises. I said, "just keep your eyes on me and whatever I give you, give me back whatever you really, really feel." We established this really spontaneous give-and-take relationship, which is what was required. We literally had a physical battle. We painted this portrait of a very, very realistic abusive mother/daughter relationship that I think hadn't been done before in musical theater. I was really proud of that work. I did the dance warm-up with [choreographer] Debbie Allen and the ensemble every morning. She got me really fit. At our first performance, Linzi went out, in her Broadway debut, and stopped the show at age seventeen. Her first number killed! And then our first section killed! Killed! The audience went insane. The audiences really responded to the mother/daughter sequences, and even Frank Rich stated in his [*New York Times*] review that he liked what we did, but on our opening night, he wrote the review about Linzi and me so carefully that a quote couldn't be lifted. People were so provoked by that show. They either absolutely loathed or absolutely loved it. And I honestly believe if they pushed through the reviews, the show could have run for a long time.

You mention studying psychology . . .

I was in analysis four times a week—classical analysis for ten years with a brilliant analyst. I would take her my scripts for whatever project I was working on. I got her counsel as to what the root psychology behind the characters' situation was and she was very, very helpful. It was the equivalent of a psychology degree.

In 1994 you took on another psychologically challenging role, Norma Desmond in *Sunset Boulevard*.

They flew me to London for a week to prepare for my audition. They put me in a beautiful hotel suite, taught me the score, and my audition a week later lasted an hour and ten minutes. Patti LuPone had opened the show in London and Frank Rich trashed it. Essentially Rich didn't think a girl with a high Broadway belt voice should be playing Norma. He basically told Andrew Lloyd Webber in the review that if he brought Patti to New York, he was going to kill the show. I think Andrew panicked. So he hired Glenn Close for the LA production. All this was going on right towards the end of Patti's contract in London. They made changes in the production in LA with the sets and everything and then they decided to close the show when Patti's contract was up in London, go back into rehearsal, make the same changes they'd made in LA, and reopen. They had never done that in British theatrical history. At this hour and ten-minute audition they really put me through my paces. Trevor [Nunn] had worked with me in *Cats*, and he knew how outspoken I was. He'd get right in my face and say things like, "The audience is supposed to feel 'ick' because Norma's so much older than Joe," and on the inside I'm thinking, "no," but I just said, "Okay." I just did whatever he said. I was really ready. It was a good audition. The day they flew me over to start rehearsals it was announced that they were going to break Patti's contract and offer New York to Glenn Close. When I arrived, Patti was heartbroken. I went to see Patti in the show and I thought she was excellent. She was just so good! I went backstage with flowers, and tried to comfort her to the best of my ability. A lot of the press asked me what my thoughts about it were, and I was her ally. Years later when she wrote her book she mentioned that I was one of the people who spoke out on her behalf, and I appreciated that. Anyway, I had my trainer for many years, Patrick Strong, who was also my movement consultant, with me. He really helped me define Norma's physicality by taking things from these silent movies of Clara Bow, Louise Brooks, and Gloria Swanson. The films were quite beautiful. Slowly I brought in other references for Trevor's consideration, and gradually he allowed me my interpretation. We got major reviews, and that was great. So I had a year in London and then a year in New York. Everybody got nervous again [when it came time to go to New York] because my interpretation was so vastly different than Glenn Close's, but Trevor stood by me. That's when I started studying with the great Joan Lader who really helped me preserve my voice. It was a divine two years of my life. It was kind of perfect. The Really Useful Company are the best producers I've ever worked with. They're also tough. I think Andrew Lloyd Webber is a tremendous producer, tremendous, and he was very, very good to me. I loved, loved working with him. In every job capacity they hire the best possible person and no expense is spared. Whatever it is, it's the best. And Trevor Nunn is a genius. I love him.

After you left *Sunset* you took *Triumph of Love*. Ben Brantley said in his *New York Times* review, "If you're human, you'll find yourself delivering a silent prayer of thanksgiving for Betty Buckley."

Such a lovely review for me from Ben Brantley! Well, *Triumph* was an interesting story. My character only had one song that was very brief, so I was asking them to consider the possibility of writing more for me. They weren't really open to that. But I decided to do the show anyway. I was thrilled to get to work with F. Murray Abraham, and I thought it was a good project. My song, "Serenity," became such a beautiful piece. Susan Birkenhead wrote such moving additional lyrics for that song, and it stopped the show every night. It was an amazing experience. They had also written a second song for me. Michael Mayer decided he wanted to cut it. It was a matter of ego and pride to me, so in my mind it became this big showdown. I really didn't know what to do. So one night after the show I'm in the quick-change booth and

I hear this voice backstage: "Where is she? Where is she?" Elaine Stritch comes all the way across the stage, catches me in the quick-change room with my dresser, and says, "What's wrong with you? Something's wrong." I said, "I don't know what you're talking about," and she says, "Yes, you do. You tell me what's wrong with you." And I said, "Well, if you must know, they want to cut my second act song." And she says, "What song?! Give them the damned song. Who cares? Your first number is fantastic. Go out there right now and tell Michael Mayer he can have that song, and let it go." And I said, "Okay." She just turned me around. I walked out of the stage door, and Michael is out on the street looking really upset, pacing in front of his car. I said, "Michael, you can have the song. It's fine. Take it. I don't need it." He was relieved. I think Elaine Stritch is my guardian angel. The show closed after a few months. It was too bad because it had so many lovely things about it.

You followed up with *Gypsy* at the Paper Mill Playhouse.
I'd done that show when I was fifteen. I played Dainty June and I watched our Mama Rose like a hawk when I was a kid. I knew I would do the role someday. Our Paper Mill production got amazing response from the critics. I was very, very happy with our version. I thought we did a tremendous job. Arthur Laurents and Stephen Sondheim came to see it and we got several full house standing ovations during the show. It was crazy! I was so nervous that they were there because I had placed Laurents on such a pedestal. He wrote my two favorite musicals, *West Side Story* and *Gypsy*, and as I told you, I am a total devotee of Sondheim. I went offstage, and I was thrilled at what we'd done. I said to my dresser, "I can't do it any better. I hope they liked it." Sondheim was waiting for me in the hall. I went running up to him, and he said, indicating my dressing room where Laurents was waiting, "He'll tell you, he'll tell you." This is after a show where I thought I had nailed it. I went into my dressing room and Laurents said, "Well, without a doubt, you're a virtuoso, yes, you're a virtuoso. But you don't know how to play Mama Rose." I said, "Oh. OK. Well, I'd sure love to talk you about it. I'd really like to make you happy. Can I call you and speak to you about it?" They wanted to move the show to Toronto because it was a great production but he wouldn't let it move. All these people really tried and tried to make it happen. But Laurents said "No." Before this experience I was completely in awe of all of the "greats" in musical theater, but something broke after that. I was no longer intimidated. Sure I'd prefer it if he had liked me. But at a certain point you just have to let it go.

I am astounded that he was so rude as to say that to you in the middle of your run. That could have seriously damaged the production, had you handled it less well.
I totally loved my interpretation. If I make a painting and it stirs up that much feeling, I must be doing something right.

It wasn't that long after that you moved to Texas.
After 9/11, I had this epiphany that I had to get my cutting horse, which is a kind of competitive show horse that I always wanted since I was twelve. I remember coming home one night after teaching and realizing that the majority of my days were spent in some kind of response or reaction to gossip and the business. I needed a horse. I just thought I needed a relationship with a horse because horses are absolutely authentic. If you're not your true self with a horse, you can't get along with a horse. Horses have deep empathy with humans. They're about the immediacy of the present moment. I found this beautiful horse, Purple Badger, near Fort Worth. I was commuting and staying at my mother's and learning to ride and compete and the emphasis changed for me. Badger was all I could think about, and I realized I just

needed to live where my horse lives. So the next day I put my apartment on the market. In short order, I found this ranch, my apartment sold, and I moved back to Texas.

What a gift for yourself after a full career . . .

It's been a really good career. I've done television, film, musical theater, recordings, concert work. I've been so blessed to do all of it. I love my career. I wouldn't want it to be any different. I've been privileged to work with some of the greatest artists in this business. I've had to learn the lessons I've learned. I'm an outspoken Texas woman who had to learn to soften my manner with some of these dudes. The fact is that they have let me collaborate with them and afforded me some beautiful portrait work. If I die tomorrow, it's fine. And I finally get to ride these horses. I don't know how long I'll be able to do all of this. And, for now, I wouldn't have it any other way.

PATTI LUPONE

April and May 2012

"CAN I BUTTER IT FOR YOU? Or maybe some jam?" Patti LuPone asks excitedly as she toasts a couple of slices of the bread she baked that morning. She's positively giddy at the prospect of feeding me and I am surprised. I've been surprised since I set foot in her gorgeous, remote, South Carolina beach house, which, like her Connecticut farmhouse, is totally devoid of any clue that an actor resides within. Actually, I was surprised by the weekend invitation to the house to begin with ("bring your bathing suit," she said), and then by the offer to pick me up at the airport, an hour away. This warm, welcoming mother hen bore virtually no resemblance to the woman I had expected to meet based on my preconceived notions of Patti LuPone, the firecracker of Broadway with the reputation for temperament and ego. And while it became clear in our conversations that elements of the star personality lie within, it took very little time to separate the woman from the myth. "My job is on the stage, and once it's over I'm out the door and into my life," she told me. The evidence was all around us.

Patti LuPone grew up in Northport, Long Island, knowing that she was destined for the stage. But first she trained intensively. She was in the very first graduating class of Juilliard's drama division and that class famously became the founding members of John Houseman's The Acting Company, with which she toured the country for four years, performing the classics. Their first new musical, *The Robber Bridegroom*, brought LuPone her first Tony nomination. Two flops (*The Bakers Wife* and *Working*) followed before LuPone's career exploded with her casting in the title role of *Evita*. Though reviews for both LuPone and the show were mixed, audiences and awards poured in and a star was born.

Except not really. While *Evita* certainly gave LuPone fame, it didn't insure steady work. She had dry spells and then seven years (which included a stint in London, originating the role of Fantine in *Les Misérables*) until she had another hit on Broadway, this time as Reno Sweeney in the Lincoln Center Theater production of *Anything Goes*. The television series *Life Goes On* followed before LuPone found herself at the center of one of Broadway's most public scandals. After contracting her to star in both the London and Broadway productions of *Sunset Boulevard*, Andrew Lloyd Webber replaced LuPone for the New York production with Glenn Close without so much as a call to LuPone. She was paid handsomely but her ego took a very public beating.

Subsequent work had LuPone replacing Zoe Caldwell in Broadway's *Master Class* and fulfilling a lifelong dream, performing the work of Stephen Sondheim, first with the New York Philharmonic (*Sweeney Todd*) then at Chicago's Ravinia Festival (six Sondheim shows in six years), and finally on Broadway (*Sweeney Todd*, playing the tuba, no less, and a hugely triumphant *Gypsy*, which won her a second Tony Award).

Blowing off the roof with "Blow, Gabriel, Blow" in *Anything Goes*. (Photofest)

LuPone has peppered her career with concert appearances, television, film, straight plays (with a specialty in Mamet), and even forays into opera. But she is thought of, first and foremost, as a Broadway baby.

As we sit, overlooking the ocean, about a million miles from Broadway, we settle in for the conversation that follows. She is colorful, candid, and open, but sadly the page cannot fully

Patti LuPone

The Robber Bridegroom, National Tour
  and Broadway, 1975
The Baker's Wife, Los Angeles and
  Washington, D.C., 1976
Working, Broadway, 1978
Evita, Broadway and Australia, 1979
  (Tony Award)
The Cradle Will Rock, off-Broadway, West
  End, 1983, 1985 (Olivier Award for
  this and *Les Misérables*)
Oliver! Broadway, 1984
Les Misérables, West End, 1985 (Olivier
  Award for this and *Cradle Will Rock*)
Anything Goes, Broadway, 1987
Sunset Boulevard, West End, 1992
Pal Joey, Encores! 1995
Patti LuPone on Broadway, Broadway, 1995
Sweeney Todd, Lincoln Center, 2000
Matters of the Heart, Broadway, 2000
Can-Can, Encores! 2004
Candide, New York Philharmonic, 2004
Passion, Lincoln Center, 2005
Sweeney Todd, Broadway, 2005
Gypsy, Encores! and Broadway 2007,
  2008 (Tony Award)
*Women on the Verge of a Nervous
  Breakdown*, Broadway, 2009

capture the energy, passion, and sheer theatricality with which LuPone speaks. She strokes her dogs; guiltily grabs a cigarette ("If I am going to talk about myself all day, I am gonna need to smoke"); coos to her husband, Matt; puts her feet up; and lets fly.

You started performing at a very young age.

We started musical training—serious musical training—in the third grade. I learned how to read music in the public school. There were two huge posters of musical instruments and we were told to choose one. I wanted harp. I'm telling you, I was always left of center. They didn't have a harp so I took cello. I was in charge of a cello on a public bus. I kept breaking the necks off. We had extraordinary, innovative, passionate music teachers from elementary school through high school. If anybody chose that path, they were going to be supported and trained.

Playing instruments as a kid takes discipline.

I wasn't disciplined, I was forced. The thing I was interested in was singing. Esther Scott was my inspiration. Not only was she an inspirational music teacher, she picked really interesting music for us to learn—there's where the discipline was. I started with her in junior high school. We did art songs and classical music. Esther was also the kind of teacher that would protect or understand a student in any kind of distress. I used to get in a lot of trouble.

When you say you got into trouble, you mean typical teenager trouble?

Oh, I was a hellion. I was a rebel. That's who I am. I'm an Italian, and I have this sense of adventure and risk. But the thing that kept me on the straight and narrow, because I would have been dead, I would have abused my body with drugs or I would have gotten in a car crash, was Esther.

Given that you were so into music, how did you end up training as a classical actor?

Well, when I started to get serious at school, I fell out of love with musicals and in love with classical theater. I wanted to wear corsets. I still want to do classical theater. And I love doing contemporary theater. I'm lucky I can do it all. Actually, it's not luck. It's an investment in a craft. A lot of people today don't understand that it takes training to do anything well. The other thing I realized when I was sixteen was that my face . . . this is a stage face. It's a very mobile, theatrical face. I had to grow into my lips. Now they're falling. But people can't see beyond their nose so I was out of work a lot.

You have said after *Evita* . . .

There was nothing. A reputation followed me from that thing. I was made difficult. I wasn't born difficult.

What does that mean?

It means that you have to survive. You have to fight for what you need to get on the stage. My fight has always been "please do not prevent me from doing my work." And there are so many machinations and politics that have nothing to do with the theater. In *Evita* especially it was quite, quite difficult because they treated me like a chorus girl backstage but they wanted me to turn in a star performance onstage. And it's like, if you don't help me get out there, if you don't prevent the little obstacles in the way, it's going to make my job harder, and it's already a ball-busting part. I had a really ineffectual stage management team and it was a constant battle. It was Beirut from my dressing room to the stage. For some reason, costume designers like to design with wool and they don't ever air condition the backstages of theaters. I remember seeing kids backstage sweating and fainting. I said to the stage management, "Can't you just get those square fans and hang three on each side so that there's air back here?" They ignored me for about a month. One day it was blazing hot and I came off the stage after "Rainbow High" and screamed as loud as I could, "*Where are the fucking fans? Where are the fucking fans?*" The conductor heard me and went out and bought them the next day. But that's what it took to get air for all of us to put the show on.

Why do you suppose, in a situation like that, you get a reputation for being difficult instead of one for fighting for the company? You'd think the rest of the cast would be thrilled that you were leading the charge to protect all of you.

You talk to any leading lady in this business and they'll tell you the same thing: it's because you're a woman. Is it a boys' club? I don't know. I can't tell you. I know perhaps my tone has never been—I haven't got a really soft edge and I'm not political. I'm Italian. That's what I've been all my life. And I didn't have agents to fight my battles. Now I have a rider that one general manager says looks like every mistake in Patti's career. That's exactly what it is. So that this mistake never happens again. However, every time you go out there, there's some new set of circumstances. But I love being onstage and I love performing. I love serving the playwright and if it's a good director I'm happy as I can be. John Doyle said I always feel the story because I'm always looking where the plot is. That's a huge compliment. I give the focus to where the plot is, the continuation of the story. That's my thrust. I love getting lost in it just like an audience. But the job is to get it on and give it to the audience. They're paying a lot of money for that. Anything that gets in the way doesn't belong there. David Mamet says, "Wipe your feet at the door." You're entering a temple. Respect it. And help everybody get onstage.

You did your first Broadway musical under the auspices of The Acting Company: fourteen performances of *The Robber Bridegroom*. You have described that as one of your happiest memories of ever being onstage. Why specifically?

Well, it was the actors that I spent eight years with. It was my boyfriend, Kevin Kline. It was one of the funniest musicals I've ever been in and it was a great part. All of that combined to be just wicked fun onstage. It's a very sweet musical.

You got Tony nominated for *The Robber Bridegroom* and as you describe it, you weren't even aware of the Tonys.

It was unbelievable. [Playwright] Alfred Uhry and I were like, "*What?*" We were so excited. I mean, I knew I wasn't going to win. We were up against *A Chorus Line* and we were onstage for one month seven months before. But my brother [Robert LuPone] and I were nominated in the same year so it was a very exciting time.

Why do you think it didn't work when they brought it back?

I didn't see it. I was so angry with our company because we were the reason they were bringing that back. Our production, our actors. But all of us had to re-audition for our parts and it was a slap in the face after eight years, four years at school and four years in The Acting Company. I said, "Forget it. I have a Tony nomination for playing this role and you're making me re-audition? It's not going to happen." It's a bad showbiz story.

Your next musical was *The Baker's Wife*. You said about it "The show was a terrible experience for everyone, and when it finally died, the whole cast yelped for joy."

We were in hell. We did what they told us to do, and it just got worse and worse. I guess I don't know why it didn't work, but it still doesn't work. We rehearsed 'til Equity said no more. And there was a power struggle between [producer] David Merrick and [composer] Stephen Schwartz and we were caught in the middle of it. Stephen wrote a spectacular score but David may have assembled a creative staff that was not right for this piece. Maybe we didn't have the right playwright. But if we see each other, we're blood. That's the thing we remember. That company was very caring for each other because we were all in pain.

Well, with the exception of your leading men.

Oh, my God. Well, Topol was an idiot. Nobody liked Topol and nobody really liked Paul Sorvino when he came in [to replace the fired Topol]. You can't be a cheerleader [which is what Sorvino tried to do] when people are bloodied. People are falling down, broken legs on a field. You can't be a cheerleader.

Do you remember David Merrick on a personal level?

Oh, yeah. David Merrick was great. I mean he was a showman. We don't have showmen around. Now we have corporations running Broadway. I miss the Alex Cohens and the David Merricks. They're not bean counters. You want people that have show business in their blood. Robert Whitehead; a gentleman, a creative producer. I would like to work with individual producers, not a group of producers that all have opinions and none of them know much about show business. And when did someone die and give the angel a voice? Somebody said, "Give me a million dollars and you can have opinion?" That's when I feel sorry for the creative staff. They have to take notes from people that have never ever done anything in theater before. That's crazy. During *Noises Off* they didn't even know backstage etiquette. The producers would come back at twenty minutes to eight and want to see me and introduce me to people. I'd say, "Excuse me, but this is an Equity rule. Nobody backstage after half hour." The stage manager couldn't keep them out. I'm thinking, "Get control of the theater and get these producers out. I don't care who they are."

How much do you care about being thought of as difficult?

Oh, a lot.

So when you have to say to your stage manager, "Get them out," does that take a toll?

Of course. It all takes a toll. You just want to do your job. You don't want to have to deal with anything.

And do you then spend time thinking about what people are going to think?

You don't ever want to be put in that position. Nobody does in any profession. I wonder why I have to go through that, too. I wonder why I have to deal with that. It isn't about an arbitrary attitude. Backstage has to be done in a particular way. Politely and respectfully. And everybody should be in there for the same purpose: to put the play on. We're getting paid. It is our job, and the audience expects it. We didn't have good stage management on *Noises Off* and you know what? Now I have stage management [approval] in my contract. Stage management. Company management. I have the backstage keys. Your backstage atmosphere will determine how actors go onstage and it should be supported. What do you need? Within reason, of course. You have to really be about the play and not about your personal shit. I love the stage and I love the audience. Nobody wants a bad experience in the theater. Because when something in the theater goes bad, it goes really bad. It's kind of rancid. But you are put in situations where you have to deal with those kinds of things and you always go into them hoping they are going to be minor issues. When they are major issues it's like, "Oh, God. Why? Why!" Most of my experiences have been really, really great ones but isn't it interesting that the things people remember are the bad ones? I always remember the bad ones. I look out at the audience and I find the one that's not listening.

You made news when you yelled at somebody for taking pictures at *Gypsy*. Some of the chatter was, "Can you believe she did that?" I saw it as, "She's protecting an entire audience from being distracted by this selfish person!" I don't understand why people weren't thanking you for speaking out, rather than gossiping about you.

It was during "Rose's Turn!" What did they think was gonna come out? You cannot have a theatrical experience anymore because you have texting, filming, phones going off. Now you have crinkling water bottles. That person is taking everybody out of the play. Not just the actors but the audiences who want to be taken out of themselves and into that environment. [Those distractions] remind them of where they are. And they have just wasted $150 to $300 to $500 because somebody was selfish. Friends of mine just told me they went to the theater and someone was texting. When they tried to get her to stop she turned around and said, "Get over it. It's 2012." Where are our public manners? Where is the sense that we are in a communal experience? Where is the sense of community? I will fight for it and I don't care what they think of me. I am very realistic. My eyes are open. I'm not asking for anything other than what audiences deserve and that is our best without fucking distraction.

Speaking of demands, Arthur Laurents said in his book that when *Gypsy* was moving to Broadway, you had a lot of them.

Some people have everything they need, and so they can just concentrate on art. Some people love art, and also need to survive. My demands were, "This is what I need to give you a year of my life." I can't lose my house. This is the hardest role I've done. I'm already fifteen years too old for it. I'm going to need transportation to and from the theater, I'm going to need a trainer, I'm going to need body massage. Which is everything I got! I got it all. I'm going to need concentration. I was exhausted in the first three months of the show. . . . Boyd [Gaines] and I came off the stage panting. I finally went to a nutritionist. I do what I need to get onstage. My demands are not green M&Ms. It's like this bullshit that people create when people are simply trying to do their job as best they can. It's unfortunate.

Do you think that the line gets blurry sometimes? When Yul Brynner was touring in *The King and I*, he wanted every dressing room painted chocolate brown before he got there.

Good for him. He is walking into an environment that is recognizable and he doesn't have to adjust, it's adjusted to him. He is on the road. It's hard. He is the star of the show and people are paying to come and see him. He has every right to demand everything he wants. He was in show business for how long?

But you get how that could be perceived as green M&Ms.

And you know what? If people want to waste their time with that, I say, "Get a life." This is what we need to get onstage eight shows a week. It is very hard work. It's hard mentally, it's hard physically, it's hard emotionally. This is what we need to keep ourselves in a Zen place. [So if Yul Brynner feels grounded in his brown dressing room] at the Belasco, then when he's at the Fox in St. Louis, [paint can help him feel like] he's at the Belasco. It helps focus. It's about craft.

Back to *The Baker's Wife*. What do you remember about Stephen Schwartz?

Stephen did his best, but you know, it was doomed. But he's had great success ever since.

Except *Rags*.

He offered me *Rags* but I said, "That would be pushing it." That would have been three. *Baker's Wife, Working, Rags*.

Well, speaking of *Working*, that was your next musical on Broadway. In your book, you gave it like two paragraphs.

It only lasted two paragraphs. It was horrible. After the failure of *The Baker's Wife*, I was asked to replace two people in Mamet's *The Water Engine* down at the Public Theater and it closed prematurely. So I called Stephen and said, "You got anything in *Working*?" So, Stephen kind of made up a part for me.

Well, that explains a lot. I had always wondered why they gave you a non-singing role.

Because I came into that cast late. It was already written. There were great relationships formed in that show. It was a great idea. It just didn't work as a show. We all went through a brutal time because there was no clear concept. I remember when the shit hit the fan and the producers came to the actors to ask them to take a pay cut. I was the only one that said, "No." We had just been asked that question in *The Baker's Wife*. I said to the company, "Our salaries will not keep this show open." I was chastised. For a lot of these people, it was their first Broadway show and they were not happy with the fact. I think it had to be unanimous. But I saw entire sets of orchestrations, costumes, sets go out the window. I saw how a musical can go from $500,000 to $750,000 to a million. You can't ask actors to sacrifice their salary. We are not making that much money to start off with! We're the lowest man on the totem pole. Figure out how to make it work or close it. It is so difficult to know a hit from a flop. It's that ethereal area. If it's bad material, you absolutely know it's going to be a flop but we had great songwriters and we had a great script. We had Studs Terkel's words, but it didn't work. That closed too, so that season, man, boom, down the drain, two shows back to back. I have been in more flops, haven't I? [laughs] I think whenever an audience reads a bad review they know I'm good!

LuPone's headshot from the early 1970s. (Photofest)

Your career is a bit of an anomaly in that you have had great success and yet some pretty bad reviews. But you keep coming back for more.

I have to. I got a big mortgage! I've never understood any of that. I'm not a critics' darling. It's broken my heart. I don't understand what makes a critics' darling, It's never easy to accept that one is not accepted. And I am not accepted. And you know, I was born to be on the stage and *there* is where the major push back is. I go on a TV show and they act like I'm Dame Sybil Thorndike! What the fuck? Where I belong I'm being kicked in the teeth and where I don't necessarily belong they think Laurence Olivier just walked on the set! It's bizarre. I think I should give up the musical stage and go on TV!

Well, your next musical ran. *Evita*. You said that when you got the call telling you that you'd been cast, you cried and they were not tears of joy.

I was supposed to do *The Woods* with David Mamet at the Public. I had made a promise. I had forged a relationship professionally and personally with David and I wanted to protect that. I didn't have the courage to tell him. I was so freaked out. And the hype was pretty intense. It was scary because so much was expected of me even before I started rehearsal.

You said that you heard the score and you thought, "The man who wrote this hates women."

Oh, and I still do. It's not in comfortable keys for a soprano. It's passaggio, the weakest notes. It can't be sung lyrically. It has to be sung with balls under it. I hemorrhaged my vocal chords.

Before it opened in Los Angeles, what was the process of rehearsing it and finding it?

I was in a state of absolute fear. It was a reproduction [of the London staging]. We weren't discovering it. I mean, the famous story for me was [theatrical photographer] Martha Swope telling me to put my arms in "this" [demonstrates position] and I snapped, "I don't do that, I do this" [arms thrust straight up,] and that's how that gesture was born. I was tired of people telling me what Elaine Paige did. Also, [director] Hal Prince would impose stuff on me. We didn't sit down and discuss the scenes. We were given blocking. "This is where the costume changes are, blah, blah, blah." So, it was absorbing all of that and then going to LA and playing it. That's where the work took place, really. The work took place in performance and you don't ever want to do that. You want to do the work in rehearsal.

Now, I'm not asking you to bash Hal Prince but your director is supposed to be helping you with that.

I'll tell you the problem with musicals: the actors are never given time in the scenes. There's too much to accomplish in too short a period of time. You're generally given four weeks. And that was a big show. The only time I ever sat down and investigated a role was with *Gypsy*. I can't fault Hal for not rehearsing us that way. It's just not done. I hope that the next musical I do, if there's a strong book, I have the power to say, "We're going to take time around a table." In *Les Miz*—and I missed all of it because I joined the cast late [she was shooting]—apparently there were six weeks of animal exercises. I couldn't believe it when I heard that! That's the Royal Shakespeare Company trying to discover their miserable parts.

It seems incredibly shortsighted given what the product needs to be. I guess the conventional wisdom is that you cast good actors who will figure it out.

But if you have a piece like *Evita*, which is expositional, you need to discuss how you are going to connect the dots. It's different in a play like *Anything Goes* where it's really only one-liners and then great Cole Porter music. *Evita* was a brand-new style. *Evita* was a modern opera on a Broadway stage. Why aren't you rehearsing the scenes? If I ever do another musical, I won't let that happen.

Is that really something that runs through your head?

Sure. I may never work again. I always say those things.

OK, but how much do you mean them?

What actor doesn't? It is sad. And you know, I'm holding on for dear life.

You said of *Evita*, "The worst experience of my life."

Yeah, until that point.

You'd gone through *The Baker's Wife*.

Yeah, but *The Baker's Wife* was different. I mean, I came into a show that was failing and it just got worse and worse. But this was emotionally bad. I was alone. I had terrible stage management. No support. I walked onstage and I thought I was going to just perish. It was so incredibly difficult.

Once you opened *Evita*, got past the review period, had Tony Awards, you didn't feel like you could settle into a run?

Couldn't. Vocally couldn't. The only time I could was when I went down to Australia. I still had to watch out but the pressure was off. In New York, I couldn't hang with the company, I couldn't go out. I couldn't do anything. I literally shut my mouth and went home. And then there was dissension backstage. Terri Klausner was my alternate and was nipping at my heels. She set up a little competition between the two of us and stage management did not control it. In San Francisco, when they put her good notices up on the board next to my bad notices? That should never have happened. I called stage management and all they did was placate me. They didn't take the notices down or reprimand the company. I went out that night and got drunk with [company member] Sal Mistretta and [hair and makeup designer] Richard Allen, and threw up all over a car. I was so devastated.

Was Andrew Lloyd Webber around at all during rehearsals?

No, no, Andrew was not. He wasn't Andrew Lloyd Webber at that point. They [Webber and Rice] came in at the end and gave notes. Tim Rice told me to do what Elaine Paige did and I was like, "Shut the fuck up. I'm not imitating. That's not the way I was trained. I'm a living, breathing actor, if you don't mind." But he and Elaine were close at the time. But no, I did not see them. Andrew was really around in everybody's space, to the detriment of the production, in *Sunset Boulevard* because he was the composer and the producer.

Do you have recollections of working with Hal?

No, and that says something about the totality of my fear and it says something about how he approached direction.

When you say, "It speaks to the totality of your fear," what do you mean?

I did what I could, but I was in a state of utter panic from the first day of rehearsal. I'm fearless onstage. I'm scared out of my mind in life, but I'm fearless onstage. I never, ever imagined that that would be the place where I was the most frightened—setting foot onstage. Listen, I knew that I could act the shit out of that part. I wrung a laugh out of the first act and I made them cry in the second. I knew exactly what I was doing. But I couldn't sing it and it's sung-through. So I couldn't do that part. Every day, I went onstage in absolute terror, even after the Tony. That's why it was the worst experience of my life.

You've been singing "Don't Cry for Me Argentina" ever since. Given all of the crap that you went through during that show, are you able to totally separate that out when you sing the song?

Oh sure; I loved playing the part. Don't get me wrong. When you have a great part like that, there's nothing better. There were highs onstage, believe me. But every night it was, "fuck here comes that D!" But "Rainbow High"—when I did that well, that was brilliant. Not me—Hal's staging and *it*. Forget about it. I've never done another number like that.

I still don't understand what "Don't Cry for me Argentina" is about.

You know it's taken me forever to figure out that song. The song is, "I'm dressed up to the nines, but I'm still one of you, so don't cry for me, I haven't left." But where does "don't cry" come in? Because they're not crying. They're going "Evita, Evita, Evita!" There was never anybody onstage going, "boohoo, she's left us." Whatever, you make it work. You're given material. You make it work.

So you left after twenty-one months and the phone should have been ringing off the hook but it wasn't. What went through your head at the time?

I was so depressed that I wasn't getting hired. I've never been the girl that one show built on another—ever, ever, ever. After *Evita*, there was nothing for years.

Well, it took three years but you got *Oliver!* You had the original director doing the original direction, the original set, the original costume designs. Ron Moody as Fagin. Yet it flopped.

I don't know why it closed. They did something weird with marketing, I think. We were devastated. The director, Peter Coe, was a problem. First day of rehearsal, Oliver was fired. That's what started it. And he said to a chorus kid, "I remember the woman that played your part twenty years ago." And we were all like, "Yeah, well, so? What does that mean?" It was a re-creation and we were handed our blocking. We weren't allowed to rehearse.

Years later you admitted to walking off with your entire wardrobe.

I did! I [since] got rid of all my costumes. The only costumes I have left are the Australian Buenos Aires dress and two costumes from *Sunset Boulevard*.

Did you collect them for sentiment?

No, they were just cool-looking things. I still have the Ethel Merman jewels from *Happy Hunting*.

Where did you get those?

[During *Evita*, costume supervisor] Adelaide Laurino came to me with this velvet platter right before I was making an entrance and on it were these sparkling jewels. "These were Ethel Merman's in *Happy Hunting*. You're going to wear them in the charity concert." Gorgeous! When I left, I thought, "I'm taking these with me because they're not going to pass that information to the next girl and these are going to get lost." We don't protect that stuff. I remember when I had on Julie Christie's corset from *Uncle Vanya* and I had on Rosemary Harris's dress from *School for Scandal* and I was playing the same part. I knew, "This means something. This imbues me with them." We don't protect that any more and that's why I steal costumes. I have all of my Paul Huntley wigs except for one.

Where do you keep them?

In a closet built for those wigs.

Do you . . . ? This is a stupid question.

No, I don't put them on.

No, I was going to say, do you visit them?

I do, I go look at them. Paul is a master. Every one but my Reno Sweeney wig.

Did you at least enjoy playing in *Oliver*?

I loved it! I had a ball. I came up with a better way to die. They wanted me to slide down my ass down the stairs and I said, "Feet first? Really?" I came up with a roll down the stairs, so at least I was allowed to do that.

Legend has it that Cameron Mackintosh sees you in the costume . . .

And says, "You'd be perfect for a role in *Les Miz*."

And you hear that and you think?

"Yippee!" I finally found some guy that's going to give me my next part. I should have called my agent. I got screwed. I came home $25,000 in debt. When I found out I wasn't making what they promised me? Oooh, I got pissed off. The other thing that burns my ass about that particular experience was that I was not invited to participate in the ten-year anniversary—not even invited to sit in the audience. The twentieth, I wasn't invited either. Then they invited me to celebrate *Les Miz* being the longest-running musical. *Les Miz* now out-ran *Cats* and they flew me over there and I came out and sang three bars: "I dreamed a dream of time gone by, when hope was high and life worth living," I walked off and Elaine Paige sang all of "Memory." I thought, "They flew me all this way to open for Elaine Paige?"

But contracts and reunions aside . . .

I loved it. I loved being in London. I loved that company. I love the British companies. There's a way that they talk to their directors that I appreciate that Americans don't do. They really have a communication. We more-or-less do what we're told. They question and have dialogue. I was in a great house in Hampstead Heath. I had a ball. I was so thrilled to be a member of the Royal Shakespeare Company. I felt that all the training at Juilliard—it just all came together in that company, in that environment. I didn't do it in New York because the deal was rotten and I couldn't believe that Cameron was offering it. But I had said to him two weeks after we opened at the Barbican that I couldn't do this in New York because I knew that this was my company. He said, "The part's too small?" I said, "No, it's not that. It's that this is my experience."

Not to discount what you're saying, but to go back to New York in a supporting role, when you're still at the peak of your powers could have been strategically not great.

Or great and I blew it. I mean, I've always questioned my decision. Always questioned it. But I think I would have been upset seeing how Trevor would lay on other actors the performances that I watched being created. People think [I didn't do it because] something went wrong. Nothing went down. It was a magical time. I would do anything to go back to London in a musical.

You came back from London and . . .

Anything Goes. We had a really great time. It was screamingly funny. You see those jokes coming a mile away and you still laugh. And Jerry Zaks cast it so brilliantly, brilliantly. It was a kick-ass part, great songs. Tony Walton designed a gorgeous set, gorgeous costumes. Howard McGillin [is one of my favorite leading men]. It was a fabulous company until it went bad, and it went bad because there were first-timers and people were entitled.

When the experience is so joyous, how does it turn rancid?

Working at Lincoln Center is a rarified environment. Every dressing room is on stage level, every dressing room has a toilet in it. In the Broadway houses, choruses and dancers are usually on the sixth floor and sharing a bathroom. Your windows are painted shut. [People were not appreciative.] The dancers started getting out of line—deeply out of line, shockingly so. And there was nobody there to—Jerry is not a confrontational kind of guy, and he didn't pull anybody back in line. It got bad. One of the dancers said, "I'm just as important as you are in this show," and in a way he's right, but at the same time he's in the background, his name isn't above the title. So you behave. You fill your function. You have to be happy to be there. If you're not, go someplace else. It was just a few people, but it was enough to change the backstage atmosphere. We had die-hard professionals on this who were shocked. We are lucky that we're doing what we do. We're not digging ditches. We're not going down coal mines. There has to be gratitude, humility, and respect for everybody involved when you're backstage.

Unfortunately, your next show wasn't much happier.

Sunset Boulevard. Well, it was until the shit hit the fan. It totally was. We had a great time in London at first. Great house. Great company. It was when I got my bad reviews. Andrew said he wasn't going to invite any New York critics, and then, of course, he invited them all. Once we moved to the West End the machine started pointing at me to get me out of the part. Backstage everything was fine. Kevin Anderson was a great leading man.

You described feeling undermined by them even before you got on the plane.

Oh, totally. Yeah. I should have quit during negotiations because they were ugly. And there was [so much press that the part was going to] Meryl [Streep], me, Meryl, me, Meryl, me, Meryl. That's when you start to put your foot on the brakes. More confidence, more wisdom, and I would have. I knew something was going on but I insisted on going. And I had to sing in those keys, too, which were not comfortable. It was devastating. But not the performance of it. Not the company. We had such a great time. We had lots of parties. This was a company that loved each other.

How was working with Trevor Nunn as a director?

I love Trevor. I'd like to work with Trevor again. I actually called Trevor for *A Little Night Music*, and he never called me back. Bastard! Trevor's fun. I loved working with Trevor and Bob Avian on this. I loved being on John Napier's set. I loved the way Anthony Powell dressed me. I was having a good time. I didn't necessarily think I was great when I opened. I got really good after I got fired because there was a different energy coming in.

Yeah, then you knew what it was like to be abandoned.

Absolutely right. It informed that part. It was horrible. But it was my second Andrew Lloyd Webber debacle. People say, "Will you ever work with him again?" You've got to be kidding me. That's never going to happen.

I'm going to ask you something that's hard to be objective about. I'm not for a moment suggesting that your dismissal wasn't handled incredibly poorly, but if you are the producer of a $12 million musical in which the leading lady gets bad reviews from the *New York Times*, what should you do? What would have been the appropriate—

Well, I wasn't the only thing that got bad reviews. It had a lot of problems. Andrew would not cut or supply any extra incidental music, so I was left, as were other actors, to have to run up those gigantic stairs. Trevor fought for it and couldn't get it out of him. But he's producer and composer. He has all the power, and he's unreasonable. Of course I was the first one to get reviewed for clumping up the stairs. But it tanked so it wasn't just me. If I was the only thing that got the bad reviews, I would say replace the leading lady. Absolutely. And this leading lady would want to go. Not without getting paid. I mean, I put a lot of time into it. But it wasn't just me. They had complaints about everything. When I did *Master Class* in London, I got a message from my stage manager that the stage managers at *Sunset* wanted me to come to the closing night. I sat through a very boring show. At intermission I said to [conductor] David Caddick, "Were we this boring?" He said, "No, Patti." I said, "Okay, because this sucks." And then when I saw Trevor at the party, I couldn't help it, I had to do it. He was saying how sad it was to be closing and blah, blah, blah, and I said, "Trevor, it was so boring." He looked at me with shock on his face. It was a boring show. I was doing what I could. I don't think I stunk.

But stunk isn't the question. It's Norma Desmond, and you need perfect casting. You were not perfectly cast for it.

No, you're right. I'm perfectly cast to sing it. Therein lies the diff. Glenn made a fabulous Norma Desmond, but she [couldn't sing it]. Yeah, you gotta do what you need to do to save the show. It's like sacrificial lambs. We're talking about Andrew Lloyd Webber who is desperate to have critical success. He wants to be Stephen Sondheim. And it's never his fault. I'm telling you, I saw a scene where he pulled the score from himself. I was in the mezzanine and he was yelling at the creative staff and then pulled the score. I thought, "This is loony bins, he's the producer and he pulled the score from himself." I turned in, I guess, a good performance at Sydmonton [in the workshop]—enough that Andrew offered me the part because I could fuckin' sing it! I think they would have preferred to have had a star. It was ill-fated, Boy. I shouldn't have done it. I should never have been cast. I probably stunk up the stage. I don't know.

You know by the audience response that you didn't stink up the stage. You said . . .

My closing night? Oh, it was intense. It was brilliant. They wouldn't let me sing. I had to turn to the audience and acknowledge them twice before I could start to sing.

What did that feel like, in the moment, given all the shit?

It was a vindication. It was a British farewell.

The restrained British?

Oh no. Uh-uh. I've never seen them restrained. In *Les Miz*—"Braaaavo!!!" That was my favorite thing: Trevor and John told us not to expect anything from the Barbican audience because they do not want to see musicals, they want to see Shakespeare. "Braaaavo!!!!" I'm not kidding you. There were people that came back to see *Sunset Boulevard* twelve or thirteen times.

Right, so you know you didn't stink.

No, I do know I didn't stink. I did get better though, after I got fired. That's the truth. I got much better. But the whole thing missed—direction missed, choreography missed, set missed, costumes did not miss. Casting missed. Everything missed a little bit on that. Kevin was fired. That's not talked about. Kevin was brilliant. Andrew totally disowned the British production. He was starting new with the LA production and they kept saying all these changes were made. Nothing changed except the color of the set. Now what does that tell you about Andrew Lloyd Webber?

You made a point in your book about the fact that Glenn Close never called you.

I just saw her, by the way.

At the Kennedy Center Awards honoring Barbara Cook. How did that go?

Well, I worried about it. I didn't want to see her. You know, you just want to hang out with people you want to see. When we went to the Kennedy Center for rehearsal, I said to my hairdresser and my makeup artist, "I don't want to see Glenn Close. Close the door." Then there was some commotion in the hall. Two doors opened—mine and Glenn's. We locked eyes and I closed the door and thought, "Well, there goes that." Anyway, we did the show. Then, there's a dinner afterwards and my son, Josh, was my escort. I get there and Barbara hasn't taken her seat yet with her date. There's Audra McDonald and Will, Sutton Foster and her brother, Josh and me. I put Josh next to Sutton—boy girl, boy girl—and there's two empty seats right next to me. Who sits down at the table but Glenn right next to me! Oh, fuck!! She didn't do very well [in the show]. She was way off. They're terrible, these things. They don't even give us a sound check. Anyway, she says, "That's the most nerve-wracking thing I've ever been in." I say, "Yeah, it takes minutes off your life. It's the worst." She says, "I'll never do it again." I say, "They're tough." Then all of a sudden she hugs me. She says, "You know what this is for." I say, "I do." She says, "I had nothing to do with it." And poof, it's gone. Get rid of that crap. It's over.

You came home from London and you did *Pal Joey* at Encores!
I couldn't believe the ovation. It was, "Welcome home, Patti."

Did doing another role, another show, sort of put *Sunset* squarely in the past?
No, it took years to put *Sunset* in the past. Years. Because it was an assault, it was napalm. Agent Orange. It's not gone either. You know, those things never go away. The bottom line is, I have never questioned my talent. I know where I belong and that's on the Broadway stage. When these things happen, it's counterproductive to work and you wonder why they happen. Your destiny has created this horrible experience. I love the stage so much and I love what I do; it's an affront.

You're talking about your love for the craft. The obstacles are the business, and those two things have to exist hand-in-hand when you're talking about the Broadway theater. And yet, they are always going to be fighting with each other.
I think if you have really upright, upstanding producers, they don't fight with each other. They support the event. Lincoln Center is a wonderful producer. Robert Whitehead was a wonderful producer. Because they love it as much as you do and they appreciate the effort on everybody's part.

Anything you want to say about the Encores! experience?
Oh, I just love Jack Viertel and the Encores! people. I would do one for them every year. I love being in the City Center building. It's one of my homes. I was with The Acting Company there. I'm just very appreciative. I didn't want to go onstage for anything, but Lonny Price and Walter Bobbie called me and said, "Patti, you'll be with friends." And I realized, "If I have a rough time in this business, the people I shouldn't turn down are my friends."

Your next musical pieces were a series of Sondheims, beginning with *Sweeney Todd* with the New York Philharmonic.
That came out of the blue. I don't go after these mammoth parts. They find me—thank God! I actually auditioned for Bernadette's [Peters] replacement in *Sunday in the Park* and I didn't get cast and I was brokenhearted. Then they asked me to do The Witch in *Into the Woods*, and I wanted to play Cinderella. They let me audition and then they called me up and said, "We still want you to play The Witch." Negotiations broke down, and then Betty [Buckley] was hired and fired, and then Bernadette got everything.

You weren't interested in The Witch?
Don't I always play the witch? That could have been a big mistake, but then I did *Anything Goes*. Welz Kauffman [at the New York Philharmonic and then the Ravinia Festival] is really the guy responsible for me doing all of the Sondheim because I don't know what Steve thinks of me. I really don't. I don't think I'm one of his favorites. I would have done something

much sooner if I had been. It was Welz's idea [to cast me in *Sweeney Todd*]. I said, "Are you kidding? I'll do it in a heartbeat" because it was Broadway, opera and symphony all rolled into one. I felt like the quintessential New Yorker. I never in a million years thought I was going to do Nellie Lovett. Ever, ever, ever. I was scared to death when I made my entrance. It's the New York Philharmonic! You have to rise up to that standard. It's huge. You're playing with one of the three best orchestras in the world. And it's Stephen Sondheim. You can't mess up. It has to be the best you've got. It was a benchmark in my career. The two great creators that have shaped my abilities are David Mamet and Stephen Sondheim. They raise the bar for me. I have to work hard and comprehend much to be good.

It is a surprise for me to hear you say you don't know what Sondheim thinks of you.
He's a tough nut to crack. But he's been a great teacher. He's pointed out flaws of mine that were necessary to correct that I wasn't aware of.

What kinds of flaws are you talking about?
Swooping.

You hadn't heard that one before?
Not swooping. He is the first person that brought it up to me. I didn't know I was swooping. Swooping is fear. Swooping is not having the guts to hit the note dead on. "Will I be sharp? Will I be flat?" It's easier to swoop up to it. But I had never heard that before, and I didn't know I was swooping.

You also have been told about . . .
Diction. Rambling. Rushing. Those are notes that I have gotten my entire career. The diction is laziness. I think those of us that rush onstage either haven't invested in the material or you don't trust the playwright. You don't trust what you're saying so you rush. Those times where I have not been precise in my speech can also be those times I was not secure in what I was saying. I didn't understand it or I didn't feel like saying it. I get that note all the time still. I got it in [*The Rise and Fall of the City of*] *Mahagonny*. I had the greatest répétiteur. Nobody would go to her but me because opera singers apparently don't like répétiteurs. But I went, "give me more!" because I'd never had a répétiteur before. "Patti, you're flat." "I am?" "Millions of singers are flat." "Well, how do I not get flat?" "Hit the note." She was so brilliant. And she gave me diction. [But when I was doing] *The Woods*, and Frank Rich said that I was over-enunciating. I wanted to say, "All of you just fucking bite me." Over-enunciating. They're never happy. Sometimes it's bad sound mixing. I got the biggest complaints [during *Anything Goes*], but I'm sorry, that's bad fucking mixing. I've worked with great sound designers, and I'm lucky. It's the mixers you got to watch out for.

Given that you can't hear yourself, what are you counting on for feedback?
If it's a really good house, you know. You can hear it. If it's a lousy house, then you've got to trust them. The guy that I use all the time on my concert work said that the more technically advanced they become, the less technically proficient the mixers are becoming. In *Passion*, we had our final dress rehearsal/camera technical. First time onstage after ten days' rehearsal. Steve made a beeline for me. I can't remember everything that he said, except in my head I thought, "Anybody with less experience than I have would turn their Equity card in." It was an assault, a barrage. All I heard was "monotonous mush, monotonous mush, monotonous mush." I have a picture [of that moment] on my piano and on the back of it is written, "Stephen Sondheim's yelling at me."

With Michael Cerveris, making the dark *Sweeney Todd* even darker. (Paul Kolnik)

I cannot fathom how that doesn't turn you into a puddle on the floor.

It did. I went to my dresser, I went to my conductor, but you know who gave me the best note? The sound mixer! "You know, when you get emotional, Patti, people can't understand you." I went, "Thank you! Thank you! I get it now." Next day we filmed it. I performed it. He [Sondheim] came into my dressing room, and he said, "Well, it's the difference between night and day."

What did you actually do?

Committed more and when I got emotional, made sure the words came out as opposed to [*talking and crying*]. It's difficult when you don't know what the problem is and people are telling you that they can't understand you but they're not any more specific. She was specific. I got it.

Back to *Sweeney* . . .

I really felt I had achieved some sort of pinnacle doing *Sweeney Todd*, my first Sondheim role, my first experience with the New York Philharmonic. And then, of course, parlaying that into the John Doyle production, and I thank God I wanted to play the tuba to hang out with boys in high school [LuPone played tuba onstage]. That experience was extraordinary. Our stage manager likened us to a band. It was a relatively dangerous production. Everybody had to look out for each other. Very tight company. We were just a bunch of oddballs in a fabulous production. I was an East End barkeep. I loved the way I looked. I thought it was wild and sexy. I loved staring down the audience at the very beginning and I loved looking at their faces during the show. They were watching a horror movie. It was the slasher musical. And there were kids in the audience, which was great. I called Steve one night, and I said, "The theater is not dead: there are kids in the audience!" It was devastating to me when we lost [the Tony for] Best Revival. I saw the writing on the wall when they sat us in our seats, on the sides. My Sicilian instinct went, "We're done for." But oh, my God, we had a ball on that production.

At that point, you'd been through the Tonys many times but this was your first nomination in the period when a nomination means appearances all month long.

Bothered me. It all bothers me. It's too much. I wish it was a small community again. I wish the Tonys were not on TV. I wish it were in a ballroom. I wish it were about the excellence of theater. And I wish they didn't give out individual awards but celebrated the five people nominated. It's a ridiculous competition now. And I don't know what it proves. It's nice to have a Tony, but ultimately—Sammy Williams said that after *Chorus Line* he went out to LA to do an audition and the guy said, "Your Tony doesn't mean anything out here." I think it probably means even less now. If that's the case, take it back to what it initially meant: excellence in the theater. There's a game going on and it has nothing to do with talent. It's disheartening.

When you discount them that way, then what does it mean when you win one?

Everything. I am a massive contradiction. It means everything when you win it! When you lose it, it's a piece of crap. Everybody wants to win. It is an honor to be nominated but once you're nominated, you want to win. You want validation. It helps your show. You lose, and it's like, "Fuck, man, when's closing night?"

In *Anything Goes*, your not winning didn't change a thing.

But it won Best Revival. I was robbed.

Did you see Joanna Gleason [in *Into the Woods*, who won]?

Yep. I loved her in it. That's a supporting part. It's not a leading lady.

During your run in *Sweeney*, on your vacation, you did *Gypsy* at the Ravinia Festival, which led directly to doing *Gypsy* at Encores! and then on Broadway.

This was extraordinary. The bad experiences I had at the beginning of my career probably trained me for the ones that I'm having now. It's not that it's time to be rewarded. No. I learned lessons along the way that led me to these experiences. *Gypsy* was a rarified environment. That entire cast never missed a performance. On Broadway there are now those stupid personal days that they give the chorus and the dancers. Personal day? Get it done on your day off. Sign a contract for eight a week and show up for eight a week. That's the drill. That's the hard story of Broadway. Nobody missed unless they were truly sick in *Gypsy* because Arthur did something so extraordinary and gave ownership to everybody in that play. They were part of the show. He rehearsed the nucleus so that we all knew each other, we knew these characters, we knew the people, we knew the actors, and then when the chorus came in Arthur gave every last person an important responsibility. Everybody was happy to be there and we had a ball. That's one of the best companies I've ever been in just because of the sheer dedication and goodwill backstage. The crew loved the cast and the cast loved the crew. It was unbelievable. And I was sick a lot of it. Laura Benanti and I got sick immediately in that theater and both of us were sick for two months. Then I hit the wall about three months into the run. That's when I went to the nutritionist, and I ended stronger than I started. Oh, the energy I needed.

In his book, Arthur Laurents describes being so excited to get to rehearsal every day and that it was as stimulating to him as creating something new. He wasn't restaging anything.

At one point in the rehearsal, I said, "Arthur, was this done in the other production?" He said, "Patti, nothing in this production has ever been done before." And that was a great gift he gave to us. We worked every day because I didn't understand "Rose's Turn." That was just my block. I'm not the sharpest tack in the box. It takes me a long time to learn stuff and if I get stuck, I'm stuck for a long a time. I didn't get the choreography. I didn't get why she was stripping. I thought if, in fact, she's trying to show Gypsy that she is as good as her, she'd be doing cartwheels. She would be doing June's act because that's what she created, not the stripping. I didn't understand it. And they let me forgo the approved choreography because it made no sense on my body. I didn't understand the shimmy or her skipping across the stage. But Arthur worked with me every single day until I could do it. That's great confidence. It's also a great desire to rehearse on Arthur's part. He didn't say, "You figure it out." He said, "Let's break it down. I'll be here." I thought my "Rose's Turn" was so raw. I thought it's the ultimate destruction and rebirth, and that's how I read it. That's how I had to figure out how to play it. That's not the way it's been done before. I mean every "Rose's Turn" is going to be different, but he really allowed it to be not just a number.

I don't think you can say that it was ever just a number. It's a breakdown.

But if you're stuck with that choreography, you're unbelievably limited. It's really choreographed within an inch of its life—the approved choreography—what Ethel did. And if you're stuck with that, then it only gives you one option. And it didn't sit on me. I tried it. I did it at Ravinia.

Doing *Gypsy* . . .

It's a quintessential, American showbiz story. It's fantastic. It's a great musical. Just listen to that overture. That's another thing that's really upsetting me: they're putting the orchestra in different buildings instead of the pit. One of the greatest things in musicals is having that sound come out of the basement of a theater and straight up to the rafters of a house. I swear to God if I ever do another musical, I will insist that the orchestra's in the pit. They can't be upstairs on the ninth floor.

There's a story that both you and Arthur tell in your respective books about the fact that the *New York Times* review at City Center was not strong for you and that on opening night on Broadway Arthur had gotten wind of the rave *Times* review and came into your dressing room before the show and told you.

I was freaked out. I thought he was going to tell me something bad. I thought, "Not now," in my head. I was going, "Not now, Arthur, not now. I got to go out and do this." He had tears in his eyes. And what do you say to a man who's ninety years old? "Get out of my dressing room?" No. I would have to swallow it. And then when he said it was a rave, I just went "phew." I don't think he would have told me if it wasn't but I didn't know.

How did you feel?

Now I can play the part. Now I can do my run. I can let go. These guys have invested how much money in this? And if I get another bad review, that could go down the drain for these people. The revival was pretty much too soon after the last one.

Did you see that, by the way?

No. For a reason.

The reason being?

Sam [Mendes] asked me to play that part.

And?

I didn't, did I?

Well, no, but why didn't you?

That's a good question. I wrote him a letter and got a really cold answer back.

You wrote him a letter saying?

"What happened? You took me out and offered me this role." And his letter said, "Well, Arthur wants Bernadette to play it. Sorry, Patti." I have to find out in a newspaper? You haven't got the guts to tell me in person or over the phone? I thought it was really cold. I have the letter in my scrapbook. I wrote him back and said this isn't a question of good or bad, it's a question of right or wrong. Please reconsider. Never heard from him. And then they did that production. Fuck you. And I've never heard from him since. After I got this great review he sent me flowers. "Congratulations on *Gypsy*."

How was Tony night this time?

I was excited because I had won everything else, but you never know what's going to happen at Tony time. And it had been a long time. I'd been nominated and hadn't won. I was relieved and so happy. And *Gypsy* won, Laura won and Boyd won, and Arthur didn't, which was insane. That one was a relief. The *Evita* one was, "Goddammit, I should have, man. It's the fucking hardest part that's come down the pike in ten years at least!" And *Gypsy* was, "Oh, thank God." But the Tonys are a pain in the ass. It wouldn't be such a nightmare if they gave us the Sunday off, and we didn't have to get up at 8:00, for a 9:30 rehearsal, in full makeup no less, and then have to wait 'til 3:00 to perform. It's exhausting. And then you lose.

But even if you lose, your show performs a number and that helps box office . . .

Does it? The only people that watch the Tonys are the people that go to the theater and they've seen the shows already.

After *Gypsy* in that same calendar year, you were back on the boards in *Women on the Verge of a Nervous Breakdown*.

Oh, I loved it. I loved the movie. I love Pedro Almodóvar. I wish I had been young enough to play Pepa. That was a great company, too, but we had a travesty of a leading lady [Sherie

Rene Scott]. I thought it was great. If we had had time for us to learn how to play the piece it would have been better. I was happy to be a part of it. And I was really happy in the part. It didn't work, but you know what? I would work with those guys in a minute again.

After *Gypsy*, was it a choice to take on a supporting part and not have to carry the weight of the show?

Never. I always want to be the leading lady. It was the part that was offered to me. It was the only one I could play. But that doesn't mean I don't know how to be an ensemble character.

You have said of yourself, "I'm not very ambitious." What does that mean?

I'm not. I don't go pursuing—I don't read *Variety*. I don't read *Backstage*. I don't know what the next thing is. I don't even know what's on Broadway now.

In 2010, you published *Patti LuPone: A Memoir*. Was writing a book about your life and your career gratifying?

I don't know if the word is gratifying. It was interesting to look back and I'm so glad I did it now when I have the scrapbooks and I can remember stuff. I can't remember anything any more. I have no idea how I'm going to remember lyrics in a couple years. But I enjoyed the process. I enjoyed looking back. I still have a lot of stuff I left out. I wanted to end each chapter with stuff like, "Oh, and this is where Jack Nicholson wanted to fuck me," but I didn't do it.

You have said to me, several times, "If I ever do a musical again." None of us can read the cards, but—

What's going to happen to me? I don't know, baby. I'm worried, too.

What do you want to happen to you?

Maybe there'll be a musical or maybe there'll be television or maybe there'll be more concert work. Hopefully I will work to support my habit.

Do you ever think about your place in the pantheon?

No, I don't. When you're not a big fan of yourself, you don't think in that way. I think I'm a really good person, really good mother, a good wife, a good housekeeper. I'm loyal, I'm trustworthy, I'm generous. I have a big heart. I took the time and sweated the blood to train for an extremely noble craft and I'm proud of that. I don't know half of what I should know. It's all smoke and mirrors. Mamet says, "Dare to live in the area where you do not know what's going on." That's my mantra. I am the scarediest cat you've ever met. Not onstage. It's the safest place I've ever been—I'll ever be—onstage. I'm scared of the dark. I'm scared of something happening to my family. I'm scared of everything. I'm terrorized by the terrorists. But I'm safe onstage. But I know that I don't know half of what I should know for the position I'm in.

BEBE NEUWIRTH

April and May 2008; July 2011

"WHEN PEOPLE COME ONSTAGE THERE'S SOMETHING you get for free," says Bebe Neuwirth, quoting something she learned from Marilu Henner. It's a performer's essence, she explained, what an audience experiences even before the actor does anything. With Neuwirth, if her essence is free, it's some deal. Whether she's *Sweet Charity*'s Nikki, a dance hall hostess ravenous for a buck and a break; Lola in *Damn Yankees*, a professional home wrecker who finds her soft spot; *Chicago*'s Velma Kelly, an unrepentant double murderess; or even an unnamed dancer in shows like *Fosse* and *Dancin'*, when Neuwirth walks on the stage the immediate payout is bountiful. Anticipation builds. It's clear that something is about to happen. Looking at her, there's no mistaking the presence of an intelligent, somewhat cool, hard-edged, predatory champion. She will never mark or phone-it-in, never fake it, and never rest on her laurels. She's positively feline: still, but acutely alert. And ready to pounce.

I thought I knew what to expect when Neuwirth and I met. I was prepared for a tough, well-armed, somewhat serious broad. I couldn't have been more wrong. In person, Neuwirth is just as striking as she is onstage. Her exquisite bone structure and china-white skin are as arresting as the eyes that make direct and unflinching contact with yours. But there's nothing aggressive about Bebe Neuwirth. She is, in fact, unassuming, warm, a little shy, and surprisingly modest (if pressed, she might concede to being "pretty good"). While she is hyper-articulate, she chooses her words very carefully, determined never to be misunderstood. And she laughs loudly and freely. A lot. Not a characteristic I usually associate with someone sporting jet black fingernails.

Bebe Neuwirth was born in 1958 in Princeton, New Jersey, to a painter (her mother) and a mathematician (her father). She started studying ballet at five, but it was at thirteen, when she saw *Pippin* on Broadway, that she instantly identified her calling: she was going to be a Bob Fosse dancer. Amazingly, with no calculation on her part, as if she conjured her career, that's exactly what came to pass. With the exception of her Broadway debut in *A Chorus Line*, and her most recent outing, *The Addams Family*, every single Broadway show Neuwirth has done was either choreographed by Bob Fosse or was a revival of a show Fosse had originally done, bearing his stamp. Even her West End debut, *Kiss of the Spider Woman*, featured dance sequences closely modeled on the style of Jack Cole, Fosse's inspiration. Sure there were major TV and film roles in between shows, most notably a stint on *Cheers* as Dr. Lilith Sternin-Crane, netting Neuwirth a pair of Emmys that share shelf space with her pair of Tonys. But first and foremost, she is a Fosse dancer.

Now, however, in her fifties with a new titanium hip, Neuwirth has been utilizing her considerable skills differently: she is vice chairman of The Actors Fund, where she founded

As Roxie during Neuwirth's triumphant return to *Chicago*. (Paul Kolnik)

The Dancers' Resource, a program designed to help professional dancers coping with injury and work loss. And her performances are shifting gears, too. In 2008, she debuted her first cabaret show, sans dance, on the tiny stage at the intimate Feinstein's at the Regency. There, in song after song, she reinterpreted standards in ways I'd never considered. Sondheim's "Another Hundred People" was not the usual valentine to New York but a neurotic cry of panic.

Martin and Blane's "The Trolley Song" went from a breezy Judy Garland ditty to an urgent, hyper-ventilated, realization that her crush reciprocates. While she was exactly the cerebral, consummate performer I knew her to be, she was constantly surprising. And at the same time unsurprising. Because if I learned one thing about Bebe Neuwirth, it's that preconceived notions of who she is bear only passing resemblance to reality.

You started dancing when you were five. How did that happen?

I wanted to take ballet lessons when I was four because I had been taken to a ballet and I wanted to do that. My mother wanted me to love it but she didn't want me to get bored and she realized that a four-year-old's attention span is quite a bit shorter than a five-year-old's, so she had me wait until I was five. My mother had danced—not professionally, but danced—until she was in her mid 40s. She

> **Bebe Neuwirth**
>
> *A Chorus Line*, National Tour and Broadway 1978
> *Little Me*, Broadway, 1982
> *Dancin'*, Broadway, 1982
> *Upstairs at O'Neals'*, off-Broadway, 1982
> *Sweet Charity*, Broadway, 1986 (Tony Award)
> *Kiss of the Spiderwoman*, West End, 1993
> *Damn Yankees*, Broadway, 1994
> *Pal Joey*, Encores! 1995
> *Chicago* (as Velma), Encores! and Broadway, 1996 (Tony Award)
> *Fosse*, Broadway, 2001
> *Here Lies Jenny*, off-Broadway, 2004
> *Chicago* (as Roxie), Broadway, 2006
> *The Addams Family*, Broadway, 2010
> *Chicago* (as Mama Matron), Broadway, 2014

loved it. Still does. She wanted to make sure that I went to a good school because she went to a terrible school. But let me say that neither my mother nor my father forced it on me. If my brother and I were interested in something, we were given the best opportunity to pursue that.

So you had supportive parents?

Extremely supportive and also wise. They were really young when they had my brother and me. And they were very, very smart about some things with us. I am very grateful to this day.

Did they take you to the theater?

No, not much. I saw *Hair* when I was eleven. No, I was not brought up on musical theater. I still don't have any kind of broad knowledge of it. I didn't see movie musicals. I was not interested in that and I never watched them on TV or anything. To this day I have never seen *The Sound of Music*. Anyway, when I was about thirteen I was sort of subconsciously aware that I was not going to be a professional ballet dancer. It was too painful for me to consciously recognize that because I loved dancing and the ballet so much. I loved performing so much and performance for me was ballet. When I was thirteen, I danced in *Oklahoma!* at the McCarter [Theater]. That was fun. It didn't blow my hair back or anything but it was fun. But then I went to see *Pippin* that summer and that choreography resonated with me. I remember where I was in the theater and I remember feeling that choreography. I could feel it. I knew I could do it. It was like—you know how some people can see a Renoir and it moves them to tears? It doesn't for me. But the Van Gogh moves me to tears. So, like that, this choreography just resonated for me. And when the show was over I was like, "I am going to dance on Broadway and I am going to do that guy's choreography." I had no idea the enormity of what I was saying. I didn't know who Bob Fosse was because, as we earlier learned, I had no idea about musicals. I didn't know he was God. I just knew what I saw and how I felt. There was a shift inside of me of focus. It didn't manifest into anything concrete. Just somewhere inside of me, I wasn't going to be a professional ballet dancer, I was going to be a professional theater dancer.

Was that just a feeling or did you think that you weren't physically right?

It was very difficult for me to admit to myself that I didn't have great turnout, I didn't have a great extension, but there was no consciousness to it. There was pain, but it was subconscious. It was there, but we don't name it. That's what people go sit on a couch for later on.

You said that in watching his choreography, you knew. Was that because you were already so in touch with your body that you knew with certainty that you could do it? I mean you said, "I can do that" as opposed to, "I want to do that."

I guess that's the difference between people who do it and people who don't. I recognized myself. It was like, "I am that." I just had to wait to grow up.

To have that level of clarity so early is a gift.

It is and I never realized it. I remember talking to this girl in high school and she said, "You're so lucky, you know what you want to do!" And I thought, "You don't know what you want to do?" I've always been what I am. I didn't realize how lucky I was. Mind you, when I was born, the doctor who birthed me handed me to my mother and said, "She's a dancer."

So you come out of *Pippin* and have this epiphany. But before you get to follow that dream, your parents make you go to Juilliard.

They weren't stage parents; they were never forcing their will or their taste on me. But education was so important to them, it was absolutely imperative that we went to college. I didn't want to go. Seventeen. I wanted to go to New York and start dancing. I was just waiting to grow up so I could start working.

You started working pretty quickly, though.

I got my first job, to go out on the road with *A Chorus Line* in April of 1978 during what would have been my sophomore year. First I was understudying Sheila and Cassie but the girl who was playing Lois, the ballerina who was cut during the opening, didn't want to do it any more. So I got to do it. Then I played Sheila for nine months, then Cassie for five. I came to Broadway and I played Lois for four months and then I took over the role of Sheila. I was twenty-two and I was the third Broadway Sheila: Kelly Bishop, Kathrynann Wright, me. You have to understand, I still had baby fat, I was so young.

What do you remember?

[Bursts out laughing] I remember that I was doing ballet makeup, putting dots in the corner of my eyes and white bits between the black lines, putting my hair back in a ballet bun. I had been performing in ballet since I was seven and that's what I knew! I didn't know so much it was amazing. What I was doing onstage was really just instinct. I was putting one foot in front of the other. I don't know what I was thinking, I was just doing it. And I loved being onstage. I loved performing in the show.

Did you get to work with Michael Bennett?

Yeah. He coached me on Cassie. He made me cut my hair. He really liked my Sheila so he didn't tell me much. He got a big kick out of me. I realize that in retrospect. This twenty-year-old kid with baby fat, playing the hell out of Sheila, getting all of the laughs, understanding it way beyond her years—that's funny. He gave me a very great compliment which I am not going to tell you.

Too personal?

I am just going to say that he really liked me. Appearances to the contrary, I am not crazy about tooting my own horn. He came out to see the show in Milwaukee and after the show I got called to the office. I went and he told me this really beautiful thing. And then he told me that he wanted to put a belt on me. 'Cause I don't have much of a waist anyway. I'm kind of straight, I don't go in. That plus baby fat . . . "I gotta see your waist. You have to wear a belt." So that was the note. It was for wardrobe not for me. So they made this belt. It was this scrawny little thing. I don't think it worked very well.

You said he got a big kick out of you. Did you get a kick out of him?

Yeah. I liked him a lot. We're different animals. Our dancing was very different. When he was coaching me, it was not the experience I had working with Fosse. When I was working with Fosse, I could feel his body, you know what I mean? Bob Fosse I loved deeply and truly, then and forever. He is, was, and will always be the most important person in my life as an artist. Michael was great and I really liked working with him. It was not on a soul level as it was with Bob. I don't know that Bob was aware that I felt this way, but that's the effect he had on me.

During your year in New York were you auditioning a lot?

Oh yeah. The audition from which I was cast in *A Chorus Line* was my third open call [for that show]. I went to one and was cut after the double pirouette. Then I went again six months later and got cut a little further on. The next time I saw an ad in the trades and it said, "Only those who have not previously auditioned." I went, "Yeah, OK, what time does it start?" Which is a big deal to me. I am usually a little too much by-the-rules as a person. If someone tells me that something is against the law, it's against the law.

Do you consider yourself appropriate?

I am, from time to time, somewhat inappropriate. But I am more frequently misunder-stood. Deeply misunderstood.

In what way?

Here I am, fifty-three, and I am looking back realizing that I have spent a lot of time explain-ing myself to people who have gotten a wrong impression about something. It's very frustrating and it's really bad when people's feelings get hurt. I am phobic about hurting people's feelings. But that's a whole other chapter in *my* book. (laughs) Anyway, here's what I want to say about rules and laws. . . . This might sound weird but if you think about it I think you'll know what I mean. I am half German and half Russian, literally and metaphorically. My father's side is Ger-man, my mother's side is Russian. A generalization you can make about a German way of being is that it's very by-the-rules, very precise, very meticulous. I am also half Russian. Russian is very passionate and huge and romantic and lush. They are sort of diametrically opposed to one an-other. But they both live equally inside of me, so sometimes I have trouble. I dance with great passion but I know *exactly* where I am going. That's actually how I learned. I had one choreog-rapher who was frustrated by it. That was his limitation. He thought I was dancing too cleanly during rehearsal. I said, "I have to learn what it is so that I can let it go." I saw Baryshnikov on-stage once—he completely threw his technique out the window. His focus was not on his tech-nique, it was on expressing and performing. The fact that his technique was crystalline was secondary to his performance. You better believe that he was in class, working meticulously for that technique. I'm no Baryshnikov but that's how I work. I know exactly what the steps are, the specificity. I learned that from Bob. The cleanliness, the specificity and *then* you express via that.

Do you think that the seemingly opposed duality of the combustible and the exacting—that level of discipline matched with creative—is what works for any artist?

People might argue with that. I don't want to say that that's the only way to go, but that's my way to go.

Particularly when you consider a Fosse dancer.

Doing *Sweet Charity* . . . [sings from the song "Big Spender"] "So let me get right to the point/I don't pop my cork for every guy I see . . ." We spent half an hour on that one phrase of movement. And then when it happened onstage and there were eight girls doing that together, it blew the top off of the theater. It was incredible. But you have to know that once we knew exactly what we were doing, he spent a lot of time telling us what we were expressing and feeling. Gwen [Verdon, the star of the original production of *Sweet Charity*], too. Gwen taught us the entire show and Bob directed it. We were eight individual women who were trying to get somebody to dance with us so that we could afford to get a cup of noodles when we got home.

You did *A Chorus Line* and then on your very next show, the 1982 revival of *Little Me*, you got to dance Fosse's choreography. As I understand, Peter Gennaro was staging the show and, without any warning, they brought in Bob Fosse to restage the number "Deep Down Inside." Did that blow you out of the water?

Oh my God!! Now I *loved* Peter Gennaro. He was such a great man and I loved his choreography. I felt terrible. I thought, "How's Peter gonna feel." I didn't know that Peter was one of Bob's dancers. As we learned earlier, I don't know much about musical theater. That was when I learned what a gentleman of the theater Peter was. They wanted to restage the number. It wasn't working and they wanted to do what they had done in the original. Bob came in with one of his old dance captains, John Sharp. Peter Gennaro looked at us—we were all kind of sitting in the house waiting—and he said, "Now you listen to him. He knows." And I thought, "Wow, that is the classiest thing I have ever heard." If I hadn't already loved him . . . My friend Gail Pennington and I were the "Boom Boom" girls in *Little Me*. We heard that Bob went across the street to *Dancin'* and said, "If you need any replacements, you should see these two girls." We closed *Little Me* about a month after we opened and I did get to audition for *Dancin'* and got into the show.

So you were handpicked by Fosse. What did you feel being choreographed by him that first time?

I was beside myself. I just wanted to do it so well and I wanted him to like me. I wanted him to think that I was really good—I don't know beyond that what I was thinking. I remember I went to the original open call for *Dancin'*, before I got *A Chorus Line*. It was non-Equity, at the Broadway theater—600 girls showed up. Who knows how many they would have seen if *The Wiz* didn't have a show that night but as it was, they had to close the doors and take down the sign-in sheet because they had to mop the stage and do a show. Six hundred girls at the open call and he was there. That's a big deal. I got a callback. I'm tooting my own horn now, but come on, a callback when there are 600 girls?

It's a fact, though.

OK. Can you put a little note in the book, "Ms. Neuwirth is not one to toot her own horn. I shall do so in her place."

That's what I'm here for.

I was in the room for the callback. There was Rene Ceballos, Sandahl Bergman. Cynthia Onrubia. Rene just blew my mind. And Sandahl was playing Judy Turner in *A Chorus Line* when I saw it when I was sixteen. There she was and I was like, "holy shit!" I got cut from that but he was so kind. He came right up to you and said, "Thank you very much. Thank you for coming." It was private. And I was like, "Thank *you!*" I was deeply disappointed but I also saw what else was in the room. They were so beautiful. And when I eventually did *Dancin'* [in 1982], I got to do it with Rene.

How long did you do *Dancin'*?
'Til it closed. That was one of the saddest days ever.

When *Fosse* was playing in the late '90s, a lot of those performers were in physical therapy almost more than they were onstage. Did *Dancin'* wreck you guys too?
It didn't wreck me. I never felt—I mean, here I am thirty years later and I've got a pair of titanium hips. When I was doing Fosse's choreography, it felt completely natural to my body. It never felt like, "Oh God, it hurts when I do this"; it just felt like that's what it's supposed to do. "That feels pretty good."

Do you think that dancers are a little more fragile now? Are they different?
There is a certain sense of entitlement that I don't remember so much from when I was auditioning for shows and dancing. Things are different now. Specifically how? I don't know. It may be just an energetic shift. There are so many contest shows in our popular culture and I think that that has a trickle-down effect. Or I should say a seep-down effect because it implies something oozing and bad. It feels different to me than it used to be. Some of that is age and some of it is nostalgia, but I think some of that is real. I know that the generation before me felt that things were different also. And I know that Chita has said that things are vastly different now. Technology changes things. Honestly, some of the dancers have a right to be pissed off now because the show schedules are so brutal. A lot of shows are now doing five shows in three days and that's really not acceptable but we are being forced to accept that. The body doesn't have the time to recover and depending on what you are doing in the show, it's just not healthy. That's reflected in accident reports and injuries and the fact that now there are physical therapists in theaters, in house.

What came after *Dancin'*?
A comedy revue. Martin Charnin's *Upstairs at O'Neals'* [1982]. That taught me a lot. That was very interesting. There was not any fierce dancing. It was a postage-stamp stage.

It's weird that you did it.
It was very weird because it was really something for singers to do and not for dancing musical theater performers. It expanded me as a comedienne. It was still all instinct, I was instinctively funny. Martin Charnin helped bring that out of me and in so doing taught me about comedy itself.

It's interesting to me that you had the confidence to go in for a non-dancing role.
I wasn't thinking in those terms and I have got to say, over the years people have said to me, "Gee you really orchestrated your career well." I swear to you I have never calculated a moment of it. It's been a sort of a Zen, natural, organic progression. When I am working I focus very, very hard on my work. I try very hard and I want to be good. I don't think that I am going to have to do this or that next. I went into this business thinking, "I want to dance for Bob Fosse." That's the whole reason I'm dancing on Broadway. That's the whole deal. I don't even know what *The Most Happy Fella* is about. It's a really stupid thing I've done, but I have

limited myself. People tell me, and I guess it's true, that I have a very strong focus. As a result of that, things come my way. It worked that way for a very long time. Now, looking back at my story so far, I'm really a performer for hire. My baseline, the germination of it all, is a dancer. That's at the core. But I am a dancer who sings, and I act in plays, in musicals, in television, in movies. I do voice-over in cartoons. I do cabaret, I sing with symphonies, I do comedy revues. I am a performer for hire except that I can't tap or play the ukulele. I feel like a vaudevillian. *Upstairs at O'Neals'* was sort of the start of that. The branching out and the sort of, "I guess I can do this, too. I can be funny singing a song onstage, standing perfectly still." That will sound awfully egotistical, in your book.

It won't. I'll cover with footnotes.
"Why is Bebe's chapter so looong? Oh, the footnotes!" Bebe apologizes once again.

Ms. Neuwirth wants the reader to know that any ego that comes across is completely of your own inference.
Bebe Neuwirth, with apologies.

***Upstairs at O'Neals'* happens. And then, in 1986, *Sweet Charity* happens directed by Bob Fosse and Gwen Verdon. How did that come about?**
I got a call from my agent and I went in and auditioned for Bob in a theater. Cy Coleman was there. I had become very friendly with Cy on *Little Me.* I loved Cy, just loved him. He was fantastic. It was just to sing and read. I used to have a very strong sense of whether or not I was going to get a job. I'd never tell you if I was going to get it, but I always knew if I was going to get it or not.

Good trick.
Nothing to it! No, I just had a sense. I read the scene of Nickie's and Bob came up on the stage and gave me a note. I took it, I did it again and he said, "OK, thanks." And I could tell that I didn't do what he really wanted me to do and I was a little bit confused. I was speaking to him as an actress and asking about this moment and the relationship with Charity. I remember him looking at me and it seemed to me that I caught his attention. Not so much what I was saying, but I think the fact that I was saying it. So he let me do it again. He thanked me and I went home. I remember being on 7th Avenue by 50th Street thinking, "Something is wrong here. I know I have this. I know that this is mine but something's in the way." It was weird and very unsettling. My agent called and said, "They are going to call you back to dance but they don't think you're old enough and you might not be tough enough." I was twenty-six. So I toughened myself up. I had this black turtleneck shirt. I pushed up the sleeves and cut the back out and tied it at the waist. And I had trunks and hiked them way up. Up by Columbus Circle there were these people who sold really tacky, long earrings. So I bought those. I didn't cover the circles under my eyes. I've had really bad circles under my eyes since I was a kid. I went in like that, I danced, and I got the role. Working with Bob was beyond words that I could use to describe to you. It was sublime. It was transcendent. As I said, I loved him. I can't claim any kind of close personal relationship with him. I didn't call him "Bobby" like some of the others do. Just, whatever he said, I got it. He was a genius. I don't know how anybody could not get it because he was so clear in his artistic, creative gesture. I mean that physically and metaphorically. I think if you look at any movie or show that Bob directed, you look at the actors, you won't see them doing any better work in anything they've ever done since. And I am including Dustin Hoffman as Lenny Bruce. He's a brilliant actor who has given brilliant performances.

Neuwirth with Debbie Allen and Allison Williams just after bounding across a rooftop in *Sweet Charity*'s "There's Gotta Be Something Better Than This." (Photofest)

None of them were better than that. Liza Minnelli has never been better than that. She's a genius, but she's never been better. Michael York, Roy Scheider? These are great actors. Great performers. And I mean only the highest respect for these people when I say this because I think they are magnificent. But the combination of those people with him—and that was part of the evidence of his brilliance—not his genius but his brilliance.

I'm not getting the distinction between genius and brilliance.
Genius is the thing that is the artist, the creative animal and energy and talent that he is. The brilliance is how it manifests. It's the thing that he does.

It's moving listening to you talk about it.
You're talking to me about—we're not talking about just some job that I did. We're talking about a person—I am a person who is living my life as a performing artist and we're talking about a person who touched my soul and my heart. Bob showed me and taught me who I am as an artist.

What you're talking about is being in the presence of . . .
Greatness. Yes.

Walking with a giant. Giants, if you include Gwen. And really taking that in for what it is.
Yeah. And may I say that Gwen was also a genius. She wasn't just a great dancer; she was beyond, into something else.

Is there a specific memory that you can share about working with Gwen Verdon?
Gwen's images were just so brilliant and do-able. For the "Big Spender" girls, when we were in these different positions [draped over a bar], she said, "You're a broken doll." Let's think about that for a minute. These girls are dolls . . . and they are broken. How did they break? You don't think of those things. You just do it. It's not an intellectual exercise. But if you are person who likes to study this stuff, that's not just a cool phrase, that's genius. Someone who danced for [legendary choreographer] Agnes de Mille in *Oklahoma!* told me that she told this one dancer that she should think of herself as a diseased Christmas ornament! Wow! How can you *not* do it if Agnes de Mille says to you, "Do it again but you're a diseased Christmas ornament!" Gwen also told us—you know, in "Spender," there are a lot of silences. There is all of this still-ness and you are just standing. She said, "You're not just standing. Put it in neutral and rev!" OK! I can do that! I watched the DVD of the Avery Fisher concert [a 1998 all-star *Sweet Charity* benefit performance] just last week.

Did watching it bring back any particular memories?
Oh, yeah, all kinds of feelings. I was doing "Big Spender" next to Chita Rivera. It was wonderful! To perform with Chita and Gwen, to do a scene with Jim Dale, who is such a master at his craft. . . . I can't even put those things into words. It's the ultimate. I feel so blessed that I have been able to work with masters. To be in close proximity of that, let alone work with that, is a blessing for anyone in the arts.

When you danced "All That Jazz" with Chita at the Kennedy Center Honors [in a 1998 tribute to Kander and Ebb], on top of the feelings you just articulated, was it also daunting? When you are dancing your Velma next to *the* Velma, is it scary?
It could be were it not for the fact that Chita's talent is equaled by her generosity and spirit. Chita is not just the remarkable performer that people see; there is her spirit, her humanity, her generosity. Her profound kindness really mitigated any of that "Oh my God!" stuff and if I felt anything like that, it was my problem. And it *was* my problem until I allowed myself to feel what she was expressing and inhabiting. And then I was like, "Oh God, she's even more than what I knew her to be!" When I replaced her in *Kiss of the Spider Woman* in London [in 1992], I went up to the dressing room to see her. I was going to watch her. Not only was she letting me trail her during the whole show, she took me around backstage showing me her track.

Like "This is where I get water?"
Yes, exactly! "Watch yourself when you go up this ladder. There's a shin-buster. It'll always get you." Not only that, when I went up to her dressing room, she said, "I'm writing a list of all

of the things that I know that they don't know." And I thought, "Well, that could be an encyclopedia." It was a list of all of those things that you know when you are in a show that the dance captain doesn't know, the stage manager doesn't know. Only you. She's amazing.

Let's go back to *Sweet Charity*. It was during the run of that show that you started working on *Cheers*, right?

We did the show in Los Angeles and San Francisco and we had four months off before we went to Broadway because Debbie Allen had to finish off her season on *Fame*. During those four months, I did one scene on one episode of *Cheers* and that was that. We start up on Broadway, we open, we're playing for a while and I get a call asking me to come out and do another episode of *Cheers*. It was in my contract that I could take off for television. It was like snow days; you tack it on to the end. So I went out and I did an episode and then I came back. And then maybe a month later they said, "Could you do that again?" Then *Sweet Charity* closed and I was offered *Cheers*. It was a very difficult decision. I deliberated for as long as I could. Television was not ever something that I wanted to do, that I ever considered doing. Movies, maybe, but not really. I was really just thinking about dancing on Broadway. I went to Gwen and Bob for advice. And my parents. Gwen thought that there was no problem. She encouraged me to take it. Bob said that he had faith that I would not be changed by television. It's money and celebrity and fame but I would always remain at heart a person of and from the theater. And he encouraged me to take it for a couple of other reasons.

Do you want to share?

[after a long pause] He told me that making money was not a terrible thing.

Why were you reluctant to say that?

I don't like to talk about money. I don't think it's really polite. People think that just because you worked in television you're wealthy and that's just not the case. Although you do make more in television than in theater.

It's economic reality. And didn't working in TV give you the opportunity to choose more?

Well, that's what I didn't realize. But what I have discovered is that there is a certain cushion that you get. Every now and then you do a big fat commercial comedy film and you get a nice paycheck and that allows you to do *Here Lies Jenny* [Neuwirth's off-Broadway Kurt Weill show]. If you are an artist, you have to balance commerce and art. There was another element that was very strong at this time and it should not go unsaid; in '86 and '87, Broadway was starting to change to a place when leading roles were going to people from TV and film. I thought, "I've been working my way, slow and steady, doing really well. I seem to be talented. People are hiring me. But if they are changing the rules of the game on Broadway and I have an opportunity to be a viable player in that game—that is to say, get some television exposure—maybe I should do this because maybe it will help later." And that's exactly what happened.

Did you move to LA?

I commuted for the first year or so. I sublet from Betty Buckley, actually. Eventually I moved.

And the TV work *did* pay off because you came back from *Cheers* and you were above the title replacing Chita Rivera in *Kiss of the Spider Woman* in London. When you replaced in *A Chorus Line*, you were not a star yet . . .

I wasn't *anything*.

So then, I imagine that you were directed very specifically: "This is where you look to the second balcony. You put your hand on your hip on this line."
Yes.

No intention given.
Yes. "Now the arm goes here."

Going into Aurora in *Spider Woman*, you were the star. Was there more artistic freedom? Did it feel different?
[after a long pause] Yeah, I think there was less of that with Aurora, but at that point I was less likely to chafe under it. The more I respect the person that I am replacing, the more you can learn from those bits of business. You think, "Well, Chita did this" and I am not one to say, "Just because she did it, I am not going to do it." I'm one to say, "She must have done that for a reason. Why was she doing it? She's brilliant. If she chose to do that, there's a reason." And I frequently work from the outside in. So if there's a movement when you are supposed to do this [makes hand gesture], when you say the line, let me do that and see what it does to me inside. There's great value in learning those bits of business. And then at a certain point, you choose if you are going to take that or if it doesn't serve you. Some roles you can do that and some you can't.

And sometimes what works organically on one performer is not what's going to work for the next.
Exactly. That's why I say, "I see what that is and for me it's this [makes a variation on the hand gesture]."

Right after *Spider Woman*, you did Lola in *Damn Yankees*. What was that experience like?
It was a mixed experience. There were some fantastic wonderful things about it and there were some difficult things about it.

When you say "difficult," can you talk about it?
Everybody working on that was extremely talented, but they all had different ways of achieving what they wanted to achieve. Sometimes people all speak the same language and sometimes you speak different languages. There were a lot of different animals in the room and we all spoke different languages. We all thought we could translate but it turns out we were not as good at translating each other's languages as one might hope. So it was a little tricky

You had worked with Victor Garber on *Little Me*.
Yeah, actually Victor and I had less of that kind of situation. That was a very good chemistry, I felt. I hope he feels the same. I think he understood languages that I didn't understand. He got some things that I didn't get. But in terms of getting each other, I think we got each other. I love Victor.

Did Gwen Verdon [the original Lola] see it?
She did. And she was very kind to me. She said I was terrific. I actually think I heard her defending me. We were doing one of the first *Easter Bonnet* shows [a Broadway Cares annual benefit] and I was in a dressing room with Chita Rivera, Gwen Verdon, and Bea Arthur. I thought, "Oh pleeeeease don't be stupid, Bebe. Pleeeease keep your big fat mouth shut. Just sit here and listen and please try to remember everything you hear and learn a little something." Anyway, I heard a conversation [in another dressing room] get real quiet and psychically you

just pick things up. And I heard Gwen go, "Oh, no, she's *terrific!*" and I was like "Thank you! I know exactly what that conversation was." I knew that Gwen had my back.

I'm sad that I can't capture your Gwen Verdon impersonation in print.

It's pretty good, isn't it! My friend was telling this dirty joke and he said, "Angela Lansbury told me this joke" and I was like, "Gwen Verdon told *me* that joke!" Man there is nothing better than Gwen Verdon telling you a dirty joke! Angela Lansbury? Can you imagine? She's fabulous! I got to do an episode of *Law & Order* with her. As an A.D.A. I grilled her on the witness stand. She was playing this grande dame. So in rehearsal, I get to the question and she looks at me and she goes [scrunches her face, flips the bird]. That cracked me up—How fabulous! I was like, "*Wow*! That's the best thing that's ever happened!"

When you are going into a big show like *Damn Yankees*, there's a lot of anticipation and excitement. It must be disappointing to then have the experience be difficult. You had something similar happen with *The Addams Family*.

You know, I loved playing Morticia and I loved *The Addams Family*. It's interesting, though; my costume was a gorgeous dress that profoundly restricted my movements. A good metaphor for my experience of the show. I'd like to just leave it at that.

OK, then back to 1995. After *Damn Yankees*, you did *Pal Joey* at Encores! That experience for you . . .

Was *fantastic!* It was great and everybody was great. It was very, very joyous. It was at City Center. I don't know what it is to me about that theater and that building but I just love it. I am very sensitive to the vibes of a place and sometimes my experience of a place is affected by a vibe. City Center is an architectural gem. The production was just right. I would crouch in the wings and watch Patti LuPone stop the show dead cold. It was really joyful. I walked by her

Exuding the requisite gothic gloom as Morticia in *The Addams Family*. (Joan Marcus)

dressing room once and she was vocalizing or humming. I go, "Hey Patti, would you teach me how to sing." And she says "Sure doll, you teach me how to dance." Fabulous.

And of course, your next Encores! show was *Chicago*, only a year later.

Here's the way it happened. I had actually done *Chicago* at Long Beach Civic Light Opera with Juliet Prowse [in 1992]. Annie [Reinking] had choreographed it. I heard that Juliet and Annie were going to do *Chicago* and I was living in LA and a little depressed at that point. David Gibson and I went to see Chita in her act at UCLA. I was so inspired, she was fantastic. I was only acquainted with her at the time. We went backstage and she was so kind. She asked what I was doing. And I was like, "I don't know. I know that Juliet Prowse and Annie are going to do *Chicago* in Long Beach and I am thinking about calling Barry Brown (the producer down there) and asking if I could understudy the girls. Just so that I could learn the stuff. I just want to learn it." And she said, "Do it! Do it!" She really encouraged me to make the call and to follow that idea. So I called up Barry from my dressing room at *Cheers*. I said, "I'd like to offer my service. You don't even have to pay me. I just want to learn the parts and understudy. I could be an understudy for free." He said, "Funny you should call. Let me call you back about this." He called me back about ten minutes later and said, "How would you like to play Velma?" It turns out—and you'd have to get this story straight from Annie but I think she was a little ambivalent about playing Velma. I think she was more interested in just choreographing. She very happily said, "Great, let her play it and I'll choreograph."

That's crazy! "Hi. I'll do this for free just to learn it?"

It was crazy. And Chita was the catalyst for that to happen. [A couple of years later] somehow I heard—and I don't know how because I never hear what's going on on the street—but somehow I heard that Encores! was going to do *Chicago*. I called Walter [Bobbie, then artistic director of Encores!], who I knew from *Pal Joey*. I said, "I hear that you are doing *Chicago* and I would love to be considered for Velma." And he said, "You're at the top of the list." I thought, "great." Now you are going to think I am psychotic. I really thought he had a list and I was near the top. I didn't think top of the list meant *the top*. So that's how that happened.

Thinking back over the history of Encores!, there have been some great shows with great receptions but nothing at the level of *Chicago*. This thing that was supposed to be a quickie couple of weeks is suddenly so much more.

It was crazy. You know they always say, "Oh, we're going to go to Broadway." And I learned the expression "I'll believe we're going to Broadway when I see the closing notice." I was like, "Yeah, yeah, yeah." I don't read reviews but apparently the reviews were incredible. And then it was like, "No really, this *is* going to go to Broadway."

Let's talk about Ann Reinking. Obviously you had worked with her on *Charity* and she had choreographed in Long Beach, but now . . .

She was my leading lady. We have a very strong connection, she and I. Sometimes you connect to a person and your real life takes awhile to catch up to the depth and profundity of that connection. I think that was the case with Annie and me. There was an immediate connection but we didn't know each other. For me, it's kind of shocking to have a connection but not really know the person. Eventually you get caught up. There is an intimacy that we have when we perform together. I love her deeply and truly. She is a remarkable woman. There are aspects to Annie that I don't think people know. She's somewhat reticent, she doesn't talk about herself, and she doesn't do a lot of publicity. She's one of the deepest, most intelligent people that I know. She's incredibly funny, her humanity, her compassion and empathy are off the charts, and her capacity for kindness is remarkable. She's wise.

How is it to be sharing the stage with your choreographer?

When she changes the choreography in the middle of the show? I used to be a little pissed! I was like, "Annie, we're both supposed to be doing the same choreography. If we do something different, I'm going to look wrong! I'm doing what you told me to do!" It was funny. Nobody dances like her. If there is one thing I learned from her it was just how close to the pit you can dance without getting killed. I have never seen anybody travel the way she travels. We're the same height but her legs are about three inches longer than mine, they just go on and on and on, especially from the knee down. I don't know where those legs came from. I learned how to keep up with her. We just go together. She also acknowledges and respects my feelings toward Bob and his style. I find that there are a lot of times when you know somebody who has worked with Bob and was also loved by Bob, you have an immediate connection. That's how Roger Rees and I connected immediately. We met on *Cheers* and it was like, "Hello, how are you." But it was when we realized that we both worked with Bob and we both loved him that we really connected.

You danced with other Roxies after Ann left the show. Obviously you are trained and you have technique, but it's a different relationship . . .

And I danced with some Roxies who were not dancers. It was very hard. I really had to stop being such a spoiled brat about it and just get over it and know that that's the way it is. The first experience was that of working with a world-class dancer. I mean, no one can fill Annie's shoes. No one can. Unless I was doing it with Chita. But there's nobody living today who could—there are other beautiful, fantastic dancers who would be brilliant to dance with. But everything about Annie and that intimacy that we share, you can't duplicate it. I had to get over it. I remember that there was one woman I was dancing with who was not a dancer. Annie came to see the show and afterwards she took me aside and said, "Don't hold yourself back. Just go ahead. Just do it." It's hard.

Were you trying to blend?

Yeah. And I didn't want it to look like I was showing off and I didn't want it to be infused with anger. Because I was angry that the person wasn't a dancer. I know what it can be and I get angry if things aren't as good as I know that they can be. It turns out the person was lovely. I really, really liked her as a person, and I'd get angry at myself for being angry at her.

One of the things that's of interest to me with *Chicago* is that they are keeping the show running and, in doing that, there have been some questionable artistic choices. We talked before about trying to replicate an opening night performance as closely as possible but with *Chicago*, there are casting choices that make that an impossibility. Some people might say that the Weisslers [*Chicago*'s producers] sell out. If I were running a show on Broadway I might do the same thing because there's an economic reality. But as a lover of this stuff, there's something painful about it to me. What do you think?

There are two sides to this. One is the obvious side. The roles are for trained dancers. But the other side is that these producers really love this show. Obviously it's very good business but they also love the show. I know with all of my heart that they love the show and they want it to stay open because it's great material. There's a way to get your mind around it where you can say, "You know, it partly proves the point of the show when you bring in a big star. There is a subliminal message that comes through." It's an interesting thing. Roger taught me something when we were doing a Shakespeare play together. He said that people can do whatever they want to Shakespeare but ultimately Shakespeare manages to wriggle free. No matter how questionable you may think someone coming in to the show is, the show survives. It is what it is. And sometimes you get *fantastic* people coming in. Sandy Duncan comes in and plays Roxie and you go, "Oh my *God*, that's fantastic! What a great actress and incredible clown she is!"

It's good that you were able to get past the "spoiled brat" thing.
Sometimes I did OK and sometimes I had days that were not so OK.

You stayed, though. And you kept going.
I loved doing that part so much and I loved doing the show so much. I didn't even know it was an exhausting role until about a year and a couple of months into it. The material was so good and absolutely took me through the show. The better the material is, the easier it is to perform. The number "Something Better Than This" from *Sweet Charity* is incredibly aerobic, but it is so well choreographed and it's so musical that just when you think, "*Oh, My God,*" it pulls you through effortlessly to the end.

At the beginning of *Chicago*'s run, after the rave reviews and all of the Encores! excitement, was it a surprise to be quite this big?
I was so stupid. I thought, "We'll probably run eleven months." That's what *Charity* ran. I thought it was brilliant; it wasn't that. I just thought it was too good to last. Our *New York Times* review was on the front page. That's a rare thing. And still I just thought, "it's too good to last." But fifteen years later they are selling out.

When the show opened it was the toast of New York. What was it like to be at the center of that?
Surreal. It's hard for me to take in and get what's happening. Anytime I start to think, "Wow! We're good," I feel like I shouldn't. "Don't get cocky, Neuwirth!'

OK, so let's take your contribution out of it. How was it to have something so huge happening around you?
It's really fun. I think what made it sweet was knowing how good the piece was. I felt like, "the show is the toast of Broadway, it *should* be the toast of Broadway." The attention that the show was getting was warranted. We would have people lined up to get the rush tickets the night before. There were people camped outside of the box office at 3:00 and 4:00 in the morning. It was amazing. And that company! This ensemble was not your everyday, average ensemble of a Broadway show. These were seasoned, extraordinary artists. Nobody auditioned.

Was the experience of winning the Tony different this time than it was the first time?
Yeah. It was an absolute unknown the first time. I didn't have people telling me, "Oh you're gonna win, oh you're gonna win!" the first time. This time everyone was telling me that I was going to win and I was like, "You don't know that. Please, I just want to have a really fun night."

When you get nominated for a Tony Award, in addition to having to do your eight shows a week, you are suddenly caught up in this whirlwind of luncheons and appearances and press. And all of the other awards happen at that same time, too. From what I understand, it can be really dizzying. Is it fun?
Oh my gosh, somebody nominated you for an award, somebody said that your performance is something special. It's incredible! It's wonderful to have the recognition of your peers. And

you look around and think, "Look at the club I'm in! Wow!" That's nice. But you know what, when I got nominated for a Tony for *Sweet Charity*, I happened to be sharing a cab with Bob between events. He was dropping me off at Sardi's for the nominees' luncheon and he said, "Be careful with that." And I got it. He was telling me to be careful with the nomination, to not let it go to my head. Just to stay on my course, to stay focused and do my work. "Be careful with that."

It seems to me that another possible risk is that in all of the craziness you might miss the experience. You're so busy that it's hard to take stock and realize that this is a rarefied time.

That's the story of my life. It's very hard for me to hear, let alone take in and accept, a compliment. It's very hard to let myself have it. I am very self-conscious.

You are very careful about not sounding too self-aggrandizing. When we are talking about these kinds of things, is it a little embarrassing?

Yes. But I also *love* it. It's actually a bit of the shtetl mentality. Tomorrow the pogrom! Yes, I have a Tony Award in my hand but tomorrow the Cossacks could come.

Your next show was *Fosse*. Were you happy during that show?

This is where my ego will come in. I dance the Fosse style very well. I think that there is value in seeing someone dance that style very well. And I feel a bit of an obligation to him. If I can do it, I'll do it so that it's done well. I don't think that you have to have danced for him to do it well. There are plenty of beautiful dancers—I mean Lizzie Parkinson—oh my God, she's gorgeous in that style! She never danced for him. I am not saying that you have to. But as it turns out, I *did* dance for him. I do it well and because of what I feel I owe him as an artist, I feel a little bit of an obligation to disseminate whatever information about his choreography I can, whether I am talking about it or doing it. It's very important because people get dulled down. They think that if you slither around a little bit and do some hip bumps, that's Fosse. I'm here to tell you that is not Fosse. So, if I am in a position where I can, I like to help that cause. I think a lot of other Fosse dancers feel the same way.

After *Fosse* your hip began to give you a lot of trouble, right?

It's so profoundly depressing to be in chronic pain. And honestly, I had it easy compared to what some people in this world walk around with. If you're a dancer and you're in pain, the pain is a constant reminder that you can't dance. And I am a person who can make a living as an actress and a singer and doing voice-over. I can do other performance experiences but it didn't matter.

Did you think for a time that you weren't going to be able to dance again?

I couldn't put that into my head. I couldn't entertain that notion. Maybe it was lurking on the outside, I don't know; I have very finely developed denial skills. About four weeks after my hip replacement, I went to Barry Weissler's office and I asked him if I could come back into *Chicago*. I said, "I'd like to play Roxie."

Where did the idea to do Roxie come from?

I don't know. It just started to germinate somehow.

Was it surreal dancing opposite a character whose every move you know?

I did it with Brenda Braxton and Brenda's Velma is fantastic and entirely different from my Velma. I recognized the blocking but it was just entirely different. I didn't get confused. Except backstage. Sometimes I would hear a cue for a Velma entrance and freeze for a second.

Well, onstage you're Roxie but offstage you're Bebe and Bebe has muscle memory.

Right. I want to come back to something you said about coming back and being able to dance again being a profoundly moving experience. You know, dancers frequently dream about dancing. You dream you do eleven pirouettes or you do this grand jeté, never coming down. I didn't dream of doing a million pirouettes. I dreamt that I was in class and doing a grand plié. That's all I wanted. I had that dream twice. I just wanted to be able to do a grand plié. I didn't dream of a million pirouettes. So when I went back to ballet class the first time after the surgery, I remember doing a grand plié and thinking this really isn't a dream. I am really here this time and it was really moving. It was something.

DONNA MURPHY

September 2008; January, May, and August 2012

DONNA MURPHY IS KNOWN FOR her intense attention to detail. I therefore should not have been surprised that our conversations featured so much of it (down to the day of the week she had a 1981 conversation, for example) that no matter how hard we tried, we could not cover all that we wanted to in our many hours together. The conversations were fantastically detailed and also maddeningly slow. It became very easy to see how Murphy's special gift for deep character analysis could be, for her, both an artistic blessing and a pragmatic curse. Editing and condensing Murphy's words was also a maddening endeavor, because part of really understanding Murphy and what makes her tick is going down the rabbit hole with her as she describes her life's moments. To take away the detail is to take away Murphy's wonderful essence. It's part and parcel with what makes her great.

Donna Murphy was born in 1959 in Queens, the oldest of seven children, and grew up on rural Long Island and in Massachusetts. The performance bug bit early and powerfully, leading Murphy to study at NYU's Tisch School of the Arts. She booked her very first professional audition, to understudy in *They're Playing Our Song* on Broadway. More understudy work followed, along with some featured roles off-Broadway, before Murphy landed her first lead, replacing Betty Buckley in *The Mystery of Edwin Drood*. Her real breakout came, however, with the daffy off-Broadway musical *Song of Singapore*. Murphy received raves but she also experienced her first bout with vocal trouble—a malady that would force her from the show and plague her very publicly until she had throat surgery almost twenty years later.

In 1994, Murphy opened in the career-changing Stephen Sondheim/James Lapine musical *Passion*. As Fosca, a sickly, obsessive, would-be lover, she was indelible. The *New York Times* called her "spellbinding" and Murphy won a shelf full of awards. She has been a star ever since, lauded for each subsequent show: *The King and I, Wonderful Town, LoveMusik, The People in the Picture,* and the Encores! stagings of *Follies* and *Anyone Can Whistle*.

As Tonya Pinkins says of Murphy, "Donna's not going to be making you laugh all night. That's not who she is. She's a very serious person. But she can become Lucille Ball on the stage, and that's what I admire most about her. Her facility as an artist is impeccable." It doesn't come easily for her. But the payoff is bountiful.

When did you start performing?
I knew I wanted to be in the business from a very young age. I played violin, accordion, and piano. I composed music for the orchestra in my elementary school. I was lucky that at that time the public school system had the arts. My teachers were unbelievable. So inspiring.

As Fosca in *Passion*, arguably the most pitiable leading lady in musical theater. (Joan Marcus)

In Massachusetts, at the junior high level, they didn't do musicals and I was like, "What? What do you mean you don't do musicals? Oh no, we can do a musical!" I gathered a bunch of my girlfriends and I said, "We're going to do *The Wizard of Oz*." There was no DVD or VHS but it was airing on television and I had my little tape recorder up against the TV. I taped it, then I wrote it all out by hand. Samuel French had a play version of it and I said, "As long as we don't do either one of these verbatim, if we come up with our own stuff, we can do it." There was a motor going inside of me but it was also nurtured in the public school system and by my parents. When I was applying to colleges, my second choice was NYU to study with Stella Adler because a guy who had graduated three years ahead of me had studied with her. Otherwise I never would have known who she was. He talked about this woman who had changed his life and his whole way of thinking about acting. And he said, "Basically, I'm telling you, you know *nothing!*" That's exactly what she said to us for the first two years. And I left after two years when I got *They're Playing Our Song.*

So you left still knowing nothing?

Thank God I took copious notes. When I got to New York it was all about New York and all about Stella. But I wasn't really mature enough. I wasn't aware that there was *Backstage* and *Show Business.* Before I even started classes, someone in my dorm had told me about an open call for *Hair.* After I sang

Donna Murphy
They're Playing Our Song, Broadway, 1979
The Human Comedy, off-Broadway and Broadway, 1984
A My Name Is Alice, off-Broadway, 1984
The Mystery of Edwin Drood, off-Broadway and Broadway, 1985
Birds of Paradise, off-Broadway, 1987
Privates on Parade, off-Broadway, 1989
Song of Singapore, off-Broadway, 1991
Hello Again, off-Broadway, 1993
Passion, Broadway, 1994 (Tony Award)
The King and I, Broadway, 1996 (Tony Award)
Wonderful Town, Encores! and Broadway, 2000, 2003
Follies, Encores! 2007
LoveMusik, Broadway, 2007
Anyone Can Whistle, Encores!, 2010
The People in the Picture, Broadway, 2011
Into the Woods, off-Broadway, 2012

"Dream Baby" on a Broadway stage, I was thinking, "I can go home! I sang on a Broadway stage with what I now know is called the ghost light. I am really singing for a Broadway director." [Despite promises to the contrary] they never called. And I thought, "Well, that's Broadway for you. That's show business." Turns out the show had closed like two days later!

You say you weren't ready, but obviously the time you spent with Stella Adler did you well.

It was the beginning of a path. It was not the linear path that I thought was supposed to happen. What I meant about not being mature enough—the technique. I didn't get it while I was there. I only worked once for Stella. I was really intimidated because she would say things like, "Why are you all wasting your father's money?" She was very condescending, particularly to the NYU students, who she felt were on a ride. I don't think she really wanted to be teaching us, she just needed the money so she took the NYU affiliation. But I am so glad I took those notes because there was gold in them there hills. She said, "You wanna be middle class? Is that all you want to be able to play?" She was talking about the responsibility of being an artist, of lifting the material, of carrying the world, of the choice to play something higher or lower than what you know, of that being a choice, not just your only option because that's who you are. And it was intimidating. But there was something about being in the presence of the real thing, being eighteen years old and watching how hard she was on people. She was much harder on women than she was on men. I think there was a competitive thing that went on for her. The one time I worked for her—I kept signing up and erasing my name from the list because I thought I wasn't ready—I was doing *In the Boom Boom Room.* I really wanted to do something that had to do with searching for something, someone who was trying to make sense of themselves and had to come up with some emotional stuff. She would sit on a set piece: a throne. Literally, a throne with a big, velvet, purple cushion on it and gilded arms. So she says, "What's next?" And her assistant, Ron, says, "Donna Murphy doing Chrissie from *Boom Boom Room*," and she yells, "*Whores!* Why do they all want to play *whores!* There's Chekhov, there's Shakespeare, there's Marlowe, and you choose the street." Fuck. I've just sabotaged myself. My hair is in this go-go girl ponytail, I am wearing red rain boots and fishnet stockings and lashes. She's just on and on and on. I start shaking like a leaf. I am setting my props and she says, "Look at her, look at her. She *is* a whore. She's whoring herself for the theater." I was in such a state by the time I got up there. "Look at her nerve, look at her nerve." I started putting my props out on the floor and I sat at her feet and I played the whole scene to her. Well, the minute I started playing the scene to her, she started acting. And she was the most incredible scene partner. At one point she slapped me. And at one point I grabbed her by the shoulders. The whole class was applauding. I'm bathed in tears, she's bathed in tears. And she turns to the class and says, "I have nothing to say. The girl's an actress." I went back to my seat and it was completely out of body. I didn't feel good when she said that; I was a basket case. Class finishes and I am just trying to crawl out of there. I am still in the boots and Ron says, "Miss Adler would like to speak with you." And she says, "You! Don't *ever* do that again." And I say, "What . . . " and she says, "Interrupt me when I am speaking. I was telling the class why you need to choose the Juliets, the Beatrices. You'll never choose that because you are afraid of it. You decided to go to the street because it's easier. I now know that someone like you should never do what's easy for you. It may have seemed like I was just pontificating but I was trying to make a point."

You interrupted by starting, by laying out your props?

It all was valid. She was a force. She made a huge impression on me. My sophomore year one of my classes was survival in the theater and it was supposed to be teaching us practical aspects, like headshots and agents, etc. We were assigned to go to an audition and come back and report on the experience. I chose the open call for the swing in *They're Playing Our Song* and I got the job. I did try to continue taking classes while I was rehearsing but my head was, "I'm on Broadway!" It wasn't until six months into being the swing that I was like, "I'm fucking bored." I loved the whole social life of it. I was invited to all of these events and I thought the people were all fantastic. I was getting to watch Lucie Arnaz and Robert Klein every night and see the differences, sit in the pit. I tried to soak it up from every perspective. They asked me to audition to be a cover for Lucie and that was a kind of a rude awakening. They told me that when I sing, I sing like I am one of the best actresses they've ever seen but the scene work was shallow. I didn't know how to do comedy. I did it the way I would have in high school. I didn't know how to bring a full life to it. That's something I'm still working on.

Did you have to work survival jobs?

I never worked a survival job once I started working in the business, but up until *Drood* it was precarious. I did a mishmash of things, but there was never a time where I could relax financially. I was all over the map. I was singing backup with a rock band, I did *A My Name Is Alice, Little Shop*. During that time, I felt that this is what it's like to be in the business. You don't know what's coming next. You just have to keep your eyes and ears open. But I did already have the sense that I didn't want to repeat myself. And I wanted to work. I wanted to keep meeting smart and interesting people in the business.

Your next major New York show was *The Human Comedy* at the New York Shakespeare Festival.

I was the standby for Mary Elizabeth Mastrantonio and a wonderful singer named Caroline Hayden. When it moved to Broadway they said, "We want you to be onstage. It's a waste not having you onstage." I said, "I don't want to do chorus, I don't want to swing. I'll do it if you don't list me as a swing. I just don't want that kind of brand on me. But if you want me to, I'll cover ten people because I want to continue my relationship with Will [director Wilford Leach] and I want to watch the show grow." I loved watching what happened with these new pieces. The good thing is that there was never an understudy situation where I didn't go on. I understudied a lot in my early career. I went on in *Little Shop of Horrors*, in *The Human Comedy* for both roles. In that case, Mary Elizabeth had gone to the Oscars, and her plane was circling to land. I had actually just been hired. I had a bad cold and I remember thinking, "Should I go in?" because I was afraid of getting other people sick. But I showed up at 7:30. I literally walked into the Shakespeare Festival lobby and there was Will Leach with this big shit-eating grin on his face going, "How you doing?" I said, "Not too great. I've got a bad cold. I don't want to shake your hand or anything." And he says, "Well, you're on." I didn't even hear him. "I probably shouldn't sing for a few days but I'll keep learning the role." And he said—now we're in the elevator—"No, you're *on* tonight." "I don't have a costume. What am I gonna do with my hair?" All I remember was that I wore a dress that was Kate Nelligan's from *Plenty* (there was a label inside). My hair wasn't super long as it is now so we could kind of work with it. Adrenaline got me through. I was scared because I was on and I hadn't made all of my choices.

Do you consider yourself very exacting?

Yes, but then, less so. I was just starting to be able to integrate some of the things I had learned with Stella Adler. Because I was mostly understudying and as an understudy, you don't have a real process that's anything like a rehearsal process. You jump on a moving train. You work in a vacuum and then suddenly you have to be part of the whole. That was one of those situations where—bless that company—they were so excited that I was going on. It was an event. I found myself just stepping into that world. I was being buoyed by the presence and commitment and the support of the rest of the company, and being engaged in the story. It went really, really great. Will watched and he came back and said, "See, you don't need any rehearsal. That was your audition for the replacement. And I'd give it to you in a second." That was the nicest thing he could have said. The hard part was the next day. You're the understudy again. But that juiced me up to start working on the other role. When they moved very briefly to Broadway, I think if I hadn't gone on, I might have said "no." But having been on, I had a different level of investment in the show. I had that little taste. When *Drood* came along [*The Mystery of Edwin Drood* in Central Park], which was only maybe a year and a half later, I was expecting to understudy Betty Buckley. Then I was asked if I would look at the Princess Puffer material. They sent me into a room with the musical director for like fifteen minutes. If someone tried to do that to me now, I'd be like, "*Noooo. I need *days* to prepare for this!" The things you did then because you had to and you were not going to miss an opportunity. The next thing I know I get this call saying they want me to understudy Helena and Puffer and be in the chorus. I said, "No, I'm not doing that." "Well, before you make your decision, they also want you to do a reading. Jana Schneider is out of the country so they want you to play Helena." Once I did that I was totally sucked in because I thought it was so great and so fun. I got excited about that role and prepared a lot for that. Then Will [Leach, also the director of *Drood*] came up to me and said, "You just did your audition for the replacement for *this*." It was both magical and very hard for me. I became very good friends with Rob Marshall and John DeLuca during that time. Rob was my dance partner, unfortunately for him because I was not a very good dancer. Those guys still laugh and say, "You were the most miserable woman in that dressing room." I asked, "Was I mean to everyone?" "No, you weren't mean. It's just everyone was sort of buzzing around and you were down at the end in this melodramatic corner that was 'this was not what I wanted to do. I set a goal for myself and I broke my rule.' You'd never know it when you were onstage, because you had a good time." I just was afraid of being branded. I was seeing it happen around me. I remember very early in previews, standing with Judy Kuhn, waiting to make our entrance. The Belvedere Castle was behind us, the moon was up, reflecting on the pond, the wind was blowing my wig. And I thought, "Shut the fuck up, Donna. This is a pretty beautiful place to be." I was part of an incredible cast. Not just great actors but really distinctive performers. George Rose, Betty Buckley, Cleo Laine, Jana Schneider, Jerome Dempsey, Joe Grifasi. So I just said, "Shut up and watch. Learn something. Feel the breeze." It kind of released me. That's when I started getting sassy with George. There is a moment when George tells the audience to close their eyes and out of nowhere, I screamed out in this cockney accent, "Shut your bleeding peepers!" [Author] Rupert Holmes says my character, Flo, came into focus because I finally relaxed. I had such a great time doing that and then the big decision came. Everyone was so excited that it was moving to Broadway. After three weeks of agonizing, I turned it down. That was really hard. I didn't want to undo the goodwill I had established with The Public but I knew I wanted to be doing other things. I know now what I didn't know then which is how lucky I was just to have that opportunity. But I felt like I wasn't going to have a chance to grow and get the process of developing the character. So I said "no" and cried a lot about it. But luckily there was quite a chunk of time between when we closed and when they started to rehearse for Broadway. They called and of-fered me a guarantee of going on for Cleo because she had negotiated twenty-five concert dates. That did it for me. Never say never. If I just stuck by what I thought was a principled decision about not doing chorus anymore, there are so many things that would never have occurred. So many things rolled off of that for me. I went on for Cleo many times. I left the show to stand by for Teresa Stratas [in *Rags*]. Originally it was just to stand by and then they did the old, "Well, there's a small role we'd like for you to play." It was hard for me because Judy [Kuhn] was playing a principal role. Once again I broke my rule because it still felt . . .

At what point were you learning that your rules were irrelevant?
Each time. And I'm still learning it. Life is actually about becoming more adaptable.

The more you plan . . .
Yeah. Yeah. And I know it in much bigger ways than apply to understudying and chorus. Much bigger ways. After three miscarriages, [Darmia] was the child that was meant to be our daughter. But I wouldn't have known that if I hadn't had those other experiences.

You left *Rags* before it opened.
Well, I run into the *Drood* stage manager and he tells me that Betty is leaving to do *Song & Dance*. He went on to say, "Did you know that Will always thought you'd be good as Drood? You should audition." When I went in they didn't recognize me. I had slicked back my hair into a tight ponytail and tucked it under. I was wearing a boy's button-down shirt and a man's vest and some trousers. I flattened what little breasts I had. I had no makeup on and they did not know who I was. I walked in and I heard Will say, "Who is this?" They say, "It's Donna," and he had the sweetest smile on his face. "Well, I guess you're gonna go for it." I was shocked that they cast me but they cast me. They were looking at people like Laurie Beechman, Andrea McArdle, Tovah Feldshuh, and Susan Anton! Anyway, they called and said, "You're the next Drood." So I had to leave *Rags*, which I was sad about. Christine Andreas ended up replacing me. She opened the show in Boston. They got great reviews

and my mother—God love her—"See, if you had stayed with the show, you would have opened it!" And I'm saying, "Mom, I'm on Broadway, in a lead role." "I know but you've been saying you want to do something new." My mother always plays devil's advocate. She's always worried. She's one of the people who always says, "Are you sure you're doing the right thing? Are you sure?" She cares about all of it. She's great.

Jumping forward from *Drood* . . .

After *Drood* I was offered *Birds of Paradise*. I *loved* doing that show. Arthur Laurents directed. That's a book in and of itself! So I had that experience and met some of the dearest friends of my life: Mary Beth Piel, Todd Graff, Barbara Walsh. In *Birds of Paradise* I was a tomboyish character for the bulk of the piece. My agents are submitting me for theater and television and the feedback is, "She's talented but there's something kind of masculine about her." And I'm thinking, "Oh, God, because I played Edwin Drood and now I am playing this tomboy?" I couldn't believe it. So I told my agents to find me something ultra-feminine. I ended up doing this little tiny one-act on 42nd Street where I pranced around in lingerie for most of the piece. Then, all of my pilot auditions were for vixens and pussycats. Isn't that ridiculous? Just the lack of imagination? When I did finally go out to LA for pilot season, I remember being on the plane and thinking, "I am a fairly attractive woman, I am a decent actress, I am young." I got off the plane, I looked around and I thought, "I am ugly, I am old, I don't know how to act!" But I got offered a six-month contract on *Another World*. I did a musical sketch comedy show called *Showing Off* at Paulson's, and I got a lot of attention for it. I was getting recognized as someone to watch. Everything leads to something; that's what you come to trust during tough times. That led to an audition for *Privates on Parade* at the Roundabout. I played a Eurasian woman. That was an amazing experience. I felt like that was my first dramatic role, even though it was comic. It called upon things in me that I hadn't had to do eight times a week. I found that I had a facility for it and I loved it. As I think about it, it was also my first character that had a strain of darkness and pain at the core of her being. I never thought about that before.

At what point did you start meticulously researching? Was it that early?

The seeds were planted by my teachers at Tisch. When I was doing *Portable Pioneer Prairie Show* [regionally in 1984], I was driving them crazy because I wanted to do research about this character. I brought some of that to the choreographer and she didn't want to hear it. She said, "I'm giving you the steps." The director basically accused me of sucking up all of the air in the room because I had a lot of props and I was wanting to make sure they were where they needed to be. He said, "Do you think that people are going to be able to trust you to star in a Broadway show if you can't handle a tech [rehearsal]? You need to move through a tech for the company, not an individual." He had a point there. But it was a stunning moment for me. And I *have* been criticized while starring in a Broadway show for stopping a tech!

In 1991, you did *Song of Singapore* in which you brought so much more to the role than was on the page. What was it like for you?

I definitely drove those people crazy! I think that's on the record. I am making light of this, but that's not why I do it. I can't help myself. To be able to invest and live inside of something is so delicious and makes it so much more interesting. *Song of Singapore* was performed primarily by people who had written the show. [I was cast because] the producers realized they needed an actress for the role of Rose, the singer. My imagination was having a field day. I did research on Amelia Earhart and on a lot of jazz singers from that time. I watched a lot of movies from the period. I had the time of my life. But it was tough for those guys. They had done the show [in Chicago] and in their minds it was working; that's why it was happening in New York. But I'd always said, "We're telling a story, too, so we have to make sense of this on a storytelling level," and that irked them. It was like saying, "It's not enough for the show to work on the level that you think it's working." I didn't view it that way; I was just doing what I do. And it was why I was hired. I loved doing the show, but it was very stressful for a variety of reasons, not the least of which was that I was sharing the stage with guys who felt that I was making it more difficult than it needed to be. They just wanted to have a good time. I know how to have a good time but I need to know I've done the work so that I can have fun.

You told me back then that you were going through major anxiety.

Yeah, it was the first time I really injured myself vocally, too. My cords were as swollen as they could be without popping a node. I did all my own vocal arranging and I used close to four octaves. I was doing these character voices and I didn't really know what I was doing. For the most part it wasn't a problem, but we had no sound monitors onstage so I couldn't hear myself with the band. I didn't even realize what a problem that was but I was screaming to be heard. I got the reviews. You couldn't write better reviews.

So there you are, having gotten the reviews, but still fighting your cast and not feeling healthy.

It was a very bittersweet time. I couldn't really heal. I was on three rounds of antibiotics. I ended up in the emergency room because you can't have that many antibiotics in your system at once and I had an allergic reaction. My eyes and hands blew up during a show. I remember the producers sitting down with my agent and my agent saying, "She doesn't want to pull out, the show means so much to her. But the doctor is saying that she can't do all eight performances each week." The producers said, "Well then we can't sell her as the star we want to sell her as." I remember just crying during these meetings, and writing on pads because I was on vocal rest during the days. I was really trying to be as Zen-like as possible but it was becoming harder and harder because my body was telling me that I had to stop. And I was like, "I can't! This is what's gonna make me a star! I have to keep going or everyone will be so mad at me." None of those are the reasons to keep going. That's not taking care of yourself and not trusting that there is a bigger plan.

I don't know that it's possible to trust that. At that stage of your career, how could you see it as anything other than "If I blow this, how can I have a career?" That's a lot of trust.

I am still working on it! It's happened several times since, mostly driven by the same conflicts. Meaning I have had health issues and have not stopped when I should have stopped. You do learn but sometimes the same lesson needs to be pounded.

What is it that you were supposed to have learned? You are in a business where you, as a leading lady, are going to have to provide a huge amount and your body responds the way it responds.

But what you learn is, "There's no sound monitor? Then we can't do this rehearsal."

OK, so that was *Song of Singapore* but later . . .

With *Wonderful Town* I begged them to take care of certain things before we got into rehearsal and not have such a short pre-production time during which they were going to try to do everything—all the press, the costume fittings. I didn't have a day off. These things all contribute. I got a back injury because I got dropped [in rehearsal] during "Conga" and I couldn't get to a doctor because we didn't have time. Two vertebrae rotated. So I started pounding Aleve, which is a blood thinner. And then I felt like I was catching the flu. I was exhausted so I was vulnerable. I got sick but I wasn't going to miss any rehearsal. That was the mind-set: I couldn't miss. The irony was that I didn't take the time then and it cost us later. I then had a really bad cough and my cords were swollen. Second preview, I have a coughing jag and I hemorrhage my vocal cord. Three or four doctors see me that day and tell me I am out of the show. The first doctor says, "It's over. You can't do the show." And I say, "Today." And he says, "No. You can't do the show. Maybe they can postpone it for a month or two." "No, no, no, that's not happening. They have been waiting for me for years."

But I don't know what you are supposed to have learned that could have prevented any of this.

I could have said, "Let's let go of some of the press." Now I would. [For *People in the Picture*] we started the wig and costume meetings months in advance, because you can't afford to lose me for four hours. Or for me to have to be somewhere at 7:30 AM and then do a full day's rehearsal and then go to a fitting. Almost every lunch break during *Wonderful Town*, I did an interview. You try to protect yourself so at least you have a little reserve. You are starring in a show and it's your responsibility not only to show up with the goods, but to do the press. But there are ways to pace it. There are producers who do take responsibility for that in a better way. It takes time to learn these things. You are in the midst of it and all you care about is the show. During *Wonderful Town* I screamed onstage and hemorrhaged a vocal cord and it never fully healed. I wasn't allowed to talk about it. I went to my doctor three times a week for her to keep her eye on it. I kind of crawled for as long as I could on that contract. It didn't end well. [During my final absence, when I knew I wouldn't be back] I asked if we could advertise that I was out of the show. My name was above the title, people were paying to see me, and we knew I was going to be out. At this point, let them know! I felt so guilty and so horrible, even though it's not something I did on purpose, I still felt responsible.

After those experiences you got a reputation for health-related absence and now being out for a week means something different for you than it does for somebody else. Yet you have to take care of yourself. How do you combat that?

It happened again during *LoveMusik*, I had healed but I re-hemorrhaged during a show. I didn't feel it when it happened but I knew it the minute I came back onstage and started to sing. I thought I might as well move to Russia. I went home and I prayed. After a few days I went back in. After I finished that show, I took some time off, but on Christmas Day that year I choked on a crab cake and re-hemorrhaged. My doctor had been encouraging a laser procedure and in June of 2009, after a lot of research and meeting with doctors, I made a decision to have the laser procedure on that vocal cord. I had to be completely silent for two weeks. I had to go into voice therapy and pray that my voice hadn't changed. It was a scary thing. The disadvantage of waiting that long was that I might not have had trouble during *LoveMusik*, but the advantage was that the technology developed further. It was such a precise procedure. There was a new kind of laser that was being used and the risk of harm was so minimal. So I did that and I am really feeling ready to do an act.

That's a switch! You told me once that you really don't like singing when you are not playing a character.

For years I really didn't want to do it because when I sit onstage as myself, it's not fun. I like the fourth wall, I like being inside of a story. But I was having a couple of really tough years

Wonderful Town brought both a lauded performance and a health struggle that would mar Murphy's reputation for years. (Paul Kolnik)

financially. At this point I need to do some TV and put away some money so that I can relax a little bit and do the theater work I love to do without worrying that my daughter will be provided for. I have been offered a number of things but they have all been at the not-for-profits and I just can't afford to do it. My agents and managers were saying, "That you are struggling financially is ridiculous. We get requests often enough for you to be making a very good living." So I want to put together a concert evening because the venues are interested in booking me and it's also a way to make very good money. It's your own thing and you control it. I'd just like it to happen before I'm too old to sing some of these songs.

The surgery also means that you are walking in to your next shows with a new kind of confidence. Was it a challenge leading a company and feeling like they can't know what to expect of you?
It was horrible. One thing that could never be questioned was my work ethic and that was being questioned. Like I was being cavalier about showing up. Do you know how much agonizing went into my decision not to go to the Drama League to pick up my award [for *Wonderful Town*] so that I could do my show that night? Yet my own producers were saying, "You're making us look bad." My company didn't trust me. It was really, really hard.

Despite all of that trauma, was there room for any joy during *Wonderful Town*?
Yeah, because I would go through periods when I wasn't having trouble and it would be like a reunion with why I was doing the show in the first place. I was on the heels of several

miscarriages and September 11. I wanted to do something that brings joy. When I was not well, it was hard because I was negotiating, but it still was joyful for me. You couldn't do "Conga" and not have a blast. And the people I would meet at the stage door so loved that show and were so appreciative of what we did. That was meaningful to me.

When you did *Wonderful Town* at Encores!, what was it like working with Betty Comden and Adolph Green?

Heavenly. They were there every day, all dressed up. They would leave and go back to their apartments and work. They were always working on stuff. They were so supportive and joyful and Adolph would sing along. Betty or Phyllis [Newman, Green's wife] would nudge him. Very supportive. That show, doing it in nine days, was crazy. It was pretty elaborately staged.

Yet, even within the nine-day limits, the Encores! experience has never been less than a triumph for you in the three that you've done.

I think I have been asked to do some good ones.

Anyone Can Whistle **could have gone either way . . .**

Yeah, but it was a great score, and a really challenging, wacky and out-there character and that's up my alley. And it was Steve [Sondheim]. Angela Lansbury saw me do "Me and My Town" at the Drama League gala honoring her and she came up to me after and said, "Have they called you?" And I said, "Who?" "City Center. They are doing it. It must be you!" She called Steve and told him. I was so happy to be there, even though there was a point where I thought, "Fuck! This is so much more than I am prepared for!" Boy I crammed my research in. A lot of Kay Thompson.

Did you get to talk to Angela about it?

I called Angela and said, "Do I owe you 10 percent?" and she said, "No, *they* owe me!" After the last performance Sutton Foster and Raul Esparza and I were all up in the dressing rooms taking pictures of one another and not wanting it to end. And suddenly the elevator doors open and out walked Angela. We all went, "Oh my God!" and embraced her. I have a picture of the two of us crying. Pretty amazing. She couldn't have been kinder to all of us.

Let's get back on chronology. In 1994 you got to do *Hello Again*.

I was doing *Oliver!* in summer stock with Davy Jones as Fagin, and I get this call from Ira Weitzman for the reading of *Hello Again* by this brilliant composer, Michael John LaChiusa. We did a week-long reading, then they planned a month-long workshop a month later. I had such a delicious time. My eyes were bugging out of my head at the talent of Michael John. I remember coming home from rehearsal and saying, "Shawn [Murphy's husband], if I could work in a rep company with people like this and make just enough money to live as we are living now, I'd be happy." I was so full of joy and creativity and love for my company members. The feeling of connection, the meaning in everything that we were doing because of the way that we discussed the work, the freedom and love with which Gracie [director Graciela Daniele] approached everything—it makes me cry to talk about it because it was so pure. We did this month-long workshop and then they announced that we were going to do a production. It was a very sane, creative, nurturing process, handled and nursed so beautifully. I would do anything for Graciela Daniele. I left the show early because I went into rehearsals on *Passion*.

How did that come about?

My agent called and said, "They want you to come in. It's a new Steve Sondheim/ James Lapine show. Wait, it gets better. The character is a consumptive, nineteenth-century neurotic." I thought, "I can taste it!" "The bad news is they want to see you the day after tomorrow." This was like 6:00 PM and I had rehearsal the next day. They wanted me to learn "I Read" from the show. I called back the next morning and said, "I can't do it. I'm not going to go. I have a sense of what I might be able to do here . . ." because they'd sent me some scenes with the song, "But I can't bring it in tomorrow. I can't suggest this. I have to go for it. Please tell them how much I want to come in, I just—I need some time." And the response was, "Well, hopefully there'll be another casting session." I think because of some of the things I'd been through, I'd grown more trusting of my decisions. Just be clear about why you're making the decision and make your peace with that. Do not attach the decision to what the result is going to be. Then I got a call on Monday saying, "They can see you Thursday." And I wasn't called for rehearsal for two days in a row, so I just immersed myself. I wanted for there to be a kind of purity about her that didn't seem shrouded always in her pain. I could reveal a kind of clarity in this person that seemed so difficult to understand or comprehend and so intolerable to many. "I Read"—the whole character's in that song. The nature of who that woman was, the types of experiences she had, how she saw herself, how self-aware she was of how she was viewed, the rage, the self-pity, and the deep, deep yearning for connection—so many things. How many songs have all those things in it? I could only prepare it and present it, even for an audition, if I could get lost in it.

Were you also working on her physicality?

Oh, yeah. They talked about her having seizures. I didn't have the Internet then. I don't know how I functioned. But I remember doing some research about women who were having hysterical illnesses they created, and it being manifested in their psychological issues. Not that she wasn't really ill. . . . One of the things I thought about was having the flu and then coming out of it, getting better; the first time you get up out of bed, just walking takes so much effort. And I thought about being really hungover, and how every sound hurts, every step is like—like any sensory input is just too much. I had to take things very slow, very slow. I thought about the fact that she probably wasn't somebody who groomed herself daily, so I didn't bathe for a couple of days. I didn't wash my hair. I don't really sweat so it's not like I was stinking up the apartment or anything. I just didn't want to feel fresh. I remember my husband—I was eating breakfast the way that I thought that she would eat, and he said, "I really respect that you're preparing for this, but do I have to have breakfast with Fosca? You don't even have the fricking job!" I would not have been prepared to do *Passion* five years prior. I don't mean necessarily vocally or as an actress, although I do think that's true, but I think—to be strong enough in who I was, to say things during the rehearsal process . . . Steve had only written some of music when we started rehearsal, and part of the reason for doing the workshop, I guess, was to motivate him because he works well under pressure.

And he's writing based on what you're bringing to the table?

Yeah. I guess there is that as well. Not that he knew that these would be the people who would do it ultimately. In my mind I assumed this role is going to Patti LuPone. How is it not going to be Patti LuPone? And I remember when I got the workshop, I was a little anxious about working with James because I'd auditioned for him many times, and he was kind of a cool customer. I remember auditioning for one of the productions of *Merrily We Roll Along* that he directed. I sang "Not a Day Goes By" and he said, "Well, that's not how I imagined it." Now that's not necessarily an insult; at the *Passion* audition, I was in my own kind of zone. I remember Steve saying, "That was very nice."

Is that as good as it gets with him?

He has talked about my audition quite a bit when people have asked him about favorite auditions, so I learned that he felt it was a standout audition. But I do remember he was smiling, and then later when I read about it, he said it made him think, "That's pretty good, what I wrote."

He wasn't effusive at all?

He's not that guy. And I have to say that sometimes I've thought, "Is it me?" Anyway, so we start out with just a few pieces of music—and this is how I learned about how he and James work together. James would write a scene and we would stage it, and Steve would come in and watch. Now I don't know what themes he had going on already in his head, but most of the songs in *Passion*, as I witnessed it, were not written until he saw us play these scenes as scenes. Then he would adapt James's writing and poetry. He talks about it in his book; James is a poet and he wanted to maintain a lot of what James would write and how James said it. He worked hard with the language so he could sacrifice as little—just turns of phrase and communication of thought that he felt were golden. He didn't want to lose that. Steve came to rehearsal and he watched and gave notes. I had never heard a composer give notes like this in my life. Rarely was something just a musical note; it was about this whole life behind the reason why it was a quarter note and not an eighth note, or it was that the tempo would be faster because she was closer to orgasm, and then he was going to pull it back. There was nothing negative about any note that he gave. It was just more information and it was brilliant. I thought, "Oh, my God, I can't wait 'til he gets to me! This is just like manna from heaven." When I was working on it and talking to James about it, I said, "I don't think she's insane. I think she's completely sane. I think she's obsessed and deprived and ill, but I think she's aware. She's manipulative and incredibly intelligent." Steve's notes to me were about wanting things to be more extreme and manic. He would give you the note, and you would do it. We were sitting in a semicircle around the piano, and you would do what he was suggesting. Either he would say, "Right, right," or you would talk about it. It was a dialogue, an exchange. And so I was trying to do what he asked but I felt like I was pushing for something that I didn't feel connected to, which sometimes you have to do. It takes a while to get connected to it because it's not necessarily in your comfort zone or what you would immediately think of. So I'm not saying if you don't feel it right away it's not the right thing for you to do. Sometimes that's exactly what you need to do. But this was making me nervous. I went home that night and I started to cry. I was sure I was going to be fired. I'd been fired from a television job, so once you've been fired, your antennae are up. The next day, James said, "Come, I want to talk to you. Yesterday was so great, and it was really important that you asked those questions because Steve has been playing all these parts in his head, and it's really valuable to have somebody who is giving voice to their own instincts and questions and is now responsible for that character. I was so happy with that." "I'm not getting fired?" He says, "What?" and he started to laugh. "You got to lighten up!"

You are blessed with your instincts for hyper-analysis. That absolutely serves the roles you create. But . . .

There's a cost.

Sounds like your over-thinking can be a huge burden.

It is. But *Passion*, from that moment on—a lot of people would assume, "That must have been so hard." But from *Hello Again* to *Passion* was from one stage of bliss to another because I was in the room with people who I trusted. I met people who I consider masters. They'd say, "That didn't work, let's try something else." Sometimes I have to do like ten different things, and there's just a little seed of those ten things in what I ultimately do, but I've got to go full blast on each one of them. But if you're afraid to try it because it's going to scare someone that they made a mistake in their casting decision—I was not tortured during *Passion*. No, I was spoiled.

Was it exhausting playing her?

During the workshop, my whole body ached because I was carrying so much of her tension and trying to discover the physicality; experimenting with what would happen during a seizure and what then the state of my muscles would be afterwards. I had a headache every day from a week in. But the playing of the show is very different than the workshop. Because once we were actually playing, the nightly catharsis that happened for her I shared. At the end, she died loved. That sounds a little oversimplified, but she died loved and she knew it. So I did not crawl up to my dressing room. I didn't feel, "Oh, my God, how am I going to do another one?" *Passion* was surprising in that way. I worked with [voice teacher] Joan Lader on my days off. I met her during *Song of Singapore* and she and I were just like oil and water. It was very difficult because I was all about the acting first, and she would say, "That's great, but you got a vocal problem, and we have to address that. We have to build your technique." [By *Passion*] Joan and I worked so closely. We practiced finding how I was going to sing in bed and not look like somebody who was producing sound in a healthy way. I said, "I need to look like somebody who can't hold myself up." She said, "Then you've got to design how the pillows are." We worked for days trying to figure out the pillow arrangement so I was supported in just the right way, so I could appear to be as weak as I needed to be and still produce sound.

This was one of those magical marriages of actor and role.

Yeah. I did feel like there was sort of this spell cast. That sounds like magical thinking, but there—Steve always wanted there to be some secret key [to my performance]. I told him I'd tell him someday. I still haven't told anybody the full version of it. Maybe I will when I'm ninety-five. I remember one night I came offstage and Steve was there. He said, "Are you having a good time?" and I said, "Oh, God, Steve, it's so meaningful, and it's so—the challenges each night just give me a chance to find things I never expected." And he said, "Are you having a good time? Because you have to. You really must find the joy in this. Because what's happening right now, you and this part, it happens maybe once for certain actors. Maybe it never happens. You've got to enjoy it. You have to allow yourself to enjoy it." And it's not like I wasn't, but I didn't think of it that way.

You have talked to me about feeling responsible for leading a company. Were you already feeling that during *Passion*?

When everybody does their job, then you just have to do your job. But doing my job is not just acting my role. Stella Adler said your responsibility is to the whole play and to the whole world. It's so much bigger than just you and your part. My mother had five kids in less than six years, so there was always somebody who was needier than me. Very early on I decided if I want something, I had to figure out how to get it myself. So when I sense that people are not taking care of things, I feel like I better figure it out. I've examined the neurotic piece of that in therapy. It's not necessarily all unhealthy because it's a survival mechanism of sorts. But there are other people who would just say, "I'm not taking that on." But if the result is that you end up in a costume you can't work in or staging that feels terrifically uncomfortable—I don't know how to live with that. In *The King and I* there were some problems for me with the staging and with the interpretation, and the director [Christopher Ashley]. I think that having seen *Passion*, he thought the Anna that I would want to play would have a darkness. He had a fascinating big picture sense for the design of the show. And he talked about what it must have been like for this woman coming into Siam on this boat, which had to be filthy, which had animals that were foreign to her, and the truly frightening way women in that country were treated. [He talked about] the type of woman it must have taken to conquer her fears and soothe her child and confront a king. I thought, "Wow, good for you, man. That sounds real and wonderful and rich." And then I read Anna Leonowens's books, and all that was justified. But it didn't mesh with Oscar Hammerstein's book. Parts of it did beautifully, but in other parts we were imposing something that sometimes worked and sometimes didn't.

And you can't fight the text.
You can give it a subtext, but sometimes you keep hitting a discord. Or when you're doing it piece by piece, it seems interesting, but when we did the first run-through, I realized, "I'm on the wrong track. We're not balancing this right," and either he didn't know how to fix it or he didn't feel the same. But I really felt in my gut that we were off. I went to Chris and he said, "I think it's playing fine." We did another run-through, and it was torturous for me. I called my agent and said, "I don't know what to do." He said, "Well, you can't quit so we have to figure out what's going to make it work if you're there." I told him I had a friend, John DeLuca, who is a really great coach and has a great critical eye. I had him ask for John to be allowed into rehearsals. I would work with him in my dressing room on my breaks and after we finished teching until 1:00 or 2:00 in the morning. And I'd go to his apartment early in the morning, before tech. I was determined to solve this. John, who I paid by the hour—most of my paycheck, quite frankly—watched and had some wonderful, fresh ideas. It wasn't about re-conceiving the show. I spoke candidly to Chris and I put the blame on me. I said, "I just need this help to get myself unstuck, and you have so much to be responsible for. Nothing will go in that you don't approve, but I do need this person who's helping me to see the big picture." It was very awkward but I had to figure out a way to make it work.

I'm sure you can appreciate that as a director, when your authority's being undermined, that's not fun.
I got that, but I also got that I couldn't get onstage. I was falling at the end of "Shall We Dance" over and over and over because we couldn't figure out a way to end it. It was the size of the dress, it was the speed we were moving. There was a physics to it. John DeLuca figured it out.

Did you feel vindicated winning a Tony for the show?
I forgot to thank John in my acceptance speech. So it was a semi-miserable night for me. I probably would have left the show if I didn't have John. He really did save me. I'm capable of saving my own ass in many situations, but I needed somebody to be watching.

Once you opened, were you able to find joy in playing the show?
The joy in that show for me was that role, that story, the children. I loved acting that part and I kept discovering it. Lou [Diamond Phillips], was so charming and such a partner. It

Navigating the dress with Lou Diamond Phillips in *The King and I*. (Photofest)

was such a beautiful story to tell. There's so much that I credit Chris with. And the producers were very angry with me for having brought John in but they didn't reject a single thing that I brought as a result of working on the side with him. And believe me, I since found out about plenty of actors who had coaches working with them, sneaking in and watching from the back. You know, the writing was on the wall early on. We were supposed to go to The Kennedy Center and then come into town but Lou got a film. They wanted me to rehearse with Lou, then play The Kennedy Center with an understudy, then go into previews in New York with Lou. I said, "That doesn't make any sense. The whole show is about the way these two particular individuals rub each other, so Lou and I would be creating something, and then I'm going to jump and create something else with [someone else]? When that happens because you have an emergency, you do it, but to construct it that way? Why are we doing that? What are we learning? I'm going to be confused as hell and so will, I imagine, those who are in charge of watching the big picture. I want to go out of town, but if we can't do it with Lou, I don't know that it makes sense." I remember Chris saying to me, "I need you to explain it to the producers." He didn't say a word that whole meeting. Later on, I realized: Why should I be put in that position? The director should be standing up and saying, "This is not a healthy way of processing the show." So already it was like Donna is the point maker.

The Tony win for *The King and I* had some drama with it.

Yeah, exactly. I remember thinking when I was nominated, "This is going to be so much fun because I know that Julie Andrews is going to win. No pressure." But then Julie declined the nomination [though she was left on the ballot] and everywhere I went somebody was sticking a microphone in my face, saying, "How do you feel about this?" "That's Julie's business. I'm honored to have been nominated in her company." But I still believed that she was going to win. When I won for *Passion*, it was kind of an out-of-body experience. I performed [during the telecast], and I had a quick change. I was paying hair and makeup people to do my hair and makeup for my glamour look, if you will, and I paid them to do three rehearsals of it. We had like nine minutes or something like that. We made it and I ran back and I got back in my seat just in time to see a Clairol commercial for which I did the voice-over. Then, "And we're back." When they announced my name it was like a time warp. I kissed Dee Hoty, and I went right past my husband. I didn't even touch him. I went up on the stage and I just had to take in where I was. I was looking for my parents because I felt so out of body that I thought, "If I can see my family, that will be real." I found my mom and dad and I remember saying hello to them. I kissed Bernadette and Liza—Bernadette and Liza! That was a real Cinderella moment. I got spoiled, spoiled, spoiled, spoiled. It's like well, where do you go from here? *King and I* was just complicated. This thing that was just going to be happy and fun got politicized. I didn't like talking about winning and the losing in any circumstance. So I really wasn't prepared. I didn't feel it then, but I've seen the video footage. I'm in the seat, and I don't get up. My husband's kind of like lifting me out of the seat. I have this frozen look on my face.

I want to read a quote to you that I heard that you like: "No artist is pleased. There's no satisfaction whenever at any time. There's only queer, divine dissatisfaction, a blessed unrest that keeps us marching and makes us more alive than the others."

That's the opening section of the quote, Martha Graham speaking to Agnes de Mille. I do love that. It was given to me as an opening night gift—just a Xerox copy of that—by Don Jones, a musical director that I was working with. The situation was that Agnes had just done *Oklahoma!* and gotten the reviews of her lifetime, and she said she felt that it was not the best work that she'd done. And she said, "I don't know how to assess myself. That's what they think is my best work that I've done?" Not that it was bad work, but . . ." And Martha said, "It's not your job to judge your work. There's a life force that comes through each of us in a particular way, and it's your job to keep yourself open to it and not get in the way of it." I love both parts of it, and the first part of it was kind of the part that I needed to hear most at that time. I used to have it in my dressing room all the time, and now I carry it with me, and it's something that I say to myself frequently. But I do think that there is some satisfaction. I do think that there is a kind of acceptance. This is where I am right now, and I'm doing the best I can do. I've been doing this long enough, and I've been through the ups and the downs. If I go down, I'll probably come up again, and I'll probably go down again. That's what brings me back to the theater always, and will forever. You get to keep doing it again. You get to keep finding something new. Sometimes I do send myself on a quest. That's usually longer into a run where you feel stuck or it doesn't feel fresh. So I'll set myself on a quest to search for something or to focus on something. Or just because my day was different, that shifts my perspective. So I never feel like, "Okay, nailed it." No. And sometimes people will say—I don't even want to know what they thought . . .

Well, sure, because then you're self-conscious, and you'll never hit it the same way again without being conscious of it.

Exactly. It's like the thing about reviews. My husband always says if you believe the good ones, you have to believe the bad ones. I do remember reading a good one and the critic was talking about some moment. I thought, "That's not what I'm playing at all." And it made me so self-conscious. I felt like I needed to change what I was playing, because if that's what they were getting . . . Now I don't tend to think about what I want an audience to get. I tend to think about what the character needs to get. That's not to say that I don't have my radar up about audience response, particularly in comedy, but once somebody had analyzed a moment like that and said, "Well, clearly she's doing this," the level of self-consciousness is unbearable. When I was younger I had a very hard time not watching myself. I had to work really hard to stay inside of the things. Now it's not as much of a challenge for me, and sometimes there's some part of me that is watching, but it's not obsessively watching me.

You famously make notes after every performance about that stuff, right?

I do. I used to keep a notebook. Now I keep my script in a leather portfolio that has my research and notes. But the thing weighs a ton so I have a separate copy of the first and second acts.

When you take notes, is it so that you can refer back to them later, or is the act of writing down your thought solidifying that thought in your mind?

I've been mostly using it for the latter. Just putting it on paper, seeing it in front of me. It's a reminder to myself to try to address.

You have said that working in the not-for-profits is financially very difficult. But with both *LoveMusik* **and** *People in the Picture***, something clearly spoke to you with both shows to make you want to do them.**

When *LoveMusik* was presented to me, it was the combination of working with Hal, and playing Lotte Lenya, and singing Kurt Weill. I just thought it was delicious. Is it perfect? I don't know what perfect is. All I know is this is something I've never done and a journey worth taking and exploring. So that was my way in to my decision with *LoveMusik*. With *People in the Picture*, one of the producers on *LoveMusik* was a woman named Tracy Aron. She had said to me, "I have a script that I'd love for you to read at some point. It's something I'm considering producing." I didn't know how I was going to be able to afford to do it because I wasn't making a lot of money anywhere else at that time. But then *Tangled* was sort of in the mix there, and a residual check came in. By the time I had done the first workshop I was screwed because I was just so invested and felt so deeply connected to it. My world had been once again cracked open in exploring the world of this character and what had gone on during the time of the Holocaust. It was an incredibly rich experience, and one that, despite the fact that it was not received critically with consistently positive reviews, was still deeply meaningful to me. It also appeared to be deeply meaningful to many audience members. I wish we had had more time to work on it because I think there are things that we learned in previews that are very difficult to fully address while you are previewing and running. The most difficult parts of that role for me were finding the transitions and yet that became my favorite part of it. It was a crazy time [Murphy was regularly back and forth between New York and Boston throughout the run to be with her ailing father], and I was sometimes doing the show on three or four hours of sleep, thinking, "How do I do this?" Well, I did it. And I think that there was a greater force at work in helping me to get through that time.

I understand that with everything going on with your father, it was hard to do the show, but do you think it would have been even harder if you hadn't had the show as an outlet?

I was very anxious to get up there. I was doing as much as I could from a distance, but my dad, once he was out of the hospital and out of rehab, wanted to be at home. My family members were basically doing shifts. But I had this job. There was an incredible sense of purpose in the work that I was doing, and beauty in being able to channel my energy, my experience, and whatever gifts had been given to me. I was grateful to have that company to come to, to have the Roundabout who was incredibly supportive during that time. I can't quite find an adjective to describe it, but I felt so proud of my family and of my Roundabout family, so blessed that I was working with people who were so sensitive and supportive of those circumstances. I felt lucky to be me. That show was rich in ways that I could never have imagined.

You mentioned *Tangled*.

Tangled was a blast. It really was an adventure and a totally new form of working for me. I'd never done animation. My audition process was so much fun. They record you and they videotape you for the animators to catch your facial expression and your physical body language. I don't think Mother Gothel looks like me but my mother does and she said so in front of my daughter, which I was not happy about. At first I thought, "Wow, she's going to be thrilled I'm doing a Disney film!" And then I was like, "I'm playing this horrible, evil character." It was complicated as an adoptive mother. This woman steals a child! That did not strike me at first. But it was a joyful experience. The guys that I worked were so generous and open to my ideas. It was such a different experience, being a vocal performance even though it didn't feel that way when I was doing it. It felt very much like I was giving a performance that used all of me. I feel really blessed to have been a part of.

And then you did *Into the Woods*, playing Rapunzel's adoptive mother again.

I know. It's so crazy. Darmia said, "Why did you have to play this part again? Why couldn't you be The Baker's Wife?" And I said, "Because they asked Amy Adams to be The Baker's Wife," and she said, "Well, she is really good, Mom." I auditioned for the original Broadway production. I remember James [Lapine] directing me at the audition, saying he wanted The Witch to be a truly frightening figure both to the characters on stage and to the audience, and ironically he said to me, "We don't want a Disney witch." I remember his feedback after I didn't get the job, which was not negative. They thought she was a little too scary, too dark. I've always loved the show. I would listen to it and just cry my eyes out. So fast-forward to all these years later, when I knew this production was happening. I was curious but afraid to even talk to my agent about it because I thought, "I can't do it. I need to make money." I got a pilot and we were able to negotiate an agreement with CBS that put *Into the Woods* in first position as they say so that if the pilot got picked up, they would have to work around my performance schedule. It's been intense because working around your rehearsal schedule doesn't mean that you don't work on the days that you're performing that night. That's been demanding. I haven't done that week after week after week, but some weeks have been heavier than others. And I've worked at the Park before, but I was much younger, and I had much less to do.

Careful the things you wish for, because as you told me, during *Drood* you stood backstage at the same theater saying, "God, I wish I had more to do in this."

Right. I know. And believe me I'm very happy to have more to do. In the majority of the first act, you're just running around on that set, not only when you're visible to the audience, but when you're trying to get some place that you're supposed to appear. It's been a challenging journey. And it was a huge show to do in the amount of time that we had. But it seems like the company is very happy to be doing what they're doing, and I certainly feel that way myself. We witnessed audiences who are really, really loving the show and who have literally stayed up all night to get a seat. For me the show resonates even more deeply than it did when I was first introduced to it because I'm a mother, I'm a stepmother, I'm a step-grandmother, I'm a daughter who's lost a parent. I see the world in a different way than I did. So I'm so happy that I've had the chance to do this, even though I am exhausted. I just accept that I will be tired until the end of this run, but that doesn't translate to mean I shouldn't have done this by any means. And I am now back at that point where I do look up at the moon, I look up at the castle and remember the first time that I was there, and think about where my life has taken me between then and now. To be telling this story in the park, there's a fairytale kind of quality to it. I don't know how much richer it could get.

LILLIAS WHITE

December 2008; July 2009

MANY OF THE WOMEN IN THIS BOOK have careers closely associated with composers whose work they interpreted repeatedly. Carol Channing? Jerry Herman. Angela Lansbury and Elaine Stritch? Stephen Sondheim. Chita Rivera, Debra Monk, and Karen Ziemba? All Kander and Ebb. For Lillias White, it was Cy Coleman who proved her constant.

Their relationship began when White took over the role of Joyce Heath, "the oldest woman alive," in Coleman's smash musical *Barnum*. He told her shortly after that he was going to write a show for her. "Yeah, people say that. Whatever," said White of her feelings at the time. But Coleman made good on his promise with *The Life*, a show about hookers and pimps on the streets of New York in the early 1980s. Neither Coleman nor White could have imagined that it would take ten years from inception to Broadway, but when *The Life* opened in 1997, White, who, in the interim, had established herself on Broadway with a handful of memorable performances, was anointed a star for her turn as the weary streetwalker, Sonja. Her lament, "The Oldest Profession," was a song so perfectly crafted to White's skills that Ben Brantley referenced it in the opening words of his *New York Times* review: "'Fifteen thou-ou-ou-sand!' As pronounced by the actress Lillias White, each syllable in this numeral opens into a cry of fatigue to make your every muscle ache in sympathy," and went on to say that she "can't strike a note or speak a word without sounding convincing." White took home a Tony for the role and went on to star in the world premiere of what would be Coleman's final show, *Like Jazz*. After his passing, she anchored a revue of his work, *The Best Is Yet to Come*, in both California and off-Broadway.

But Coleman wasn't the only theatrical legend to whom White owes some gratitude. Back in 1983, when the original production of *Dreamgirls* was heading to Los Angeles with its star, Jennifer Holliday, director Michael Bennett coerced a reluctant White to go with them to cover for and ultimately replace Holliday in the central role of Effie. So powerful was White's performance that when the show came back to Broadway in 1987 [opening four days before Bennett's death], it was White belting "And I Am Telling You, I'm Not Going" to critical acclaim. And when *Dreamgirls* was mounted for a landmark, all-star concert in 2001, White again memorably took on Effie.

Despite her undisputed talent, however, White remains difficult to cast. Her round face, saucer eyes, huge smile, and voluptuous figure are almost as specific as her unmistakable, clarion voice. Though she was Tony-nominated for her 2009 role in *Fela!*, White has spent recent years performing more frequently in straight plays, cabaret, and concert halls. But she remains a force of positive energy. Even sprawled out on her bed after a nap (as she was for one

Celebrating Cy Coleman in *The Best Is Yet to Come*. (Carol Rosegg)

of our meetings) she is all bouncy, playful, and sparkling. When she smiles, which she does frequently, you could be fooled into thinking that joy is ever abundant.

You grew up in Brooklyn. When did theater enter your world? Did your mother take you into the city as a kid?

My mother took us regularly to Radio City Music Hall. And we lived walking distance to the Brooklyn Public Library. We went to BAM and saw dance concerts, puppet shows, a lot of cultural stuff. And my mother bought me a lot of show tune albums. *South Pacific. Annie Get Your Gun. My Fair Lady*. And then I got albums like *Harry Belafonte: Live at Carnegie Hall*, Andy Williams's *Moon River*. We saw a lot of Perry Como. I saw Nina Simone in concert. The O'Jays. The Brooklyn Fox Theatre on DeKalb Avenue. The Vandellas. Smokey & the Miracles.

So you were exposed to a lot of culture early on. When did you decide you wanted to pursue it as a career?

I think it wasn't until I got to college. The theater bug just kind of grabbed me. I never intended to get involved in the theater, but I'd always been involved in speaking publicly in elementary school. I was picked to announce the dance contest participants.

What got you picked?

I could speak very clearly. My grandmother came from the South and they came up to do better. They wanted their children to speak the King's English. I had to speak intelligently at home. My teachers noticed that I didn't talk like the other kids. I had aunts and uncles who were artists and painters. I had an aunt and a cousin who played piano. We used to all get together on holidays and sing around the piano. My grandmother would have everyone together and she would cook the most beautiful food and then at the end of dessert, she had my grandfather clear the table and she would say, "OK everyone,

---

Lilias White

The Wiz, National Tour, 1978
Barnum, Broadway, 1981
Rock 'n Roll! The First 5,000 Years, Broadway, 1982
Dreamgirls, National tour, 1983
Queenie Pie, Washington, D.C., 1986
Dreamgirls, National Tour, Broadway, 1987
Romance in Hard Times, off-Broadway, 1989
Cats, Broadway, 1991
Once on This Island, Broadway, 1991
How to Succeed in Business without Really Trying, Broadway, 1995
The Life, Broadway, 1997 (Tony Award)
Dinah Was, off-Broadway, 1998
Dreamgirls in Concert, Broadway, 2001
Like Jazz, Los Angeles, 2003
Purlie, Encores! 2005
South Pacific, Carnegie Hall, 2005
Chicago, Broadway, 2006
Fela! Broadway, 2009
The Best Is Yet to Come, off-Broadway, 2011

---

my baby's gonna sing and dance," and I would sing and dance for my family on my grandmother's dining room table.

Did your family have any sense that you had a special gift or was it just for fun?

I don't know. I think they knew that something special was there, but there were a lot of other issues between my brother and father that had to be dealt with. I was entertainment for my family. But as a little girl I thought I'd be a nurse. I was always bringing home strays of every kind. But on Sunday that's what we did; we got together, we ate, and then I got on the table and sang. I think that was a way for me to dodge what was going on in my family. And other members might have used it to protect me. "Maybe she's not noticing all of the stuff that's going on." I don't know. I never thought of it before.

Did it work? The dodging?

I think that being in the arts certainly put my mind off of a lot of stuff that was going on. When I look back on it, it's probably what saved me from being out of control or doing something really crazy or destructive. It was my outlet.

Were you doing plays at all?

In junior high and high school we did something called *Sing*. They would take Broadway shows and superimpose different lyrics and cut them down. Then in high school, instead of taking gym, you could take dance. I wanted to be a dancer. Then I got to college and I got into theater. I was in a chorus class and the teacher was going around the room to listen. She hears me singing and she stops. "Who is that? That's *you!*" I thought it was going to be something wrong. "There are auditions tomorrow for a theater company, you're going!" So I go to this rehearsal space and I audition. I didn't really know what I was getting into. But they invited me to join the company. And suddenly I have to go to all of these rehearsals and stuff. I knew nothing about acting. I was terrible. *Terrible!* I could dance and I could always sing, but I never knew *how* to sing. So I learned the hard way.

You had to reverse old habits?

Yeah, and not only that, I wasn't used to practicing. I was used to practicing dance, but singing? I wasn't into it. And I was young and fine! And I had a boyfriend to take care of. But I did it. I stayed with that company too long. Like seven years. I did a lot of shows. I ended up leaving the company and coming back a few times. I was put out of the group because I wasn't showing up. I was really young and I didn't know that people were looking for me. I wouldn't call. I was just in my own world. So they let me go but they brought me back.

You describe yourself as not all that interested in the work. What made you apply yourself?

I really liked what I was doing. I liked the attention and I think there's a sense of power you get when you can get on the stage and affect people. They listen to you, watch everything you do, and at the end they applaud!

You had talent . . .

But I didn't believe in it. It was hard for me to believe. When they put me into the theater company, The Demi-Gods, they used to tell me that I could be a star. That scared the shit out of me.

Why?

I don't know. I didn't know what that meant. I didn't believe that I could accomplish that.

Somehow you knew that in order to keep getting your applause fix, you were going to have to buckle down, though.

Yeah, I figured that out. I figured it out when I lost my voice. My voice was gone. Nothing. It didn't hurt but I couldn't speak. That scared me more than anything else. I went to this doctor and he said to me, "You don't know how to sing properly." He made me be quiet and absolutely still, no talking, no singing, for four weeks. I got my voice back and I started taking my voice lessons a lot more seriously. But after awhile I decided enough of The Demi-Gods. I got a call to come and replace someone in a show called *Amen Corner*. In the audience were the producers of the upcoming big bus and truck tour of *The Wiz*. They called the producers of *Amen Corner* and told them they wanted to see me for Dorothy. I go in to audition and there is George Faison, Geoffrey Holder. I was just amazed. Geoffrey Holder says, "Oh my God, darling, where have you been? I don't believe we've never seen you before!" They offered me the role of the Dorothy understudy. So I got in the company and I played a bunch of little roles. After five or six months, the girl playing Dorothy got married and called the company manager and said, "I'm not coming back." I had gone on for her before because she refused to take the bus. She always flew and sometimes the flight didn't make it in. So I would do opening nights and I would get the review. This happened several times and finally by the time she left, I had saved their asses all over the country. But we get to South Carolina and they had a contest for local yokels for the role of Dorothy. I had been the understudy for six months! They didn't even tell me. I heard from other company members and they told me,

"You better call your agent." I didn't have an agent. So Yvette Freeman called her agent. The agent, Honey Sanders, hears what's going on and says, "Don't worry about it." And Honey took me on.

Never having seen you perform?
Never having seen me. Just based on what Yvette told her.

Did she see the reviews?
I don't think so. We were a bus and truck tour. There were no computers back then. No fax machines. None of that shit. But Honey says, "I'll take care of it." She called the producers and said, "I am calling to make sure you treat Ms. White right." And they said, "We didn't know she had an agent." I took over the role.

So you finish out the national tour of *The Wiz* as the lead. Were you conscious at the time of having made a huge step forward or having gotten your break?
I didn't know what to feel about any of that. Except that I was working and making more money than I had ever made in my life. That was exciting. But it didn't feel like stardom. It didn't look to me like what happens to overnight wonders. I didn't know where I was with it. I hadn't made a choice; it chose me

Were you still a wild girl?
I was more disciplined with my heart and my other parts.

But not 100 percent, because shortly after you started your next job, the tour of *Ain't Misbehavin'*, you got pregnant, right?
I actually got pregnant before the tour. I knew but nobody else did. But don't print that! Oh, it's ancient history now and who cares. But I *was* pregnant and I took the job because I needed the money. My daughter's father was crazy and I knew I wasn't going to stay with him, but I wanted the baby. But he just got crazier and crazier and I thought, "Let me go to work and make some money." He put his hands on me the wrong way and I said, "I'm out." I left everything there. All my clothes, all my shit, everything. This was after *Ain't Misbehavin'*.

Out on the tour what were you playing?
I was the Charlayne understudy, understudying Jackie Lowe.

The thin one! So the moment you started showing, was it noticed immediately?
I went on and every time I did, they kept having to let my dress out a little more and a little more. And they kept looking at me funny but they couldn't say anything because when I was on I was *on*. High kicking, squatting, up and down the stairs, all that stuff. But around Christmas I had to tell them. I was getting bigger and I started having contractions after "How You Baby?" So I had to tell them. No one had been able to figure out what was going on with me because I was on my game. People suspected. They were like, "she's big up there" but no one asked me if I was pregnant.

In Charlayne Woodard's one-woman show, *In Real Life*, she talks about how the experience of doing that show took so much out of the whole cast. She was seriously, clinically exhausted. You were pregnant, which makes people tired all on its own. How did you do it?
Well, you have to remember, I was in tip-top shape. I just finished a fourteen-month bus and truck tour of *The Wiz* where I was Dorothy, running all night. I had a blue bag on wheels

which I called my kitchen bag. I had a frying pan, a teapot, condiments, I was eating well, I was taking vitamins. I was taking excellent care of myself. I did my exercise, I got air and sun. I was in the best shape of my whole fucking life.

Then you gave notice.

I gave notice. They were relieved because they knew something was up. But I was doing my job and killing onstage.

And you have a baby.

I have a beautiful baby girl!

But you were on your own. You left her father. How was that in terms of work?

It was OK. My aunts, uncles, and cousins had come together and given me all of these beautiful clothes. I got her the Cadillac of strollers! I had moved back to my mother's house in Coney Island. Three days a week, I was running, so I got back into shape. I was still working. I went to Rome for a week with a gospel chorale. And then I got to do *Tintypes* on the road with Faith Prince. When I got back I had an audition for *Barnum* on Broadway. I went and there was [composer] Cy Coleman and [director] Joe Layton sitting in the dark in the theater. I sang my audition song, "Don't Rain on My Parade." I finish my song and Joe says, "I hear you can juggle." I had learned to juggle doing *Waiting for Godot*. I dropped everything. So I said, "It gets better." They thought that was really funny. So they hired me to do *Barnum* [replacing Terri White]. I got to do *Barnum* for about a year.

This was your Broadway debut.

Yeah! I was still nursing when I was doing this show. I don't know how I did that. I would nurse her in the afternoon before I left and when I got home. But I was in great shape and that's how you do that.

You mentioned meeting Cy Coleman and obviously that became one of your most important professional relationships. What was your impression of him when you met him?

Cy was like a big full moon to me. There was always a big smile on his face. And he had big thick lips. I used to say that man has a black person somewhere in his family. He was just so cool. And Joe Layton and I got to be really tight. We all used to hang out quite a bit. Joe and Cy and Franny Lee, who did the costumes, we all hung out. Then Joe put together *Rock 'n Roll! The First 5,000 Years*. I went to the audition and every diva in New York was there. We got to the Aretha Franklin part and he had everybody come to the mic and sing a portion of the song. Three of us went for the Aretha part, doing "Respect." I wasn't really into it but I got the job. It was an amazing show. The choreography was amazing. It was a multimedia event. It was incredible. Way ahead of its time. It opened and promptly closed. Devastating! Devastating! It was a huge show, and it was a wonderful cast, brilliant choreography; it was just incredible. So it was a shock.

Your first flop.

Yeah. That was really hard. The last thing I expected was to be told that we were not going on with the show. "We're closing? We just opened!" I didn't get that. No one told me about that in school. "We just opened!"

Madonna was in that show.

She was in it for [snaps fingers] that long. She got a record deal within the first week of rehearsals so she left. She never performed it.

It was the early '80s and there wasn't a lot going on, was there?

Well, *Dreamgirls* was running and they were getting ready for their LA company. They were looking for replacements in New York. I went to the audition for Lorrell.

You thought you were a Lorrell?

Oh yeah. I didn't think I was an Effie at all. I didn't look like that, I didn't sound like that, and I liked Lorrell's costumes.

What happened?

I went to the audition, I had a callback and they said, "We want you to come back but we don't want to see you for Lorrell; we want to see you for Effie." And I said, " I don't sing like that, I don't want to gain weight." And they said, "Just come back." I went back and they had me sing every note that Effie sings. Everything. Michael Bennett puts his arm around me and says, "Ok, when you go to LA, you'll stand by for Jennifer Holliday. You'll go on because she's out a lot." I said, "I don't want to go to LA. I don't have any family there. I have a two-year-old daughter. I just bought a new duplex. I don't even know how to drive. I don't want to go to LA." He said, "You'll go to LA. Everything you need, you'll have." He didn't lie to me. Everything I needed. They taught me how to drive. My agent was a pit bull and he went up against Michael to the point where Michael said to me after I took over the role, "You need to fire your agent. Your agent is a son of a bitch." And I was like, "Oh, *really*???"

What was it like working with Michael Bennett?

I enjoyed working with Michael. Michael was never mean to me. When he would say things that didn't sit right with me, I'd straighten him out right away. Michael used to come to my dressing room and sit on my lap and we'd drink cheap champagne and just talk. People were warning me about this man [being difficult] and this is not the man I got. I didn't get any of that bullshit from him.

You were saying "No" to him and he insisted that he wanted you for this. That's a big deal, to be strong-armed by Michael Bennett and be told, "You're the one that I want." Did that register at all?

You know, I thought I was being strong, too. At that point in time I am not sure how many people would have told him no. But I had heard horror stories about him so I was willing to stand my ground. The money that I asked for, he was willing to pay me.

You were willing to walk away?

I offered to stay in New York on a pink [ensemble] contract. People thought I was crazy.

Did you ever regret it?

No, I had a great time. I was directed by someone I consider a genius in the theater. There has not been anybody like him since. He was a creator, he was a great talent. And he was a son of a bitch too. He was on drugs too. That whole thing can really alter someone's personality. But he met his match when he met me because I had already gone through what Effie went through. I'd lived that. I had a child, I wasn't married, I had been in a group and been put out. I had to pull myself back up. I approached Effie from an actor's point of view not a singing point of view. I wasn't trying to sing it the way it had been sung before. I really wanted to bring my own tale to it. I used my experience to act it differently from what I had seen. He appreciated that. It was about the acting. He saw that. He had an extremely sharp eye. Like a camera.

Where did those acting chops come from? You said that when you did *The Wiz* you couldn't act.

I studied with The Demi-Gods. And I studied with a couple of great teachers. My acting improved. So I was ready.

By this point you had already covered in *Ain't Misbehavin'* and *The Wiz*. Did being the standby in *Dreamgirls* have particular challenges?

It did, because there wasn't a great vibe about Jennifer. I had to be ready. Always.

When a show is that loved and the star has taken home all of the awards and there's tension backstage . . .

Look, for the six weeks of rehearsal, I was Effie because she was recording her album. We get to LA and suddenly she's Effie. The Shuberts, who produced it, had built her up as the big star and the one to see. When she started missing performances, people would leave. I'd get onstage and I'd bring people back. At first it bothered me but then I was like, "fuck it." I couldn't take it personally. That's how they built the show up. Eventually the people in the cast got used to me. It was just that kind of, "Is she gonna be here? What's gonna happen?" But then I took over the role. We went to San Francisco, I met my ex. I got married [shoots herself in the head]. Nice guy. Nice manners. He looked good in a suit. And I hadn't been with anyone in a long time. He was good with my daughter. I wanted it. I wanted it to work out. It looked like he was the one so I said, "Let's not wait. Let's go." Wait, wait, wait! Everybody, wait.

What went wrong?

He couldn't really support me the way I wanted him to. He was too content with me being the breadwinner. And he couldn't keep his dick in his pants. And it was at a time when they were discovering that not just gay men were getting AIDS. I wasn't in the mood to take a chance on my life with someone who couldn't be faithful. I had my son with him and when my son was a year old, I had enough.

After your marriage ended, you did *Queenie Pie* and then *Dreamgirls* again, in New York. Michael Bennett was gone and Bob Avian directed. How was that experience?

I don't remember. I do remember that it was very difficult coming back into New York with it and not having Michael Bennett, Michael Peters, Tom Eyen, Larry Riley, a whole host of other people who had passed away. It was difficult.

When *Dreamgirls* closed, you stood by for Darlene Love in the infamous *Carrie*.

I got to Stratford-upon-Avon and they led me into the dark theater and I am sitting there. Across the aisle is Barbara Cook and Wally Harper, and we are watching this scene where they kill the pig. I am looking and thinking, "Well, this is different." I hear Barbara Cook say, "I haven't been on Broadway in eighteen years and I am going back in this piece of shit?" Barbara Cook is a tough cookie, honey. Barbara Cook is a no-shit-taking cookie with the voice of an angel. I saw her say, "I am not going to do this 'cause it's crap" and I have loved her ever since I observed that moment. Linzi Hateley was phenomenal. It was a great cast. Gene Anthony Ray, Scott Wise, Charlotte D'Amboise, phenomenal talent. There was a lot of technical stuff they had to get right. Fire and things floating in air. When Carrie would do things, it took a lot to work it all out. And you had to figure out how to get the blood out of all the clothing and hair. It was the most expensive flop in Broadway history.

Wrenching guts in one of the all-time greatest Act 1 closers, "And I Am Telling You I'm Not Going" from *Dreamgirls*. (Photofest)

After *Carrie* . . .

I did *Romance in Hard Times* at The Public. It was pretty fabulous. I was going through a divorce at the time. It was a strange time. My son had some issues, had to have surgery. I had to move into a new apartment. But I loved working with [composer] William Finn, because he's so creative and a little nutsy. The play had so many possibilities. The music was melodic and different. I just thought it was a great, great piece. [Playing] Henny made me feel like I could fly, because of the idealism of it—this woman wanting to hold a baby and keep it from being born until the world's a better place? I still, to this day, wish and pray that William Finn will do whatever he thinks needs to be done to get this show mounted—and to do it before I am too old to play Henny! My life was in craziness at the moment but coming to the theater was the joy. It was my Balm in Gilead.

You were back on Broadway almost immediately in *Once on This Island*.

I was so happy doing *Once on This Island*. Dancing barefoot, swiveling my hips. It was a glorious cast of people. Glorious group. It was divine. My father was still living at the time and he had never seen me on Broadway and [he came]. That meant a lot to me.

Why was that?

We had been out of touch. Then, while I was gainfully employed at *Once on This Island*, I got the offer to do *Cats*. They called my agent and we thought it would be a career move to be the first black woman hired to do Grizabella. I hated it. Hated it! First of all I got sick from all of the gunk and dirt and gook. There was so much gook and stuff that hadn't been cleaned, it was like ornaments hanging from the vents. There were roaches accumulating around the barrels of ice that they used for the smoke effect. Roaches of every size, every configuration, One night I am doing my makeup, all of the layers and layers of crap on my face, and a roach falls out of my wig.

Did you like performing it?

Performing the show was OK but I was sick from the day I got there 'til the day I left.

From the dust?

And the mold. There were people there who had been there since the beginning and they were used to it. But I hated it. *Hated* it.

How long were you there?

Six months. And I had a stage manager from hell. He was a son of a bitch. He listened in on people's conversation through their mics.

Is it true that you once came on in slippers?

Yeah. That was my last show. That was a "fuck you" to him. A huge "fuck you." Not to the show or the company, or the producers, but to him. Ok, I'm gonna tell the story: I had hemorrhoids that weekend. Bad. Really bad. And if you've ever had them—you don't want to wish that on your worst enemy. Bleeding. So I come in the Friday of my last weekend and I say to my stage manager, my company manager, my house manager—all the managers are there—I say, "Look, I am not feeling well. I want to do all the shows. But can I just wear flats instead of putting the high heels on?" And the company manager says, "Of course, we're just glad you're here." Stage manager says, "No. You have to wear the whole costume." I say, "Look, let me explain to you, I am in pain. I should have stayed home but I want to do these final shows." He says, "You have to wear the costume." I ignored what he said. I did the show in flats for the first act and at intermission he comes to me ranting and raving. I said, "Can you let me alone for a minute, I have to go to the bathroom." Grizabella wears layers and layers of clothes and I used to get cold so I'd wear a unitard under everything to keep myself warm. So I had a lot of layers to take off to go to the bathroom. So he comes to my dressing room and he's giving me all of this crap. I was trying to go to the bathroom and I finally went off on him. I said, "Get out!" He says, "You are not going to go on tomorrow, I am banning you from the show for not wearing the costume." I am now hurting and I am really upset. I call Equity. A lot of good that did. They say, "Well, I see that he's not being nice but he's in his rights to tell you that you can't go on if you don't wear the costume." The audience doesn't know one shoe from the other! They come to hear that music and see the cats go "Meow!" And a cat in high heels, what the fuck kind of sense does that make? So, he bans me from doing the show Saturday matinee or evening. Sunday is my last show. I bring my kids, I dress them up. They are sitting there in the theater. Stage manager says, "Are you going to wear the whole costume?" I say, "Yeah." So I do the show, wearing the heels. And for the bows, what I was typically doing—me and Deuteronomy go up to the Heavyside layer and you are up at the very top of the theater. You want to talk about gook? I'd ride up on the tire, and my dresser would be there at the top of the staircase with my slippers for the walk down the long, narrow spiral staircase. The heels were hurting my knees going down. I would go down in my little pink fuzzy bedroom slippers. I got all the way down and I would usually take them off and put my shoes back on. But this was my last show. I didn't take them off. I went out on the stage and I took my bow in my bedroom slippers.

Did he say anything?

Oh, he wrote me up! He wrote to Equity. Gimme a break. The next day my agent calls and says, "Ummm, Lillias? There's a rumor going around Broadway about you. Did you, did you go out onstage in your bedroom slippers?"

Do you feel like you have to be a ball-buster in this business to protect yourself?

I try to be a sweet ball-buster. I really try to have good temperament and good character. If there are people I haven't been nice to, I apologize. But if you haven't been nice to me, don't expect me to be nice to you. One night, when I was doing *Barnum*, [I saw] Nell Carter in one of those little off-Broadway dives. Typically I am very shy. I really am. It's hard for me to talk to people I don't know. But I sat down and I talked to Nell Carter at this little place. I said to her, "I have heard all kinds of things about you, that you can be so mean to people." And she says, "Sometimes you have to let people know where you stand. Because people will take advantage of you." And I totally got that.

Actors spend so much time worried about getting or keeping a job and they spend so much time pleasing. Do you think you take a risk when you decide to assert yourself?

Well, the way I look at it, I have nothing to lose.

The job?

I wasn't going to starve. I have unshakable faith.

Where did that come from?

I think it came from surviving and overcoming obstacles in my young life. I could have turned out a whole different way. I came from what you call a broken home where my father and mother couldn't get along. I witnessed my father kick the shit out of my mother on a regular basis.

That explains the instantaneous reaction you had in your own marriage.

Yeah. As soon as he put his hands on me I said, "I'm out." I was thinking of ways to kill him. I thought, "If I kill him, I'll go to jail and what's going to happen to my baby?" I had to go.

So Broadway was comparatively small potatoes.

Yeah. I ain't scared of Broadway. I ain't scared of the road. I learned how to stand up for myself. I think that people who come from a broken home miss something in the parent giving you self-esteem. I mean, my grandmother put me up on the dining room table and I had a cousin who was like, "That bitch, she's always showing off." And I loved her, but everybody that you love doesn't love you.

That's a great lesson for an actor. Do you read your reviews?

Yeah. But I gotta say this: most of the reviews I've seen of myself are dynamite.

How does that feel?

It feels great, because when I get a good review that helps the show. And I'm all about that. Let's help the show. I want the show to fly. I want people to feel something when they leave the theater. Theater is supposed to change your life in some way. You can't go and fix everybody's heart or everybody's problems, but if I can touch you in some kind of way, that is my job. That is what I hope to do each time. Because you need it. I'm not trying to fix everybody but I am trying to put it out there so that you can get it.

When you were talking about *Cats*, you said you were conscious of the career move of being the first black Grizabella. Are you conscious of being a leading black Broadway actress now? Audra McDonald, it seems, is the only one who is regularly cast in roles not written for black women? Do you think about that?

I thought about it when I did Grizabella but the producers didn't do anything with that. I thought it was going to spark a revival of people coming to see the show because there was someone who looked like them. I think that Broadway has not done what it said it was going to do in terms of non-traditional casting. It has been very slow to move on that. Producers haven't reached out. They don't understand that there are people of color who will buy a Broadway seat if they think that people that look like them are on the stage. I'm that way. I want to see a good show first. I also want to see a show with someone who looks like me on the stage. I want to see everything that's good. What am I trying to say? I'm trying to say that Broadway used to open your eyes and open your horizons even more. I don't need to see all black on-stage. I want to be considered for roles not traditionally thought about for a black woman. I think my name has come up here and there. My name came up once for [Mrs. Potts in] *Beauty and the Beast*.

You described yourself as a shy person and also as a person with unshakable faith and confidence.

I had to build that confidence. I am at a point in my life where it's waned a little bit but it's coming back.

Why?

Seeing people that I think are mediocre getting all of these accolades and they aren't all that good.

Do you think that's different than it ever was?

Probably not. But as I get older I see how superficial it all is. It's a lot of factors. Timing. Who are you willing to kowtow to and how much bullshit are you willing to eat?

In your case not much.

I don't see why I should have to. The things that I see people do for the attention . . . it's revolting.

Your next show was *How to Succeed* . . .

For the most part, that was great. The producers were strange. They would come into the theater and look at you and not say, "Hello." I didn't get that part. And [director] Des McAnuff was not nice. They threatened to fire me during rehearsals in La Jolla.

Why?

Because for three weeks we rehearsed and everybody had to be there from 10:00 AM to 7:00 PM. I had my kids with me and they needed me. They needed my attention. So for three weeks I was coming to rehearsal, sitting all day, not doing a god-dammed thing. This particular Saturday I decided I was going to take my son for a haircut and sit down and talk to my daughter. I called in and said I won't be in until noon. "Well, we're doing your scenes." And I was thinking, "Right, of course. The one day I decided to take time." I took care of my kids that day. I took them to lunch, I looked them in the eye. As a single parent, I have to give them some of myself. I get to rehearsal and he says they are going to send me home because I didn't show up and I disrupted the rehearsal day. And I say, "I am sorry that I disrupted your rehearsal day but you have everybody coming in here and sitting around for weeks. My kids needed my attention. I'm sorry. If you want to send me home, I'll go home and pack. Before I had this gig, I ate well and I will always eat well. So don't threaten me." He calmed down.

After that it was a good experience?

It was a good experience because Jeanine Tesori and Ted Sperling got together and did a fabulous arrangement of "Brotherhood of Man." People think I won a Tony Award for that.

Did it feel great to stop the show like that?

Oh, yeah.

And then you got to do a Disney character.

It was so, so, so delicious to do *Hercules*. When we were recording it, the animators came and watched us and they said, "Tomorrow we are going to come in and film you guys. We want you to look like you want your characters to look. So I wrapped my head up and did my eyes. I said, I want her to look tall and thin. And she did! I loved it. And the sound of it is just magnificent. We had so much fun. We giggled, we laughed. We had the finest background singers, studio singers on the planet. It was just magnificent.

Were your kids too old to be impressed?

My daughter was a teenager. When it was time for the opening, she didn't want to go. I told her, "You are going to this opening and you are going to like it." My son was over the moon. They closed 42nd Street and did a parade! My kids had a ball, honey. David Zippel is still a very good friend. We are going to do something together soon.

After *Hercules, The Life.*
Again.

Again?
Yeah. Sonja was mine since the beginning. Cy Coleman and Ira Gassman wrote Sonja for me and they told me that when we were doing *Rock 'n Roll! The First 5,000 Years.* For ten years we did backers' auditions and private presentations. We did staged readings. Ten years. We never let go of it and I think that that is a tribute to the tenacity that you have to have in the business when you believe in a project—particularly when it's being written for you, in your key, in your flavor and all of that. It's worth holding on for the dream of it all coming together. And we finally get to Broadway and we weren't sure.

It's uncomfortable material.
Yeah, it was for me, too. When we were doing the workshop back at Westbeth, I was divorced and I was saying to my mom, "I don't know if I want the kids seeing this rehearsal." My mother said, "It's Cy Coleman music, ain't it? They're goin'. Don't worry about them children." But listen, they saw a lot of different things over the course of my career!

What was it like to have Cy Coleman, one of the true greats, write his last show for you?
It's the best. He paid me the highest compliment. He said, "You are a force of nature." He would tell anybody who would listen. He allowed me to mess with the notes to an extent. He gave me latitude. I think it's some of Cy's best work.

When the show finally opened what was the experience of the run?
Chuck Cooper and Pam [Pamela Isaacs] and I and some of the other members of the original production were so happy to finally be in the rehearsal process. We were happy to do the press. It was a dream come true to celebrate the opening of this musical. Coming to work every day was a joy. I felt like a mother hen, bringing in lipstick and glitter and nail polish. And it was a gig, of course. Eight shows a week is eight shows a week, no matter what you are doing. But when you are doing something where you feel like you've been part of the creation of it, it makes it even more worthwhile to do. That was always a trip. We got to where we'd recognize certain people who'd be in the audience over and over again. I thought that there would be stage door Johnnies but there weren't. Because I figured it's a show about hookers, boobs, and butts hanging out and shaking up, I thought there would be a long line of stage door Johnnies with flowers and jewels and candy but it wasn't that way.

Maybe you should have put the word out that you were expecting that.
Well, I am gonna put it out there for the next show I do.

When Tony season came around, it seemed inevitable that you were going to win.
Did it seem like that to you? Really? A lot of people have said that to me. Tony time was absolute madness. Between the rehearsals—and my kids were younger then and they were just working my nerves. So between the kids in school and rehearsals and interviews and Tony luncheons, it was maddening. I wanted the rehearsals and stuff to be done with but when they called my name and I was standing there with my beautiful cream-colored ensemble. . . . They hooked me up, I looked really nice. It was Radio City Music Hall where my mother had taken my brothers and me when we were kids. And we would wait in line for seats up front and see the Rockettes, and see the camels and sheep drop their dung, and here I am

Bemoaning being "too old for the oldest profession" in *The Life*. (Photofest)

on that stage receiving the top award in the theater. It was surreal. My kids were there and they were weeping with joy. I said, "Look at those little buggers. Last week this time they were working my last nerve. Now they're crying, 'My Mommy won!'" My mother and my boyfriend at the time were there and it was glorious. It was a lot of weeping and a lot of smiling and a lot of thank yous.

With this role you became a headliner in the theater world. Before you were a solid working actor but now you were getting press. It's different. Did you feel that shift?

It was great. Who doesn't want to be in the *New York Times* and recognized by your peers? And having people stop you in the street and say, "I love you, I love your show, I love your work." That's rewarding. As actors we don't always believe in ourselves and we don't always believe in what we give out. It's nice to have that kind of feedback. Where the average Joe on the street or someone like Liza is excited and appreciative of your work. . . . I remember standing backstage at Radio City and Whoopi Goldberg says to me, "You know you're gonna win." I don't even know what I said. I didn't want to be cocky or assumptive, as if I had it in the bag. I am not that person. I had no idea how much of an impact it was going to have on my life. Career-wise, it's been good but I am still waiting on some bigger results.

In September of 2001, you performed Effie again, opposite Audra McDonald and Norm Lewis, in the landmark *Dreamgirls* concert. This was fifteen years since you first did Effie. Do you remember her being different?

Yeah. She was better. She was stronger, she was gayer, lighter sassier, more intense. That night was spectacular. The energy was crackling and sparkling! It was almost as if you could see sparks flying in the house. And I was so glad to be the one chosen to do that role that night. That was one of the times I felt like I was flying because I really loved Effie. Effie kicks butt. She was a big challenge. Very taxing. The second day of rehearsal I cracked a bone in my foot. Total freak accident. So it was a challenge. But I am unstoppable, except by my God. I am grateful, for my life.

In 2003 you had the opportunity to premiere what would turn out to be Cy Coleman's last show, *Like Jazz*.

Like Jazz was fabulous, Cleavant Derricks, Patti Austin. Fabulous cast. The direction wasn't clear but the talent was superb. Some of the best music that Cy and the Bergmans have done. I'd love to see that show press forward and get produced again. Cy left us very suddenly.

When Cy passed . . .

I was devastated. I had just seen him a week and half before. He was the picture of health. And he was Cy: swaggery and funny and fun, looking great, wearing a beautiful blue pinstripe suit. He looked fabulous. Two weeks later he was gone. Death is something that we all know is going to happen but we are never really prepared for it. There is still that feeling like you are being punched in the gut. That was tough. I remember crying and moaning. It was not good. But luckily I felt blessed that I had been a part of his life and he had been part of mine in such a great way. I am a lucky girl.

In 2006, you did *Chicago* on Broadway.

It's a machine and it churns people in and out. Interesting. The role of Mama Morton, it's a small role. I don't know if what I did was that memorable but I had fun doing it. It was a good gig. The producers are making a lot of money on it but they are not sharing it. I'd like to see the theater in better condition for the actors. It was a gig that I needed to have at the time. I needed the work.

Why do you think there wasn't more work for you after *The Life*?

I don't know. I can't say what's in other people's minds. Maybe the content of what I was doing. Or how I look. Or how I don't look. What's popular.

I think casting you was never the easiest thing. You have a very special voice and you are a unique entity. In becoming a Tony Award–winning star, you aren't likely to take smaller character roles again, so maybe it's that much harder to cast you.

There is an assumption that because I have a Tony, I might charge too much or that I won't do certain things. Why don't you call me and ask me? Because I may want to do that little show off-off-Broadway if it's something that I think is really interesting. We'll work out the money part. I don't have that kind of attitude about the Tony. But I did think the Tony was going to lead to roles on TV and film and that didn't happen. So I don't know. I think they don't use a lot of people like me, if you know what I mean . . .

No. Be more specific.

I think that Hollywood and even Broadway to an extent still has issues with race. This country has issues with race. I am pulling the race card because it's real. It's a real dilemma in this country. We don't look at people for who they are inside; we're still basing everything on outside and not on talent. This country should be at a point where a black person can play any role. It shouldn't matter. If I am doing something wrong, nobody has said so. The country and the industry are still stuck in a racist corner, if you will. I think the country and the industry are sick with this prejudice. There have been many roles that I have been up for and told, "We're going in a different direction."

So if we accept that, how do you keep doing what you do?

Well, in spite of all that bullshit and in spite of all that's wrong, I love what I do. I love the reaction that I get from people. I love getting onstage and doing songs that move me and with which I can move people. It gives them that feeling that they get. They want to cry or laugh. They feel different from when they came in. And because of that, I have been blessed to keep going. I do what I can and I keep going. I am not really concerned about the rest. I do what I do to the best of my ability knowing that there are people who accept me for who I am and enjoy my work. If they could give me the world they would. I am very optimistic about the future. Maybe somebody out there will get it in their heads to try to do something different. Directors, producers, casting directors, artists of every ilk; it's time for people to wake up.

KAREN ZIEMBA

May and September 2008

KAREN ZIEMBA'S UPPER WEST SIDE APARTMENT IS exactly what you might imagine. Like Ziemba herself, her space is bright, airy, unfussy, warm, and relaxed. But it's the guest bathroom that she especially wants me to see. "There's a photograph in there," she tells me, "of somebody who's very important to me. It's during a performance, backstage between numbers . . . the whole . . . everything about it—the scene, the sweat, the fatigue is what's so beautiful about it, about her." I am unsurprised to find a picture of a winded, unsmiling, but radiant Gwen Verdon. Who else? We had been speaking of performers Ziemba idolizes, and, after all, there are precious few women in the history of musicals who, like Ziemba, are true dancing/ singing/actors. But Ziemba is one of them. In his review of Ziemba's breakout show, the 1991 off-Broadway revue, *And the World Goes 'Round*, Frank Rich said of her "She's got what Chita and Gwen have with her own singular daffiness." Unlike Chita and Gwen, however, she was born in an age when vehicles for her particular brand of leading lady are far more scarce.

Karen Ziemba was born in 1957 in Michigan to a mother who harbored unrealized dreams of the theater. She didn't push her daughter but she certainly encouraged her. And Ziemba took to it "like a duck to water." After graduating from the University of Akron with a degree in dance, Ziemba came to New York. Within a couple of years she was cast in the national tour of *A Chorus Line* and then, in 1983, the Broadway production of *42nd Street*, with Ziemba playing the lead role opposite Jerry Orbach. She had a small role in the 1987 flop *Teddy and Alice*, and a few more regional appearances before *And the World Goes 'Round*. With that show, a revue of Kander and Ebb songs, Ziemba accomplished something that's become increasingly rare: in a tiny, off-Broadway show, she managed to become a star. The show also launched the careers of director Scott Ellis, choreographer Susan Stroman, writer David (Tommy) Thompson, and musical director David Loud, who along with Kander and Ebb, became her self-described musical family with whom she worked steadily for the subsequent two decades.

With *And the World Goes 'Round*, Ziemba was suddenly Broadway's "it" girl, appearing in such hallowed halls as The Kennedy Center, Carnegie Hall, and the White House alongside established stars like Bernadette Peters, Julie Andrews, and Liza Minnelli. Even after notable performances at New York City Opera and Encores!, however, there was not a new musical to show off Ziemba's talents. So she toured the country in *And the World Goes 'Round* and then in Stroman and Mike Ockrent's *Crazy for You* before replacing the Broadway lead a year into the show's run. Finally, after a short-lived off-Broadway revival of *I Do!, I Do!* in 1997, Ziemba had her name above the title in a new Broadway show. Reuniting Ziemba with Ellis, Stroman,

Ziemba's turn as Roxie in *Chicago*, one of the finest dancers to essay the role. (Photofest)

Thompson, Loud, and Kander and Ebb, *Steel Pier* was so eagerly anticipated it bumped the then-new revival of *Chicago* from the Richard Rodgers Theater. However, despite eleven Tony nominations, including one for Ziemba, the show closed within two months.

In 1998, after touring in *Chicago*, Ziemba joined the Broadway company, replacing Marilu Henner as the third Roxie Hart. The following year brought Stroman's and John Weidman's *Contact*. Ziemba portrayed an abused 1950s housewife who escapes into her wordless fantasy

Karen Ziemba

A Chorus Line, National Tour and
   Broadway, 1982
42nd Street, Broadway, 1983
Teddy and Alice, Broadway, 1987
Nunsense, off-Broadway, 1985
Jerome Robbins' Broadway, Los Angeles,
   1990
And the World Goes 'Round, off-Broadway,
   National Tour, 1991
The Most Happy Fella, New York City
   Opera, 1991
110 in the Shade, New York City Opera,
   1992
Crazy for You, National Tour and
   Broadway, 1993
Allegro, Encores! 1994
I Do, I Do, off-Broadway, 1996
Steel Pier, Broadway, 1997
Chicago, National Tour and Broadway,
   1997
Ziegfeld Follies of 1936, Encores! 1999
Contact, Broadway, 1999 (Tony Award)
The Pajama Game, Encores! 2002
Never Gonna Dance, Broadway, 2003
Bye, Bye Birdie, Encores! 2004
Curtains, Broadway, 2007
On Your Toes, Encores! 2013
Bullets over Broadway, Broadway, 2014

life, via dance. She was heartbreaking, and she won the Tony, Drama Desk, and Outer Critics Circle Awards for her work. The short-lived *Never Gonna Dance* brought her another Outer Critics Circle Award and Tony nomination before she went back to work with Ellis, Loud, and Kander on *Curtains*. As Georgia Hendricks, the wisecracking lyricist of the show within the show, Ziemba, at fifty, was doing some of the most eye-popping, athletic choreography of her career.

"My first Broadway musical was starring her," says Kristin Chenoweth of Ziemba. I thought 'if I'm in a show with Karen Ziemba, I've made it.' I would come to rehearsal sometimes when I wasn't needed because I just wanted to watch her work. You can't get a bigger compliment than that."

You grew up in a household with three brothers. What was that like?

It was great. My Dad was a jock. We all had to do that athletic kind of stuff. I had to compete against three boys. My dad always said, "God, if you had played tennis as much as you danced, you'd be pro by now."

You have a picture of you and your three brothers in tutus at the age of five or six. There has to be a story there.

I didn't force them to wear the tutus but a couple of my brothers did dress up to play some of the women's characters in my scenarios. The boys had really short buzz haircuts back then, so I took my tights and put them on their heads so they'd have pigtails. I'd put bows on the legs. My mother was a wonderful seamstress so she always made our Halloween costumes and my tutus for the ballet. We had boxes of wigs and costumes.

And your mother took you to classes from a very early age, right?

Yes. She'd studied dance but stopped when she entered her teen years. When I came along she handed down the thing that she always loved but never realized professionally.

She got to be a nicer Mama Rose.

Yes! She was present but not a pushy stage mom. She knew every actor's name in every A, B, and C movie. She introduced me to all of the actors who sang, danced, and did comedies. So now, I'm a TCM whore. I love old movies.

How did you get to New York?

Excelling as a ballet dancer. I joined a little local company, Michigan Ballet Theatre, and my teacher, Evelyn Kreason, brought us to New York in the summertime and said, "You're going to take classes at the Joffrey, Alvin Ailey, ABT [American Ballet Theatre], and you're going to know what being a professional is about." I caught the bug. We'd go to see dance at Lincoln Center— Cynthia Gregory, Baryshnikov, Judith Jamison, and then we'd also see a Broadway show.

At what point did musical theater enter the picture for you?

I did musical theater in high school. My first experience was with *West Side Story*. Because of my training, my Maria was able to dance her own dream ballet.

Where did the acting and the singing come from?

I don't know! I don't know!

From the living room with the tights?

I guess so! And the watching. Watching actors in movies. I always had a natural singing voice. I sang in chorus in school and in church. I played piano well enough so that I could read music. I had this great choral director in high school who made us sing six-part harmony a cappella. I always loved choral singing and wasn't afraid to lift and project my voice. It trained my ear so that I could sing harmony. I was in the middle . . . second soprano. After coming to New York I got serious about studying voice and worked with Nancy Evers and Joan Lader.

And the acting came naturally?

I studied acting, more so when I got to New York. I remember I took my first important class when I was working on Broadway in *42nd Street*. I studied with a teacher named Wynn Handman. He ran the American Place Theatre. He had a scene study class filled with terrific actors but I really wasn't sure what I was doing. I had a good speaking voice and good presence but I didn't really understand how to express what I was feeling deep down inside. Wynn recommended I study with his colleague Fred Kareman. With Kareman I learned acting 101. The Meisner Technique. For me, it was one of the best things I did as a fledgling actor. Fred was a mentor and phenomenal teacher. I learned more about my emotions in one year from taking his class than I had in twenty years of life. I had been too busy looking at myself, which is what I did as a young dancer because that's in the training. It's about line and aesthetic, not necessarily about how you feel.

Well, you have to make sure you're not kicking someone in the face.

Yes. But what I learned from taking that acting class is how much I needed to start at the beginning, as if I was learning to dance for the first time. I had to start with simple steps. I had to learn to really listen and pay attention, to allow whatever I felt to come out without thinking, "Oh, I look bad," or, "I look like a fool." At the same time, doing *42nd Street*, I was trying to practice my new technique with my leading man, Jerry Orbach, and I thought, "No, he's got his show down already, don't try anything new." I mean, Jerry was solid as a rock. Never missed an entrance or an exit . . . never missed a show! I learned, through his example, about comic timing and consistency. But interestingly enough, six months down the line, Jerry and I seemed to have morphed into our own show, as opposed to the show he did with the actress before me. We bonded onstage and eventually, shared something new. We weren't changing the original blocking; we were just making a few new choices.

And your stage managers allowed that?

It was subtle. It wasn't as if we made major changes. It was more about the relationship between our characters.

I ask because I knew a number of cast members who were in the revival of *A Chorus Line* and they felt somewhat stymied by their direction. They felt that they weren't allowed to create. Rather, they were told, "Your hand goes on your hip at this moment." And it was up to them to justify gestures, which, once upon a time, came from the original actors' motivations. Some of them had the technique to do the work to fill the gesture, but others just made the move and it was empty. I wonder if the kind of opportunity you describe has changed.

I think in any long run of a successful Broadway show, especially a big musical, you're going to get very specific stage movement and direction from stage management because a show is like a machine they need to keep up and running. Every individual that replaces an actor in a role is going to bring their own personal qualities to that role. Each has his or her own sound, their own look, or the way they may kick their leg. But *A Chorus Line*—and I know this from my own experience in that show—is its own entity. So I know what they mean. But what's so fantastic about that piece is that the collaboration of the lighting design, how the music seamlessly meshes into the dialogue, the choreography, all the show's contents, are so perfectly . . . down to the last millisecond . . .

Calibrated?

Calibrated! So, to break from that could make it a lesser piece. If that machine isn't kept going at that same speed and precision, the momentum and intent gets lost.

I think it makes all the difference when the stage managers were in the original rehearsals and they understand the director's intent, not just the blocking.

Yes. It helps immeasurably but most stage managers don't always have the luxury of time. They get just a few hours to put a replacement actor into a show. Stage management is one of the most difficult jobs in the live theater. They must wear many different hats and multi-task like crazy. They're in charge of everything. They practically live at the theater!

Let's get back to your early career. After doing replacement work in *42nd Street* and *A Chorus Line*, and the short-lived *Teddy and Alice*, you got to work with Jerome Robbins.

Getting to work with Jerome Robbins was a major milestone for me, but Robbins was mean and demanding. We had just closed the first production of *And the World Goes 'Round* in New Jersey at The Whole Theatre and we didn't know if the show was moving to New York yet. In the meantime, I auditioned for the tour of *Jerome Robbins' Broadway*. I was so entranced by the Broadway production. To get the chance to possibly dance his choreography made me giddy. I felt that the show was so up my alley because they needed people that could dance, sing, and play character roles. There was a part open for the road troupe that was going out to LA for a while. Because they were cutting the cast down to thirty-five or forty performers from their usual sixty-four, we had a lot to do, and so I was dancing throughout the entire evening, playing Fruma-Sarah in the *Fiddler on the Roof* sequence, Mama Crook in the *High Button Shoes* "Bathing Beauty Ballet," and my favorite, the hooch-guzzling collegiate in the "Charleston" from *Billion Dollar Baby*. And of course, all the *West Side Story* stuff. It was the tour, so he could have had his assistants map the show, but he was so hands-on with his work. Unfortunately, when dealing with me . . . he never called me "Karen," "Miss Ziemba," just plain "Ziemba" or even "Z." Never uttered my name. It was always like, "Hey, Fruma" or "Miss Bennington." I guess because I was the most white-bread-looking of the Shark girls. He'd yell, "Get a wig or something! Put a flower in your hair!" He was just rude. When we were working on the "Bathing Beauty Ballet," I was rehearsing Mama Crook and I wasn't doing it the way he wanted me to, he yells, "You're terrible! You're terrible!" I was literally on Michael Kubala's shoulders performing Fruma-Sarah in the final rehearsal at the Gershwin Theater and he screamed, "You're doing it wrong! Put the understudy on!" He would berate me in front of the whole company. I was one of the older members of the cast and I was humiliated. I remember going into the bathroom afterwards and just sobbing. But the flip side was that it was the most amazing choreography I had ever done in my life; and when I was onstage doing the *West Side Story* dream ballet—it was so hard, but it was so beautiful. Everything in Robbins's work is so full and clear. Every move is for a reason.

That's the price you pay to get to do that choreography.

Yeah, for me it was. One of his assistants on the show, Victor Castelli, who had danced with the New York City Ballet, approached me opening night in LA and said, "Karen, you did exactly what you were supposed to do. He knew you could deliver so he pushed you. You responded the way you should, which was to just dig in and do it. Don't break down, don't talk back." It would make me sick to my stomach but I held it in. When being admonished by Robbins, I went back to being that little girl in ballet class who was reprimanded. I would hold back the tears and just dig in and do it.

Later in your career, as you were having experiences with other choreographers and seeing that there are lots of other ways to get results . . .

I remember one time in rehearsal for *And the World Goes 'Round*, telling Susan Stroman that I didn't want to do a certain bit of stage business. She knew the bit would work great, and after I blabbed on awhile about my objections, she said, "KZ, just shut up and try it, please." She didn't yell or even raise her voice, but gave me a straightforward direction. I finally said, "Okay." She was right. It turned out to be one of the biggest laughs in the show.

And that's eye-opening too.

It is. And I learned to always try it. Try something at least once. I've read interviews with Susan Stroman and she has said, "Karen Ziemba's fearless." Whenever I work for her, it's like, "Okay, what do you want me to do?" and I do it. I trust her and want to give her ideas a chance. Just as I want a director to trust that I will deliver.

Coming back around to Jerome Robbins, he wasn't the only Broadway choreographer famous for bullying, but do you think we are past that now? I think that the current generation of choreographers don't feel the need to treat people that way to get their end result.

I don't personally know of anybody who does that psychological warfare anymore. I've worked for Rob Ashford and he creates some very exciting and risky choreography. Executing it is difficult. You really have to pay attention to your fellow dancers coming at you from every direction at high speed. You can't be one inch off your mark. It's dangerous. Pitting people up against each other doesn't work when you need to be responsible for someone else's safety.

Did you notice while dancing Jerome Robbins's choreography that it felt different from dancing the work of contemporary choreographers? Obviously the style is different . . .

Jerome Robbins's work was so ballet-based, but there was a real human movement element to all of the choreography, too. You would do a very human, pedestrian move and then all of a sudden do a triple pirouette. If you didn't have ballet training, you couldn't do his choreography justice.

Do you think that choreography now is different in general? Is it less character-based?

Dance has changed in the media and so how people view dance has changed. I'm not talking about concert or ballroom dancing, I'm talking about some theater dancing and music videos and that kind of stuff. Dance has become a lot of quick takes and about tricks; how impressive can you be in a short bite of time, as opposed to telling a story. I think that's in conflict with what choreographers really want to achieve. They really want to tell a story.

The need for eye-popping tricks is something that I think Susan Stroman pioneered. *Crazy for You* was the first show I remember that relied on props and "gimmicks" and not just technique to make dance numbers. And they were incredibly inventive. There was so much that I had never seen before. But it set the bar for utilizing props in a whole new way. Just like *Phantom*'s chandelier changed set design, *Crazy for You* changed dance. Now we have numbers with jump ropes or people dancing with license plates on their feet.

Well, Stro has a unique way of incorporating props as part of her vocabulary in telling a story. She's very inventive. She creates in a style that really speaks to her. She was hugely influenced by the golden age of movie musicals. Look at *Singin' in the Rain*. Gene Kelly's umbrella. Or the couch in "Good Mornin'." Or all of "Make 'Em Laugh." Prop heaven! And Stro has this way of drawing on those ideas and making them fresh . . . creating something new in her own vision. And I do think other choreographers have been influenced by her work. Do everyone's ideas always work? Does anything?

Something occurred to me when you said that we have become used to viewing choreography as fast impressions. I am frequently disappointed by the *American Idol*-ization of theater in which people scream for the money notes whether or not there's anything going on behind them. Or people applaud mid-song for a great note and the applause totally drowns out the rest of the lyrics. They aren't responding to the storytelling in song, they are responding to the fireworks. Are you talking about the same thing in choreography? That perhaps people don't have patience for watching something develop and unfold; they just want to see the eye-popping moves?

Yeah—but I don't think it's always true. For example, the TV show *So You Think You Can Dance*, where they have the different couples performing hip-hop, Broadway, Latin tango, story ballet. . . . If that's done well by the performers and by the choreographer, and the dance partners have a real connection between them, it's exhilarating, because everyone's emotionally invested. But we are living in a time when we view everything in fast cuts. Movies are full of digitalization and action. It's fun, but the way it's thrown at us, our attention span is shortened.

Let's get back to you. After *Jerome Robbins Broadway*, you did *And the World Goes 'Round* and you became a star. That kind of attention doesn't usually come from a small off-Broadway show. But you were suddenly performing at Carnegie Hall, performing for the president. How did that feel?

I was ready. In *And the World Goes 'Round* I was working with the right people, doing the right material. It just suited me. I wasn't straight out of school. I had been in New York for ten years. A lot of people thought that it was the first thing I ever did in town, because I had only been a replacement up to that point. When you replace an actor you don't record the cast album, you don't get the reviews, so people didn't really know me. But the roles I played in *42nd Street* and *A Chorus Line* gave me invaluable experience. They were major steps. When I finally got to originate a role, people took notice.

During the run of *And the World Goes 'Round*, you also played Cleo in the City Opera revival of *The Most Happy Fella* and you got quite a bit of attention when you performed both shows on the same day.

That's the kind of stuff I would do. Cynthia Nixon did the same thing [performing in *Hurlyburly* and *The Real Thing* in 1984]. When you're young and you're hungry, and will try anything, you take your costume off, quick change, jump on the subway and do the next gig. It was kinda crazy.

But you would do it now, wouldn't you?

Yeah. I would. In the year and a half of doing *Curtains*, I can't tell you the number of readings, charity benefits, and awards shows I participated in while I was still doing eight shows a

Ziemba sang "Arthur in the Afternoon" in *And the World Goes 'Round* and a star was born. (Photofest)

week. It was a busy year, But wonderful because of the people that I got to work with. Deb Monk? Not only is she one of the funniest women you'll ever meet, she was generous and loving to everyone in the cast. I love watching her perform and being with her onstage. And then, of course, there's David Hyde Pierce. Such a quick wit, such intelligence. He can say something cryptic and naughty and yet is always kind, with a glint in his eye. He remembers everything that's going on in your life. On his one vacation from the show he had just a few days off and on the last day where was he? In the audience, watching the show, supporting his extended family. He's grade A.

When you get that great alchemy and that great mix of people, how did it feel to be losing it when the show is closed?

When any show closes it's bittersweet. When you're doing eight shows a week, live, which is unlike anything else, whether you are onstage or backstage, you know where you're supposed to be, where your responsibility lies. Being onstage is fun, yeah, but it requires you to be a responsible grown-up for a few hours every night. You can't screw around or nod off, or kick too high, or drop a prop, or miss a cue line. You're supporting every detail and every other person on that show and if you screw up it can fall down like a house of cards. That's where I find my strength and identity. I am proudest when I'm in that team mode. It gives me purpose.

After *And the World Goes 'Round*, in 1992 Scott Ellis cast you in *110 in the Shade* at City Opera.

110 was one of my favorite shows. It pushed a lot of buttons in me. I loved the character of Lizzie Curry. N. Richard Nash, who wrote *The Rainmaker* [the source of the musical], was at rehearsals and he was able to add, at my request, some beautiful passages from the play that had been deleted from the musical. I think Scott Ellis did great work on that production; and the score, in my opinion, is Tom Jones and Harvey Schmidt's best.

And after that, you reunited with Stroman for the tour of *Crazy for You* before replacing Jodi Benson in it in New York. What's the difference between originating something and replacing for you?

I originated the role in the first national tour opposite James Brennan. We had a long rehearsal process before we opened in Dallas but I got very little time when replacing in the Broadway production, which was well into its run and a well-oiled machine. Harry Groener had been doing the show for a year and a half and was used to it. Suddenly, he's dealing with a leading lady who weighs a different amount, whose body moves differently, and it was an adjustment for him. It can be difficult to fill someone else's shoes. And leading a company that's already bonded takes work.

In 1997 you got to do an original Kander and Ebb, *Steel Pier*. The show was written for your talents. How did that feel?

Pretty daunting. It was the first time I had done anything like that. During previews the show would change from night to night, so my job was to keep my head above water doing the newly written material and choreography. Kander and Ebb wrote terrific songs for the show but you'd be surprised how many great ones were cut. In this show, every cast member was literally dancing in the arms of a partner all night. Talk about intimacy. It was an exercise in emotional and physical trust. I missed the fact that we didn't get the chance to do an out-of-town tryout. *Steel Pier* didn't get that luxury and I think it might have really helped.

In his book, Fred Ebb said that in the studio, he and John Kander were in love with *Steel Pier*, and what ended up onstage totally surprised them.

It was a labor of love, but sometimes intimate details viewed in a rehearsal room get lost in a 1,500 seat theater. *Steel Pier* was a dark story mixed with soaring melodies and sprinkles of hope. It's one of Kander and Ebb's greatest scores. It will be done again. For me personally, it was the one that got away.

Fred Ebb, I'm sure you know, said that if there was one show he could do again it would be that one.

Yeah. I mean, do it again and maybe from a different . . . Find it.

What happens the day after a flop opens?

Our lead producer, Roger Berlind, really wanted the show to go on, regardless of our notices. He's a real gentleman and spoke to the cast, crew, and orchestra with conviction and truth about the show's prospects and that we were going to move onward. I know the show meant a great deal to him. He wanted us to feel proud of our work, no matter what happened.

You got your first Tony nomination for *Steel Pier*.

Yes. It was a thrill for me to rub elbows for the first time with all these artists from the straight theater world and the Brits who are always up for awards who I wouldn't normally cross paths with.

When you are nominated, are you fielding a ton of calls from designers asking you to wear their stuff?

My first Tony dress was designed by my friend Stephen Yearick. It was a fully beaded black beauty. I also like to borrow exquisite jewelry, because it's something I'd never buy for myself. I'd go to Fred Leighton's or to Verdura and look through their jewels and you see pieces that were designed for Cole Porter's wife and famous designs that they have continued to make through the years. Vintage pieces. When I was nominated for *Curtains* I wore earrings encrusted with aquamarine stones, beautiful things, and a simple diamond bracelet. It's scary, though.

You are walking around with $500,000 on your body.

Right, it is a bit of a rush but it gave me the jitters.

After *Steel Pier*, you went into *Chicago* in 1998. When you started in that show, it was still an artistic triumph. You were there as it was transitioning a bit into something more commercial.

Yes. Absolutely.

From a producer's standpoint—this will sound like I think poorly of a producer's stand-point and I don't—the Weisslers did what they could to keep that show running. I am not implying that they did it to keep their house in the Hamptons, although there would be nothing wrong with that. But let's say they did it to keep Kander and Ebb's score on Broadway. Here's this show that relies heavily on the specificity of a knuckle move or a hip placement, and suddenly you have non-dancers up there who have been cast to keep the show going. You were there as it was happening.

When I came into the show, Bebe Neuwirth was still playing Velma and she wanted to work with someone who could skillfully dance the Fosse choreography that Ann Reinking re-created. I didn't know Bebe well and we had never worked together before. She had this integrity about the show. She had, of course, worked with Fosse and she had a mania about *Chicago*. That's part of why she was brilliant in it. She's still my favorite Velma to play opposite. She shares the scenes with you—singing with you as one, dancing with you as one, the way Bob Fosse meant for it to be when he created the roles with Gwen Verdon and Chita Rivera. Bebe and I were a great team. What has happened since then . . . sometimes they vary the choreography to fit someone who may not be as skilled a dancer. God bless John Kander and Fred Ebb. Especially Fred Ebb in this case because he wrote a lot of that book. Along with that score the show's pretty foolproof.

It's just a different show.

Yeah, it's different. But if you deliver that stuff with gusto and conviction, most people who see the show now are not going to say, "Oh, that's not really a good Fosse move." You've got that score, that rip-roaring band onstage, it works. It's a great production.

For me, it's always a feeling of disappointment. Like you, I grew up on cast albums. The shows are precious. When they start to dilute and become something less than everything that they can be, although audiences might not notice because they have no basis for comparison, that doesn't make it good; it makes producers lucky. They scraped by and no one noticed. I can't blame the Weisslers because there aren't that many people who can do this role as well as it should be done. Did you notice it going on around you?

There were a lot of Broadway veterans in *Chicago* when I joined the cast. Most of the original company was still in residence. Later I played opposite Ute Lemper who came from the London company of the revival. She was a different kind of performer. Annie Reinking and Walter Bobbie continued to help me to evolve in the role of Roxie and adjust to the cast changes. It took work. A few months later, Bebe came back and I felt I was sharing the stage again. Bebe was a real mentor to me. Even though she'd occasionally say things that would make my jaw drop, she really looked out for me and made sure our producers treated me well. She kept saying, "You're the leading lady!" She was always in my corner.

***Chicago* was your third Kander and Ebb show out of five that you've done. John Kander said of you that there are a couple of people he and Fred Ebb would consider "our actors." You and Debra Monk were among them. For somebody who grew up on cast albums, to have become part of that world and find yourself embraced and in that circle, do you ever pinch yourself and think, "How did this happen to me?"**

Yeah, I do. Every once in a while John will say something to me or somebody else about me and I think, "Wow!" It's great coming from him because I've been so involved in and inspired by his work. It's a mutual admiration society. I owe so much of my career to him. I've known John Kander for over twenty years. His hair has gotten whiter but he's just as creative, lively, and full of wonder . . . still songwriting like mad. Debra Monk, Scott Ellis, David Hyde Pierce, and I were given honorary doctorates to Niagara University. The afternoon before the reception, there was a talkback with students, faculty, and family members. John asked me, "When we first worked together, you had a nice singing voice, but what has happened to the size and sound of your voice since then is just astonishing to me. How did you do that?" I was a bit dumbfounded. I answered that I really worked at it, but it was so much more than that. It was more like . . . I studied to become a better actor . . . I got more confident, and I grew up. But it didn't hurt that he and others gave me opportunities to work on such rich material.

Have you ever said "yes" to a show and regretted it?

A couple of times. Some projects may not turn out to be as good as I thought at first. Hindsight is twenty-twenty. But if I've committed myself to something, I'm in. On every endeavor, whether it's successful or not, I usually come away with something decent. I learn new songs, meet new playwrights, sometimes even make a lifelong friend. So it's never a total waste of time.

A year after *Chicago*, in 1999, you were back with Susan Stroman, doing *Contact*, the best musical Tony winner that so many people insisted wasn't a musical.

That particular show consisted of three interesting stories that were told very well. There were no live musicians involved and no singers singing, but it was a great piece of theater with music. It's semantics. For me, it was the culmination of my work with Susan Stroman. I portrayed an Everywoman. There was something haunting and sad about that character, but she was a survivor. The collaboration with Stro was intense and fulfilling. She wanted me to "fly" in every sense of the word—physically and emotionally.

It's a particular challenge and skill to pull off non-verbal acting that way.

People mentioned to me, mostly women, that they were very moved and transformed by the show. It inspired them to make decisions about their own life, to . . . [Ziemba mentions an actress who came to her whose name she prefers to keep off the record] came to me backstage and she was crying and said, "That was my life for twenty-five years." [She mentions another famous woman] told me, "I got it. That was me." I got a letter from a woman who ran the

Heart-breaking (but Tony-winning) in *Contact*. (Paul Kolnik)

abused women's program at Roosevelt Hospital. She said, "I work with these women every day. You nailed it."

You won the Tony!

Yes. I was white-knuckling it Tony night. I was up against Eartha Kitt. When the announcement for the award was moved to the end of the telecast, after she performed from her show, *The Wild Party*, I thought, "It's gonna be her." Lucky for me I was wrong! A few years later, Eartha and I did a workshop of Joe Stein, John Kander and Fred Ebb's musical adaptation of *The Skin of Our Teeth* at the McCarter Theatre. When we met the first day of rehearsal she gazed at me pointedly and in her signature growl, snarled, "So you're the one." She was one of a kind with a deep soul and great sense of humor.

How did you feel about doing *Never Gonna Dance*?

I got to work with the terrific director Michael Greif. I got to sing some Jerome Kern songs—not too shabby—and I was crazy about my leading man, Peter Gerety. He's a sexy, funny guy and a really fine actor. That was a show that we really needed more time with.

It seemed odd that they cast you but didn't have you dance much.

Michael Greif had seen my performance as Lucy Brown in a revival of *The Threepenny Opera* at Williamstown. Lucy Brown was a comedic, singing, acting role and based on what he saw he felt the character of Mabel Pritt was right for me. Mabel wasn't originally written as a dancer but Jerry Mitchell ended up creating some lovely choreography for her. The creative team added an obscure Jerome Kern song, "Shimmy with Me," at the top of Act 2 for Mabel to do with the company. She was the piano player for the dance school in the story and we come to find, hey, she dances, too. Jerry Mitchell was one of my first dance partners. So many great singer/dancers that I've shared the stage with have become successful director/choreographers . . . Jerry, Casey Nicholaw, Rob and Kathleen Marshall, Rob Ashford, Sergio Trujillo, Andy Blankenbuehler, James Brennan, Josh Rhodes, Randy Skinner, Lorin Latarro, JoAnn Hunter, Noah Racey . . . it's overwhelming and their work is all so different and uniquely their own.

How often do you take class now?

I take yoga and do Pilates, but not dance class. I was at the opening of a new ballet studio and I thought, "You know what? I should take class again. I shouldn't feel embarrassed that I don't look like I did when I was twenty."

But you've got nothing to be embarrassed about.

Well, that's what's in my head.

That's why you don't go to class?

Partially, and because I'm thinking, "I'm not going to be able to remember the steps. I'm not going to be able to keep up." It's just my personal insecurity stuff.

Do you save a lot of stuff from your shows?

I do and I've got to let go of some of it. But I like to save the handwritten cards and letters that I've received. I'm reminded as I read them that what I have the privilege to do has the power to really move people. It's life affirming in a business that's so filled with rejection. Sometimes I wonder if what we do actually matters. It does. Look at the power shows can have.

Wicked is about the outcast who saves her country from evil and hypocrisy. We have the power to inspire. Theater matters. But in terms of the rest of the stuff I save, I love that I can donate it to the Broadway Cares/Equity Fights AIDS Flea Market and someone else will hopefully enjoy it as much as I did.

As one of only a few singing/dancing/acting ladies, in an age that no longer builds musicals for those kinds of stars, where does that leave you?

I have to continue to stretch, not just because I won't always be able to dance like I did at twenty-five, but because I want to grow. I have abilities that haven't even been tapped. So I've been doing more straight theater, more concert work, a solo act . . . taking new steps. It's about saying yes and jumping.

So in an ideal world in ten years . . . ?

Someone would say without hesitation, "Yes, Karen Ziemba can play anything." It seems like a small wish.

DEBRA MONK

May 2008; March 2009

THERE ARE PLENTY OF PEOPLE who can't afford to go to school. Debra Monk literally couldn't afford to leave. After being berated by her teacher at Southern Methodist University during the beginning of her first term as a graduate student, Monk admits, "I said to myself, 'What am I doing here? I'm gonna go home.' But I had no money to leave so I had to stay." Thank goodness she did because her training led to a career that's lasted more than thirty years.

Not that she took New York by storm when she got there in 1975. Quite the contrary. "I came thinking I'd be doing Ibsen," she says, "but I couldn't get a job." So rather than wait to land a show, Monk and her friend Cass Morgan went to work creating one. Monk had never performed in a musical, let alone written one, but their show, *Pump Boys and Dinettes*, ran for more than 500 performances, was a 1982 Best Musical Tony nominee, and remains a regional theater staple. Monk and one of her *Pump Boys* co-stars also wrote her next show, the off-Broadway hit *Oil City Symphony*. And suddenly, after so many fallow years, Monk was cast in an eclectic array of shows, straight and musical, on Broadway and off, contemporary and classic. In musicals, she worked steadily in high-profile pieces, which were almost always high-profile flops. There was her turn as Gerald Ford's would-be killer, Sara Jane Moore in the original production of Stephen Sondheim and John Weidman's polarizing *Assassins*; the infamous Charles Strouse/Arthur Laurents/Richard Maltby adaptation of *The Thin Man*, *Nick & Nora;* Harry Connick Jr.'s *Thou Shalt Not;* and Kander and Ebb's *Steel Pier*. For that show, Monk was nominated for another Tony (she had won two years earlier for the play, *Redwood Curtain*) and stopped the show nightly with a song that would become her signature, "Everybody's Girl," but more important, she became part of a theatrical family that included Kander, Ebb, Karen Ziemba, and director Scott Ellis. All of them reunited on *Curtains* (though Ebb didn't live to see the finished product). As Carmen Bernstein, the tough-as-nails producer of the show within the show, Monk was once again Tony-nominated. It was her first big hit since *Pump Boys and Dinettes* and she loved it, but *Curtains* took its toll on Monk. She spent much of the run battling a persistent sinus infection and her knees gave her a lot of trouble. She stayed with the show for its entire fourteen-month run, however, her longest run to date.

It was during *Curtains* that I met with Monk the first time. Though she was well into the run, her dressing room was without clutter. The only personal item on display was an opening night picture with co-stars David Hyde Pierce and Ziemba. Monk isn't a collector of trinkets and souvenirs. A self-described unsentimental person, she saves just one manila envelope of items from each of her shows. "Who has room for all that stuff in New York City?" she says pragmatically. Her memories, too, are straightforward and unadorned. Not that Monk isn't

Proclaiming, "I'm Everybody's Girl" in the underappreciated *Steel Pier*. (Photofest)

Debra Monk

Pump Boys and Dinettes, off-Broadway,
    Broadway, 1981
Oil City Symphony, off-Broadway, 1987
Assassins, off-Broadway, 1990
Nick and Nora, Broadway, 1991
Company, Broadway, 1995
Steel Pier, Broadway, 1997
Thou Shalt Not, Broadway, 2001
Chicago, Broadway, 2005
Curtains, Broadway, 2007

warm. She is. But she's also in and of the moment and totally lacking in any pretense or artifice. She is earthy and grounded and to hear Ziemba tell it, more than meets the eye: "She makes fun of herself and she can tell a joke better than anyone in the world. She's this steely bitch onstage but she's so soft inside. The fragile soft ingénue."

You were born in Ohio and grew up in Virginia. When did the stage bug bite?

I'd never seen a play. We never saw plays when I was a kid. We hardly ever saw movies; we just didn't have any money. So I watched TV; we were TV babies. In high school I was a screamer and a fainter in *Bye Bye Birdie* but only because the football team was in it. I was literally gonna get married to my high school sweetheart and have kids. I didn't want to go to college. And then we broke up. All my friends went off to college and I worked as a secretary in Dupont Circle. You know those tests where you just fill in the marks? I would work on the high school equivalency tests for prisoners. It was so depressing. And finally I said, "Okay, I got to get to college. I don't know what I'm doing with myself." All my friends were at this little school called Frostburg State College, so I went up there. At the time, if you said you'd be a teacher they'd pay your tuition. Dr. David Press, who taught speech class, said, "You have to try out for a play." I thought, "I've never even seen a play. I know nothing about plays." He gave me *The Birthday Party*, Pinter. And to this day I don't know what the hell it's about.

Who does?

Who does? So I auditioned for it and I got it. I didn't know what anybody was talking about. He said, "OK, let's block it." And I'd just sort of look at him and he'd say, "Well, okay, say that line and move to the refrigerator and make a cup of tea and then come back and sit down and then close the window." And I did it. And then the next day we came back and he said, "Let's run it." I had no idea what he was talking about, didn't know any of these terms. I started doing it all different and he said, "No, no, we blocked it yesterday." I said, "What do you mean?" He said, "You know, blocking is when I tell you to go here and you say this line." And I thought for a minute, I said, "Oh, you mean you do it the same way every time? Oh all right, fine." So I did it and I had so much fun. See, my whole family worked so hard, blue collar, really hard jobs, to support a family. And none of them enjoyed their work. Work, to me, was to pay the rent, feed the kids. The idea that you could actually work and enjoy yourself was not something I'd ever witnessed in my family. I remember turning to somebody and saying, "Do people do this for a living? I want to do this." And then I was told, "You'll never make it in New York. You're not good enough. You better go get your master's because at least you'll be able to teach." I could only apply to two schools, 'cause it was $50 per application and I had $100. That was it. Dr. Press suggested Yale and Southern Methodist University. I auditioned for Yale, didn't get in. So I sent away my application for SMU and they wanted me to fly out there. I said, "I don't have the money to fly. Isn't anybody gonna be here on the East Coast?" And they said, "Well, Dr. Hosgood, the head of the department is in Washington, but we don't do this." I said, "Please, you gotta do it." I don't know where I got the guts to say all this stuff, but I did. I drove down and met him in a conference room and I did my horrible audition, Juno from *Juno and the Paycock*. Afterwards I got on my knees in front of him and said, "Oh, I'm terrible, I'm terrible. I'm really bad.

You've gotta get me in. I didn't get into Yale. If I don't get into this school I can't afford to send another $50. I don't have $50. I'll work so hard, please." And he brought me in, thank God! They had a terrific, terrific acting program. I mean, they had Shakespeare, Shaw, a comedy class. . . . It was so intense there. I was so well trained. But I still had never really seen a professional play.

If you were as terrible as you say you were, what do you think made Hosgood respond to you?

I don't know why he did, but thank God he did 'cause I don't know what I would have done, I really don't. I would have had to wait a whole 'nother year to apply for graduate school 'cause I'd have to scrape up the $50. Back then $50 was a huge amount of money for me. Huge. You live a month on $50.

You said, "I don't know where I got the guts to be saying all these things." Thinking about it now, do you have any sense where that was coming from? I mean, did you somehow innately know that you were meant to be doing this?

I don't know. I knew I wasn't good enough, I knew I didn't have the training, but I had to try. I think for the first time in my life I had a passion to do something. I fell in love with all things theater and I think that's what drove me. That's what gave me the courage. And I still feel that way about it to this day. I still feel it's the most exciting, fun, most wonderful thing I can do. And I'm so thrilled to be able to do it and make a living at it. It's amazing.

All of this was probably very foreign to your family. Were they supportive?

You know, bless their hearts, everybody was doing their thing. My mother was a single mom raising kids. She worked two jobs. She was fine with it but it wasn't like they were thrilled. They didn't really—they'd never seen plays and they didn't really know what I did. They still don't really know what I do.

Did they ever come up to see you in anything?

Not really. My mother only got to see me do one show. I remember having done all these plays and I was so proud of 'em, but I did a Tide commercial and, to them, that was the biggest thing I could do. It's just relative. Nobody who's not in the business really understands what we do. They're very proud of me, but it wasn't like I was encouraged. The four of us kids had to make our own way. But David Press, who put me in that first play at school, has come to New York to see every single play I've ever done.

You came to New York after SMU. How did you end up writing *Pump Boys and Dinettes*?

I didn't work for four years. I was an out-of-work actress. Out of work. I didn't even have an agent. I had nothing. I couldn't get my Equity card and I was so frustrated. I was waitressing and I found New York waitresses fascinating. They could be so tough and at the same time turn around and be the greatest, sweetest, dearest. I'd keep a little diary about them. I met Cass Morgan and we decided to write something so that we could each learn from each other: I would help her with acting, she would help me with singing. And we decided to write about waitresses because I had been working as one. We really wrote this piece because we had nobody sending us out, no agents. We were writing to create something for ourselves. Then, when she married Jim Wann, and when we combined forces, we did a little run of it one hot summer on 43rd street at the Westside Arts. It was really so dangerous over there back then. They let us do it at 11:00 at night after the other show finished. Nobody showed up. We had our friends come and we were like, "if you just buy a beer, we'll comp you in." We just needed enough money to pay for the air conditioning. And all of a sudden we became this phenomenon and we had producers wanting to produce it. But up until that point, none of us had thought about it really being a show. Then when it went to off-Broadway all of the dreams were like "Oh my God, what if this really went?" And then Broadway. It was thrilling and not at all expected.

Did you get your Equity card out of *Pump Boys*?

No, I actually got my card before *Pump Boys*. I had done extra work on soap operas. So I paid to get in. In fact, when I was married, my husband had his Equity card and I would take it and go to those auditions. I'd put my hand over his name and just flash it. Sometimes I'd get through and sometimes I wouldn't. They'd say, "That's not you!" Well, I tried. But I thought, "What the fuck are you gonna do? Kick me out of the union? I wasn't even in Equity." But that's how I got in the union—I had to pay my way in. You know, I have to say, my whole career's been like that. I've had a wonderful career, I'm so thankful. But always just, like, step, step, step, step, step, step. Today, too.

Do you think of yourself as still struggling?

I'm not struggling, but I have to say I have to work hard. In New York theater I'm pretty well known, but not in LA.

You have an Emmy.

It doesn't matter. You audition for everything out there. I have to audition to this day for everything I get, especially in film and television. I'm not too proud to do that. But you know, these days everybody has to work hard to get in, I mean, everybody. You can go in for an audition and there are like twenty great gals sitting in the room. And you can go, "Emmy, Emmy, Emmy, Oscar, nominee, nominee." Everybody wants a job. I think it never stops. I think you're always looking for work and having to prove yourself.

You seem to have no anger about that.

Well, you're angry when you're younger. You're angry about everything when you're younger. I was just angry all the time. I didn't do good auditions, either. I do much better auditions now. It doesn't mean I always get the part but at least I can go in, have a great time, do my audition, leave and not let it plague me for the next week like it did when I was younger. I saw Tommy Tune last night and I reminded him that when I was younger I had a non-Equity call for *Best Little Whorehouse in Texas*. I kept getting through, called back, called back, called back, until Tommy came over to me and pulled me to the side, put his arm around me and said, "You're very talented and I'm not gonna use you." That was the first time I realized that you could be good but not get the part. I just thought every time I didn't get something it meant I was terrible, I should have worked harder, I was ugly. That kept me in New York. I don't think I'd ever been to an audition where people were nice to me before. He actually treated everybody like they were real people. It was so lovely. And it really changed everything for me, gave me hope.

After *Pump Boys*, you wrote and starred in *Oil City Symphony* with another *Pump Boys* alum, Mark Hardwick. What made you guys decide to write another one?

Mark called me 'cause I play the drums and he said, "Deb, my friend Mike and I are playing this Lawrence Welk music; it's so funny. Can you come over and play the drums with us?" He would play these silly renditions of these songs. It just kinda grew and evolved into a show. I remember the night we opened down at Circle in the Square on Bleecker and I was leading people in "The Hokey Pokey." I was thinking, "My career's gonna be over. I'm making the

Monk (far left) and the original cast (and creators) of *Pump Boys and Dinettes*. (Photofest)

critics do 'Hokey Pokey.' They're gonna hate this." And they loved it. Some of the best reviews I've ever gotten.

So there's a lesson—

Yeah, I know. I've never waited for an agent to find me work. I keep trying to do everything I can do to get a job. Those things happened because I just went for it. I loved doing that show. It still runs all over the place.

Do *Oil City* and *Pump Boys* still pay dividends?

We still get little royalties and stuff. It's lovely. Yeah, from *Pump Boys* on I never had to work a second job. I was able to always just do theater.

Your next musical was *Assassins*. Did you feel like you might be transitioning to the big leagues, working with legends?

I didn't think about transitioning. I was in a shock that I was in that show and I was very, very nervous. 'Cause I don't read music so I was scared about keeping up with everybody. The first day we all had to sit as a group and learn these difficult songs. At the end [musical director] Paul Gemignani says, "Does anybody need me to put it on tape?" and I was so embarrassed because I thought, "I'm going to be the only one." I raised my hand and everybody raised their hand with me. Everybody was just as nervous as I was. It was great, that one. That was a wonderful experience for me. And also my first big flop. It was very interesting being in something that people hated. People hated it. They would leave in the middle of our scenes. They would actually get up and leave. I had never experienced that. People thought this show was about encouraging assassins and wanting to kill our president. I remember Sondheim did a talk back after the show and people were saying that to him. Sondheim almost started crying. He was like, "If that's what you got from this show then I've written it wrong." That was frustrating. However it made us bond even further as a group. I am still actually very close to many people from that show.

Did you feel vindicated when the 2004 *Assassins* revival was appreciated?

Not really because it wasn't our show. It was a different show. But I was happy that people who never got to see it saw the show. But no, it had nothing to do with us; I thought it was great but it wasn't our show.

Do you have specific recollections of working with Sondheim?

He is one of the most supportive people ever. He is so excited and helpful and generous. He writes you great notes. He really wants you to be the best you can be. He's also so emotional. He cries all the time. Always crying. Just so moved by it all, always. I still get nervous when I know he's in the audience, when I sing at a benefit honoring him. You know he's out there and you want to do really good. You want him to like you, you want him to be happy.

Your next musical was the infamous *Nick & Nora*.

Nick & Nora was a totally different situation. It was troubled from the minute we started. *Assassins* was troubled as well but we were unified. *Nick & Nora* had no direction. It was very confusing. No one knew what we should do to make the show better. It kept getting more and more hard to do it. When I first read the script I thought it was great. The songs were great, too. I *still* think it's a great script. But the creative team wasn't always getting along. When you don't have that, that trickles through everybody. Arthur Laurents was well known for giving you pretty harsh, tough notes, so nobody's feeling really centered and like you know what you're doing. You're not really sure how to make it work, you know? It was one of the longest previews ever. [Seventy-one previews—a record bested only by *Spiderman: Turn Off the Dark*.] Any kind of creative togetherness seemed to be dissipated. People were not talking to one another.

So as it was getting tinkered with you didn't know which way to turn?

Well, during previews Arthur Laurents was giving notes and he comes to me and he says, "And Debra . . . I don't know. Try anything." And then he looks at the rest of the cast and he says,

"Does anybody have any ideas?" Christine Baranski said, "I can't believe he said that to you. I mean, what do you do with that note? Try anything?" But I have to tell you about what Arthur did for me; in the months between the first reading of *Nick & Nora* and rehearsals, Lanford Wilson sent me a play with a note saying, "This might be a piece of shit, but I wrote it with you in mind." I didn't know him. It was *Redwood Curtain*. So I read it and I thought, "Oh my God, this is a great part." We did a reading of it and then they decided to take it to Seattle. Now all of a sudden *Nick & Nora*'s starting up and I have a conflict. So I call Arthur and I'm so scared. I say, "Arthur, I don't know if I can do *Nick & Nora*. Lanford Wilson wrote a play for me and we're going to do it in Seattle." "Is it a good play?" "Yes." "Is it a good part?" "Yes." He says, "I'll tell you what, open my play, then I'll let you out." Unheard of. He said just get to the opening and then I could leave. He did that for me. So I'll always be thankful to him. I didn't have to worry about it because *Nick & Nora* closed. But I got to do both of them. And we're still good friends, I love him. He's like a force of nature. I don't know how he keeps doing it, he's amazing. With *Nick & Nora* I think it was just not happening and nobody could really fix it. I don't know if it was fixable. You try to tell a story and some people just don't like that story. With *Thou Shalt Not*, people *hated* that story.

With shows like *Steel Pier* and *Thou Shalt Not*, by opening night did you feel like you knew whether or not it was going to work?

Steel Pier was so much fun and such a great rehearsal period. I wish that show had had a chance to run. I think we would have found our audience. I always thought it was a really wonderful, beautiful show. The rest of 'em I understand, you know? *Steel Pier* will come back some day.

After experiencing a few flops that were so highly anticipated, did you start to develop a suit of armor?

If I thought that way, I'd leave the business. I just do the shows that I like and want to do. Just because one person or a couple of critics don't like them doesn't mean that they're not good shows. It's heartbreaking and it also means that I have to get another job. But I don't seek a show or pick a show because I think it's going to be a hit. I do shows that I believe in. So I've never felt like I have a suit of armor. It's sad when they close and I'm upset that they're closing, and I go on to the next one. But it doesn't mean that I am going to give up theater. It's part of this business. Even in a hit you're going to close eventually. Nothing lasts forever. And I might not have had the TV and film career that I've had if my shows had run. You never know why things happen. The workshop and the rehearsal period of *Steel Pier* was one of the best times of my life. That was great! *Redwood Curtain* got the best reviews I've ever had in my life and that closed in six weeks so who's to say? What can you do? I just try to do the shows, and enjoy every day, knowing that they will close. If we have a long run it's great and if we don't, there's another one around the corner. I'm still friends with many, many people from all of the shows that I've done. Some of them are my best friends. We keep working together again and again.

Kristin Chenoweth was one of those people. She calls you her second mom. Could you tell during *Steel Pier* that she was going to explode?

Who knows. I bet a lot of people will say, "Oh, yeah, I could tell she was going to be a big star." I don't know if that's true. But I never heard anybody able to sing that way consistently eight shows a week. I thought that was phenomenal. And I never met anyone like her. We became very close and we're still close. I think it's great for her that she's had this career and she deserves it. But there are a lot of women who come to New York and are talented, funny, beautiful, and perfect, and one of them gets to get through. I am so happy for her. She's great. But there are another fifty girls that deserve it, too.

Karen Ziemba was another *Steel Pier* alum whom you worked with again.

Karen Ziemba is one of the strongest people I have ever met. She has never missed a show; she has a voice that is like a beautiful, shining, silver rod that goes right down into her gut; she has that body that is just unstoppable. The energy and passion of her dancing is so thrilling. She's an actress. A wonderful, beautiful, sensitive actress. They throw that term triple threat around a lot but she really is. She's so caring and loving and dear. She's a really remarkable person. What she does, she does in such a way that she makes it look easy. I don't know if she's always appreciated for doing what she does because she makes it all look effortless.

Before *Steel Pier* you were in *Company* for the Roundabout. Was *Company* daunting?

It *was* daunting. More daunting than almost anything I've done. But Elaine Stritch has been a great supporter of mine. I have never sung that song ["The Ladies Who Lunch"] since. I never wanted to sing it at a benefit. It's a tough song. I was really proud of it and glad that I got to do it. But there was always the pressure of being compared to the original. Sondheim never made me feel that way, though. He was amazing.

You've only come in as a replacement once in your career. That was in 2005 in *Chicago*.

Yeah, I'd never wanted to do it, but it was just one of those things that worked out so amazingly. I had scheduled a hysterectomy and my doctor said, "You need to put aside four months for recovery because it takes a long time." So I just blocked off time to have this operation. And right before, they called me for *Chicago*. I saw the show and I thought, "Wow, for this role, you just sit there on the side and then you sing your one little song and you go back and sit down. That might be perfect." I had my operation and then I was in that show, like, a month and a half later. I was a little tentative about it. But I swear to God that show helped me heal. It was one of the greatest things I ever did for myself. I made a little bit of money, I got to work with Huey Lewis and Charlotte d'Amboise and Brooke Shields. And to sing those songs! It worked out perfectly. I loved doing it. Loved it, loved it, loved it, loved it. The Weisslers were so amazing to me. They said, "Anytime you want this role, let us know." So you know, it's one of those great things of "why not? " As you get older you might want to have a little somethin' you could fall back on. Plus I'd never been in a big, fat Broadway hit. I thought it was fun to be in a show you didn't have to worry about opening and the critics. I'd never experienced that before. There's something so relaxing about that. You just show up and do your job and you act.

And you don't have all the added press appearances or the Tony Awards. When you do get nominated for awards and you have all of the extra commitments that go along with that, is it fun, is it a drag, or is it both?

Well, it's better to be nominated than not be nominated. But there's always something to complain about right? Like, you're not nominated and everybody else is going to the luncheon and you're, "I wish I was going to the luncheon." And then you're nominated, you're going to the luncheon, and it's, "ugh, another luncheon." But most of all you do that stuff to sell the show. You want your show to run. I mean, it's part of our jobs to show up to all these luncheons. You show up to try and get as much publicity as you can and get people to come to your show. It's about selling tickets.

Have you been able to enjoy the times that you've been nominated and to sort of revel in it at all?

Well, let's see. I was nominated for *Steel Pier* and then it closed, that was sad. I was nominated for *Redwood Curtain* and we were already closed. And with *Curtains* everybody said, "Oh, this is Christine Ebersole's year." I had the honor to be nominated. With *Redwood Curtain* they were writing columns about who was gonna win and I was never listed. So to win was, like, a total shock for everybody. The press always has their favorites and I'm usually not on those lists. So I always go to these things just happy to be there. You can't get caught up in it, you can't. You do! But you can't. I'm thrilled to have won and every time I get nominated it's exciting and wonderful. Every time you don't get nominated you feel like you're left out of the party.

Do you have specific memories of the night that you won?

Well, because everybody else thought I was gonna lose . . . it's a story! I was sitting next to [actor] Paul Kandel, and his beautiful wife, a gorgeous black woman. Unbeknownst to me, when they said, "And the nominees for best supporting actress, Debra Monk . . . " they put the camera on her, not me. And then they said, "And the winner is Debra Monk," and they put the camera on her. And then you see me walking and all of a sudden the camera swerves to me. Now, back when my show closed I got a call from Circle Rep and they said, "Christine Lahti is leaving *Three Hotels* and Mercedes Ruehl is coming in to replace her, but there's a week there that is open and we don't want to close down. Would you want to come in and do that week?" I saw the show and I thought, "I *do* want to do this, this is great." And then all of a sudden Mercedes Ruehl dropped out. I never really heard the whole story but something happened. So they asked me to stay and I did that show for seven months. So now, I win the Tony for *Redwood Curtain* and I look up and it's Mercedes Ruehl giving me the thing. I went, "Oh dear, this is a little awkward." But I went up and I said whatever I said. And then they take the Tony away and they whisk you out the door and across the street to some bar where they have all the press. First they take you to the TV people and they're going, "You know what? You can just go on. You don't have to really talk to the TV people. You can just go right down to the newspapers." So, I go down to the newspaper and the newspaper guys say, "So why did Mercedes Ruehl leave—" that's the first thing they asked me. And I said, "I don't know, but she's upstairs; she'll be down in a minute. Ask her." And then I go to the radio people and they say, "Congratulations. So why did Mercedes Ruehl . . . " that's all they wanted to talk about. Nobody asked me a question! Then they said, "Now just go wait over here." So I wait over there. Andrea Martin had won that night for *My Favorite Year* and her show had closed, too, so nobody really wanted to talk to her, either. So we kind of bonded that night. We said we were winners but losers. We were just hanging out. Now, that year they were honoring Agnes de Mille and all the winners were gonna sing "Oklahoma!" at the end, right? So slowly people are coming in and taking people back to get ready for this big number and Andrea and I were, like, left there. Finally they took Andrea and I said, "Aren't I supposed to go, too?" "Just wait there, we'll come back." I was the only one there and nobody came back. I thought, "I'm gonna miss this whole thing!" So I walked back across the street to the Gershwin and I punched the elevator button and I end up downstairs wandering around with the set designer from *Tommy*. We finally get back up just as they are starting to sing "Ooooooklahoma—" and Barry Bostwick grabs my hand out of the elevator and pulls me around so I can be onstage. That was my Tony night. Isn't that hysterical?

You have said that your career has an element of "Wah, wah . . ."

It was *totally* wah-wah! The night I won my Emmy was the same thing! Nobody wanted to take my picture. Thank God, Rob Marshall was my date and he was so sweet. By the way, when you're nominated for an Emmy for featured, you are not at the big Emmys; you're at the—I call it "the Emmys at the Holiday Inn with the beer nuts and the keg." You're at the one with the technical guys, right? But they never wanted to talk to me either! I call it winners but losers. It just never stopped. But you know what? I'm still thankful. I'm just so thankful.

Of course you are, it's just funny and—

I know! You can take home the award and still feel like a loser sixteen years later. I won that award in 1993? I was at the opening of *God of Carnage* and a reporter comes up to me . . . and Marcia Gay Harden, who was up against me when I won the Tony, is right behind me. It's *her* opening night. And he says, "So you won Marcia Gay's Tony?" I looked at him and I said, "No, I won my Tony." Sixteen years later, making me feel like a big loser! So, you know, it never stops. Don't get me wrong—there are great press people who write lovingly and beautifully about the theater. And then there are schmucks.

With the exception of your first show, *Pump Boys and Dinettes*, you've never had a long run until *Curtains*.

This is the longest. I always wanted one. This has been great. It's a great show. I love everybody I'm working with. I have been involved with this show for six years so it's a long time. But when a long run comes, there are a lot of injuries and things. It's exhausting. It's a hard show for us. So you're trying to keep your health. That's what it's been for a lot of us in the show. I love that it was a success for John [Kander] and Fred [Ebb], which is why I wanted to do it. I'm happy for them that they had another show on Broadway that ran. But I am going to take some time off for a while. I am too unhealthy and until I really feel well again, I can't do it. I've missed shows and I never miss shows. This illness has been really hard to let go. So that's the hard thing about a long run.

Has doing a long run given you the opportunity to find more in the role than you otherwise might have?

Oh, yeah. Those things are great. It's like you whittle away everything until it becomes the simplest, purest form. Most of the shows I do run six weeks. Really! That's it. Or even shorter

With David Hyde Pierce in *Curtains*, devouring a role Fred Ebb tailored just for her. (Joan Marcus)

if you're at places like Second Stage or Lincoln Center. It gives you the opportunity to get through all of that first period—publicity, opening night, the awards thing, and then you can just play it. It's lovely how you can just simplify, simplify. It's all about simplifying to me and just really talking and making it as real as possible. It's really fun to do that. This cast is so good—soooo good—and so professional. There has not been one instance where someone hasn't shown up to do their show. Nobody has an off night and nobody marks. Ever. I've never seen anything like it. If you're not feeling your best, they buoy you up. We have David Hyde Pierce as our leader and he sets the standard. And he has such a high standard because he's such an incredible person. Everybody has risen up to his level. He's the most generous, kind, incredibly talented, very thoughtful—he's a really special person. He's a very rare human being in this business and it's great. For all of our young kids, making their debuts, I am so happy for them that they get the experience of being with him. The crew, the staff, the front of house, everybody loves him. That permeates throughout the whole show. And I think the audience also feels it. It looks like we are having a good time and we always are. It's a smart show. Our director, Scott Ellis, and [book writer] Rupert Holmes really homed in on the book and made it as clear as possible. It's one of those very rare shows where everything about it—the producing staff, the theater staff, the creative staff, the company and all of our crew—we all get along, we all like each other, and I treasure it because I know it happens rarely. So I'm very happy to be part of it.

Will leaving this one be hard for you?

It's always hard to leave shows and it's not so much the show. This show, I feel like we did the show the best we could and I am really proud of it. What makes you feel sentimental is not seeing these people every day. The family you create. That's really hard. I won't be sad not to do the show; I will be sad not to see these people.

You talked about John Kander and Fred Ebb and being happy for them. In their book, they called you one of their dear friends in the business. Does that ever make you go, "Oh my God"?

It does. The very first musical I saw in New York was *Chicago*. I'll never forget sitting there. I mean, more than the fact that they're legends, that they are the people they are. John is just one of the greatest men I've ever met. He's just such an incredibly sweet, dear, wonderful person. Open and lovely and smart. I just adore him. Because they are such good friends I forget sometimes about the legendary thing. 'Cause I think of them more and more as just these wonderful, sweet, dear men that I love and love to hang out with. John's a very shy guy. He doesn't like to play the piano in public. He really only wants to be up in the country in his house, walking around in the woods. He and Freddie had such a work ethic and worked so hard for so many years.

Chita Rivera told me that even though Fred Ebb is gone, she feels comforted being on-stage with his words and it helps her feel like he's around.

He's totally in this show every minute. Everything I say. "It's a Business" was not changed a word from the way that he wrote it. He coached me on it. I got to work, luckily, with him and John. Yeah, he's in the show so much. He would have loved this show. I am sad thinking about all of this—that he didn't get to see it open. This was his show. It was his humor. I still feel that he's with us. What Chita said is true. Nobody writes lyrics like him. The way he writes is so smart. Only a really smart, well-read, educated person can write like this and also make it so base and funny. I feel very, very privileged to have known him, to have had him as a friend. To have been able to do three of their shows, was thrilling, thrilling, thrilling. I miss him terribly. With him and John—John's music is so beautiful. Sondheim is this type of writer, too—when they write a song, there's so much information to feed you as an actor. Not only musically, the rhythm and notes—they really give you a lot of information. And, of course, the lyrics as well. Not everybody writes like that. You're given so many wonderful clues about who these people are without ever seeing the words on the page.

Your career is unusual in that the roles don't seem to follow any sort of path . . .

I have not planned my career. Well, I planned to do theater. That was always my first love and the thing that I wanted the most. Every TV thing I got was cast in New York. I never went to Los Angeles trying to get something, to try to land TV or film. It was never like, "OK, now, I am going to do TV," or, "Now I need to do a musical." I never planned that way. I've been very, very lucky. The timing has been terrific for me. To be able to do both plays and musicals is very rare. A lot of people don't get to do that. They get kind of cornered into one area and I've been lucky to be able to go back and forth. And I've been lucky to be able to do TV and film. It's just something that happened, not because I planned it. I've been with the same agents for more than twenty-five years. They are not a big high-powered agency. We do career planning in that we make choices; if I turn something down it's because I think, "I shouldn't do another part like that because I've done it already. We'll just wait and see what comes up." In that way, yes, we make decisions. Sometimes it's very painful for me to turn down work. When this closes I don't have any specific plans.

I've seen you when you've been rail thin and I've seen you heavier. Has weight been something that's been an issue for you in terms of getting cast?

Well, I don't know. I keep getting cast no matter what size I am. Now, if I'd been different sizes would there have been other parts? I don't know.

Did you ever want to be a different size for the sake of work?

I fought my weight all my life. My whole family does. Up and down, up and down, up and down. I always struggle with it. But I was a character actor even when I was in my twenties. I was never an ingénue. You can be a character actress and be heavy or thin. I have been both my whole career and it just so happens that whatever weight I am seems to fit into whatever's gonna come up next, or it doesn't seem to make a difference and I love the parts I've done. Believe me, for my own health and for my own vanity I wanted to be thinner, forget theater or film. I've tried off and on. Sometimes it works and sometimes it doesn't. It's not about getting a part. I just want to be able to sing better and do eight shows a week and feel physically better. I want that more than anything. More than a role, I want to feel healthy. So I'm losing the weight now because of that. Every time I've tried to lose weight for a role, forget it, it doesn't happen.

You have a willingness to go from a tiny, off-Broadway house to a big musical and back again. That's pretty rare.

I guess I was trained as an actress. I was never trained as a musical person. And everything I did comes from the acting standpoint. The singing . . . I was trained afterwards, but that kind of came through the back door. I sang in church but I never thought I'd sing like this. That's all kind of added on. But everything is approached as an actress. If you have a base of being a good actress you can do a small house or a big house. You're trained in that and that's what's helped me the most to be able to do all these different things. I approach all of these things the same—whether it's TV, musical, a play, a film, a small house, whatever. It's all the same. What are you trying to say? Who are you talking to? All the stuff is there. In a musical like this—I always say to my actor friends who don't do musicals that it's like doing Shakespeare. It's almost like the world is bigger. You still have be truthful, you still have to be real, but you have to get it out there to the gods. It still has to be based in reality—it can't be just big for big's sake. The truth has to be there. Having good training, which I did, having gone to graduate school and really studying hard, that has served me the best. I find that the environment doesn't matter to me. I have had some of the great, great directors direct me. Scott Ellis is one of our great directors of all time. James Lapine, Dan Sullivan, Nicholas Martin, Arthur Laurents, Joe Mantello, Jerry Zaks . . . So when you're in some of those different venues, if you have good material and a great director, that's half the battle. I really like going back and forth between all of those different things. I find it very appealing. For years I didn't even look at my contracts. I was so happy, I would just sign anything to work.

VICTORIA CLARK

August 2012

FOR THE 2013 PRODUCTION OF Rodgers and Hammerstein's *Cinderella*, Douglas Carter Beane re-imagined the role of the fairy godmother. Marie, as he named her, was the traditional, poised image of a fairy godmother, a beautiful soprano in a massive twinkling dress, reminiscent of Billie Burke in *The Wizard of Oz*. But she was also a dotty bag lady with a lusty laugh and a twinkle in her eye. She was Victoria Clark. (It helps, of course, that he fashioned the role for her.) Marie allowed Clark to deftly combine the elements she has perfected in the two halves of her career, the first part of which was defined by spot-on comic character women (see *How to Succeed in Business . . .* ; *Titanic*), the second by straight-spined, serious women with emotional heft (see *Sister Act, Follies*). The dividing line between the two was Clark's superlative performance as Margaret Johnson, a 1950s Southern housewife at the heart of Craig Lucas and Adam Guettel's *The Light in the Piazza*. Clark's performance was universally hailed. In his *New York Times* review, Ben Brantley raved, "Hands down the best musical performance by an actress this season. . . . Ms. Clark emerges as a star not through show-stopping flash but with the quiet confidence of an actress who knows every bumpy inch of her conflicted character." Clark won every conceivable award and the redhead previously known as a second banana was suddenly a major player.

As Clark approaches her mid-fifties, though, she is not at all sure what path she'll choose. Could she continue happily in musicals? Absolutely. But along the way, Clark developed an equally satisfying career as a teacher and coach, and she says she'd be just as happy committing herself to that work. And in the last few years, she's done some straight plays quite successfully, thank you.

And, of course, there's always directing, which she studied at New York University. Looking at her "books" (which are sort of combination journals/visual guides/scrapbooks), it's clear that Clark maps performances and her journey with a character much as a director might map a show. The skill and the talent are there, waiting to be tapped. As far as Clark is concerned, the opportunities are all exciting and she wants to do as much as she possibly can.

These books are big, and they take up a lot of shelf space in Clark's sunny upper West Side apartment, which she shares with her son TL. There is also a grand piano in the living room, marking the territory in which she teaches. But the home is very much a home. It's warm and relaxed, like Clark herself, who somehow manages, like Marie, to simultaneously take things very seriously and not so seriously at all.

Clark's game-changing role, Margaret Johnson in *The Light in the Piazza*. (Joan Marcus)

You were born in Texas. When did you decide that the arts were for you?

I was the youngest of three. I had a lot of energy, and my grandmother enrolled me in music lessons when I was six. We started singing and playing piano, and it just seemed a natural outlet for someone who had a lot to say. I remember feeling very early on that I would like to try to do all the things that interested me. Everything that I do is about storytelling. I see

Victoria Clark

Sunday in the Park with George,
    Broadway, 1985
Cats, National Tour, 1985
Les Misérables, National Tour, 1987
Guys and Dolls, Broadway, 1992
A Grand Night for Singing, Broadway, 1993
How to Succeed in Business Without Really
    Trying, Broadway, 1995
Titanic, Broadway, 1997
Cabaret, Broadway, 1999
Urinetown, Broadway, 2003
Bye, Bye Birdie, Encores! 2004
The Light in the Piazza, Broadway, 2005
    (Tony Award)
Follies, Encores! 2007
Juno, Encores! 2008
Sister Act, Broadway, 2011
Follies, Los Angeles, 2012
Cinderella, Broadway, 2013
Gigi, Broadway, 2015

myself in a very long line of people that want to communicate stories for all kinds of purposes: for educational purposes, entertainment, to make people laugh, to make people understand, to chide, to admonish, to scare, to illuminate. I really don't care how people see me or what people say about me. It's more important how I feel about the short amount of time that I get to be here on this earth. Even when I went off to college I thought maybe I wanted to act, but then directing came up very soon after, and then I wanted to be the next amazing opera director, and then I sidestepped into acting. But it's all storytelling, whether you're directing or parenting or being a friend. I think in telling our stories, we share grace and healing. There's a lot of receptivity involved, obviously. You have to be listening and receiving. It's always felt to me like [theater] is its own form of ancient healing, just like being a shaman. This is our way to heal others and ourselves.

It's interesting that you saw yourself as a director more than an actor.

It's so not linear, this career. Even just a year ago, I hit a really hard patch, and I thought maybe I should just direct and stop performing. Just go back into teaching—which I love—and directing.

Did you have a moment of clarity that led you to focus on acting?

I had so many moments of clarity. I don't know where to start. The first one probably was at NYU in the Graduate Musical Theater Writing program. I had come there to be a director and to work and collaborate on new musical theater works. But I didn't know how to fit in in New York. In those days, I literally had to build up my strength to go to Fairway. All the little old ladies would knock me down with their shopping carts as I was reaching for the ground coffee. I thought, "I really need a sign that this is the right career for me." I was praying. And I'm not kidding, within five minutes the phone rang, and it was Ira Weitzman calling, saying, "I don't know if you're interested, but someone is taking a leave of absence from *Sunday in the Park with George,* and I need someone who's really versatile who can learn music really fast to cover three women. Nine roles. Are you interested in auditioning?" That was my sign. And I booked it.

You were a directing student. How did Ira Weitzman know you as an actor?

NYU. Ira was a casting director then, and he would come to watch the writers present material and none of the writers wanted to do their own scenes and songs, so they would hand me material: "Vicki, read these five roles" or "Sing these twenty songs." In six months Ira had heard me do everything that I could do. That's how he knew I could cover, bada bing, bada boom. So that was my sign. Another good one was when my son was nine months old. I was sitting, breastfeeding him, and the phone rang. It was Cameron Mackintosh. About seven years prior,

I had been dance captain in the first national tour of *Les Misérables*. I played Madame Thénardier at twenty-eight. So I would do my part but I would also direct and put people in the show. About seven years later, when I was performing in *How to Succeed . . .* , and my son was not even a year old, Cameron said, "How would you like to take over supervision of all the American companies of this production?" So I went down and met with him. I literally just thrust my baby on my husband, slapped some clothes on, and went down there and met with Cameron and John Caird. They were very serious. I said, "I've got to tell you, I'm on the fence about this because I came to New York to do what you're saying, but now my performing career is just starting to bloom. This conversation would have been good about five years ago or maybe ten years from now, but right now I can't do the amount of traveling that you ask because I have an infant." Cameron said, "Do you actually think you're good enough to have a real career as an actor?" And I said, "Yes, I do." That was one of those moments. It was a risk because that would have launched my directing career in a major way. Financially I would have been set for the rest of my life. But it didn't feel right for my family and I knew I had more to learn in the acting category. I just see things as a director. Even when I act, the best directors have to say, "You have to shut up now and let me take control. You're going to have to trust me." But there's a part of me that always zooms up, looks at the trajectory, looks at the function of the scene, the function of the character. The set should be moving there, that's the wrong lighting. It's really hard for me just to stay in my assignment. It takes a lot of grace and humility to say, "It's not my job." All the great directors know what they want. You may not agree with them, but they know the story that they're telling.

What about when a director lacks that clarity?

I try, in a very kind way, to get them to articulate what story they're telling. If a director can tell us what story they're telling, we can all be in his story. If you can't articulate your point of view on a story it's very hard for us to fill in the blanks. They don't have to take you by the hand and walk every step with you, but just like a traffic cop, they tell you the way to go. When you say, "I don't know how to get to Columbia University," I might say, "There's a gate at 116th and Broadway. If you want to go over yonder and go around and get your ice cream and sit down there, that's up to you, but that's where we're all going to end up." You have to let the actor wander off. You have to let them have their process, otherwise they won't own it. They'll feel like you own it, and that they're doing it for you. They have to feel like they're doing it for themselves, and that there's so much of their own blood in it that it can only belong to them. But surprisingly a lot of directors won't tell you the final destination is 116th and Broadway. They don't know. In a way I feel like I've taken this thirty-year graduate course in directing because I've watched how everybody does it.

It started when you saw *Pippin* on Broadway when you were in sixth grade. That inspired you to want to direct?

The point of view was so strong. I remember actually thinking, "I wouldn't do it like that but I appreciate how theatrical it is." And I remember I liked the energy of the city. It just seemed magical to me—a place where magic things happen.

When you got here after Yale what was New York like?

It was exciting. Sondheim was king, king, king. After *Sunday*, I was offered a part in the Fairy Tale Musical [which became *Into the Woods*], which I turned down in one of my shrewd career moves. They were calling it the fairy tale thing and James Lapine specifically called and asked me. But I turned it down for a steady job in the tour of *Cats*, believe it or not. I saved a bucket of money. I understudied the Gumbie Cat and the Opera Cat, then Jennifer Butt left the tour to do Madame Thenardier in *Les Miz*, and I replaced her. They just bumped me right up without blinking an eye. Boom. On.

Where did that dancing come from?

I don't dance. I'm a terrible dancer. But I danced in every show except for *Piazza* and *Sister Act*. I danced my ass off in *Cabaret*, in *How to Succeed*. . . .

How do you end up in *Cats* if you're a terrible dancer?

They wanted somebody with a high C. I popped it out. Did a split. Made fun of dancing. They thought I was funny. They talked for two seconds and said, "We'll see you Monday morning in Chicago." It was Friday at 6:00 PM. Tuesday morning I was in Chicago Ballet Studios, walking through three feet of snow. The dance captain, wonderful Richard Stafford, was mortified because they had sent him someone that couldn't dance at all. I went down to the laundry room in this little furnished hotel in Chicago, and I worked on [the Gumbie Cat number] every night between midnight and 3:00 AM, and I got it. I can still remember the way the routine starts. That's why when kids today come to me and say, "I don't really want to." I say, "Are you kidding? You always say 'yes,' and then if it's not a skill you have, go out and get it, and get it fast, and make it look like you know what you're doing." That was a major dance show. I lost 152 pounds.

When you first got to New York . . .

Well, remember I came here to be a director. There were five women in the program and seventeen men. There was George Wolfe, Winnie Holzman, just totally brilliant. New York for me was seen through the prism of these brilliant people. I had an illegal sublet on 74th Street right by Fairway. I was studying voice with the renowned soprano Eva Likova who had one glass eye because her husband had thrown a chair at her in a fit of rage. She had a cat that she would throw at me when I was late, and I was always late. I was terrified of her. So that was my life. Going to these weird seminars with these brilliant people. We were the first cycle and no one really knew what to do with these directors. We were always being invited to parties, and Sondheim would be there, Ted Chapin, Ira Weitzman, Andre Bishop. We were in these rarefied circles of people who had or were about to shape the future. And our teachers were Betty Comden and Adolph Green, Stephen Schwartz. So when I got pulled into acting, I already had these connections. They didn't know me as an actor; they knew me as a director and collaborator.

You go through this program and then the *Sunday in the Park with George* thing happens. Nine roles is a lot of Sondheim music to learn at once.

I learned it overnight. Paul Ford played it for me, and put it on a tape recorder. I came in the next day and it was all memorized. I wanted to be indispensable. But I never went on. The minute I arrived the woman who was the first cover came over to me and said, "You will never go on." She actually pushed me onstage once during rehearsal to try to get me in trouble. I didn't really care, I was just happy to be in the building. I was only two years out of Yale. I watched the show almost every night, I learned in the dressing room how unhappy a lot of the actors were. Everybody was brilliant but they didn't have a ton of stuff to do. I didn't like the negativity, so I was out, watching from the balcony. I'd watch how James Lapine had constructed it. It was a soaking-up time.

After *Sunday*, did you ever have to wait tables or—

Never. Because at NYU, I once mumbled under my breath that a lot of the songs that the composers were writing were completely un-singable. So the head of the program asked if I would teach a master class in voice. I said, "Well, that would be hilarious since I have never taught at all." I was twenty-two. And they said, "Just tell us what you know." So I started with thirty minutes of material, and I just talked about basic range. Four hours went by. And one of the composers in the program who also coached, Steven Lutvak, came over and said, "Guess what? You're a teacher. And I have four people that I want to send you right away who need vocal work." And so that's how it started. During the time in between acting jobs or when I've wanted to spend time with my son and take a break from acting, I teach. I never have had to advertise. People know that I do it. I've worked with famous people, children, people who are just interested in singing but they don't know why, people who have technical issues—everybody. I love having someone come in, and I just focus 120 percent on them. It makes me very happy.

You almost did *Edwin Drood* . . .

I auditioned and the very same day they called. I was replacing Paige O'Hara who was leaving, to make a movie "cartoon" [*Beauty and the Beast*, playing Belle]. Everybody thought it was a big mistake. "You're leaving a Broadway show to do a cartoon?" Anyway, the stage manager called and said, "Please come to the theater Thursday night, and you'll meet the cast, and you'll see the show." I got there a little bit before a half hour, and everybody was sort of around the callboard. The energy was very odd. I had no idea what was going on. The stage manager came over to me and he was crying. He said, "Our closing notice went up so you do not need to rehearse. You will be paid for two weeks." So for that audition I made two weeks of Broadway salary, and I stayed and watched the show.

Your next show was *Les Miz*. How was that experience?

Two years on the road, saving money for my wedding, unbelievable. And that's when the directing and the acting came together, and I was really happy because I was doing both.

Shortly after *Les Miz* . . .

Guys and Dolls. And I really didn't want to do it because I had been doing principal roles and I felt like a principal actor. I didn't feel like an ensemble member even though I was there to be in the mission band, and to cover the roles of Adelaide and Sarah. I was thinking, "My whole life is going to be about people calling me to understudy." It was very difficult for me because I think you have to have a very specific kind of personality to understudy and I don't have it. You have to be in the background, not in anyone's way, and then all of a sudden when the time comes, you have to take the stage and, like a vacuum cleaner, clean up and make magic. What I did learn from it is how to behave oneself when one is the star and when it's all about you. Faith Prince behaved so beautifully, with so much grace and humility. She was a wonderful person to learn from, and she was very kind to me. I think everybody should understudy in a situation like that at least once because then when understudies go on, you know what that feels like. You know that if they turn right instead of left, it really doesn't matter. So now when understudies go on, I say, "You can do whatever you want. Just come on, and we'll have fun." Because it's absolutely terrifying. It's an impossible situation.

What was that *Guys and Dolls* experience like overall?

It was hell. I really needed people to know what I was capable of, and there was just no opportunity.

When you went on, you went on with Nathan Lane . . .

He didn't know who I was. Didn't care. I wasn't Faith. I wasn't going to be as good as Faith no matter who I was, no matter what I did. I was a waste of his time. And it wasn't until I finished her first week away that he said, "Great job this week." I thought, "Even if you didn't know I was going to do a great job, if you had just lied a little bit and told me on Tuesday night, 'you're going to be great,' this would have been a much easier week." But instead he called extra rehearsals with stage management because he didn't like the way I was doing my handkerchief bit [during "Sue Me"]. My parents had come to see me and I snuck them into the theater early to watch one of those rehearsals. They didn't believe me when I told them how exacting he was going to be. Now, in all fairness, ever since then, every time I see Nathan he always gives me a huge hug. He and I have come a long way.

That was also your first experience with Jerry Zaks.

Jerry's very musical in terms of his rhythms. He hears things in a certain way, and comedy is very rhythmic for him. So you have to find a way to have the lines be musical in the way he hears it. The challenge is to make something real within a rhythm that you didn't make up. But I've worked with enough directors and I see the genius of what he does. And I've seen how he can take mediocre material and make it—now, Abe Burrows was not mediocre and neither is Douglas Carter Beane [the writer of] *Sister Act*, but I've seen other things that had been so-so material, and he's been able to elevate them. I love Jerry. His humanity and compassion allow him to draw out the heart from both the writers and his actors

Guys and Dolls **was "the" show that season, and you were part of—**

A phenomenon. We didn't get it. I personally didn't get it. I remember my dressing room overlooked 45th Street, and the day after we opened, we looked out the window and the line was all the way down to 9th Avenue and was starting to go around the corner. Remember how cartoony the sets were? I thought, "You know what? It's not what I would have done, but Jerry and his team have gone for something and they're sure it is the right way to go." I didn't agree with it, but we were all telling the same story, and it was clear what the story was, and that's one thing Jerry's a genius at: getting everybody on the same page.

After *Guys and Dolls* in short order, you were at Rainbow & Stars doing *A Grand Night for Singing*, directed by Walter Bobbie.

I caught Walter's eye during *Guys and Dolls*.

When you went on for Faith?

It wasn't what I did onstage; it was the way I worked with Nathan. He said, "I'm very impressed by the way you handled everything so professionally and so sweetly." It was really fun and Walter did what he does all the time—he casts really well, and then lets you go.

When *Grand Night* moved to Broadway, you were a principal. Did you feel a shift career-wise? Were you thinking of it in those terms?

I did feel it was a break, but my dad died of a massive heart attack on press night. I got the call right before I was leaving for the theater. My brothers and my mom said, "You have to go on. Dad would have wanted it, and there's no way you can fly home and be with him."

Do you remember the experience of performing that night?

I remember feeling like he was there and that he was present in the light. It was almost like he was just surfing on the beam that you could see when it was coming at you. I just felt, "there he is," and then he just sort of turned around and walked the other way. That theater was haunted anyway. There was a ghost that used to wander around in top hat and tails. The first time I saw him I asked the fly guy, "Do you guys have a ghost?" "Oh, yeah, the guy in the tails? He's here all the time. He just walks back and forth across the back like he can't find the exit." I'd already seen that, and it didn't scare me, so when I started feeling my dad's presence, I thought, "We're all here together. Let's all have a party."

After *Grand Night for Singing*, you did *How to Succeed . . .* , but you had just given birth.

I got a call from Ted Sperling. He was out in La Jolla doing *How to Succeed . . .* and Dawnn Lewis, who was playing the part of Smitty, was leaving. Ted says, "Des [director Des McAnuff] really wants to bring you in." I said, "Well, I don't know. I can't even put on my shoes yet. I'm really tired." But I came in and then they called me back on a Friday. They offered it to me, and we had to make the deal in two hours because rehearsal started Monday. I was like, "Des needs to know that I need twenty-minute breaks instead of fifteen because I'm breastfeeding, and I need an extra apartment when we're in Washington because I'm going to have either my mother-in-law or my mom there to help. And I need my own dressing room at the theater because of the baby." They gave me everything, and I've never regretted it. I don't believe in regret. I have a picture of my son at five months sitting in my lap looking up at me as I'm getting my wig on backstage at the Kennedy Center, and his expression seems to be saying, "You don't really look like my mom, but you smell like my mom—it's all good." And that's really been the way he's dealt with my career his whole life. He is a very flexible and wonderfully optimistic person: "Let's roll with it and see."

A lot of the women I have spoken with have had a hard time balancing career and motherhood.

In the beginning it was easy. He waited until I got home at night, and I put him to bed, and then we would both sleep late. It only gets hard when they start school, and you're getting up at 6:00 AM or 6:30 AM to make their lunch and get them going. Now that he's a teenager, he sets his alarm and gets his own breakfast, but I think, just because of the way I was raised, I need to be up and starting the day with him. But the only thing I can say is being an actor has made me a better mom and vice versa. I know that being a mother has made me a better actor. There's no question. Motherhood has taught me to trust first instincts and to stay in the moment. I think that having something that I love to do and being able to share that with my child is so important—it's a good lesson for him—pursue your dream, do what makes you happy. It's not all of who I am, by any means, but it's a big part of who I am—I think it's always good when children see their mothers are happy. There have been so many things I've said "no" to because I'm a mom, and he knows it. I've almost exclusively done work in New York for his entire life. And there have been things that I've been offered in New York that I haven't done. And once I'm in something, I do nothing on my nights off. No benefits, concerts. I know that he knows what I've given up. And he knows for sure what he's given me in terms of the experience of being a mom and all that that has taught me. I don't really think I knew who I was until I had a child. I realized I have so much more to learn. Motherhood is and always will be my favorite role.

Back to *How to Succeed.* . . .

It's kind of a blur because I was sleep-deprived the entire time. And every time I looked down, I had baby vomit, cottage cheese, yogurt, or banana on me somewhere.

It kind of works for the role of Smitty.

Totally. I feel like these roles come into our lives at the appropriate times. I know *Piazza* very much coincided with my grief about my divorce. I used Margaret to forgive myself and to

"It's Been a Long Day" with Megan Mulally and Matthew Broderick in *How to Succeed in Business Without Really Trying*. (Photofest)

find grace and forgiveness, even though I knew the show was majorly disrupting my son's life. Experiencing the guilt of Clara's accident in the piece was a way that I could chip away at my own grief. And I felt that by the end of our run—I can think about this now without bursting into tears—I could manage. It's because of that role. I think that's what moved people so much. And now with *Cinderella*, what Douglas Carter Beane has written is very interesting; the Fairy Godmother and Cinderella form a close relationship in this piece. The Godmother has to push Cinderella out of the nest to find her own life—to leave the *known*, as horrible as it is, to search for a life that is *impossibly* rich, but *un*known, and that's exactly what's happening for me this year—the term of the contract will take us through my son's senior year and first semester of college. And I am learning how to say goodbye and to launch my child into the next phase of his life. I think every single role that I've done has somehow lined up like that. Isn't that interesting? You couldn't plan it. It's a miracle. It's a gift. It's a blessing.

How to Succeed . . . **was your first of several shows where you were an expert second banana.**

I fought hard for it. I think that was the first show when I realized that I can have an opinion about this. That was something else that being a mother brought. I threw my first diva fit in *How to Succeed*. . . . I've probably only had five that I can count in my whole career. They had already cut "Cinderella, Darling," which was Smitty's big solo, so I had no solos in the show. I came in and they said, "We're going to cut this section in "Coffee Break," and you're not going to do that. I was operating on three, maybe four hours of sleep. I talked to Des, and there was some kind of argument. I walked out. I just walked off the stage. I've never really done anything like that, but I was so tired. It was during a blizzard—it's always a blizzard in these stories. In my costume, I just pulled on my galoshes and left the theater. All three stage managers are chasing me, "You can't do this! You can't just walk offstage." "Yes, I can. You know why?

Because I have an infant. You've now made this a part that anybody can play, and I'm too tired, and I'm not at home. I'm breastfeeding. I need this to be worth my while to come and be in rehearsal all day long. So please find somebody else. It's too much." And Des had also said something demeaning about me in front of the cast.

Do you remember what it was?

No, but I remember it wasn't nice. So I said, "Des owes me an apology. I don't want to come into the theater unless I have an apology." It wasn't like I planned to say that or that I planned to walk out, but the mother wolf in me realized we had crossed the line. "This show only works for me as a young mother if I get something back, if career-wise it's enough that it warrants my being away from my son X number of hours a day." I had this equation in my head, right or wrong, of how much I wanted to stand out or shine based on what I was sacrificing. I felt like Des violated an understanding that the two of us had had in previous discussions. He apologized. These collaborations aren't without conflict.

Beyond the diva moment, how was playing the show?

One of my favorite nights was many months into the run. I was stage right and it got really quiet onstage. Any time that happens, everybody's heart starts to race because you think, "I missed an entrance! It's me! I'm supposed to be talking!" We couldn't figure out what happened. Then wonderful Matthew Broderick came offstage and he very calmly walked over to one of the crew guys and said, "Do you know what my line is?" And the guy, very calmly, said, "No, Matthew, I'm sorry, I don't." So he went back out and said to the audience, "I'm really sorry. I'm editing a film every night after my performance from 11:00 PM until 3:00 AM, then I sleep for three hours, and then I go to shoot a film all day with Jim Carrey until I eat dinner, and then I come do the show. I'm just super tired, but don't worry, I'll be right back." Meanwhile my dear friend, Marty Moran, Matthew's understudy—I heard his heels in the stairwell. And Matthew says, "Marty, just in time. Can you just stand in the wings and give me my lines or just help me remember what the scene is about?" It was just a miracle that I happened to be standing right there when this happened because I would have missed the whole thing. And when Matthew came back on to start the scene again, he got a standing ovation. And at the end of the night during his curtain call, a roar like you've never heard. I'll never forget thinking, "People just want to see something real." And he just handled it so gracefully. He is a true star. One of the greatest. It isn't just his talent. It is his big heart. And that show had an extraordinary cast. When Sarah Jessica Parker came in, it was really fun getting to know and to work with her, and she made that part her own, asking for new wigs and costume designs. Watching the way she handled that essentially taught me how to handle *Follies*. How do you replace Bernadette Peters? The answer: You don't. You don't replace her. You do your version of it. Period.

Titanic was next.

Every day I expected the phone to ring: "Hello. This is your stage manager. This is silly. Forget it. Don't come in to rehearsal. The show has been cancelled." It's a musical about the Titanic! Every time the phone rang I was sure. Even when we started rehearsals. Even when we were in previews. It wasn't until after we opened that I thought, "Okay. This is going to run. For a long time." The thing that was frustrating about that show was that the ship was the star. So here we've got Michael Cerveris, Judy Blazer, Alma Cuervo, John Cunningham, Brian d'Arcy James . . . You would kill to have half of these people in any show. They were all so freaking great.

And there you all are with the ship—with this huge hydraulic thing. Was it scary?

The only thing scary is when—we had this piano with the innards taken out. You couldn't be anywhere near that when it smashed against the wall of the set. But the safety on that show was top notch.

The show was so episodic . . .

Every day scenes were cut and edited. The late great writer Peter Stone would make notes. He would sit with this briefcase and yellow pads. I was kind of schmoozing with him just to find out what was going to happen to my character, but meanwhile, I went and researched. I'm a nut about research, so I was reading bunches and bunches of things on the Titanic. In the musical, I played Alice Beane, second-class passenger. I found the woman that my character was based on. Her name was actually Ethel, not Alice. And I found her family outside of Rochester. I called and learned a lot of things. In the show Edgar, Alice's husband, dies, but in real life, her husband lived. He was one of the people picked up in the lifeboats. But his wife didn't know he had been rescued. The survivors were all in shock. No one could find anyone. And he was very ill. So here was Ethel on the Carpathia. She sailed all the way back to New York, and when she disembarked, she was checking in with someone on the dock who said, "Your husband is right over there. He is alive." And she had no idea! And to this day, their descendants do not swim. No one in their family goes near the water. When I told Peter Stone all this, he said, "I can't write that because no one would believe it."

Were you shocked when the show was well reviewed and then won Tonys?

We all thought the show was good, and we were very excited when they put the ending in because we had all these crazy different endings. The crew kept saying they should bring all the dead people back. The crew always knows. And so one by one the cast would go talk to the director and he got so tired of hearing everybody ask for it, he said, "Let's just try it and tomorrow we're going to go back to the other ending." We just did a very small reprise of the opening number at the end, "Sail on, Titanic . . . " The crew was sobbing. That's when the response to the show turned around.

Your next show was *Cabaret*, and . . .

It was just a miracle that that job came along because by that time my marriage was—we were deciding to spend some time apart, and an extra apartment means extra furniture, extra rent. Where's this extra money going to come from? So that two-year *Cabaret* period was very intense because I was teaching full time and doing a Broadway show at night.

Given that, it seems fortuitous that you were not the original so you didn't have the all-consuming rehearsal process. Plus you were walking into a hit so you knew it would be steady work.

I've been very, very blessed in the opportunities that have come. And I didn't have to go through the agony of creating it. I had my second diva fit in that because I was so different from Michelle Pawk, and I had such a different take on it. I was going through my divorce, too. Sweet B. T. McNicholl, Sam Mendes's assistant, said, "Sam isn't going to like what you're doing." I said, "Well, here's the deal. I am Kost. Kost isn't something out there. My connection to Kost is the character. That's it. That's what we share." He said, "Well, it's not working." I said, "Well, let's do this." I'm so terrible. "I'm going to go over and lift the window. Who do you think's a size eight down there? You see her? Let's get her to come up and she can do the part. Because now what you're saying is that you can give anybody who can fit the costume a pretty good idea about how they're going to play it. So let's do that. And I want you to tell Sam that

that's what I said." And I'm not a pushy person! But I think when somebody like me says some-thing like that it's shocking. I'm not a bitch, and I don't go around telling people what to do, but I know what's right and wrong. I said, "This is nothing against you at all. I'm telling you that I know what I'm doing with this part. Every moment of this has been carefully crafted. This is not a random performance." Then Sam Mendes saw the performance, and in front of the whole company said, "Let's talk about Vick's performance and why it's so fantastic. " He was able to see that it could be so completely different from what Michelle did and still work. Once I got Sam's stamp of approval it was great. But I was so exhausted that two years into the run I fell asleep onstage. There was that moment at the very end where the four principals walked down towards the audience, and then when we turned upstage, and walked away from the audience, you could see people through the fog, and you knew that they were all walking into the gas chambers. I remember facing the audience, and when I opened my eyes, I was walking away from them into the fog so I had walked ten or twelve feet, turned, and walked five or six more steps—in my sleep. I hadn't fallen down. And that night I went to the stage man-ager and I said, "I'm giving my four-week's notice—I'm out." The casting director asked me to give them more time. I said, "I can't. I just fell asleep onstage. This means mother needs to sit down. I have had a grueling two years. I must sit down now." Then I took a lot of time off. I took two or three years off.

How did *Urinetown* come up for you?
It was fun for me to just try something like that, and also musically challenging. But I had already signed on for *The Light in the Piazza* in Seattle, so I said, "I can only do it for eleven weeks." It was kind of a similar thing to the Paige O'Hara thing. They're like, "why are you leaving a Broadway show?" No one had heard of [director] Bart Sher or the Intiman Theater. What the heck is that? But there was another good "aha" moment: Thanksgiving, 8:30 in the morning, the phone rings. "Hi, this is [playwright] Craig Lucas." It was before my final callback for *Piazza* in the Seattle production. "Who is it really?" "Craig Lucas." "Who is it really though?" "Craig Lucas." It was another one of those miracle phone calls. He said, "The last thing Bart saw you do was *Marathon Dancing* eight years ago. He thinks you're a clown so in order for you to get this part, you're going to have to show him that you've got the chops." I literally played a clown in *Marathon Dancing*. A mute clown. Who did cartwheels. And I was pregnant at the time.

Obviously you managed to convince him.
[The character] Margaret Johnson is from North Carolina. A typical Southern woman is not going to show you her hand. And everything's going to be just fine no matter what because that's what we do. We're survivors, and we're funny. Humor, humor, humor. If you're not from the South, you don't know how that goes. But Bart was concerned that I was going to make everything a joke, so with his help, we were able to explore the more serious aspects of her interior landscape. I knew it was my time 100 percent. I knew who she was inside and out, and I was ready to play her. I had grieved enough. I had been through enough. I knew the mother struggle. I knew that woman. And [musical director] Ted Sperling had already played "Fable" for me months before, and I started weeping two seconds into the song. I knew her entire history just from hearing that one song. I've never felt a connection with a role before or since where I've known like that. I just knew her.

The role required a huge emotional output every night.
I feel like it was a gift of healing for both me as an actor, to have to relive the pain of that woman every night, and for others to watch me go through it because I wasn't pretending.

I was actually showing people a piece of my grief. So I think for people to watch it, it was very painful.

And cathartic?

And cathartic because in the end what Margaret Johnson realized was that even she could be forgiven. That show is about grace. I always look for roles that explore grace because what unifies us as a race, as a people, is that none of us have ever gone through anything that someone else hasn't been through. We're unified by our imperfections and by our mistakes. And that's what draws people to our story. Who wants to look at a perfect person with a perfect body and a perfect face who's never done anything wrong, or said anything mean, or hit the wall, or had a crisis, or grieved? I can't relate to that. Our greatest secret, our deepest guilt is what gives birth to humility and a way into everyone's heart. I didn't really understand that. I adore my ex-husband. We are best, best friends, but we couldn't be married to each other. We were just not a good fit as husband and wife. And I didn't know that my greatest joy of discovering who I am as a person would come out of so much grief, but there it was. It was the greatest gift. That's the story I wanted to tell, even though it hurts to tell it. It's a story everyone needs to hear.

Do you ever think, "that's the pinnacle. That's it?"

I do. I think it probably was a pinnacle, but who says there can't be more than one, or two or three? All the right roles have found me at the right time. I'm not worried. There are enough things to be neurotic about. Hopefully the projects that need me specifically will come my way. I'm praying that they do, and it's a blessing that it's happened so far. But if that ever shifts and stops happening, I have to pay attention to that, and why it's happening.

That doesn't even have to apply just to roles. It could be true of coaching, directing, the ways in which you are needed in the world.

That's exactly right. I come from a family of ministers and missionaries. When I felt like I wasn't doing enough to save the world, my aunts always said, "Don't you see? God put you where you're supposed to be. You're doing your work in your world. God uses us wherever we are." Not that I feel like I'm a missionary, but there is a tremendous healing that occurs when we connect with audiences, and we all need each other—wherever we are. And my faith does keep me strong. I pray before every performance. Prayers and thoughts are real things. Powerful and sustaining and life changing in the best sense. I try to see my life as one long road leading to God. *Love* has to be the main ingredient of my work, *whatever* that work is.

Even though *Piazza* was your first famous collaboration with Ted Sperling, you had a thirty-year relationship before that show.

We were best friends from Yale, so when I directed at Yale, he was always my musical director. We did *Merrily We Roll Along, Side by Side by Sondheim* and *Once Upon a Mattress.* He was principal violist in the Yale Symphony Orchestra, and I said, "You should be a conductor." He didn't really know that much about musicals, but I played *A Little Night Music* for him and he was very excited, "What's that?" I joke that I take credit for his career, but he would have found it on his own—it was his destiny. He is a true genius, and I don't use that word lightly.

Do you have anything to share about the process of working with Bartlett Sher on *Piazza*?

Bart, like all the great directors, knows what he wants. And he is masterful. He actually inspired me to work on that character in a completely new way. I'm very in the moment as

I go through my work in a show. I know the parameters of where I'm going and what I need to accomplish and then it will change night to night. Bart liked that to an extent, but [he also liked to have more parameters than I did]. I resisted that at first, and then he said, "You're going to have to trust me. I want that particular scene to be what you did Tuesday." I had no idea what I did Tuesday. "Well, you did this, and this." "Okay, well, the triggers for that scene are three scenes earlier." "I don't care how [you get there], but in that scene, I need this." The scene he was talking about was the "Dividing Day" scene. I had to know myself and my process well enough to know where the seeds for that scene came from and what I would need so that I ended up on target. So I made a chart, and I figured out how I was prepping every scene so that I knew the things that would trigger me to get what he needed. That was the turning point scene. If we got through that scene, the rest of the show fell like dominoes. If a certain number of requirements were met and we could check them off, he was happy and I was happy and the show went the way Bart liked. It was such a puzzle figuring it out and I'll always be grateful to him. But since then I've learned not every show works like that. *Sister Act* was my next big Broadway show after *Piazza* and [that approach] totally backfired. I hit the wall on that show and had to leave early. But I learned something extremely important from that experience too: there's always rebirth. By God's grace, what happened in that show was that I found the Alexander teacher and mentor that I've been waiting my whole life to find. Beret Arcaya is somebody who knows so much more than I do. You think, "Hey, by my age, I should know X, Y, Z," and then you go see her, and you realize you're just beginning. To know that I have an ocean of knowledge still to acquire and that I'll never learn it all is so thrilling, so freeing. But if I hadn't slammed into the wall and left with all of this tension and injury, I would never have sought out someone to help me correct it. It turned out that Alexander work was the perfect technique for me to learn and it came at the perfect time!

What happened in *Sister Act*?

I had a very difficult time in *Sister Act*. I left that show with a jillion injuries. I had a trapezius injury, a rhomboid injury, a neck injury.

From what?

Well, it's a good question because I just stood there. But the costume was tremendously heavy. When people would come backstage, I'd say, "Here, hold this," and their eyes [would go wide]. Every single person. [She covers her ears with her hands.] Do what I am doing. See how it distorts your own sound? Even though the costume is just this thin piece of fabric, acoustically you can't hear your own sound. It would be like asking a musician to put earmuffs on when they play. It's insane. Apparently, over time, my stress about being disoriented slowly crept into [my body]. Everything got very locked. I thought, "I guess I must be ready to retire." But gradually, through the help of my teacher and my family and friends, we got through it. Now it's a blip on the screen. Artists tend to see whatever we're in passionately, in that moment. It's very hard for us to back off and see that every project is just a piece of the continuum. I never expected to win a Tony. I never expected for like anything like *The Light in the Piazza* to happen. I was always the second banana. I was really good at the second banana. There's nothing wrong with a career like that. So to be handed something like *Piazza*, which was very much front and center, was so beyond my expectations. There is a big part of me now that says, "You have already accomplished so much more than you thought you would, so now what are you going to do with your blessing and gifts? What's your response?"

With *Piazza*, you were recognized in the community in a whole new way. Do you remember feeling differently?

It was kind of weird because I feel like I'd always been doing good work.

Well, during the season that yours was THE performance to see, were you just doing your work as usual, or did it feel different as people were talking about you in all of the media?

It was more work. It was like a whole different game that I had never played before. But I'd seen so many of my friends play it, and I'd watch a lot of people go through it. I felt like my press agent was calling me every Monday saying, "Congratulations." And I was like, "What's Drama League?" "Congratulations." "What is the Outer Critics Circle again?" It was a whirlwind. "Congratulations." Norman Vincent Peale Award. It was kind of fun but it's still a part of the business I don't really understand. I think it's very mysterious who captures the affections of the media. Because I think there are so many talented people who don't. I can't think about it too much. It's enough to just try to show up at the theater on time and do your part.

What do you remember about winning the Tony?

It's always weird because you can't see your competition in their work so you never really know what your chances are. It's kind of like a blind date. You sit there, and gosh, it's hot when they turn the AC off because it makes too much noise. That's the main thing I was thinking about. My son had a little polyester tux on and it was stuck to him. He was uncomfortable, so I was worried about him. [Then I won and] it was surreal. I remember thinking, "This is like an out-of-body moment." I remember thinking I have to run to the stage, and I have to talk really fast to thank everybody I love in under sixty seconds. You're up at 6:00 AM, at the theater, getting your costume and wig on for the dress rehearsal, then you go do your matinee, then you change into your red carpet outfit, then you do the red carpet, then you sit in the seat, then you run backstage, you change back into your costume, to perform onstage live at Radio City Music Hall, then you change back again. It's exhausting. And I was forty-five. It wasn't like I was a spring chicken. The recognition part came pretty late in my career. TL wanted to do all of the press junket with me so he went to all the interviews. He just wanted to be there. He was ten.

After *Piazza* you did two back-to-back Encores! shows, *Follies* and *Juno*. Do you like doing Encores!?

Love it! Love it! I'm on the board of New York City Center and they're an amazing organization. They've got that Encores! thing down pat. It's a formula that works.

What do you remember about *Follies*?

Well, everybody was nervous. And needlessly so. Victor Garber, Christine Baranski, the great Jo Anne Worley. What a fun group of people! [Director] Casey Nicholaw was amazing. He had a very strong vision for it and really knew what he wanted. It was just magical. And we had a lot of room to experiment and be wrong, which is always a great atmosphere for actors.

That's amazing given the amount of time that you had.

Casey's very much that way. "We'll see." Which is so freeing. I think Donna Murphy really shone. I really, really loved what she did with Phyllis. She was just a killer in that part. I really loved working with her. She was a new mom and she was exhausted, and yet she was still so good. Unbelievable. I never missed her performance of "Could I Leave You?" I sat in a chair

As Sally, losing her mind in the Los Angeles Center Theatre Group 2012 Production of *Follies*. (© 2013 Craig Schwartz Photography)

that was as close to the stage as I could be so I could feel her energy and listen to her do it. Every single show—well, it was only six performances, but still, I didn't want to miss it. I think she channeled that part.

How was it working with Sondheim on *Follies*?

He thought what I was doing with Sally was great. His one note for me was that "Losing My Mind" is not a book song, it's a pastiche number, a torch song. That's really hard for an actor, because you can't ignore the character and just say, "Cut to torch song." We did six performances of that, and he would come back and say, "No, no," and then after the last show, he grabbed me by the shoulders, and he gave me a big hug and said, "That's it!"

Did you know what you had done differently?

No. I mean, I know I prepped differently, and my sense is there was probably more of a sense of detachment. A lot of the times when people have trouble with my work it's because it's too emotional and too personalized. Sometimes what it needs is more of a sense of distance, more of a sense of detachment. That's certainly what Bart was always looking for. It's hard to tell an emotional creature not to be emotional.

How was it returning to the role five years later?

It was really fun to revisit the character. She felt familiar in my bones. I knew her history, I knew how she moved and how she was. I feel like I really found what "Losing My Mind" should be for that production. But if we did it again, and the role was mine from the beginning, I would do it a third way.

After *Piazza* and *Follies* and *Juno*, were people forgetting that you're comedic at heart?

Yeah, they can only remember what they just saw. That's why every time I do a cabaret I'm always half stand-up, half singing. I just have to. I'm so silly. Who can be serious for that long? I can't. Life is too short.

You got back to comedy with *Sister Act*. What made you decide to do it?

I really wanted to work with Jerry again. And I really wanted to work with Douglas Carter Beane. And I wanted to be back on Broadway. I'd been offered lots of different things, and I had turned everything down. I thought, "If I keep waiting and waiting and waiting . . ."

What were you waiting for?

I think I was waiting for another *The Light in the Piazza*. But that clearly wasn't going to be coming. Adam Guettel and Craig Lucas created a masterpiece. Period. Do I think I will have another opportunity to create a role in a groundbreaking show like that? Yes! In the meantime, I realized that there were projects I was being offered that could teach me something. And I thought, "Well, no time like the present." The idea of playing someone who, on the surface, has to be an authority on God, but has lost God, was a very interesting challenge. Somehow redemption for that character comes from a very unlikely place, as it always does. I did some research on Benedictine nuns and I just fell in love with them. A few of them came to see the show. I met the wonderful Dolores Hart who left acting to become a Benedictine nun. She was my fairy godmother on that project.

Were you disappointed to have to leave *Sister Act*?

I felt tremendous shame about it. I was always very proud of my record. I was embarrassed and humiliated and felt like I was letting everyone down. I was devastated, thinking, "Maybe I'm not an actor anymore." We have to remember, too, that Broadway acting, eight shows a week, is like the Tour de France. It's so athletic. It can't be compared to anything else. As you get older, it gets harder.

Well, you did come back, somewhat triumphantly with *Follies*.

It was such a gift. It was very redemptive because I was really scared. I didn't know how it would feel, I didn't know if I would really be able to pull it off. But it turned out that I could and that I started to feel like my old self again. My confidence started to come back, and everything started to fall into place. And I was surrounded by strong, funny women—I was the youngest one, I think, of the older group. I would hear their voices get tired, and I would see their bodies get tired. It looked like a triage unit after "Who's That Woman?" People walked off and the ice comes out, the ACE bandages come out, the Band-Aids, the propping the feet up. That dance number was really hard and really long. I think that it was just a huge gift because I realized I really love being onstage. I'm really, really happy. And most important of all: it doesn't have to be perfect. People don't expect it to be perfect. My take on the character was radically different [from Bernadette Peters']. It changed everybody's performance. Danny Burstein was so dear and open and generous to me. We would work on trying new things and before you know it, a whole new marriage started happening, completely distinct from what had been. That meant that the Ben/Sally thing had to be completely different, and because Ron Raines was different, Jan Maxwell had to adjust, so all four of us kind of [shifted].

One final question that's impossible to answer without sounding completely egotistical, but do you ever consider your place in the pantheon?
Every day. I think, "What have I done today to make a difference?" Not in terms of how people will remember me, but "what have you done today to make somebody's life better?"

So you're not talking about your place in the annals of theater history; you're talking about your place on the planet.
Yes. Healer, storyteller, mother who sang, who tried to make a difference. I worry about it because I know how fast life is going, and I've been given so many blessings, I don't want to have squandered any of them. My parents worked hard. My grandparents worked hard. And their ancestors worked hard to put me in a position where I could pursue a life that is essentially dressing up and playing pretend.

So when you look at yourself and say, "Am I contributing in a real and meaningful way?" how are you doing?
I don't know. And that's okay. I don't know. And that's sort of the state that I live in now. It's okay not to know. I know that I'm striving. I know I'll never stop striving, and that that striving is what keeps life interesting. And very beautiful.

AUDRA MCDONALD

May and June 2010; July 2012

THREE HOURS BEFORE THE FIRST PERFORMANCE of *Porgy and Bess* at the American Repertory Theater in Cambridge, Massachusetts, Audra McDonald spills out of a final, grueling rehearsal, exhaustion all over her face and in her voice. She greets me sounding utterly defeated. I
tell her how excited I am for the evening's show. "It's gonna be what it's gonna be," she says with
a shrug. What it was, was glorious. In his *New York Times* review, Ben Brantley called McDonald's
performance "as complete and complex a work of musical portraiture as any I've seen in years."
But to qualify McDonald's assessment of her own work as modesty would be inaccurate. Ego
isn't what drives her. Not that she doesn't have it, but her focus is on the work and whether she's
satisfied with it. As praise and awards are heaped upon her, McDonald is grateful, gracious, and
even incredulous but unimpressed. In 2014, she won her sixth Tony Award (for *Lady Day at
Emerson's Bar & Grill*), setting the record for the most Tonys won by an actor in history. But there
is nothing in her bearing or attitude that says "star." McDonald is approachable and easygoing.
Her range seems to have no boundaries. She fits no type. She has played flirty and shy, murderous and saintly, simple and intelligent, strident and coquettish, defiant and wounded, impoverished and moneyed, coveted and plain. She has also managed to make the fact that she is African
American largely irrelevant in the eyes of both directors and audiences. While a few of her roles
(in *Porgy and Bess, Marie Christine, A Raisin in the Sun, Ragtime*) were written for black women,
just as many (in *Carousel, Master Class, 110 in the Shade, Annie*) were not. Her talent regularly
trumps her color and sadly, in the theater, she is alone in that consistency.

Audra Ann McDonald grew up in Fresno, California, the child of educators who fervently
believed in the arts. Her stage debut came at age seven, as one of the Siamese children in a
local production of *The King and I*. At the king's death, she burst into tears, displaying an
easily accessible emotional life that would serve her well throughout her career. She trained
classically at Juilliard but longed for Broadway and got it almost immediately after graduation
in the form of Nicholas Hytner's acclaimed 1993 production of *Carousel*. McDonald was Carrie Pipperidge, a role that allowed her to show off her spunk, guile, charm, and lush soprano
all at once. Every subsequent Broadway outing (including musicals, straight plays, and Shakespeare) has been a triumph. Even *Marie Christine*, an adaptation of *Medea* written for her by
Michael John LaChiusa, one of the emerging young composers championed by McDonald in
her first two solo albums, though financially unsuccessful, was an artistic bull's-eye for
McDonald.

McDonald has done a good deal of work in television (including a four-year run on *Private
Practice*) and in concert halls across the country, but she consistently returns to the theater. It

As Grace in the TV version of *Annie*, one of McDonald's rare frothy roles. (Photofest)

was there, in *Master Class*, that she met her mentor, Zoe Caldwell, after whom she would name her daughter, and it was there, in *110 in the Shade*, that she met her husband, actor Will Swenson.

Though McDonald describes her life as being in a constant state of disarray given her commitments (in addition to performing and parenting Zoe and Swenson's two sons, McDonald is deeply committed to several causes, most notably the fight for gay marriage), her upper Manhattan home shows no sign of that. It is relaxed and tasteful, like McDonald herself.

You were, shall we say, an active child?
That's a very sweet way of putting it.

Audra McDonald

The Secret Garden, National Tour and
   Broadway, 1992
Carousel, Broadway, 1994 (Tony Award)
Ragtime, Broadway, 1998 (Tony Award)
Marie Christine, Broadway, 1999
Sweeney Todd, New York Philharmonic,
   2000
Dreamgirls in Concert, Broadway, 2001
Passion, Lincoln Center, 2005
110 in the Shade, Broadway, 2007
The Gershwins' Porgy and Bess, Broadway,
   2012 (Tony Award)

You've said that your parents chose to get you into performing instead of administering Ritalin.

Yeah. Well basically I was really, really hyperactive and really dramatic. I would overreact to everything, whether it be a thunderstorm or I cut my finger. My parents were like, "What do we do, what do we do?" They knew I had musical talent—I mean everybody in my family has musical talent—and they just started putting me in everything that they possibly could, from piano lessons, to voice lessons, to dance lessons, to channel that energy. They were both educators. People weren't medicating nearly as much as we medicate today. Hyperactivity was diagnosed but just dealt with. I really applaud the way they handled it. They could have been evil parents and put me in a corner or something like that. But they didn't.

With all of this dramatic energy, once there was a channel for the stuff, did you become less of a drama queen?

Noooo. I just got tired. I was busier. More of my time was being spent onstage.

At sixteen, you were Eva Peron in *Evita*.

I'll never forget. I was in high school, in class. A note got dropped off from the principal of the performing arts section of the school. She was like a second mom to me. It said, "Audra," and then it had a big heart and it said, "love Eva. Exclamation point, exclamation point." That's how I knew I had gotten the part. I'll never forget it. I was so obsessed with the role, and one of my closest friends, Lindsey June Garbett, was double cast with me. People always asked if there was a rivalry. Noooo, we absolutely adored each other. We watched each other's performances and stole from each other. Fresno could be a bit conservative. Still can. There were people who were confused by my being cast in the role. There were other people who would call and say, "Is the white or the black one on tonight?" It was kind of crazy. I was just so excited doing the role I didn't care. I was having a great time.

How aware were you of the fact that it was unusual for a black woman to be playing the part?

For me, it was only just that I was young. I did the role again in summer stock, my first summer out of college. The difference between that time and the time before was that I was no longer a virgin. The role made so much more sense to me, you know? So while I may have had the intensity and a sort of raw vocal ability to do it, I don't think you'd look back at it and say, "Oh that was so well sung." But there was so much more that I understood doing it at nineteen than I did at sixteen.

Anything else from that period that was particularly memorable?

I remember figuring out certain things. I guess you'd call them milestones. There was a time when we were doing a pre-show cabaret and I had been assigned a solo, "The Birth of the

Blues." I guess I was about twelve. I remember the reaction from the audience and that being the first time I was like, "They are really responding!" But that same year, I decided I wanted to do one of those teen pageants and I decided to do "The Birth of the Blues." I only did the talent part because my Mom was like, "you're not doing the whole thing." There was a girl in blue spandex, big red lipstick, hair in a side ponytail, and she was dancing and singing "[Flashdance] What a Feeling." Whatever. I sang and I didn't even place. My mom reminded me—think what you want but this was the '80s in Fresno, CA—"You're still an African American girl so you are going to have to work even harder." Whenever I would get really depressed about not being the most popular at school or having a boyfriend . . . I had friends, but I wasn't always in the popular group, and when you're that age you take that stuff to heart. Back then the thing was to be really cute and petite and short. I wasn't. I never have been. I was probably born this size. My mom and dad always sort of comforted me by telling me to look inside and work harder at what you *do* have. And for me that was my performing ability. So even now, if I am having a hard time or getting bummed out, I immediately go to my work. "I should practice, that will make me feel better." Or "I should practice piano." For some reason, that was my retreat.

How great that your safe haven is something you can generate.
Yeah. I am never satisfied with my work, but yeah.

You play piano?
I used to. I am trying to get it back. I started when I was four. Everyone had to in my family.

When you came of age, you said you were going to New York and your parents said, "Fine, as long as you get your degree."
My parents were all about education, so I auditioned for UCLA, UC Irvine, NYU, and Juilliard. My mom and I flew out for my audition and the night before my audition, we went to see *Into the Woods*. Phylicia Rashad was playing The Witch. And then I auditioned and made a fool of myself, but for some reason they were like, "Oh, let's try it . . . "

What do you mean you made a fool of yourself?
I didn't know what I was doing. I had studied voice but not classical music, not vocally. I was so into musical theater. I was singing soprano repertoire, and I didn't know what I was doing.

How cool that you saw Phylicia Rashad and then years later you got to work with her. You have had the opportunity to work with and be around lot of people you grew up loving.
Yeah, it's crazy. I went to see *Dreamgirls* in San Francisco as a junior in high school. I had [the star of that production] Lillias White's picture on my wall; I had Patti LuPone's, Phylicia's. To look back on that now and realize that I know these people and have worked with them and can call them "friend," and "good friend" and "sister friend" is mind blowing. I was driving into the city the other day and I was having a shitty, shitty day. I turned on the satellite radio and "Buenos Aires" [from *Evita*] was playing and I was listening to it with a whole new set of ears. I was listening with my entire history and then my history with Patti, and I got so happy I started to cry. I pulled over and I was like "I am going to text this woman." "Oh, Patti, I am having the shittiest day and you just made me so happy. I love you." And she texted back, "Oh, Audie!" I realized, "Oh my *God*, whose life am I living????"

Do you still have moments of being star-struck?

All the time. . . . It's like they are separate people. There's Patti LuPone, and then there's Patti. There's Barbara Cook with the soaring voice and the 500 high notes in "Glitter and Be Gay" and then there's Barbara who came over for Thanksgiving and brought adorable stuffed animals for my kid. You separate in a way. You start to compartmentalize.

That's how Barbara Cook describes her career. She says that things happen to the "other her."

I understand that. Absolutely. Boy do I get that. I still can't keep my house organized. I still have issues with depression. I am trying to bring home the bacon so my kid can go to college. You are faced with the fears of what's gonna . . . Judy Garland used to say, "Is this the time they are going to figure out that I am a fake? Is this it? Is this the night they figure it out? Is this the night?" That is a real, real fear. Maybe it doesn't make sense to other people. I remember the first time that I read that Barbra Streisand has terrible stage fright and I thought that was crazy, but now I get it. I absolutely get it.

Do you still have stage fright?
Sure!

I think it's a universal feeling that we will all be discovered as frauds. And I also think that it's easy to stand outside of someone else's life and say, "I have insecurity, but her?"

Yeah, it is so very true and very real. Maybe . . . I don't know, but in a way, if we were to lose that part of ourselves, maybe we wouldn't need to perform any more.

Or you become the person who believes the hype and then you are insufferable.

Insufferable. And then you have nothing else to offer. Once you believe the hype and believe that you are the diva, the part that makes you genuine and real and organic onstage goes away. I have never been very good at the façade. I think people have always seen me warts and all. Maybe because I started out so young, at a time when I didn't really know how to cover up the warts or didn't know that I should. Or just didn't feel that I should. People would see me pass out onstage or forget the words.

You gave me a couple of examples but from where I sit . . . What warts? I mean, in the entirety of your career you've not had a bad personal review.

Ohhhh, you've not seen them all. They are there. And yet . . . you know, in the end it doesn't matter, because you feel about yourself the way you feel about yourself no matter what everybody says. Halle Berry doesn't necessarily feel all that beautiful. There's something about that that makes us continue to get out there. Are we seeking approval, are we seeking validation? Are these things we have to say? I don't know.

I am not suggesting that good reviews and awards are supposed to put you at peace but I think the public perception of you is pretty damned great.

But with that comes a certain amount of trepidation, too. There's always someone ready to shoot you down out of the sky. It's like, I made it past that, *now* they are gonna find out I am a fake. You know what I mean? I am dealing with this in therapy!

You mentioned fighting depression. . . .

Yeah, I tried to off myself at Juilliard. I don't know how serious of an attempt that was but it landed me in the mental hospital for a month. I look at that period in my life and I do remember quite a bit about it but what I remember most is the dreams I was having at the time. And all of them involved me just fighting in the ocean. Waves. Sometimes they were clear but most of the time they were dark. I was just really confused. I was at Juilliard and going down this path which, for the first time seemed wrong. It seemed, "Where am I? I've known what I wanted to do since I was nine years old, but where am I headed? I am being stuffed in a box. And where's Broadway? Why isn't it here? I am headed in this direction and doing poorly. I am not going to be a shining star in this direction, I have just lost my way." This guy cheated on me and . . . whatever I was going through in terms of my personal relationships . . . I had some wonderful people at Juilliard who took care of me and got me on the right path. When I got out and was getting ready to go back to school, the opportunity to audition for *The Secret Garden* came along. And Juilliard, which normally would have said, "Absolutely not, you have to finish school," said, "Yes, this is the right thing for you. Take this time off. Go." They all understood that this wasn't my path. What had seemed like the enemy to me actually set me on the right path. When I look back I can say I was on the right path all along. I just couldn't see it. So I did the *Secret Garden* tour and then the last two months on Broadway.

What do you remember about that period?

Some of the people I met during that tour are still the closest people in my life to me today. [Actors] Andy Gale and Bobby Wilson. I get emotional when I talk about them. They are like my fairy godfathers. You don't realize when you meet people in your life that you're going to travel together. It's been since '92—a very long time that we've been traveling together. I met people who would have a major impact on my life and I saw the country for the first time. When I did it on Broadway, at the put in rehearsal, we did this one part and Rebecca Luker was like, "I have to see who this new voice is I am hearing from back there. Very nice to meet you." She marched herself right up to me and I was like, *that's Rebecca Luker!* It was my Broadway debut! It wasn't in English [the character of Ayah was Indian], mind you, but it was still my Broadway debut.

You did *The Secret Garden* and then you graduated . . .

And I went back out on the road with *Secret Garden*.

And during the tour, that's when you started auditioning for *Carousel*. So you had no down time, no period of having to hold down a survival job?

Oh, I got very, very, very, very lucky. You know, what's the quote: "What do you do when your life exceeds your dreams?" I started flying in from wherever we were on the road. On my first audition I met Ira Weitzman and Daniel Sweet, who were casting it. They said, "Could you please go out there and sit down for a minute? We'd like to have you come in and sing again but you have to wait for a little bit." They brought me back in and two other people were sitting at the table. It was Michael John LaChiusa and Graciela Daniele. They were working on *Hello Again* [also at Lincoln Center that year]. I was too young for that but they wanted to call me back for both shows. When I came back a week later for the callback and I sang "Tom" from *Hello Again*, Michael John said to me, "I am going to write a musical for you someday."

So there you are at nineteen, and some guy you never heard of is telling you he's going to write a show for you. What were you thinking?

Well, you don't believe it. You think, "Oh, he's being polite." Not only would he write me three shows, now we're working on four and five. I will be the first to admit I have been very lucky.

Sounds like the stars aligning. You have talked about the numbers of incredibly talented people you've worked with who don't have the same success. But I don't know if it's luck

Luck to me is being at the right time and right place. I remember there was one baritone from Switzerland at Juilliard, who told us, "I was a violinist in an orchestra and the baritone got sick one night and they asked me if I knew the part. I was like, "yeah, I think so." So he played it and then became an opera singer! So not only did the stars align, he tripped and fell into his career. I am not saying that I tripped and fell into this career because I was doing it my whole life, but still . . .

No, but what you did trip and fall into was classical training.
Yes.

You passed out cold during your audition for *Carousel*.
What was going through my mind was that it was one of those moments—and my fainting is a medical condition with a very specific reason—but in that moment I remember thinking, "This show could happen, this could happen and I am freaking out. What if I fuck it up at this moment? This could happen, this could change my life." Whereas before it was like, "Oh, I got this. That's cool." In that moment it was like I felt the stars converging, I felt the planets lining up and I couldn't handle it.

It's a medical condition, you said?
It's Vasovagal Syncope Syndrome. I have an overactive parasympathetic system which basically means that when I go into situations of high stress my blood pressure goes up, which everybody's does, but instead of your body going, "OK, let's downshift it back down," my body goes "OH, BOOM!" I go from high blood pressure to no blood pressure and my body goes, "reset, reset, reset." I take medication so that my blood pressure can't get super high in high-stress situations. If my body starts to go, "We're nervous, fight or flight syndrome, let's just shut down," my medication never lets it get to that.

What do you remember about the experience of doing *Carousel*?
Just magic. Being at the Vivian Beaumont Theatre. Meeting the people that I met. Meeting Lovette George who would go on to be like my sister. We traveled together until she passed away at forty-four. And just the magic of that entire process. We all knew that this was something special. Being in the rehearsal room, being with [director] Nick Hytner, the incredible convergence of talent from such different aspects of theater. There was incredible spirit in the room. Just being down in the basement at Lincoln Center. That first preview, I'll never forget right before the curtain was going to go up, Sally [Murphy] reached over and grabbed my hand. I knew that this was going to be the greatest experience of my life and it was. Everything about it was charmed.

Do you feel spoiled by that?
Oh sure. I have had other incredible experiences but it was my first. Yeah. I do.

That production really tapped into your comedic skills but since then you have been cast almost exclusively in dramas.
I don't know why that is.

Do you want more of that?
You know, I don't know. Comedy scares the crap out of me. Drama is easy, comedy is hard!

But you have said time and time again that you always want the next thing you do to be something that scares you.

Oh, yeah. That's why I am getting ready to play the piano in front of a bunch of people at Tanglewood! No, of course. It depends on what people want to cast me in. I just gravitated toward the roles that have felt right to me. Carrie was somebody who was a lot of fun and very funny, but maybe some of it has to do with the voice. The voice is a bigger, heavier thing.

Some of the songs you have chosen for your albums are very funny.

Maybe that's where my outlet comes in. I remember Steve Sondheim saying, "Why don't you sing any happy songs? You don't sing happy songs and you don't sing any of my songs." His songs scare me! But we had to call my third album "Happy Songs."

To have Stephen Sondheim say, "Why don't you sing any of my songs?" That's crazy!

It *is* crazy. Once again you have to compartmentalize things. Because Steve is just Steve to me, and then I'll get in a rehearsal room with him and he instructs, "Your U's need to be more lyric. And the rhythm here is a bit wrong." He's a taskmaster! And then there's Steve after a performance, hanging out and drinking, and I'm listening to all his stories. "Tell me another, tell me another." And then I go home and think, "Where was I? And what the fuck was I just doing and with who? I was just hanging out with *Steve Sondheim*???" It always kind of hits me after, you know what I mean? But in the moment, what I am learning is to just soak it in and learn all that I can. I believe in the adage "respect your elders." And I am not calling him an old man or anything like that but respect is a word that encompasses more than that for me. Learn from your elders. They have made it as far as they have for a reason. The true greats want to share that knowledge. They want to pass that torch. So any chance I can get Zoe Caldwell or Steve to tell me a story or for them to smack me and go, "What are you doing? That's fake!" Or whatever, to teach me. I take it. I take it. That's manna.

On the subject of learning from the greats, at the Sondheim birthday concert, you, Elaine Stritch, Patti LuPone, Donna Murphy, Marin Mazzie, and Bernadette Peters all performed essentially for each other. What was it like to be one of those women in that semicircle of chairs, one of them and at the same time, watching them?

It was *scary*! When [director] Lonny Price told me that's what we were gonna do, I was like, "I'm not doing it! I'm not doing it! Oooo! I would rather sing for Obama and the Queen and everybody else on the planet than have to sing in front of some of the people I admire most in the business. And with Steve sitting right over there and the New York Philharmonic?" Talk about a scary, scary, scary, *scary* moment. Even though I know, admire, and love all of those ladies and they have been nothing but lovely and supportive to me . . . that makes it *scarier*! But then we do the rehearsal and you realize that everyone is feeling the same way. Everybody's nervous, everybody's afraid. I wasn't getting out of my head enough to realize that I was going to get to sit and listen to them from that close. I got so wrapped up and carried away learning from it and experiencing it, it ended up being a hell of a good time, soooo much fun. I just didn't think I was gonna have fun. I thought I was gonna be freaked out and then it would be over, but that was a freaking ball.

Are you better now than you used to be at taking that stuff in and experiencing it?

I am learning to. I just sang "America the Beautiful" at the Rose Bowl in front of 50,000 people plus something like forty-five million on TV. I had invited Will and his dad and brothers to come because they are football fanatics and I knew we'd get to be on the . . . What is it called?

The *field*! I remember thinking to myself the night before, "you better be there because this is never going to happen again and it's going to be amazing. If you are freaked out about how you are sounding or afraid of passing out, you are going to be really pissed off." More and more I am learning to do that. I sang at Lena Horne's funeral and it was the same thing. I was thinking, "I am going to be facing Lena's family and Lena's casket and Chita Rivera and Cicely Tyson and all of these people" and I am learning more and more to be in the moment because that's all you got. Life is made of moments so be there.

Faith Prince said to you at the time of your Tony for *Carousel* that you should try to take it all in. Did you? Do you remember?

I don't remember a ton, I have to admit. I do remember first seeing Carol Channing when I gave my speech. She was the first thing I spotted. Tony Danza handed me the Tony and then . . . if you look at it in terms of a POV [point of view], your POV is the stage as you are walking toward it and then the presenter and then the Tony. And you're like, "Oh, that's what it feels like." You really haven't had a moment to take in the house at all. From that, they usher you to the microphone and you look and it's like [inhales deeply], "Oh my God!" Then right there in the front row with glasses and a short dress, Carol's was the first face I saw. I was just like, "Hiiii, Carol Channing! Oh! Hi!" She just calmed me down. It was all glasses and face and it just made me happy. I remember being with my Mom and my Dad and my sister afterward and that was the first time we had all been together as a family in a while. I remember having a cheeseburger when I got home, which is kind of a tradition. I just want a cheeseburger when I get home from an event. A couple of years ago at the Emmys, we had a great big ol' limousine and we left the Emmy ball and went straight to In-N-Out Burger in the drive-through. In our gowns and tuxes! That's all I want, because you've been starving yourself leading up to that.

After *Carousel*, *Master Class* was not long thereafter. We are focusing on your musicals, obviously, but *Master Class* is such a big part of your overall story because it's where you met Zoe Caldwell.

I have her name on my neck [shows me a tattoo on the back of her neck]. What can you say about Zoe? As much as I had learned up to that point in theater, I learned the exact same amount in the two years I was with her. I just learned. I just saw what all of it could be, standing onstage with that hurricane, with that power, with that love, with that fierceness. Some nights she was pissed off at you, with that anger.

Pissed off at the character?

Pissed off at me! She would get upset if I missed a show and rightly so. Or if I wasn't working as hard as I could, or focused. She's deeply human. I think people probably see this grand actress pontificating from on high but she is Mother Earth. She is all that encompasses. Loving, fierce, loyal, dangerous if need be. I am using such dramatic words. It's such a deep love I have for her. It started off as just respect and fear. Awe. And then you realize that that hurricane is swirling around you and you are inside of it and it's protecting you. She understands what it means to be a mentor. She understands what it means to be in the theater. She respects it.

What do you mean "understands what it means to be a mentor?"

She is not someone who would say, "Yes, you may call me Ms. Caldwell. I will see you onstage, don't talk to me offstage." She'd say, "Come in, talk to me!" I had to go by her dressing room on the way my dressing room. She was at the theater waaaaayy before anyone. She'd get there by 5:00 for an 8:00 show, going over her lines every single night. She is the epitome of professionalism. Setting up, getting into character, checking the stage, doing her exercises, saying hello to the stage hands and the ushers, every single night. I mean that's a creature of the theater. That's someone who respects the craft and expects no less from you. It was all very genuine. She's like the Wizard of Oz but she was a wizard you could touch and feel and the power was real. To be with that every night onstage, how could you not learn?

I think you have to be open to that and not everyone is. So many actors onstage are stuck within themselves. Being open enough to learn and take in isn't something everyone can do.

Maybe it's because I have had very powerful people in my life, particularly powerful older women who mentored me. I developed huge crushes on them. Whether it be my Mom or my grandmothers or the woman who ran the performing arts high school I went to or Zoe, I developed these huge crushes. I thought: teach me. I wanna be like you. I want to crawl into your womb. I am very much in awe of the female spirit.

Your next show was *Ragtime*. To me that was one of the great musicals of all time. Being in that from the ground up and seeing it develop around you . . .

When we did the first workshop in Toronto, there was only a first act and only Stokes [Brian Stokes Mitchell] knew the songs. Having [director] Frank Galati and [composers] Lynn Ahrens and Steve Flaherty there and the big, bombastic ego of [producer] Garth Drabinsky . . . that man had passion and a lot of ego. I had maybe four lines. Steve sat at the piano and played and Lynn would sing the songs. Stokes sang "Wheels of a Dream" and he had tears in his eyes at the end of it. In that moment I knew it was a hit. It was just magic in the room. I watched my part develop from nothing. At a later workshop, when Terrence [McNally] wrote the line, "You've been polishing that car so hard there ain't gonna be anything left for us to ride home in." I have my script where he was like, "You know, she needs a line here." And he wrote it in pencil on my script. I've still got it. I was like, "Terrence, will you sign this!" and he wrote, "XXOO, Terrence!" Then just being up there in Canada for an entire year. That was a long hard year for all of us. Especially because they went and opened the production in Los Angeles. We were the American cast and yet a whole group of other people [were premiering the show in LA].

Did you see the revival?

Oh, yeah. It was interesting sitting in the audience watching it. I thought, "Wow, this is a fantastic musical. I am so drawn in to this." Even though I was part of it ten years ago, I don't know that I or the rest of the community appreciated its full value. It's hard to have an objective opinion about it. When you have Garth Drabinsky saying, "We're the best thing since sliced bread," it made everyone go, "Fuck you" a little bit. There was a lot of gunk that wasn't part of it.

What was it like watching someone else play the role you created?

It was Pavlovian. I think she gave a lovely performance but I don't know—I was aware—this is no slight to her but I was living it. She walked out with the baby and I started reliving the experience of it. I was reliving what I was doing backstage at certain times. I started reliving doing pushups with the guys before the show. I remember thinking this is the point I need to get into the coffin. I remember thinking during the second act that I used to go back to the offstage mic and sing that with the girls if I got bored in my dressing room! I was there watching it but I was reliving it and appreciating it all at the same time.

You won another Tony for *Ragtime*. Your third. What do you remember of that night?

That one was very emotional because I felt that as a cast, we had been through so much. And with any of my Tony wins, I never thought I was going to win. I really never have. Especially with that one. I wasn't nominated for either of the two awards leading up to the Tony, so I was surprised that I even got nominated. I just thought, "My hair is straight, I'll go have a good time with the cast." And then Gregory Hines gave it to me. I was such a fan of his. It really felt "this is for the cast."

As you talk about it you seem almost tired. Your whole aspect changed.

I *do* get tired talking about this show! It was two very, very long, full years. Being away from home for a year and just the relationships that you forge, the drama. It was a time of great growth. And I don't know if you believe in this sort of thing but those were my "Saturn Returns" years, too. There was just so much that went down. And the *role* was hard too! My God, being beaten to death every night and singing that? Maybe that's why it's fatiguing for me to talk about. It was my first really dramatic role where I had to drop into a dark place every night. When people go "*Ragtime!*" I go, "Yeah. . . . *Raaaagtime!*" and I want to take a nap. As [co-star] Peter Friedman used to say, "Find another vein, find another vein." The roles are very heavy.

So working on it wasn't joyous?

It was . . . full.

You also got to work with Graciela Daniele. What can you tell me about her?

She's another one of those women I have a huge crush on. Another mother. She's someone who just trusts all of her instincts. She's so organic. Whenever I work with Graciela I drop so much weight! You don't feel like eating, you just feel so satiated by the creative experience. You don't need food, you know?

That's a diet plan we should all be on.

I know! I was never thinner than when I was working with her.

So at that point you had three Tonys and the rumor is that you sent them home.

Yes, I sent one to Mom.

And two to your sister, right?

Yes.

Why?

[Long pause]

You know, I felt arrogant having them out. I did. It's a little silly now.

Emma Thompson keeps her Oscar on the toilet.

Yeah, I know! I've seen it. With Oscar polish next to it! You're in there with all these books and whatnot and it's like, "feel free to polish the Oscar when you're on the loo!!!" But for me, "*Look* at my *Tonys*!" just wasn't me.

At some point you reclaimed them.

I got a house!

After *Ragtime* you did the TV version of *Annie*.

That was nice because I had all of these theater people around me. [Producers] Neil Meron and Craig Zaden are good old-fashioned theater lovers at heart. Victor Garber, Alan Cumming, and Kristin Chenoweth. We had full-on rehearsal for about two weeks, so by the time we started shooting, there was comfort there. It felt great. And for me it was an exciting experience to get to play a role that I would never, ever be considered for normally. There were some battles that had to be fought with that production. We shot the finale where Daddy Warbucks presents a ring to Grace, and then we were informed that the powers-that-be wanted us to shoot an alternate ending where there was no proposal, just in case there were any issues because of the interracial thing. Craig and Neil and [director] Rob Marshall were so apologetic but their hands were tied. I was devastated and embarrassed. It was a terrible day for me to go in and shoot that scene. Rob Marshall is just about the coolest man on the planet. He said, "Well, we all know why we are here. Let's get the shot." We did all of one take with it. "OK, did we get it? Got it? Good." And then he brought the ring back in and we used the rest of the day to re-shoot it *with* the ring and get better shots with it. In the end they ended up using the one where he gives her the ring. *Newsweek* ended up commenting on it saying, "Daddy Warbucks takes a black bride and nobody cares."

That same year was *Marie Christine*, the show with which Michael John LaChiusa delivered on his promise to write a show for you.

We had a big workshop before I left for *Ragtime*, in the summer of 1996. That's where the piece really came together and came to life. I felt so creatively alive. Before that he had given me a few songs that we had worked on for a backer's audition. Mary Bond Davis [was in it] and she had gotten into numerology and name work and all this stuff. She's crazy. I love her! I asked her, "Will you do my name?" At that point I was still Audra Ann McDonald. At

In the daring if unpopular Medea retelling, *Marie Christine*. (Photofest)

the backer's audition, while Michael John was talking, explaining the piece to the producers, Mary Bond Davis goes [whispering], "Audra! I did your numerology work. Drop the 'Ann!' You gotta drop the 'Ann.' There's no power in it! No power! Audra *Ann* McDonald, no power. Audra McDonald, power!" I am listening to her, completely engaged until Michael John turns around and he's like, "Do you mind?" But because of Mary Bond Davis, my name is Audra McDonald. Anyway all that led to Lincoln Center. We started rehearsals right after I got back from *Annie*.

The show was built around you, your name was above the title; did you feel the weight of that?

No, I didn't. It was just another piece. Obviously, it was pretty wild, to see your face flapping in the breeze on a banner at Lincoln Center, across the street from where I went to school. That was kind of crazy-making. But I was surrounded by such support and safety and creative buffers. That experience was life changing. I was sad that a lot of people didn't get it and I wish it had had a longer life. That was disappointing but I never felt that pressure. I felt the pressure to get it right and do well but I never thought, "if this show fails it's because of me."

That show happened right as what were then called the new breed of composers—Jason Robert Brown, Michael John LaChiusa, Adam Guettel, Andrew Lippa—were all coming into the public consciousness.

And their shows weren't the big, big hits that everybody hoped they would be. Sadly, we've turned into a community where everybody is afraid of doing anything new. Anything that is not a jukebox or isn't going to be an instant success . . . the show may have had its flaws but every show has its journey. I never felt like it was a failure. I remember certain moments of growth throughout. One of the biggest ones—I had already built this great relationship with Zoe Caldwell and she came backstage early in previews. She let everyone say their hellos and then essentially told everybody to get the hell out of my dressing room. She said, "Stop trying to make people like you. You are not supposed to like Medea. Your journey is to make the audience understand why she did what she did. Do not make them like you." I have never forgotten that lesson. It was so freeing! Instead of going, "Is it OK that I am killing my brother now?" . . . the audience doesn't want that. They want to be led on a journey, but they don't need their hand held.

After all that lead up . . .

I was disappointed, I was. We closed in January and I had just gotten engaged. Four or five months later, at the Tonys, it turned out I was pregnant and I didn't even know! But at the Tonys people were saying, "Oh, well, you finally lost." And I was ecstatic: "Hooray! I finally lost!" It happened, it's no big deal, the world didn't come to an end, I don't think my career was in the toilet because I have now not won a Tony. *Whatever!* The Tonys are fantastic and it's an honor but at the same time I have work to do. We all have work to do. I still have to get up in the morning and sing for my supper. That night was one of the most fun nights I had ever had at the Tonys. I ate my cheeseburger, I was partying all night at George Wolfe's house with *The Wild Party* cast. I had a great time. I did not know at the time that I was knocked up or I wouldn't have drunk so much! So *Marie Christine* kicked off a fertile part of my life! I look back on it with really fond memories. No regrets.

You mentioned the *Marie Christine* poster. Your face was also on the *110 in the Shade* posters. What's it like for you living in the city and watching your face go by on a bus?

Ummmm. It's weird. It's you but it's not you. There's a part of you . . . coming up to the theater every night during *110 in the Shade* and seeing this picture, it would take my breath away. Not in the [grandly], "Oh, *look* at me!" But, "Oh my *God*! That's me." But then I realize my apartment is still a mess. I still have crazy, messy, frizzy hair and I always will, even though my face is on a billboard. That reaction happens almost immediately after I see those things. I go, "Wow! Oh."

How much of the mythology about yourself can you tune out?

It can get to you, absolutely. Especially if a lot of it is untrue or blatant falsehoods. I remember when I went on bed rest and I had to cancel this event that I was participating in. Something ran in the *Post* that Audra can't seem to show up at her shows. I was like, "You asshole. Do you know anything?" Or the *Daily News* ran something saying that I was "very married" and stepping out at an event with Will Swenson. Meanwhile I had been divorced for a year. That's hard. But you just have to know what's true about yourself and hold on to that. And what helps, honestly, since motherhood, is perspective. I can't even think, "Did I write the note saying that she's coming home on the 96 bus today? Do I have carrots for her lunch? We have a recital on Saturday." There is too much real life that you have to organize and that takes up so much of my brain space these days. It's easier to let all that other stuff be noise. I'd be lying if I said it doesn't affect me in any way, but more than anything I aspire to be a good person and I don't ever really want anybody angry with me. I think of myself as a generous person and a nice person, so when there's bad press, it's hard. But as I approach forty, I am getting better. And as my personal life gets fuller, it gets easier.

Your next musical theater performance in New York was September 24, 2001.

Oh, *Dreamgirls*! That was such a journey because of what had just happened. And more than that, just the incredible generosity of spirit that came together that night. I have always wanted to do that role and to do it with girls who I love. The night was just explosive with love. My memories are always kind of coded by color, as if there is a picture and someone has put a colored haze on it, and for me, the colors of that night are this magenta purple. That's the blues in there. Then there was the warmth of the red of heart and love. I remember these incredible magenta hues all night. And I was *hugely, hugely* engorged. Zoe was still nursing and I was still very heavy from the pregnancy and so happy to be there. I'll never forget that communion of spirit.

After that you were gone from the stage for a while. And then you came back and did *Henry IV* on Broadway.

It was scary. I learned a lot. I tripped and fell through a lot of it. And I was no less afraid of Shakespeare at the end of the run than I was at the beginning.

We are not going to spend a lot of time on your non-musical work but *A Raisin in the Sun* was next. At the time, you said your director, Kenny Leon, called you on all of your tricks. What do you perceive to be your tricks?

Well, because I am an emotional person, it's easy for me to act with emotion but just getting there wasn't enough for Kenny. He wanted me . . . Audra McDonald . . . to disappear. I have never been pushed that way by a director. Ruth was a character who was, on the page, more like me than any role I had ever played and the hardest for me to get to.

Did being pushed to your place of discomfort and then being successful and winning the Tony feel that much more gratifying?

Sure. I was . . . I guess you could say that, if I were to say that about getting an award ever. Because there's a part of me that feels that winning an award shouldn't be gratifying. But that was a very difficult [role]. I went deeper than I had ever gone before and I accessed a lot more pain. As sad as it was when *Raisin* closed, I was ready to not be living with Ruth for a while. She was a lot. You try not to bring your work home with you but she was a lot.

110 in the Shade **was eight years after your last musical on Broadway. But in between, you did a series of Sondheim pieces at the Ravinia Festival.** Passion, Sunday in the Park with George, Sweeney Todd, Anyone Can Whistle . . .

It was a great opportunity to do roles that I would never be considered for on Broadway, in a place that is somewhat insulated from the New York press, and do the work of this incredible composer. In a way we formed our own repertory company; me and Patti LuPone and Michael Ceveris. It was like, "What are we doing this summer? What's our summer camp project gonna be this year?" And for me to get to work with yet another great lady of the stage, someone I adored, admired and feared . . . to get to know her intimately both onstage and off . . . I look at it all as an education. And it was great because I was able to develop a relationship with Steve. Being around that genius! He is just so affable. Ask him to tell you a story about the '70s and he'll spew for hours! It's fantastic. There are no words.

When he talks about his career now, it seems as if he doesn't take himself too seriously.

No, he really doesn't. When he talks about *Anyone Can Whistle*, he says, "We were just showin' off how intelligent we could be." He's the first person to take a shot at his own stuff.

110 in the Shade. **There's another role for which you wouldn't be the first person to come to mind.**

Lonny Price had to chase me for that one for a long time. He gave me the CD and I have to admit I wasn't bowled over the first time I heard it. I just didn't connect with it immediately. Now I look back and I wonder why. That's a story that could be close to anybody's core, regardless of how one is viewed. It's about how one feels about oneself. Lizzie thinks, "I'm plain, but I don't want to settle and be less than who I am." I think those are very universal themes no matter what a person looks like and what they project. But I just had a wall.

What made you ultimately say "yes"?

Lonny Price is the most tenacious man on the planet. He is my gay, Jewish husband. That was one of the favorite roles that I have ever played.

Isn't it interesting; that something that didn't especially speak to you ended up being your favorite? What makes it that?

There's not a single color that she doesn't show; there's not a single emotion that she doesn't go through. The music and the writing is so beautiful. "Your whole life you cry for a star and you know you'll never get it and then one night you look down and there it is shining in your hand." And the relationship with the father, that was more poignant than I ever realized. It was hard to do those scenes for a long time [McDonald lost her father during the run]. John Cullum is just a master and so full of love. That's what got me through. I knew that whatever happened, he was gonna catch me. That's . . . hard to talk about. I had never been in a situation before where the cast was full of such love and joy. I felt so safe.

You once told me that before you leave the planet you wanted to do *Porgy and Bess.* **And then you did!**

The universe is always listening, isn't it? Bess had been in my consciousness for many, many years, but it was really interesting to now go in and look at her with an analytical

With Steve Kazee in *110 in the Shade*, the show in which McDonald met her husband. (Joan Marcus)

eye. I had never read the book. I've heard people say, "You're not doing what DuBose Hey-ward wrote." As a matter of fact, I am doing what he wrote. It's all right there [in the book]. It was fascinating to analyze it. I was always a little confused by Bess's choices. Why does she go off with Sportin' Life in the end? For me, I had to really start with her addiction. Once I looked at that, that's when all of a sudden she started to unpack herself for me. Maybe this sounds flowery but she started to hand off little secrets about herself. Even though Bess comes on full of spit and fire, for me it's more about trying to keep Crown from exploding. She's in pain. She needs drugs. She can cover all that up by being big and loud, but she also knows what these women think of her. She wants their respect, and she can't have it. And she has to make sure that every man in that place wants to fuck her. That's protection for her. Because if something happens with Crown . . . So there's a lot going on. She's struggling to survive.

That's a whole lot to play eight times a week.

It's really hard. Trying to find a vein to pick every night to get that blood, that juice. I've actually got cuts all over because one of the tics I picked for Bess is that she scratches and picks when she's scared. I don't put stress on having to be emotional, I stay on my verbs. It's always about "what do I want?" And then the emotion kind of takes care of itself.

Are you going home exhausted, triumphant, or both?

Not triumphant.

Not ever?

No. I push myself really hard, but I am not one to go, "I nailed it!" That's just not me. There are nights when I think, "Okay, I felt pretty open." But every day, the show that you just did is gone. It's a whole new show you've got to do. Don't try and recreate what you've done, but try to learn from it.

Is this the biggest you've ever bitten off? Do you feel like this is the most you've asked of yourself?

Yes, in every way. It's a bear of a role. And when I go home I'm a mom. So balancing the two together is very challenging. It was a goal of mine to play this part someday and now I can check it off my list. I can't check off my list that I played it as brilliantly as humanly possible but at least I got the chance to play it, where I wanted to play it, on Broadway.

We can't really discuss this production without mentioning Stephen Sondheim. [Sondheim, in an infamous response to a _New York Times_ article, accused director Diane Paulus, writer Suzan-Lori Parks, and McDonald of disrespecting the show.] A lot of people read his letter as objecting to the changes. I didn't see it that way. I saw him as objecting to hubris. For Suzan-Lori Parks to say, "I think that's what Gershwin wanted . . ." and if he had lived, he would have changed it, I think to call that hubris is a valid perspective.

Yes, it's absolutely valid as a perspective. However, he was reacting to a few quotes in an article that were out of context. How many times has he been [misrepresented in the press]? What wasn't in the article was [how much passion and respect] we all have for this piece.

When his letter hit, you were in the middle of final rehearsals in Cambridge.

Yeah. There was a lot to negotiate. It felt like we were being attacked, like the plane being shot down before it had even taken off. There was still a lot of exploring to be done. This was an out-of-town tryout—that's what it's for.

Many of the proposed plot changes reverted back to the original. Did Sondheim influence that, or do you think that would have happened on its own?

That had nothing to do with Sondheim. They were trying different versions and they'd check in with the cast to see how it felt; they'd gauge audience reactions. Once that letter happened we closed ranks. We were in a huddle working, staying focused.

Is there any way in which that was good?

Hell yes. It's the closest group of people I've ever worked with. I don't necessarily mean that we all go party on a nightly basis, but there is so much trust that you can go anywhere on that stage and go as deep as you want to go. I think it's because we went through a battle together.

Having taken on something so huge, do you have a sense of what direction you now want to point your compass?

I never know exactly. I just hold onto the mantra, "Keep evolving, keep evolving, keep evolving." It may not feel good, but this is going to help you evolve. Certainly that was the case in _Porgy and Bess_. I know I've emerged stronger than I was a year ago. I feel like a different person. And I still have miles and miles and miles to go. But I will always dive in and try. I mean that's my stupidity or brilliance. I don't know. I'll figure that out when I'm old.

KRISTIN CHENOWETH

September 2009; November 2010;
November 2011

KRISTIN CHENOWETH IS HOLDING MY TAPE RECORDER to her mouth to make sure it captures every word she has to say, having had firsthand experience with lost audio. "For my master's thesis I interviewed Jerome Robbins and my tape was broken and I didn't know it. He did two hours with me and then he died," she exclaims. We're in a tiny West Hollywood café and Chenoweth is gobsmacked by the presence of Gabriel Byrne sitting at a nearby table. It is she, though, who is repeatedly interrupted by adoring fans. "Why do you think I live in West Hollywood?" she giggles. "It's like *Soapdish* every day."

Kristin Chenoweth was born in 1968 in Broken Arrow, Oklahoma, and adopted by parents she still considers her closest friends. The road to Broadway wasn't a direct one for the pint-sized blonde with the freakishly versatile voice and untouchable comic timing. In fact, it very nearly didn't go that way. Chenoweth's training (which she paid for, in part, with money earned on the pageant circuit) was in classical music. She was on her way to a fellowship with the renowned Academy of Vocal Arts in Philadelphia, to which she had a full scholarship, when she allowed herself to be distracted by an audition for the musical *Animal Crackers* at Paper Mill Playhouse. The rest is a history that included memorable turns in *Steel Pier* and *A New Brain* before her explosive turn as Sally in the 1999 revival of *You're a Good Man, Charlie Brown*. Chenoweth stopped the show cold with the song "My New Philosophy, " penned just for her by one of her idols, Andrew Lippa. The show did not do well but a star was born. A slew of varied opportunities followed including extensive film work, four television series, albums, concert tours (including evenings at Carnegie Hall and the Metropolitan Opera House), but Chenoweth's most indelible creation came with her next musical, *Wicked*. As the bratty Glinda, who learns through love and acceptance to be the Good Witch of the North, Chenoweth was the perfect foil to Idina Menzel's Wicked Witch, Elphaba. Together they took Broadway by storm and earned their places among the theater's most memorable marriages of performers to roles.

Chenoweth's subsequent shows, *The Apple Tree* and *Promises, Promises*, were less successful, though both gave Chenoweth the opportunity to display her unique gifts to great advantage and, in the case of the former, the most glowing reviews of her career.

A Little Bit Wicked, Chenoweth's memoir, is full of folksy charm. That's not artifice. When you spend time with her it's very clear that that's who she is. She is also, of course, a big star. So while she may be home making her Butterfinger pie, she may just as easily be running off to get new hair extensions for her appearance on an awards show. That's her dichotomy. Or, as Karen Ziemba pointed out about her turn in *Charlie Brown*, "she's got a cultivated coloratura

Playing a six-year-old Sally in *You're a Good Man, Charlie Brown*. (Carol Rosegg)

and is playing a five-year-old kid." Dichotomy. She is also a self-described control freak who believes strongly that a higher power is in control. A small needlepoint pillow hanging from her dressing room door during her run in *Promises, Promises* read: "Good morning this is God. I will be handling all your problems today and I will not need your help, so have a great day." It's dichotomy and it's Chenoweth.

You went to an audition on your second day in New York.

I went down to the Equity lounge and I waited for about five or six hours. I loved every second of it. Listening to the people out there with me: old-time Equity members talking about the olden days. I was like a sponge. They talked about the old school and how it was way back when. I heard a guy talking about working with one of the Marx Brothers! Some random lady came and gave me an Equity pin and I said, "I'm not a member of Equity." And she said, "You will be." I didn't think I'd get to be seen and that would have been OK with me because I got the experience of getting to talk to those old-timers. But I got to get in there and audition for [director] Charlie Repole.

Kristin Chenoweth

Animal Crackers, Millburn, N.J., 1993
The Fantasticks, off-Broadway, 1995
Steel Pier, Broadway, 1997
A New Brain, off-Broadway, 1998
Strike Up the Band! Encores! 1998
You're a Good Man, Charlie Brown, Broadway, 1998 (Tony Award)
On a Clear Day You Can See Forever, Encores! 2000
Wicked, Broadway, 2003
Candide! New York Philharmonic, 2004
The Apple Tree, Encores! and Broadway, 2005, 2006
Stairway to Paradise, Encores! 2007
Music in the Air, Encores! 2009
Promises, Promises, Broadway, 2010

Your training was in classical music, but your comedy timing was, it seems, innate. Why do you think that is?

I think it's a combination of a couple of things. I'm a believer in the Lord so I say "Him." I also watched the Carol Burnett show, and I watched cartoons. My father was a huge Pink Panther fan. So, look at who I watched.

It's a very rare thing to have the voice of an ingénue and the comedy chops of a character woman.

People always ask me what I played in high school. "Did you play Ado Annie? Did you play Adelaide?" No, I played Laurey and I played Sarah. And when I got to New York, people said, "You can do either one."

But they don't like that, when you can do either one.

No, they don't. I wanted to play Belle in *Beauty and the Beast* more than anything. The musical director said, "You know, you're not cookie cutter." And, in a way, it devastated me. But in another way I knew that that meant that I could create parts. I was lucky enough to be given that chance. I know so many of my talented friends who should be given the same opportunities that I've had. But somehow . . . it's a combination of talent, luck, being in the right place, your time, your journey, your attitude. All of it.

Can being so specific that they don't know what to do with you be a curse? This is probably a key area when your faith really comes in, no?

Thank you for bringing that up. Just because I have faith in God doesn't mean that I don't doubt myself, that I am not insecure, that I don't love gay people, that I don't question things. The list goes on and on. I have my insecurities like everybody else. Sometimes it's good problems to have like, "What do you want to do next? What do you want to focus on?" No one has a crystal ball. You have to ultimately get quiet and hear. Whether you believe it's the Lord, yourself, or Buddha, you have to hear what you're supposed to hear.

That's where I can imagine faith being really helpful, in just letting go and trusting.

Lots of people think that I made a huge mistake in not doing *Thoroughly Modern Millie* and doing the TV show *Kristin* [which was canceled after thirteen episodes]. Here's the thing: the right person played Millie and the right person got the TV job. Yes, it failed but I am proud of that failure and I learned.

And it gave you the chops to do more . . .

Yes! And it launched another career of a talented person [Sutton Foster]. And I like that.

Who, incidentally, said of her time in that show, that it was incredibly stressful. It's easy to imagine that she would have been on cloud nine, but that wasn't the case.

It's hard to have perspective. I don't know how Sutton feels or any other actor but sometimes the Internet, as much as I love it, can be the devil. So I can go online and read 5,000 really nice things and five other really mean things and I'm curled up in a corner. There are people who will read this book who don't like Kristin Chenoweth. They think, "I don't buy it and I don't think she's all that and a bag of chips." They are allowed their opinions. I have finally gotten to a place—and I really mean this—where I don't care. It's cost me a lot of money and therapy. I want the respect of people I work with, I want to be someone people want to work with again. These are the things that matter to me. I want to keep continuing to grow as an artist. But I can't care any more if a couple of people on the Internet don't like me. I would lose my mind. I just have to do my thing and hopefully 70 percent of people will like it.

When you are at a benefit and working with legends like Chita Rivera or Barbara Cook, do you worry that you might come off as a super fan?

I try very hard to keep my cool. I did a Stephen Sondheim thing with Barbara Cook. To be the age she is and be able to sing like that—that's my dream. Long after Broadway and Hollywood stop calling I will want to sing because that's where my heart is. Always. Always. I said to her, "Barbara, I know that you know how I feel about you. You're my idol." And I said this to her right before she was getting ready to walk out onstage, and she just said, "Oh, fuck me, kid." I am so shy when it comes to famous people. My mother used to say, "Go up there and say 'Hi' or get their autograph," and I would run the other way.

So what happens when you're backstage at the Oscars or Emmys?

I ignore everybody unless someone says something to me. Believe it or not, I am shy around celebrities. When I met Madonna my manager said, "She really wants to meet you," but I barely said a thing. I'm a weirdo

Back to that very first audition in New York. In your book, you said that Charles Repole said to you, "Who are you and where have you been?"

I said, "I'm nobody. I'm just here. I'm heading to Philadelphia to the Academy of Vocal Arts to be an opera singer." He said, "You need to think very seriously about what you're doing. Because you look like one thing, an ingénue, but you're really a character." He did offer me the part. Turns out they had been looking for several months. I had a decision to make and I got quiet. I had a full $75,000 scholarship to study with the best coaches in the world, or I had a show, *Animal Crackers*, at the Paper Mill Playhouse for about $500 a week and I'd maybe get my Equity card. Most people would say, "What, are you nuts?" My whole life, all I ever wanted to do was be an actor. People think it was to be a singer. Yeah, singing was what I connected to but I am an actress first. In opera, acting is second on the list. They want to hear the voice.

And I knew that I would fit some of the roles in opera but I know I am an actress. So I made a decision to follow my heart. I went and I got my card. I moved to New York and every day I took a cab to 890 Broadway because I didn't understand the subway.

That would be $500 a week right there.

It was. I lived on ramen noodles because of my cab money. And then I would walk all the way home. I didn't understand the 1 and the 9 trains. The chorus guys had seen me getting out of cabs every day and they said, "Are you rich?" And I said, "No, I just don't know how to . . ." And they took me under their wing. So one afternoon, we got out early and they made me practice. I learned how to at least get to and from. And that's what the Broadway community will do. I love making movies, I love television, but there is a part of a Broadway person that you do not get anywhere else in the world and that's why my loyalty always will be there. I miss it every time I go to see a Broadway show. It's almost a little depressing to me. I go to a show like 9 to 5 and I am watching my friends Marc Kudisch, Allison Janney, Stephanie Block. I am beyond happy, and yet I leave sad because I am not onstage. I think a lot of people who are performers will understand that.

Because you want to be a part of the community?

I do. And movies are not live. Movie stars aren't going to come out after the movie and shake your hand. Or make a mistake. If there's a mistake onstage, we all experience it together. That is why shows like *American Idol, Dancing with the Stars*, etc., are popular. It's the only chance that we have to watch people live. I miss it.

What do you remember about *Animal Crackers*?

I was a freak. We would take vans out to the theater and I was the first one there, always. I would remember what the people in my van wanted to drink and I would go and get it so that everyone was settled. We would get to the theater and I'd say, "If anybody wants to warm up with me . . ." I was the eager beaver. I remember hearing a guy saying, "Oh my God, the *enthusiasm*! I just wanna slap you." He said it in a kind way. But he said, "One day Kristin, it's gonna be a job to you. You're still gonna love it but it's gonna be a job." Well I am happy to report that as of the last time I was on Broadway for a length of time, it was no job. I did it for the sheer love of the role and the opportunity to do it. I also got to experience young people having their Broadway debut and I got to be the person who looked at them and said, "I'm so happy that I am getting to do this with you." It's never been a job. People always say, "You're always so happy all the time." They're almost bitter toward me. Sorry.

Not to cast a pall on the positivity but when you were winding down in *Wicked*, you told me you were over it and ready to go. So at a certain point . . .

It *was* a job. I'm glad you brought that up. I really am because even in my sadness and tiredness . . . you know I had been with the show since the beginning. So even though I had only done the show on Broadway for nine months and in San Francisco for two, I had been doing it for a long time. I was tired. And I get a little ADD. There comes a point when I need a break from the character.

I am not asking you to defend being ready to leave. But I want to know how you deal with that. You're still going out there and doing your show. So when it becomes a job, what you do to keep it fresh and exciting?

The audience. That's what got me through. Every audience is different and every show is different. I am also extremely hard on myself. So I never nailed the show—for me. I am happy with a lot of what I did and what I was able to add to the role. But on every show, I have this journal—my dresser would tell you—and I write down my mistakes. I just wanted one performance where I had a blank page and there never was. There never is. Also, I was injured. I had a bad neck and there was a lot of numbness down my arm. There still is. So that, compounded with a long hard run, I felt lots of pressure. But it was still not a job for me. I didn't do *Wicked* for the money. I made money but I didn't do it for the money. I was offered *The West Wing* and I chose to do *Wicked*.

Speaking of money, you came back from *Animal Crackers* and, in your book, you describe a living situation where there were bunk beds and you didn't know which bed you'd end up in from night to night. Your description lacks any element of, "Oh, my God, I can't believe I have to live like this." Which was either artifice, an amazing ability to look on the bright side, or insanity.

I think it might be the latter. You are absolutely correct and no one's ever nailed me on that. I lived with my best friend, Denny, and he *was* aware of how we were living. He was more upset by it. I remember a situation when the shower curtain was filthy. I guess it really had been bothering him. He came in and said, "Do you think one of us can buy a clean shower curtain?" And I was like, "You bet-'cha! I will, I will." I guess the point is that I didn't know what I didn't know. I say that to a lot of young people. Nothing was gonna stop me and I didn't know what I didn't know. Now I would think, "Four roommates? Are you high?" But then, I didn't know what I didn't know and I loved it.

Did you work survival jobs during that period?

I was lucky enough to go from [acting] job to job, but I did an extra job called The Masquerade for additional spending money because I like to shop. Now, granted, I would go to cheap stores, but I still liked to shop. So I would take these Masquerade jobs and perform at bar mitzvahs. One time I was the Statue of Liberty. I didn't care, I had fun! I met fun people and I made $150 a day. The only thing that I hated was that the costumes never fit me.

But you never had to take a regular job?

No, thank God. And I did not want to take money from my parents; I wanted to make it on my own. I am going to live with four people so that I can do *The Fantasticks* for $230 a week.

Speaking of *The Fantasticks*, in your book, you described a few performances when there were two people in the audience.

We used to be able to scan the audience during "Try to Remember." During "Follow, follow, follow . . ." you'd turn your head and scan the house. And I thought, "What do I do? There's one person there and one there!" I remember the air conditioning breaking in the dead of summer. I got parasites. A lot of things happened to me during *The Fantasticks* but it remains one of my all-time favorite parts. She doesn't know what she doesn't know, either. And she's a little odd, but she's also growing. I could relate to her. I loved doing that show. I had been offered other things. I had been offered *Phantom* overseas for a lot of money, but I really wanted to do that part.

That's a recurring theme in your career. Just like when you turned down *Forum*. You turned down your first Broadway show offer. Even though it was to understudy, a lot of actors would never have done that.

I knew myself. I knew what I wanted and I knew I wouldn't be a good understudy. I would be upset that I wasn't up there doing the work. If you take a job, the important thing is to have a good attitude about your position in that play. If you are taking an understudy part and you are going to be bitter and unhappy . . . I had enough faith to know that there was something coming around the bend. I didn't know what, but I knew I'd rather stay doing *The Fantasticks* where I'd get to be working.

Your next show was a straight play. That was an unexpected turn.

My Broadway debut was *Scapin*. I remember getting the call and Marc [Kudisch, her then boyfriend] said, "You can totally do this." He helped me a lot. He said, "You just be you. That's what Bill Irwin wants." I had the *Steel Pier* workshop, so I had nothing to lose. When you have that attitude, that's when you get it. Bill Irwin let me open the show and then leave six weeks early so that I could do the *Steel Pier* workshop. For that I will always love Bill Irwin. It gave me the experience and an opportunity I would not have had.

That was your first experience working with non-musical people and that's a very different experience. The environment in a straight play rehearsal is very different from a musical. What was that like?

It's a different beast. I viewed it as one big class that I didn't get in college. You have to pace yourself very differently. You don't have to worry so much about how you sound. Usually you're not dancing your butt off. But the words are the focus. With Bill Irwin it was like clown school. It was the most fun I've ever had in my life. With Jerry Zaks [in *Epic Proportions*], it was working with a master. He was one of the first people to say, "I am going to help you hone the comedy. You have so much that's innate but I am going to clean it up a little." He helped me focus. I just learned. Every director I have had has been a teacher. Gary Griffin, when I did *Apple Tree*, was my teacher. That's why when I agree to do a project, the director is more important to me than anything else.

Let's talk about *Steel Pier*.

It was so underrated. Daniel McDonald is no longer with us and, of course, he played an angel in the show. Now I believe that he's a real-live angel. They were looking for a tall showgirl that could maybe hit a high C. There was big hype about this. Kander and Ebb's next show! I had made it through the dance audition and got a callback—and by the way I was there with all the tall people. I went in and there was John Kander, Fred Ebb, Scott Ellis, and the producers. I sang "Art Is Calling for Me." Many people have done it but I have my own trills and frills that I do. I go up to high E. I saw John Kander sit up straight. I knew I was singing well that day. After I sang it got really quiet which I thought was either a good sign or a bad sign. I saw them really looking at me. They asked me to read. Of course I had memorized it. I put the sides down which isn't always a good idea but in this situation it was. I did the audition and Scott came over and said, "Thank you so much," and shook my hand. And I thought, "I am not getting this part." My parents lived in Pennsylvania at the time so I took the train to meet them. I was devastated. We met at The Olive Garden, which is my favorite place, and I remember crying over dinner and saying, "I know this is my part and if I don't get this part, I am not sure if my heart can take it." I'm sure it was very dramatic. I thought, "Some tall showgirl is going to get that part. They get everything, the tall people!" But I got it and that was the first time in my life that I felt, "I'm gonna make it. My way." John Kander wrote a whole new aria for me. You don't get better than that. I got to do the part and I am sorry to the tall people: Finally a short girl got the part. They get the Rockettes.

I am interested in your *knowing* from that moment that you were going to make it. What gave you that feeling?

John Kander. He said—I am just repeating the feedback—"I haven't heard a voice like that in forty years. I want that." And I knew that he was classically trained. I thought, "If he said that about me, I have a prayer."

You had more than that; he wrote a sixteen-bar F for you.

People thought it was canned, lip synched. And I was never prouder, ever, in my life, than opening night of *Steel Pier*. It was my Broadway debut in a musical. I was singing opera. Freddy and John were down there and I met my second Mom, Deb Monk. I get emotional because I think about Daniel. And I think about Scotty Ellis just taking a chance on me. My favorite moment of my career, besides winning the Tony, was doing that show. I loved it. Every night I was never happier—I was just happy to be in the Richard Rodgers Theater.

What can you share about working with Kander and Ebb and watching them develop a show?

You get really close when you develop a show with people. For me, John was a mentor. He called me his little Brunhilde. I love him very much. I am still waiting for him to write me a show. With Freddy it was a little more relaxed. He would tell me a dirty joke and make me repeat it just because he wanted to hear the word "fuck" come out of my mouth. I miss him every day. He came to my *Wicked* opening. C'mon, he didn't have to do that! He's Fred Ebb! And John Kander, too; he came to see me in *Candide*. And don't think I wasn't nervous about him being there. I wanted him to be proud of me. I can't believe Fred's gone. I still think he's on a long vacation. I loved him.

What was your experience of Susan Stroman?

I just didn't want to disappoint her. I would have spun on my head. I would have clucked like a chicken if she told me to. I still would. Even though I am at a certain level now, I'd do anything that she asked me to do. It broke my heart that I didn't get to do *Young Frankenstein*, mainly because I didn't get to work with her. I trust her. I think she is going to go down as the best Broadway choreographer of all, in my time. I'm gonna hang my hat on her.

Do you remember what you felt when the *Steel Pier* reviews came out?

Devastated.

Did you read them?

Every single one of them. Not for me personally; I don't believe I was mentioned in the *New York Times*. But all I cared about was the show. This is what I think happened and you can tell I've thought about it; *Titanic* had all kinds of problems in previews and they fixed their problems. So when you fix your problems, you're going to be perceived as better. When you're perceived as the show to beat and you come out and you're good but not great . . . you see what I'm saying? I think that's what happened to *Steel Pier*. I think people will look back one day when they do it at Encores! and think, "this is a good show." It's got an incredible score. Unbelievable. It broke my heart. Our audiences began to dwindle. I'd see empty seats at a Kander and Ebb show and I didn't understand. I cried like a baby. I might have been twenty-seven but I was still young and I was still looking at the business like, "How can people not come out to this?"

Your next show was *A New Brain* at Lincoln Center. How come you gave it less than a sentence in your book?

That's a good question because [composer] Bill Finn is a genius. And that was my first meeting with Malcolm Gets who I fell in love with. I am not sure why it wasn't included in the book because, like every show I am in, I have so much to say. I remember Graciela Daniele asking me to do it. She also asked me to do *Annie Get Your Gun*. She was very good to me in my career. I should give her more homage. She's been an encourager, and she's so talented. I remember Chris Invar was in it at first and he got really bad acid reflux and had to quit so they brought Norm Lewis in, who I fell in love with. It's a small show so it was like family. Still. I see them. And Mary Testa! How could I not have brought her up? God, she's a genius. I didn't know what I didn't know. I always say that. I was just trying to be good and concentrate on my job. Sometimes you get into a situation where people don't want you to be good but these people—everybody wanted everybody else to be great. During *New Brain*, that was the first time I was hit with an inner ear problem and I didn't know what it was. I couldn't walk. I had to be out of the show for about three weeks. I thought it was interesting that it happened during *A New Brain*. Talk about art imitating life. Now I know it's Meniere's disease but then I didn't know. I still fight that.

After *A New Brain*, Graciela asked you to do *Annie Get Your Gun* and you had to decide between that and *You're a Good Man, Charlie Brown*.

Everyone I know was saying, "Do *Annie Get Your Gun*! Job security! It's Bernadette Peters!"—who is my idol. I was really torn, and Marc Kudisch said, "I think you should do *Charlie Brown*. You'll be one of six people and you'll have a greater chance for your talents to shine through." And the rest is history. I didn't even know what part I'd be playing. I auditioned for Patty. Not Peppermint Patty, but Patty who is the amalgamation of all the girls. And Michael Mayer said, "I have an idea but I can't tell you about it. I have to get it cleared through Charles Schulz." I took a part not knowing the part I was going to play. I showed up [the first day of rehearsal] and at everyone's place at the table, there was a script, a character mug and a hat that had their character on it. Mine said "Sally." I credit Michael Mayer with that. He said, "You are going to get to make up your own part." And then Charles Schulz sent me every comic strip he had ever written that had Sally in it. We got to play with sketches and see which ones worked. It's so funny: the ones I thought would kill were kind of like "eh." And the ones I thought were kind of off-beat killed.

Did you know at that time that Andrew Lippa would be writing new songs for you?

I knew that there was a chance he might but they wouldn't commit to it. So I signed on to do a show—let me repeat that the other show would have had two big solos and dance numbers with a guy, and I would have worked with Bernadette Peters. And this show, I didn't have a song for sure and I didn't know what part I was playing. It's that inner voice thing. I just knew.

During rehearsals did you ever think, "What did I do?"

Oh yeah! I thought, "Is this working?" I had no audience and I needed to be in front of people to know. Michael Mayer kept saying to me, "Don't worry."

Was that frustrating?

Yeah. Roger Bart and I were left alone to make up "Rabbit Chasing." But to Michael's credit, he let us do it. It wasn't until the opening night in Chicago that I got a great response. We all did, but the character just went over so well and I thought, "Phew." Michael came backstage and he says, "I told you!" And I said, "No, you didn't, you didn't say anything." And he said, "I told you, though. I knew." I guess he did. I don't know. That's his genius.

During *Charlie Brown*, Michael Mayer said about you, "Kristin has this comic ruthlessness. She's one of those performers who'll stop at nothing to make it work." Does that seem accurate to you?

That's so nice. Yes! I do not stop until we've got it. That may require time, it may require an audience, but I will not rest. He knows that about me and I am glad that he does. I expect the best from myself and I expect the best from people working with me. If it's not right, if it's not working, then we need to figure out what is. People are paying a hundred and some odd dollars to see us, I want it to be our best.

So what happens when you are not in harmony?
It's tricky. You have to figure out a way to get beyond that and make magic.

When the reviews came out for *Charlie Brown* . . .
I got a call from my doctor, Barry Cohen. He called me at 12:30 or 1:00 in the morning. I was just getting home from the party with my parents. They were staying with me in my apartment up on 107th. And he said, "Go get the paper." My dad ran out and the first paragraph, my Mom bursts into tears ["giving one of those break-out performances that send careers skyward," it said.] They were so proud. Someone was actually writing something like that about their kid. The next day my phone wouldn't stop ringing and my life was never the same. But it will never happen like that again.

You also had the challenge of getting that kind of reception, but seeing your close-knit company not getting recognized. How could you express being sad about that to them and come off as sincere?
You can't win. That's why I made a promise to myself that if I was ever in a dramatic part or in a part that wasn't flashy and getting noticed, I always wanted to make sure that other people felt safe enough around me to be able to celebrate. That's why [during *Promises, Promises*] when Michael Riedel began writing untruths about me having a problem with Katie Finneran, I went right to her and said, "Katie, I *want* you to be great. You don't need my permission. I want you to *kill it!*" And I meant it.

What do you remember of your first Tony Awards experience?
I have no idea how I won. It is a roller coaster. I just remember having fun, and I remember my agent at the time, David Shaw, said, "It will never happen this way again. It will happen, but in different ways. So you need to remember it, and you need to enjoy." Best advice because I did. I just had fun. I didn't worry. It was amazing. I remember Ben Stiller and Swoosie Kurtz calling my name and then it feels like—I don't remember that whole moment of winning. I go back and watch the video so I know I won. I remember getting to meet Bernadette Peters. To be in the same room with her, I mean it's—Martin Short saw me on the red carpet and picked me up. You just have these surreal moments where people that you look up to are acknowledging that you're alive. It's really fun.

Your first couple of post-Tony projects, the show *Epic Proportions* and the series *Kristin* didn't take off.
What *Kristin* did was taught me about camera work. It taught me that world and I got to make money. I also loved the show. It's so funny because people view certain things as failures. I view not one thing I've done as a failure. It's all been—it's the way you look at things, I guess. You're not going to knock every single thing out of the ballpark. Not everything is going to be *Wicked*.

After *Kristin*, you did back-to-back TV musicals, *Annie* and *The Music Man*, then comes the call from—
Stephen Schwartz. I thought he wanted me to play one of the midgets or something.

How's that self-esteem thing working out for you?

Because I always think "what am I right for?" And when you think *Wizard of Oz*—He said, "I have been working on this script and I've written this part with you in mind." At that point, Glinda was very much like the third or fourth lead. But I knew that she had the best song and I was like, "that's mine." I knew I wouldn't be happy sitting and watching somebody else play my part. I did the reading with Stephanie Block as Elphaba and we became fast friends, very close. We started doing reading after reading after reading and then it started becoming apparent that what people were responding to was Glinda and Elphaba. Winnie Holzman went ahead and started changing it and it became about the two women, though it's still Elphie's story. I knew that that show was going to be huge.

When? At what point?

Opening night in San Francisco I knew. And our reviews were not great. It didn't matter. I knew. I kept telling Idina, "It doesn't matter what the reviews say. Look at the audience every night."

In your book you dance around the question of Idina a bit. You say, "I am not a hater" which may be true but is not an answer to the question of whether or not you got along. It's clear that the two of you are very different. So you are both working to be the best that you can be, but not necessarily the same way or harmoniously and you are on a journey together. I don't just mean on the show; I mean press, the awards, etc. When you are together all of the time but not together . . .

I think what you do is you remember what you are there for. We certainly found our way. I don't think anyone can deny that we did. It was up there. I just kept reminding myself what the show is about: lack of acceptance, then tolerance, friendship, love, and ultimately forgiveness. So I did that every night. I had it on my mirror and I remembered every night that that's

Stopping the show with "Popular" in *Wicked*. With Idina Menzel. (Joan Marcus)

what this is about. I can only speak for me. And I also knew that this show was affecting people in a big way and I wanted it to continue because I loved the piece and I loved the parts. And I love her. I respect her. Idina and I went through an experience together that we may or may not ever have again. *Wicked* is a juggernaut. [When Idina won the Tony] I think she deserved it. She was great. I think Idina would have felt the same if I had won. Idina and I both know our experience together and what we experienced together in those parts and the bottom line is there've been no great onstage couples in a long time. I think Matthew [Broderick] and Nathan [Lane] and I think Idina and Kristin. It's still very much a big huge part of my life. It was the perfect marriage of person to role. And I wanted to be part of a big hit. Boy, was I! I love it. I love that I will always be connected with that. I came down in a fricking bubble! I can't believe how lucky I was.

That show created a fan base for you who were especially passionate. Does that ever get a little scary?

Yeah, because on Broadway you are accessible to fans. But I also love people, I really do. I find people fascinating. What's been hard for me is learning that wall that you have to kind of put up when you feel something isn't right because there are those people, too. But for the most part I like that people come up and say, "This changed my life." I like to hear those stories. People always say, "You're not curing cancer [when you're acting]," and no, we're not, but we can affect people's lives in a big way so I do take it very seriously. That's why we do it. Certainly there are nights after a show, when I'm exhausted and I want to go home but I really do try to [be available for fans]. It's not hard for me. I battle a lot of other things, but that's not something that I have to work at.

Joe Mantello said, "Kristin can go straight to 100 percent. It's a question of editing with her."

He's so not wrong. He's a great director. When we were doing "Popular"—this kind of sums it up. He said, "I'm going to go get some food, and I'll be back. You go ahead and do your thing. Let me see it when I get back." And the reason that worked for me is because I do have 10,000 ideas. He came in and streamlined it. He trusted me enough to find it and then comes in and does his magic. And he's not wrong in anything that he said. I do have an edit problem definitely.

Given the opportunity you'll try everything?

Yeah, yeah, yeah.

Did you end up with glitter all over your house for a year?

Yes. I think it came out of parts of me that I can never—I still have it! I'm very clean. I have a maid come every week, but I still will open something up, and there'll be glitter in there, and I just smile. It's like Glinda's little way of saying, "I'm not done with you yet."

Even though you said that when you left you were ready, how was the actual leaving?

Heartbreaking, heartbreaking. I remember coming down on the bubble, and there being quite a long time before I said anything—I'm fine if you don't give me a moment to think about it, but I am very much a crier, and I immediately lost it after ten seconds of the audience applauding. I lost it. And then I remember looking at Idina in "For Good," and I remember her looking at me, and I remember her lip starting to kind of shake. I couldn't even look at her. I just got through it. We both knew we were doing something special together. It was tough.

I haven't been able to go back into the Gershwin since. I can't even walk by it. That's sad. I don't know what that's about other than it's such a lovely, singular memory. I can't. And I've had friends play Elphaba and Glinda and stuff. I haven't been able to go. But I'll get there, I'll get there. And then I got to go into *Bewitched* and *West Wing* and everything. Thus began a new chapter.

Your next musicals were at Encores! *On a Clear Day* and then *The Apple Tree*. Two Barbara Harris roles back to back.

It was awesome. Encores! are my favorite and here's why: I have ADD, and I get to go in, concentrate on just one thing for a week and a half, and then perform it five times and it's done. Perfect for me. I wish I could just do Encores! all the time.

For someone with ADD, *The Apple Tree* seems especially perfect. Four different roles in one show.

I loved it. I remember thinking, "I don't know if I can do this. This is hard. How did Barbara Harris do it?" Jerry Bock—God rest his soul—and Sheldon Harnick would say, "That's why we waited forty years. We never had the right person." That meant a lot to me, and that's why it was so important for me to do it right. To this day, I wish I could just relive that. Act I of *Apple Tree* is perfect. There's not one flaw. It's the perfect piece of musical theater. I miss it so much.

There's a show that requires stamina. It's an insane amount of singing and then add all of the costume changes, the wigs . . . How did you pull that off?

[After the Encores! run] we did it for three and a half months at the Roundabout and I didn't miss one show. I lived like a nun. I lived on Airborne. I got nine to ten hours of sleep a night. I had to. And people don't get it. They don't understand that going to a luncheon when you have an 8:00 show might not be the best idea because you have to talk to people and then maybe you have to talk over people because you have to be heard. If you're quiet, you might be considered rude. I've had people get mad that I wouldn't come to stuff or support something when I'm in my show. My first priority is my job. I have to do it. They don't get it.

You said of *The Apple Tree* that it was the most enjoyable theater experience of your life.

Yes, yes, yes.

You also told me before about the joy of leading a company and having people doing their first shows and how—

I love that. There were three or four kids making their Broadway debuts. It made me feel so proud, I just get goose bumps when I think about it. I want them to be able to look back and say, "Kristin was a good example." I've seen a lot of bad examples and I don't want to be that. I want to be a positive force. I have to see you every day. You have to see me every day. I don't have to be best friends with everybody but we're going through this journey together for a year. I don't want to misbehave. That doesn't mean perfect. But also I find when you're not a big complainer, when you choose your battles, people will listen to you more.

Can you describe working with Bock and Harnick?

I'm so sad Jerry died. He was an incredible artist. He'd draw me little cartoons all the time. His heart was massive. Every time he would come to the run-through, tears, tears at the end of Act I, tears at the bows. Every time he came to the show, period. Oh, my God. I miss him.

From chimney sweep to goddess in the *Passionella* section of *The Apple Tree*. (Joan Marcus)

Sheldon is still very much a part of my life. He was probably more hurt about the Tonys that year [Chenoweth was not nominated] than I was. He just couldn't understand. He does not suffer fools, and he does not mince his words, which is why he is who he is, and that's why he's very much still in my life. He's almost like a protector, a guide, he's a sounding board. I love him.

After *The Apple Tree*, you did another series, *Pushing Daisies*, and then *Promises, Promises*. What made you choose it?

I am so happy with my choice to do *Promises*. I knew Sean [Hayes] would make it great. Never did I think that I would extend in that show. I had commitments. But I wasn't done with her. I do things only to get better, as an artist, as a person. I have somewhat lived this girl. Not getting any sort of recognition from the Broadway community, again . . .

You mean not getting nominated for a Tony?

Yeah. Even after [not getting nominated for] *The Apple Tree*. It really sent home a reminder. "That's not why you do it, Kris. You do it to get better and to grow. You do it because you love the cast and you love Rob [Ashford, director]." Then the Emmy nomination came for *Glee* and I thought—I am going to be brutally honest—I really didn't want to take part in the Tonys if they were not going to acknowledge our show. I'll pass. My dad called me from Oklahoma and I said, "I'm not gonna do it. I just don't feel right. They just totally ignored our show and our cast." And he said, "You know, I understand that that's where you're at, but the kid in Idaho or Wyoming or Oklahoma that wants to see you on the Tonys and you're not there, he doesn't understand the politics of it. He just wants to see you. Who is it hurting, really? Practice what you preach: if it doesn't really matter, you shouldn't really care." So I told my manager that I would do it after a week of saying "no." I was so glad that I got to be a part of it.

Why did you feel like you wanted to extend?

My [character] Fran evolved. I was finding more moments of joy for Fran. I think that makes the drama pay off more. I was still getting better and better. And I also loved the chemistry with Sean. It's funny when I read the *New York Times* review and it said I was miscast. Ben Brantley didn't see that something like this could happen to someone like me. It was a lovely slam. It really was lovely! I mean it!

I am surprised you read the review.

I always do. I used to not, then I went back and forth. Then I realized, "Read it. Everyone already knows. You might as well know too." I read it and to hear that he thought this couldn't happen to me . . . I thought, "You are so wrong. I lived it. I am not proud of it but I was with a man who was emotionally unavailable to me for many years. I put up with things that are not OK. I did that. Kristin Chenoweth did that." I was healing in doing this role. I loved it! And Mr. Brantley publicly said that he didn't like the show when they did it at Encores! But it doesn't matter because people loved the show and that's what I care about.

That's a huge leap forward from when five negative things on a chat board could leave you curled up in a corner.

I've grown. I have tougher skin. I still don't go in the chat rooms but I can pick up a magazine in a hair salon and see that someone thinks I have cellulite and I laugh. What can I do? No one died. Trust me, I know where my flaws are. It's funny, on Broadway, the theater eats its own. I never really understood that. They build you up but then there can be some mean . . .

How do you mean?

There is a feeling of "We own you. You started here. We are going to bring you down a peg or two, because you haven't been around." That's what I've felt. It could just be me.

Other than not getting nominated for a Tony, how have you felt that?

After I did *Charlie Brown*, I went to do *Kristin* and I remember an interview I did. They said, "You just won a Tony and you are going to Hollywood?" And I said, "I am going to go get better at something else. But I will come back as many times as you'll have me." But there's this sense of abandonment, like I've just . . . I don't know, it's so weird.

But this many years later, when you've proven that you keep coming back, do you still feel that?

Well, I mean, I had the best reviews of my career for *Apple Tree* and I wasn't nominated.

Well, let's put Tony Awards aside. Don't you feel embraced by the community?

By the actors and audiences, yes, I do. I don't know . . . there is a sense about me, according to my friend who is in the theater and shall remain nameless. She says, "People look at you and think you have it all. You don't need it." And I think, "Should I get punished for that?" *Apple Tree* was a real sock in the stomach. I had to stop caring and let it go.

Often when you stop caring, that's when you do your best.

That's right! I thought some of the best performances I have given in *Promises* were when I was tired or sick or injured. I just let it go and it was some of the best performances ever. It's such a great lesson. If I care about the right things—my work, my colleagues, the people coming to see the show—as my Dad keeps saying to me, "Focus on that, Kris. Would you rather have the critics say you are the second coming or would you rather have people come?"

You've had the reverse. With *Charlie Brown*, you have the reviews and the Tony but no audience.

Same with *Pushing Daisies*. It's just up and down. I know every woman that you are interviewing has said the same thing: you can't rely on this business to make you happy. That's why I have other things in my life. It may not seem like it, but I do. I have another life and I love it. I have other goals. I love what I do, though. I will never quit it as long as people keep hiring me. There is so much I want to do, revivals and original stuff, too. I'm bound and determined. I'm going to go down trying.

IDINA MENZEL

July 2009

MEETING WITH IDINA MENZEL WAS A GAME of beat-the-clock. Between the time she agreed to participate in this book and our actual meeting, she became pregnant. I knew that if I didn't catch her before she gave birth, I'd have a very hard time getting her attention for the foreseeable future. I was therefore very happy to meet her five weeks before her son, Walker, did; it was on a Sunday morning in the airy Los Angeles house she and then husband Taye Diggs were renting. Diggs, who came to the door in his boxers, ushered me into the living room, where a very pregnant Menzel hoisted herself up to hug me. She had the serenity that expectant mothers sometimes possess and absolutely no trace of the fiery characteristics of her most famous roles; *Rent*'s vixen, Maureen, and *Wicked*'s witch, Elphaba. Both of those characters act and react from their gut emotions, while Menzel is far more cerebral. She is also fairly soft-spoken and even-keeled, the polar opposite of the roles she's known for. But she laughs heartily and her eyes are always alive, occasionally flashing with the kind of spark she ignites so freely onstage.

Born on Long Island in 1971, Menzel grew up wanting to sing rock music, but her interest in acting led her to train at Tisch School of the Arts at NYU. Still, a career in theater was by no means a forgone conclusion in Menzel's mind. But her casting in the small, off-Broadway musical, *Rent*, changed that. *Rent*, of course, was not only a global smash; it was among the handful of musicals credited with changing the art form. Its cast of unknowns found themselves on the cover of *Newsweek* and besieged nightly by adoring, screaming fans. So instrumental was the contribution of that original cast to the show's development and success that they, like the original cast of *A Chorus Line*, receive royalties for what they helped to create.

Most actors don't ever experience a show of such magnitude, but seven years later Menzel did, yet again, with the opening of *Wicked*. Playing Elphaba, the misunderstood Wicked Witch of the West, Menzel was not only in another blockbuster; she along with Kristin Chenoweth was at its center. Menzel took home the Tony Award for *Wicked* and recreated her role in London, during which time she was the highest paid female performer in the West End.

Since *Wicked*, Menzel has been off-Broadway, on film and TV (memorably on *Glee*, where she sang both *Les Misérables* and Lady Gaga), and in concert but not back on Broadway for a decade. She was also busily raising a son. But in 2014, the same year that she voiced Queen Elsa in Disney's *Frozen*, belting the year's most popular song, "Let It Go," she returned triumphantly to Broadway in the new musical *If/Then*. The show garnered mixed review, but fans and critics alike were thrilled to have Menzel's singular talent back on the boards.

In the short-lived off-Broadway *The Wild Party*, which played during the same season as the short-lived on-Broadway *The Wild Party*. (Photofest)

You grew up in Syosset, New York. When did you decide that you wanted to perform?

I had a grandfather, Grandpa Nat, who was always singing to me, with me, creating little scenes behind the couch. I had a little toy, this wood thing that looked like a microphone, so I used that all the time. He sort of encouraged my creative talents. And then in school I auditioned for choral concert things and it was apparent that I had some sort of vocal talent. I went to a teacher, Mrs. Steadman, and I screamed a bunch of *Annie* tunes. She didn't want me to hurt my voice and she also wanted me to find my own voice and not imitate those girls, so she took me on and she taught me breathing and to read music. I loved her. So from then on, I just studied in school. My mom wouldn't let me do anything professionally; she didn't believe in that.

Idina Menzel

Rent, off-Broadway and Broadway, 1996
The Wild Party, off-Broadway, 2000
Hair, Encores! 2001
Aida, Broadway, 2001
Wicked, Broadway and West End, 2003, 2006 (Tony Award)
See What I Wanna See, off-Broadway, 2005
Chess in Concert, London, 2008
If/Then, Broadway, 2014

Studying vocal technique might be pretty boring for a kid. What made you keep at it?

It wasn't boring to me. It felt very mature and sophisticated and like I was being let into this club ahead of schedule. I felt special in some way.

And then at fifteen you decided to find your way in professionally, since your mom wouldn't let you.

Yeah. My parents split up that year and it was really traumatic for me because I didn't see it coming at all. Back then you could get karaoke tapes on cassettes and if you set up a four-track recorder right you could make a cheap, cheap demo. I had about eight of those—"Evergreen," "Flashdance"—and they were the only contemporary songs I knew, because I had been using arias and classical music with my teacher at that point. I remember hearing them back years later and it's like the most legit versions. . . . It's always funny to me when people think I come from this rock world. The technique and discipline of singing has always been important to me, so it's funny when people think you're raw or unstudied. Anyway, I wanted to work, because you get the sense when your parents are splitting up—well I got the sense—that I should. They were taking care of me as much as possible but Dad was strapped, so I just wanted to get a job. I worked at Tony Roma's, at a deli, at Macy's. Then I lied about my age and I went and auditioned for this [wedding] band called Tony Sietta & the Echoes. I knew just enough songs in each genre to get by. I did that every week. It was very empowering as a young girl to walk in and do that. I felt like this cool, professional singer chick. It was a really wonderful educational tool. I was driving around in my car illegally because in Long Island you had to be sixteen to have your junior license. That really laid the groundwork for me as far as always wanting to be self-sufficient. I just loved it. But there came a time when I became very jaded by it and wanted to break out. The more I knew how good I was, I felt I should emerge from that. I always had self-confidence. Where it's gone the last . . . the older you get, and the more successful you get, the more neurotic and introspective. I was much more fearless back then. So that's what I did, on and off through college.

You went to Tisch at NYU and studied acting. What made you decide that acting was . . .
Well, both were in me.

And you hadn't really explored that part of you?
Not really, not in an intense way. The trajectory of my life has always been to have somewhat of a balance of both—to want to be an actress and to also be a recording artist. I've gone back and forth in how strong my passion is toward one or the other at different times in my life. When I was little and I was following all the Broadway musicals, my parents would take me to see stuff all the time. That's what I wanted to do. And then when I became a kick-ass wedding singer, singing with a band, I said, "Oh, I want to be a recording artist and sing rock

'n' roll." But I was always afraid that I would be abandoning a side of myself. So I've always just tried to balance both and study both. What was nice about getting *Rent* as my first professional job was that it was both. It became a Broadway show, but it was singing a style of music that felt really natural to me.

When you auditioned for *Rent*, did you have a sense that it was something you really wanted to get?

No, not really. I didn't really know what it was. It reads funny. A lot of musicals read funny in script form. This especially did. It was hard to imagine what it was and that "Over the Moon" monologue was like, "What is this? Is this some kind of joke?" But I just went in and did my audition. Every time I go back to theater, I'm reminded of how much I love it. I think it's the nostalgic part of it—being a kid and being in a school play and how much fun you had. I think it's always reliving that. It's that communal aspect of the cast. People all have the same mission and are accepting of your artistic talents and your individuality. In school there were always kids, including yourself, that were not fitting in, but when you were part of the arts you stood out in a positive way. I think that stays with us as adults and so when you find that, it's like your playground again. I just love it and I miss it. It exercises parts of my personality that I feel I had a lot of when I was younger. I was really good at meeting people, making friends, being a leader. And so that idea of being back in a play really strikes that chord.

You say you had a lot of that when you were younger. Do you feel like you're less gregarious, less outgoing, less . . . ?

I can be. I come off as being shy and soft-spoken. I don't know what's changed there. I don't know, maybe I became more aware, or more self-conscious about being too "big," standing out too much. A girl who's a bitch, or knows how to express anger, or a girl who's powerful can be scary. That's what we're taught in our society. So, maybe I tried to combat that.

Is it that you realized "I don't need to work so hard to be noticed any more because I'm actually getting noticed?"

Well, for me, ever since I was a kid, people were always doting on my singing. I actually hated that. Maybe because there were a couple of girls who were one or two years older than me that were always making fun of me. You don't want to be too good because that will evoke some kind of envy or jealousy. That was me. I wasn't that girl that just took the stage. Once I was up there, it was always a place to let go. But I was always a little sensitive to having people not like me because I was good. I found that *Wicked* actually helped me to sort through that. So often your characters mirror things in your life that you don't realize. They're going through something that you sort of need to experience yourself.

A lot of what you described sounds very Elphaba.

I know, yeah, whereas *Rent* was this very body-confident woman. Boom, comes in, wrecks the room, everyone loves her. That was probably very confidence building for me. A take-no-prisoners kind of person. Elphaba was more . . . there's a big gap between those two shows.

Let's talk about *Rent*. Jesse Martin once told me that it was a bizarre rehearsal process because it was kind of anything-goes. Did it feel odd to you?

I didn't have as much experience as Jesse did, so I didn't know what to compare it to. For me, I just knew I felt very comfortable with [director] Michael Greif, and I didn't know what you do when you're in a "professional" show. It was very freeing and open and I guess set the tone for me. Staging "La Vie Boheme" was a perfect example. We did it for a couple of weeks where he would just play around and Michael would remember a tableau that happened spontaneously and organically and then he shaped it. It was just a free-for-all party. Nobody was holding back. It was great. [Now] when someone just blocks you before you discover a scene, it rubs me the wrong way.

It's part of Broadway legend that Jonathan Larson died the night before the first performance. Personally, for you . . .

It definitely shaped the way that I think about things or aspire to lead my own life. "No day but today" and living in the moment. I only knew him six weeks, but I'd gone to a feast at his home and sat at the piano with him. That show just took off like gangbusters and we were doing *Vogue* shoots and *Harper's Bazaar*, the cover of *Time Out* and *Newsweek*. Most of us didn't have a template for that. We all could have gotten really swept away but there was the importance of us putting out his message first and foremost. Every night, everywhere we went, the responsibility to his work so overrode anything that we were doing, anything superficial. It really taught us how to stay in the moment and serve the work and the people coming and not to be jaded eight shows a week. Not one of us missed a show for the first six months. That's pretty unheard of, especially with the young kids these days. It kept us grounded and because of that we really were able to get the most out of the experience. It sticks with me. Every single time I'm doing a show you can lose sight of how incredibly rewarding being a stage performer is. In the rigors of eight shows a week or when you're not feeling well you can really start to focus on the negative. It's a constant thing for me to try to remind myself. [There are] those Sundays or those two-show days where you wake up and there's a sheath of mucus and infection going over your cords and you think, "Should I call in or can I get through?" I've gotten through, by sticking to my technique, to my routine—whatever it was—and keeping a positive outlook. To get through to the end of that is so empowering. It's invigorating. It takes all different ways of doing that throughout the year of being in a show. I've been lucky enough to have shows that go that long. You have to exercise that part of yourself. *Rent* sort of laid that groundwork to touch base with that at all times. "Get over yourself. So you're not feeling well? These kids came in from wherever. They're coming to see you. Get it together." There's a responsibility to youth and the message. It's bigger than the actual show. I'm lucky to have that, but it's a great responsibility.

Both *Wicked* and *Rent* had a rabid fan base. As wonderful as that is, is it also sometimes a little scary?

Scary wouldn't be the word . . . it's just about learning to carve out a space for yourself and when to compromise that because there's a young woman or boy crying in front of you, confiding about how you touched their lives. Sometimes it's too big for what you feel about yourself. And I'm not saying that to self-deprecate or try to be extra modest. It just feels like they're giving you this gift that I don't know I've actually earned. I mean, the show is bigger than me. I also think I'm helped by being in an original piece because you're working with the composer from the beginning and so, what's the chicken or the egg? The character's there but then he writes songs because he starts to know your voice. The dialogue gets written with a couple of inflections that are very similar to something I've inspired, just because of the way I speak. It becomes this living, breathing, character, person. I feel spoiled and frustrated because it's harder to find jobs that I really want to do now that I've had those experiences. You'd think, "Oh, you can pick all these different things," but for me, I can't just step into something.

But when you did *Aida* or *Chess* and it wasn't being crafted around you, you still managed to find your own stuff.

I hope so.

Is it still a satisfying experience?

Oh yeah, because performing is satisfying to me. With *Aida* I chose to embrace the idea of having to learn a role in four weeks, which I'd never had to do because I get these long rehearsal processes with these writers and these original pieces. That was a challenge and I wanted to just prove that I could do that. I really respect women that come in [to a show] and make it their own. Because there is someone saying, "Well, your predecessor normally ends up here at [this spot on the stage], could you just be here and then go stage right . . . ?" It actually happened to me when I went to London to do *Wicked* because they had all these fucking other people who were telling me [based on the stage manager's book], "Oh, you always pick up your luggage in your right hand and put it down over here." And I'd have to say, "I don't think so. I'm a lefty, first-of-all, so it just doesn't feel right." How do I say that without sounding like I'm being a diva?

Donna McKechnie told me something similar about when she went back into *A Chorus Line*. It's kind of like, "I get that that's what you *think* that I do, and maybe that's what I did then, but I did it because it was coming from some place organic and it's still got to come from some place organic and not because you tell me it's my left hand."

I don't know if I always responded in the best way. I [might push back] and then I'd see the look in people's eyes and I'd quickly try to get rid of that. I constantly combat the part of myself that wants to be really liked by people. Like I said, especially in my later life, the more successful I am, the more I don't want people to think that I've somehow gotten too big for my britches or something. I'm constantly saying, "Well, if I complain about that, will they think this?" London was a really great experience for me, because having done the show and having had positive feedback and an award, I had the confidence of knowing people like this show and like me in it. I was able to go there feeling good and solid. I hadn't looked at the show in a year and a half, or two years, so I actually went back to a coach. I really wanted to rediscover things. I felt more grounded. And I reminded myself that I used to be good at making friends really easily. Maybe the pressure of not having to learn the role wasn't there so there was more time to be social. I had more time to enjoy the cast. It was really good for my confidence going back there and working from a place of being confident. I took more risks and tried different things.

With a show like *Rent* where you have to be vulnerable eight times a week for over a year . . .

That's how you learn technique. I think that's why movie actors are often in awe of theater actors. You have these couple of great rehearsals where it's magical and something happens that you don't expect to happen with your fellow actor and you're in the moment. You take note of it and you sculpt it and carve it out. Then the fear is, "Will I be able to find that again?" What happens with eight shows a week is muscle memory. It actually becomes easier to find those things—they just come out naturally. Your body just learns it. The first time you try to sing that ballad with all the emotion you sound like a dying cat. It might be really beautiful and everyone's crying but it's not going to serve the piece if you do that every night—especially in theater because people like to hear really good notes. Somehow, your body learns to divide itself. The heart and all the emotion is there and yet your vocal cords can still find a way to ride on top of that. I love that, when you hit that stride. [Sometimes] you think, "I'm just too tired today. I'm

With Adam Pascal, Jesse L. Martin, and then husband Taye Diggs recreating their roles in the film of *Rent*. Also pictured: Rosario Dawson (far left). (Photofest)

not in this." And then all of a sudden, you're onstage and it just comes, or you find ways to surprise yourself. I always find it weird when people say, "When I'm in a show too long, it just gets boring," because the audience really is different every night. It truly is. The audience is incrementally this much different and you're in a tiny bit of a little different place that day. A line comes out and all of a sudden you don't get a laugh, so you're thinking about it, and then you're four lines down and so you miss that one and you have an off show. Then that night, for the evening show, you want to get that song right again. So for me, it's this living breathing thing. I also don't sing it the same every night. I stay within the parameters so the composer will be happy, but I find a little something I can do. Then the keyboard player says, "Ah, she put in that little nuance, cool," and then I can hear him play a little something different. I find these little dances to have with people, whether it be the actors onstage or the guys in the pit. It's very subtle, but it's those games that keep you fresh.

Ben Brantley wrote an infamous article about the *American Idol*-ization of Broadway in which he noted that Broadway audiences now prefer money notes to interpretation in singers.

It's not just the *American Idol* of it. I'm a creature of both worlds, right? So I appreciate and respect a lot of different styles. But someone like a Rufus Wainwright or Bruce Springsteen or Alanis Morissette—we love them because of the quirkiness, the tones, the truisms of their voice, the imperfections as well as the perfections. Whenever I sing pop songs, the keys are always much lower. If you looked at pop sheet music where it starts, it's much more like how I'm speaking to you right now. It's down here. If you're in theater, the verse would never be that low normally. The whole thing is just pitched in a whole different place, which I think is to enhance the acrobatics and the sort of "wow-ism" of it. When you've listened to Seth Rudetsky go on about "who I love so much"—he loves that vibrato and the long, high note. He rarely ever talks about that beautiful thing, that moment where you hear a voice crack a little bit. I find that in the theater community, I'm applauded for my acrobatics and when I work in the studio, the producers always want to get this more intimate, sexier, vulnerable sound. Granted, there's a reason why things are higher; back in the day, you didn't have as much amplification. If I was singing to you down here, you're not going to hear that in the back row—it just doesn't project. I just don't think that it's all *American Idol*, because before that we had *Star Search* and before that we had Barbra Streisand who fucking sings her ass off and held these amazing notes.

But Barbra Streisand was never disconnected from the music so she's doing both. Whereas, I think part of the *American Idol*-ization is that it's just about the notes.
And the riffing.

You're known in the theater community as being one of the practitioners of this particular art form.
I know, and it's not where I come from. I've never been an *American Idol*. I've actually tried to take on things where I can put things in keys where I can show dynamics. But it's one of the things that I wrestle with—wanting people to see that side of me versus being perfect and hitting that note. Especially in this YouTube generation, people examine everything note-by-note. "Did you hear, she missed that F, she must have been sick," or "she has no technique." That's stuff that drives me a little crazy. Should I have stayed home that day because I wasn't feeling well and you would have seen the understudy? I came in and I gave the best I could give and it was a little growly or whatever but I was still there. It's something I grapple with. You can really be successful and not have to sing those crazy high notes. And yet, there's always this other side where someone's successful because they do that. So there's no answer. It's really hard.

Let's get back to *Rent*. So, the thing explodes, and you're suddenly doing it on Broadway.
I was really unaware of the politics of the Broadway community during that, which was probably a blessing in disguise. I didn't know about Tony voters coming and what weeks those were. That can undermine what you're doing. When I got nominated for a Tony in *Rent*, I had no idea that I was even being considered. That's how out of it I was. . . . I didn't know the whole rhythm of the season. The only thing I knew was that it was cool that we were off-Broadway and we were moving and not closing. If you compared it to *Chorus Line* or *Hair*, we were having a similar experience. The money . . . we didn't become really aware of that until we re-negotiated the second time. So all of a sudden, you get all of that stuff in your head.

That's a lot to sift through at once.
Yeah. But we had each other. And I met my husband, so that was another thing.

How was leaving the show for you?
It's always bittersweet. You're ready to let go of the character, to move on creatively, but when something's made an imprint on who you are, it's very powerful. You're excited about moving on. For me, I'd gotten this really nice record deal. That dream was coming true and so I was really excited about that. And yet you're scared to leave.

After you left *Rent* and you recorded an album, your next show was *The Wild Party*. The producers were very confident that the show would move to Broadway.
I wasn't convinced. All I knew was that this was another group of people, another cast that really clicked big time. So once again, I felt spoiled. It was another great gift for everyone to love each other that much and want to hang out all the time. That was what it was about. The

music was unbelievable. That was the first time I'd read a review. I don't even remember reading reviews in *Rent*—I'm telling you, I was oblivious. I remember Taye and I read a review and it was really scathing about both of us. Ben Brantley wrote something like, "They should each take a little of whatever the other has. He's too subdued and she's too shrill and hyper." That loud and shrill thing really stuck with me. So I wanted to show more vulnerability in different parts of my voice—I felt that people weren't seeing the spectrum. But also, I'm asked to do that in the things that I'm in. Like, in "Defying Gravity," you're the Wicked Witch of the West. Shrill? I grapple with that all the time, finding the right keys in *Wicked* so that you have this really organic, earthy girl—that tone—those keys that would evoke those sounds and emotions in my voice and then also, call on those more treble-y tones that a witch often lives in. That was a dance for me all the time because I didn't want to just "be singing up here!"

Do you still read reviews?
Yeah, just after the fact.

After you're done with the show?
Not that late. After the sting won't be as bad, and it won't change my performance. I remember after I read [*The Wild Party* review] every time I was singing one of those high notes, I couldn't get it out of my head that I was just too loud and shrill. Taye and I found that we worked together really well in a show situation. We have good boundaries.

You didn't find that out during *Rent*?
We did, but this reinforced that for me. Back then, we were more feisty as a couple—we fought a lot more. But we laid down ground rules as far as not dragging things into characters, not slanting a line just to . . . you can do really mean things onstage to each other if you want. Just that look in someone's eyes if they're mad at you. You can make it personal and that's not OK with me. And because we played arch enemies in *Rent*, you had to be careful. And Brian d'Arcy James was just the best. When we didn't get extended, we all went to the Dominican Republic together.

Then, your next show was *Aida*. We talked about why you did it but do you have any other specific memories of performing it?
Yeah, well my opening day was supposed to be 9/11. Broadway closed for three days. So that's what that time represents to me. It's not even the show as much as what was going on in New York. When I finally did get up there, talk about getting out of yourself: I'm the third replacement, I've been dropped by my record deal, I'm in a humbling place in my career. But then 9/11 happens and it's supposed to be a comedic role? The theater was only a quarter filled and nobody was laughing. You just wanted to get offstage. It was just a weird time. It was another time to say, "Ok, get up there and do your work and help people forget." The other good thing about playing Amneris was reuniting with Adam Pascal—that was fun.

***Wicked* was next for you. You said that you felt you screwed up your audition when you cracked on "Defying Gravity." You cursed.**
I screamed, "Fuck!" at the top of my lungs, which apparently had a very good *Wicked*, fierce, tone to it. I screwed up in my *Rent* audition, too. You know how sheet music for pop songs often has the repeat sign at the end? Because it just fades out on the radio? I forgot to figure that out with the accompanist before my audition. I was singing "Let's Give Them Something to Talk About" and I just kept going on and on, kept repeating and repeating it. It

was messy and not very professional of me. Years later, I'm in *Wicked* and I had to learn "Defying Gravity" for the call back. It was so emotional, my notes weren't all . . . I was doing a really good acting job and connecting to the material, but it affected me. But [when I cursed] I stayed in character, which I think is what [director] Joe Mantello liked.

Stephen Schwartz said of you. "[She's] one of the most diligent and hardworking performers I've ever worked with." Was the rehearsal process of *Wicked* hard for you?

It was demanding, it was really demanding, because it was being rewritten every day. I wasn't great at cold reading at the time. I've since worked on it a lot because it became an anxiety of mine that I wanted to get past. There'd always be new pages and it's hard to work in the moment if your head is down in the page, but the writers need to hear the lines because they're trying to get plot across and fix things. So that was difficult for me. Also, they wanted to see if things were working and quite often, for that role, she's at a very heightened state of emotion. So, if they didn't see it start at six and go to nine, at ten in the morning, they weren't sure if something was working, so I always had to start there. I also found that when you are making yourself really vulnerable, it's just a really fragile place to be in rehearsal. I know a lot of people look at *Wicked* as this little fairy tale, but there's a lot of real core emotion going on there. The cast constantly screaming at you and hating you? A lot of times it was very emotional and it was hard to . . . I would sometimes just go into the bathroom and kind of let it go there so not everybody would see it, so I could clear the slate and then go have lunch with people or come in and do the next scene. I had high expectations of myself. I really wanted to satisfy Joe. I had this huge respect for him as a director. I was pretty intimidated by him as much as I knew he loved me. I just wanted to do really good work. It was very trying for me. I'd come home and cry to Taye all the time—"I'm not getting this," or, "They gave me these new pages and I'm not quick enough." I learned that my way of working is to sit in it and not be perfect right away, so I can find those idiosyncratic moments. Her magic and her gifts all come out of this place of extreme emotion. She can't harness it—at least not in the first act. It was all working for me, but the perfectionist, the professional, wanted to have it together.

There was a lot of chatter about you and Kristin. In terms of working together . . .

I learned a great deal from her. First off, I found her to be one of the top ten most talented people I know. I liked to watch her work and figure out the timing of things—comedy, all that kind of stuff. And her abandonment! Just being able to "go there." It was a real treat to be able to work with her that long, to watch that. It wouldn't work if we were the same girls with the same backgrounds. It's who we are and it's what made us appreciate each other for our differences.

How do you work through the gossip that you hated each other? Do you just ignore it?

That's just a reflection of society not being able to be okay with two women being leads in a show . . . having to make some kind of drama. When people work together that long— men and women, whatever, my husband and I—there's always a day where . . . but she and I had the utmost respect for each other. We worked our asses off and really cared about the success of the show. We were involved with it for so long. We were really invested in our characters, their relationship, what the show was saying. We were like sisters. Some days we'd be more in tune with one another and visit each other in our dressing rooms, and other days we had our lives and didn't see each other until we were onstage. But that controversy always happens, and it only happens with women— when two men star together people don't manufacture a fight.

Taking a triumphant curtain call with Kristin Chenoweth in *Wicked*. (Photofest)

Do you have specific memory of working with her?

The first day that Kristin was working on "Popular" in rehearsal and just watching her work. She's just . . . so free! Watching her construct a scene . . . she just fluttered around like a bird. Walked over to the lipstick and started putting the lipstick on me and she's singing at the same time but she's not worrying about hitting the marks. She's in her body and doing these ballet moves and just like . . . she was just floating. Like jazz. I can relate to that. It doesn't manifest itself in the same way in my body but . . . I just really respected that. It was just all free and everything she did was kept . . . it was just a way of working that I will always take with me of . . . letting go and riffing, sort of riding a wave and it was just a really magical thing to watch.

You told a reporter when you were going into the London production that you hadn't had a glass of wine for a year and a half during the run. Was that because of the demands of the role?

I never drank in the beginning. I never know what to expect for myself, as far as endurance. In the beginning I'm somewhat . . . anal. And alcohol dries my voice out so that's one of the things I'm really good about. And I try to get a certain amount of sleep, which is hard when you're nervous about the role. It's all about sleep for me. And not going out to a loud place after a show and talking. That can do me in. It takes me a while to let go and have a glass of red wine with dinner. Maybe because I don't want to rock the boat because as soon as I start let go a little bit, I'll get sick. So I'm a little tightly wound when it comes to my preparation.

Does that make the prospect of doing a show that much more like, "Oh, God, I'd love to perform but I have to go through all that endurance and living like a nun again . . . "

Yeah. But I still want it. I still want to find that next thing.

What was the San Francisco experience of *Wicked* like for you? Because that was the first time you tried an out-of-town—

It was okay. A lot of people were giving me the feedback that my part was underwritten. So that was worrying me. It was like, "Damn it. After all this work . . . it's coming off as very one-dimensional." But when they decided to take off the summer, and get back in there and work, I was excited about that. I knew they were trying to figure that out.

Did you read the reviews?

I was told it was a love letter to Kristin. My manager said, "There's nothing bad about you. There's literally two lines about you in the whole thing and the rest is a love letter to Kristin and the show he didn't like very much." That felt bad to me and sad. I was happy for Kristin but I felt bad. But you keep on going. We got so much wonderful feedback from people that I knew not to let that get me down. I was touching people in a way, and that's all that really mattered. And the fact that his review wasn't making a dent in the sales was very gratifying. There is nothing that compares to the closing of that first act and what the audience feels and therefore what I receive back. That was like a gift every show, that amazing rush of emotion and applause and knowing I had this incredible theatrical moment in a musical. So it just fed me and I kept doing my thing. I think my performance got better and better as the year went, too. Joe would constantly say, "Be a star. Get out there. Sometimes you are too subtle, too introverted. Fucking Wicked Witch of the West!" I was finding places in the show where I realized, "Oh! Just stand here. Enjoy this silence in this moment. Have the power and the confidence in yourself to know you are holding the stage." Discovering all these moments that I let go because I was afraid to sit in them or whatever.

How was being nominated this time different from the first time?

I had to enjoy it. I'm not going to be a freak. Go to the luncheon, enjoy being in the company of all these amazing actors and have fun with this. And I did. I couldn't believe that I won. It was so amazing.

Who did you think was going to win?

Well, everyone was telling me it was going to be Tonya [Pinkins], but I don't know. I felt like I was always the outsider. And to actually win that award and join the club, a little bit . . .

You felt like an outsider?

I was always kind of this hybrid girl. I've had some wonderful opportunities and everything but I just didn't think I'd be the one to actually win the award. It was a great feeling. I tried to take a yoga class before the Tonys to chill myself out but I had this horrible zit and I have really good skin. Even with the green makeup my skin is really nice. But I had squeezed and picked at it for like three days before out of nervous energy. I went to yoga and all I could see in the mirror was this big red blotch on me. I came home obsessing about this pimple and how ugly I was going to look that night and how my agent had sent me an e-mail saying, "Don't be your self-deprecating self and assume you're not going to win and not prepare a speech" So I came to Taye, "I haven't written anything because I don't want to get my hopes up. I have this big pimple. I wanna win but I know it shouldn't be important to win." All this stuff. He was trying to take a nap and I was having a cry, literally snotting all over his bare chest. It was so disgusting. And I remember, instead of him being like, "Get your shit together" he said, "Ok. Well, what do you want to say if you get up there?" We were going through it, and I remember when I won he was so in awe of the fact that I remembered. I nailed it, exactly what we had done in the bedroom. Once in a while some-thing will happen and it's nice. It doesn't really amount to much. It adds a lot to ticket sales and the way producers see you, but it doesn't amount to much. You still have to audition and prove yourself.

Taye joined you during the run.

Yes, Taye came in for Christmas time. It was really fun. Nerve-wracking. I was almost more nervous to kiss him in the scene in this musical . . . it's not even a big deal. It's just a kiss, but for some reason . . . maybe it's the dynamics of him being this movie star, and this is this show that I was the lead in, and wanting him to think I was good up close. Also putting your intimacy in front of people is a fine line. I remember having to sing that duet with him and being a little shaky. It was funny. But he was too, because he hadn't been singing a lot and doesn't even consider himself a singer. So annoying.

When you left the show, that's another story . . .

Which I like to tell just because I love when things are so dramatic and then afterwards just so comedic. I fell through this hole. One of the automation people, a substitute, was filling in and she cued the floor two minutes early. She was a cue ahead of herself. And so the hole that normally would be flush to the stage was already down. I walked into a five foot hole in smoke, in the dark, and caught the side of it with my ribs. The stage manager pulled me out . . . and I couldn't breathe. I thought I had punctured my lungs. The show stopped and it was like your typical, "Is there a doctor in the house?" I was in full costume, wig, green makeup, lying on the floor. I always remember those amazing crew guys, who I love to this day, who always took my safety so seriously, they all were around me . . . these hot, macho guys and they were like, "Come on honey, do your yoga. Breathe. We know you can do it." I felt like I was in a Lamaze class or something. And then some doctor from the audience came and asked me if I could feel my toes and meanwhile the audience is out there. My vanity came up first. I said to Joey, my dresser—because the green makeup only came off at the right temperature of hot water with the right pressure in the shower, and a specific brand of Neutrogena soap that I had learned worked best—so I said to him, "Joey," they were wheeling me out to the ambulance, "make sure you bring the Neutrogena. And don't let them take pictures of me like this! Please!" Just a couple days before I had asked, "How much does this dress cost to make?" $16,000! I get to the hospital, and nice doctor comes into the ER and says, "We have to get this dress off of you." I said, "Just cut it off. These producers are making all this money, they're fine. Just cut it off." But apparently they have had people sue them for stuff like that. She had three big guys come and hold me in traction, turn my body so that they could get the dress off without cutting it off. And I was thinking, "You're risking my spine for this fucking dress?" Because I hadn't been X-rayed yet. Then the next thing . . . the nurse starts to wheel me down the hallway for X-rays, and I notice that she stops immediately. Why? Because Taye Diggs walked into the hospital. She sees him and she's star struck. She doesn't know what to do, and she's like, "Oh, um, I forgot your folders." And I said, "Listen. If you don't leave me here in the stretcher I promise I will introduce you to my husband." And we went from it being two guests to . . . all of a sudden it was like a party. All my friends came. I'm high on morphine. Finally the X-rays come back and we see I broke my rib but everything else is OK. My mom, my sister, everyone is in town because it was my last show, so my mom and my sister are like the women of the Nile, with this bowl of water—because I'm still in the green—so they are like taking cloths with the Neutrogena trying to . . . so now I'm like a putrid shade of . . . it's like yellow now. The doctor comes in and starts to give Taye prescriptions and all the instructions. And she says,

"You can take her home tonight. Just put her clothes on and get her home." And he goes, "What clothes?" I literally put on those plastic surgeon pants and someone gave me a sweatshirt and I walked out of the hospital. . . . There was one camera guy outside waiting. The entire audience was not waiting outside the hospital to see if I was OK; they sat in their seats while Shoshana [Bean] took twenty minutes to green-ify and finish the show. And I was appalled! I was like, "What???? They are not outside waiting to see how I am? They stayed to watch the show?" I was so mortified! And then the next day the producers said, "If there is any way you could drag yourself up to get to the theater somehow, we want to give you a send-off." Shoshana was so great because she did the show and then she left for the last two minutes so that I could come in. It was really gracious of her to do that. I walked out . . . it was so wonderful. And I remember even though I was stoned on Percocet, Joe Mantello gave this really beautiful speech which meant so much to me, and then the applause just went on and on. And then a year and a half later I get to go to London.

When you went back to the show in London, you said that was life changing. In what way?

Just being in a new city by myself, having to make friends, coming in as the star of the show and all the things that brings up for me. Wanting to make friends and belong with these people and yet having to be in a leadership position with them. I felt like I did that dance really nicely, so it was confidence building for me. I like the person that I was when I was there. You can discover things if you start from a place of trust in yourself. All that fear really doesn't serve you. As artists we often say, "Oh I won't do it unless I'm terrified to do it," but there has got to be a place you start from that says, "I'm here for a reason. I was hired. I have something to give. I may suck from day to day, or fall, take a couple of steps back, but I will emerge and bring something very special." You just have to know that. That is something I am trying to bring with me now to everything . . . that I have something to give and that people want me there. It's also a relief to the people who work with you, to feel like you have some kind of strength and you're not just going to fall to pieces.

You're describing taking ownership of that role.

And that it's not ugly to be—it's rather attractive to be—confident. And less tiring for people when they are around someone who believes in herself. Not to say that on the next role I'm not going to come home crying to my husband, "I don't know what I'm doing! Why did I take this role?" but there is a template to get back to.

Your next show after *Wicked* was a really interesting career choice. *See What I Wanna See.* What made you choose it?

I just always wanted to work at the Public and with Michael John LaChiusa. I just wanted to do good work and challenge myself.

By doing a small, off-Broadway show you defied expectations.

I wasn't thinking strategically. I just wanted to keep working and do something that would challenge me and get me into a new group of people I hadn't worked with. That's all it was. And it was nice that it was a mature show, mature themes. The one thing I have learned a lot about the fan base—which does span a lot more than just teenagers but for some reason certain people, critics, like to harp on it—is that even if it was just those young people, they are a really sophisticated audience. They're not just going to Britney Spears concerts. They appreciate and learn and soak up anything and everything that you're doing. They would come to this and be supportive of it. When I do my own concerts and things, I don't think, "What's for the fifteen-year-old girl?" I'm thirty-eight years old; I can't clean up my potty mouth the whole time. I just have to be who I am. I have this young audience but I don't dumb down to them. So it wasn't a fear of mine to do something like that. But I do feel a responsibility to these kids. My manager put on my website, "Parents should be aware that for young kids this may not be the right material" because I was getting raped onstage and I don't want some mom bringing her thirteen-year-old girl who likes "Defying Gravity."

Let's talk a little bit about *Chess*. What made you want to do it?

To get back to London and to work with Josh Groban. I just knew it would be a real honor to be onstage with him and to reunite with Adam Pascal after all these years. Usually things are about the creative people involved before the material. Because the material, especially if it's new, gets worked on and massaged and changed. It's the talents of the creative people involved that will make it amazing. Or not. I've learned that. *Chess* was just gonna be fun. What was challenging about doing a concert version is that it's a concert. It was in Royal Albert Hall for 5,000 people. I am trying to find the intimate beats and the director is saying, "Can you just make sure there is never less than three feet between you and Josh because I need you to open up so the people in back can see you." It was also being recorded for television . . .

So you have to play for the camera and the huge house at the same time.

Yeah. And we really didn't have enough time to discover the nuances of the roles. It's a rock concert and I didn't want to accept that. I'm playing a role. So I tried to do as much preparation as I could before I got to London. But we were pretty much shot out of a cannon. I did the best I could. I listened a lot to Elaine Paige. She has her own morning radio show where she talks about theater, so after the concert I was one of her guests. She's fucking funny! That was great. I listened a lot to her and tried to copy a lot of her shit, because we only had eight days. I look nothing like her, I sound nothing like her, so I might as well take what I can use.

We didn't talk about the *Rent* film.

It's funny because people keep asking me about the *Wicked* movie and I say, "Please, they're never going to ask me and Kristin to be in it. We'll be too old or they'll want some big name." But I did get a shot at the *Rent* movie which was ten years after so I should be counting my lucky stars with that one. That was wonderful, and another opportunity to come back with some confidence. I work differently now. I'm older and I've had more experience than when I was in *Rent*, so it was nice to go back, to watch a couple of things; try to capture that innocence and that rawness. There was such an amazing sense of total abandonment in what we were doing but I don't know if you can repeat that when you are ten years older. And back then I didn't delve into the work in the same way that I do now. I think for that show it helped to be "This is who I am! Take it or leave it!" But the responsibility of being a professional now, when I sat down with the movie script, I really came at it from a different place. It probably helped the character in a lot of ways. It was just such a great experience to be with Taye again in the same costumes with pretty much the same cast and be living a dream. That movie was the most screen time I had had. You know, when you have these smaller supporting roles you come on for three days. When you're a lead, you're there for three months. You know everyone, you get to know the crew. I'd ask the camera guy, "What does that mean when he says he wants to take steady cam?" and all that stuff. When you feel like you're part of the family you can ask. So I learned a lot about movie making with that.

You talked about being a hybrid of the two worlds. Looking forward, is there one world that you're favoring?

I see myself as encapsulating it all and just telling everyone to go fuck themselves when they try to label it because I just can't do it anymore. It's exhausting. The kind of music I want to sing in my concerts: I like to sing an old Pat Benatar cover, I like to sing my own music, I like to sing swing and do standards and I'm good at singing them, and if it doesn't fit into one crappy little box then so be it.

SUTTON FOSTER

September 2008; September 2009; July 2012

ONCE UPON A TIME BROADWAY'S leading ladies could count on a career of going from show to show to show from season to season. That's no longer the case. Unless you are Sutton Foster, who, between 2002 and 2012 appeared in six musicals (with Tony nominations for five) and has spent at least some part of every one of those years on Broadway. "I'm jealous of her," says Patti LuPone. "She's the go-to girl." That's true, in large part, because so many of Broadway's leading roles are built on spunk and nobody does spunk like Foster. Be it earnest (*Little Women, Annie, Grease!*) or wisecracking (*Shrek, Anything Goes, Thoroughly Modern Millie*), Foster's brand of pluck is simply unmatchable. She is also one of the very few true triple threats who can act as well as she sings and dance as well as she acts, regularly transcending her material, making adequate look good and good look great. When she opened in *Anything Goes*, Ben Brantley's *New York Times* review remarked of her rendition of "Blow Gabriel Blow," "You figure that if no horn-tooting archangel appears, it's only because he's afraid of the competition."

Sutton Foster grew up in Georgia and Michigan, studying music and dance from a young age but not sure, for many years, whether performing was what she wanted to pursue. She dabbled, though, and amassed a few professional credits (*The Will Rogers Follies*, national tour; *Grease!* on tour and on Broadway alongside her brother, Hunter) before fate gave her a shove with her first starring role in *Thoroughly Modern Millie*. Her casting was, of course, the stuff of legend: understudy takes over lead at last minute, wins Tony Award and becomes a star. While the story seems now to have had a happy ending, the road was a rough one with Foster suffering for several years and asking herself repeatedly, "Can I sustain this?"

It took a few more at-bats for Foster to find her footing, learning to conquer roles without them conquering her. Now, as she approaches forty, she seems finally at ease as a Broadway star. I met with Foster the first time in Seattle, during previews for *Shrek*, and then again in the homey Hell's Kitchen apartment she shares with her dog, Linus. On both occasions I was struck by how relatively simple Foster keeps her life. She has no assistants or publicists hovering, she wears no makeup and has no pretense about her. She is simply Sutton, fresh scrubbed, accessible, self-deprecating, addicted to cupcakes and amazingly talented.

You have gone out of town with almost every show you've done and so many of them have undergone major revision on the road, even from night to night. How do you handle that?

It's actually the part of the process that I love most, oddly enough. I love being a part of things at the beginning. With *Shrek* I was part of the very first read-through of the first act.

With Bob Martin in *The Drowsy Chaperone*, a show that provided Foster six costume changes in one number. (Joan Marcus)

They didn't even have a second act written. [To see it evolve] is exciting. And the fact that they continued restructuring and writing and putting in new songs . . .

And writing around you?
Yeah, that's always wonderful. I love the process.

What about it do you love?
On that project in particular, I think what I loved the most is how this creative team was so game. They were so willing to just try anything or to scrap stuff and start over, as opposed to letting it be good enough. They were really brave and very much willing to rewrite and rework. As an actor, it makes you feel like you can try new things. I came in [one day during previews] and our director said, "We're restructuring the first twenty minutes of the show." And I thought "All right, here we go!" We got a packet of twenty-five new pages. It's all about storytelling. That's what I find fascinating. When you see good theater, there's nothing like it. Truly trying to tell a story, trying to make it clear . . . The show was already good but they wanted it to be exceptional. How cool that they were not settling for "good."

Was it particularly challenging recognizing what's not good enough with an out-of-town audience? No offense to the Seattle audiences, but they don't get great theater as frequently as we do in New York.
New York audiences are definitely trickier. When I was in Seattle with *Young Frankenstein*, the audiences were like at a rock concert. We got to New York and their arms were crossed.

Were they like, "Show me?"
Show me. And you're like, "Shit!"

It's a particular skill to be able to look at it and say, "the audiences are going crazy but it's still not there yet." I would think it would be very easy to get sucked into the audience energy and go . . .

"We're a hit!" Totally. [For *Shrek*] they brought in a lot of really smart people with fresh perspective. That's another thing, too; you lose perspective. We have no perspective because we're in it. They were smart and brave enough to bring in people they trusted to say, "Actually, what if you tried this or this. This isn't coming across. You think it is, but it isn't."

When you're out of town, the rest of your life is far away and out of focus. You don't have to worry about the laundry and your social obligations, you can just stay focused on the show.

Sutton Foster

The Will Rogers Follies, National Tour, 1993
Grease, National Tour and Broadway, 1996
Annie, Broadway, 1997
The Scarlet Pimpernel, Broadway, 1997
Les Misérables, Broadway and National Tour, 2000
Thoroughly Modern Millie, Broadway, 2002 (Tony Award)
Chess in Concert, Broadway, 2003
Little Women, Broadway, 2005
The Drowsy Chaperone, Broadway, 2006
Young Frankenstein, Broadway, 2007
Shrek: The Musical, Broadway, 2008
Anyone Can Whistle, Encores! 2010
Anything Goes, Broadway, 2011 (Tony Award)
Violet, Broadway, 2014

I love going out of town. You're right; my only focus is [on the show]. What else am I going to do other than sightsee or rehearse? I love having that intense focus. And I love getting away from the everyday of New York and all of the responsibility that is ultimately there. Being in theater, you're never doing just one job; you're always doing five. You're constantly trying to find your next job.

How is it for you rehearsing during the day, performing at night, and putting in changes? Is it fun? Overwhelming? Both?

Totally both. I love the challenge of it. There's something about just going for it. You can't even get in your own way as an actor. There's no time. Sometimes that can be so freeing because if you think about something too much . . . Oftentimes we make things more difficult in our minds than they are. It's kind of fun to explore new material in front of an audience. I love being able to have a list of notes before a performance, things to focus on and things to really think about and then go out there and . . .

Play it. Maybe only once.

Right! You have to be really adaptable and willing to let go of stuff and not take it personally when things get cut. It's hard because you get attached to things. That's really hard.

When you went through that during *Millie*, you didn't have quite the clout.

Oh god, no! I had no clout.

Are there now times when you challenge things a little more? Would you ever challenge a director?

I am a big fan of trusting the creative team. If I strongly disagree with something, most of the time it will come out as, "Can we have a discussion?" Because I don't quite know, it just doesn't feel right. But I don't really *know* anything. I really trust them that they know. They're the writers. But I definitely feel like I'm heard more now. And maybe I'm braver to speak up now too. Maybe my opinion is asked more now. Just from experience. But you have to have that complete trust and faith.

Let's go back to the beginning. You were born in Georgia and lived in several places in Georgia, ending up in Michigan, performing as a kid, and taking dance by the age of four. You enjoyed it but never thought about it professionally?
Never even thought about it.

You went to Carnegie Mellon and left after a year because you were not sure about what you wanted to do. So how did you end up on Broadway?
My parents were always incredibly supportive. They probably believed in me more than I did. And at nineteen, does anyone *really* know what they want to do? I had done the national tour of *Will Rogers Follies* professionally at seventeen . . .

Did Tommy Tune direct you in that?
Yup. It was awesome. He was great. I was so young and grew up really fast.

All of those women . . .
It was intense. I was still reading *Sweet Valley High* and teen magazines.

What's interesting to me is that you're a self-described dork, and there you were up there with all of those leggy beauties. Some part of you decided you could fit in with that group. And you went for it and got it.
That's how I knew I could do Inga in *Young Frankenstein*: because I was, at one time, a showgirl. I went to school and I had no idea what I wanted to do. My parents were so supportive of my acting but I didn't know if I wanted to do it because *I* wanted to do it or if *they* wanted me to do it. So I moved home and then I went to visit Hunter in New York and went to an open call for *Grease!* Jeff Calhoun [who had worked with Foster on *Will Rogers*] was sitting behind the table. I was nineteen and at that point I had cut off all my hair and put on twenty pounds. I was anti-showgirl. He cast me on the spot. He said, "We want you to come out on the tour" and I burst into tears and freaked out. I had no life direction at all, and all of a sudden the universe said, "You actually do need to be doing this. We are going to make this decision for you."

Why were you at that call to begin with if you weren't really interested in going after it?
I was a ballsy little fucker. I think I was getting antsy at home and decided, "I'm going to see what New York is like." I auditioned not thinking I was going to get it, but I did. I have to have walked in with confidence to get it.

You went in not knowing if you wanted it or not . . .
But I think I did. I think maybe I was fighting it because I was scared. Scared of failing or rejection. Even on that tour, I was still unsure. Obviously, I went and I had a good time. But not until *Millie* did I finally sort of realize, "Oh my gosh, this is what I want to do." Ever since then, it's been "owning it."

You are crazily confident onstage. You are so in command of everything you do. . . .
It's smoke and mirrors!

Do you think if you had chosen something else you would have approached that with the same ballsy confidence?

I don't know. My confidence was being onstage. I wasn't confident about anything else.

Back to *Will Rogers*, do you remember anything specific about what you learned on the road your first time out? Do you remember if it met your expectations?

I think the thing that I didn't really understand going into it was the social aspect of how to belong and fit in with a group of people you're working and living with. Touring is so different from working in New York in that way. I think that was the aspect that I didn't understand or expect and I ended up making a lot of mistakes. I felt like, in many ways, I wish I had had the experience of college because I made all of my mistakes in the workplace as opposed to in school. You say the wrong things, you piss off the wrong people. You're just stupid.

You're just young.

I had a lot of confidence at seventeen. I was not trying to be confident or trying to be obnoxious but it can be seen that way. I walk in with this big voice and I want everyone to hear it. I'm not trying to show off but I guess I am because I want to be noticed.

But in *Will Rogers*, you probably learned almost immediately about the power of everyone working together as a unit and blending.

I didn't like that so much.

So you had to learn discipline.

Well, of course, but I wanted everyone to look at *me*!

Did you have to be whipped or did you figure it out?

I remember being noted and talked to about it, I guess. It was something that I learned.

Donna McKechnie talked about being seventeen in *How to Succeed* and how the women in the dressing room taught her so much about life.

Yeah. I learned a lot, but I also learned a lot of negative things, too. Like body image stuff. I was a kid who had no issues at all and I was surrounded by eighteen women with issues. I had no idea that people thought about this or that. Boyfriends coming, staying in your room. I was so naïve, so young.

So that was a major crash course. Then you go out on *Grease!* and you're playing Sandy. You're the lead. And you get to play it for three weeks in New York.

It was a crazy, crazy time. But again, I think I had a lot of balls, a lot of confidence. I think you have to. I have learned so much as I've gotten older. I was so fearless. I look back, especially on that girl who did *Millie* (me) and I *love* that person. I guess I still have all of the things in place but I know so much more now. But I think my naiveté and greenness protected me in a way. Because I would just go for it, not knowing any of the crap that isn't useful anyway. It's business crap.

Like what?

Millions of dollars. Reviewers and critics. Awards season. It's all promotional stuff, which wasn't even on my radar. And then right after we opened, I thought, "Wait! If I had known, I'd have dressed a little better."

So you do *Grease!* and then . . .
Annie!

Tell me a Nell Carter story.
I *loved* Nell Carter. She had beautiful flowering plants in her dressing room and I swear to God she ordered fried chicken every night. I know, it seems so wrong, but every night at intermission came the call from the stage door, "Nell Carter, your food is here." She was lovely to me. Amazing. We got along very well. I would not have gotten that job if it weren't for Jeff Calhoun. I walked into the audition and he thought, "The girl I found in Detroit, Michigan! I'm gonna hire her again." I finished the *Grease!* tour and I went in on that audition. The only sheet music I had was "Oklahoma!" I don't know why. I didn't have a headshot because everything was still in my suitcases that were being shipped. I was wearing clogs and a dress. No headshot. "Oklahoma!" [director] Martin Charnin said, "Change your shoes, bring a picture and bring another song, come back at 5:00." So I changed my shoes, went to Woolworth, got into the photo booth and got a color 3 × 5 photo of myself. I did "Since I Don't Have You" from *Grease!* The musical director [who had been with *Grease!*] played it for me since I didn't have music. I obviously had balls. I broke every rule.

And you had to know them at that point. You knew what the rules were.
Yeah, I didn't care.

Why was that?
I don't know. I have no clue.

It wasn't cockiness or you thinking you were somehow above the process . . .
I don't think so. I always tell people when I do master classes, "Why do you want to look like everybody else? Why do you want to wear a black skirt and a white top? Who told you to do that?" My best auditions were when I forgot that there was an audition and I was wearing jeans and no makeup. I end up doing the best job because I'm me. Your best asset is your individuality. I guess I just refuse to play into any . . . I still make Jen [Cody, sister-in-law] and my brother mad that I got the part with my little picture from Woolworths and sang "Oklahoma!"

Was that show your first taste of being disappointed after great anticipation?
I was bummed that we didn't do an album. It would have been my first cast album, so I was disappointed in that. And even though it was a revival, it was my first original role. I had a solo on Broadway! That was really cool. They offered me the opportunity to stay with *Grease!* and play Sandy on Broadway but I said "no" because I always believed in doing new stuff. And then when I was doing *Annie*, I auditioned for *Scarlet Pimpernel*. I sang "Since I Don't Have You." I sang that dammed song for everything. I got cast in the ensemble, and that was exciting because it was my first time originating a new musical. It didn't go out of town, it rehearsed in the city. I stayed in that for about six months and then I left to do the Burt Bacharach revue, *What the World Needs Now* at the Old Globe in San Diego. That was a failed regional that was supposed to come in to New York. But again, I was cast for the first time as a lead.

Was Liz Callaway part of the show at the time?
No. That would have been amazing. I'm still obsessed with her. My entire family is. I'm amazed that she knows my name. And that goes for all of the people that I like . . . Liz, Patti LuPone, Lea Salonga . . . Lea Salonga came up and introduced herself to me while she was

doing *Flower Drum Song* and I was doing *Millie*. She said, "Sutton, I'm Lea." And I was floored. "Hell-ooo! You have no idea, Oh my God!" Freaks me out. And Patti LuPone, she was with my voice teacher before me. I walked in and I freaked out on her. "I used to listen to you on the Sondheim Carnegie Hall concert repeatedly! You basically taught me how to sing!" She couldn't have been more lovely. Now we write notes to each other and stuff. Anyway, *Pimpernel* and then the bad Bacharach show and then *Les Miz*.

What do you remember about doing *Pimpernel?*

I don't remember a lot of it. I remember I had big hats. I liked the music. It was after *Jekyll and Hyde* so Frank Wildhorn had cachet. I loved Doug Sills. He was amazing. Christine Andreas, so great. It was actually a really great experience even though it didn't do well.

What happens when a show opens to less than ecstatic reviews? Does the director sit the cast down and talk about what's what?

It depends on the show. The day after *Young Frankenstein* opened and it got—I don't read reviews any more. I stopped after *Millie*. It was just too hard. It's not useful for me. So I didn't read the reviews. But of course we have a meeting onstage half an hour before the show and it's basically like a pep talk from [director] Susan Stroman. "We got a lot of mixed notices, one really good one, one really negative one, but this show is fantastic. I really believe in it. We're gonna go out there, our time will come. Blah. Blah Blah." That happens quite a bit. After *Pimpernel*, I guess I read the reviews but I liked it. Of course, I wasn't in the reviews and I thought, "It's fantastic. These people are stupid. I love it! I'm happy." And that's all that mattered. Until your name starts getting put in there . . .

So after *What the World Needs Now*, *Les Miz?*

Yeah. I went to an open call. My agents said, "Why are you going to open calls?" Again, I'm just a ballsy little shit. I saw that there was an audition and I wanted to go. They put me on a wait list and then out of nowhere I got a call to do ensemble track/Eponine cover on Broadway. It was awesome. *Les Miz* was one of my favorite things I've ever done. I did it in New York for about seven months and then I went on the road as Eponine for about a year. *Millie* happened in there, too. I did a workshop in the ensemble.

How did that come about?

I heard about it and I called my agent. Again, very ballsy. I hear things. I went in and it was a terrible audition. But the casting director was Jim Carnahan who had cast me in the bad Burt Bacharach show. He told them, "Actually she's much better than this." My agent was really good friends with Dick Scanlan, the writer, and they gave me a part in the ensemble. I fell in love with it. I thought it was so funny, so good. I went on the road and I flew back. I kept flying home for auditions for it. I flew back multiple times. First there was the workshop that Kristin Chenoweth did and then La Jolla. And at this time I was also heavily pursuing being in *Rent*. I was flying back for auditions for that, too. Getting down to the end and then not getting it.

For which role?

For Maureen! Because I'm a perfect fit! I'm not. But I was trying to be edgy.

You seem not to think about yourself as having any limits.

I decide things. I decided I had to be in *Millie*. [I had been offered *Les Miz* in New York] and I turned it down to do *Millie*. It was a really hard decision. *Les Miz* was offering me $1,700 a week and that was the most I had ever been offered. I was going to go to a $400 a week paycheck. I didn't care about money. I'm still that way. I don't think about it. I just pay my bills. It was a really hard decision. One of the factors, too, was that I was dating a guy who lived in LA. I thought, "Well, if I do the show in San Diego, I'll be closer to him." That was part of it too.

So you go off to do ensemble in *Millie* and then . . . the story is now legendary.
Me and Anne Nathan and Kate Baldwin, we would all gather in my apartment and learn our lines. We were all the covers. We would drink bottles of red wine from Whole Foods and learn our lines. It was great. We had so much fun out there. I was up visiting the boyfriend and I got a call from the stage manager saying—and this was the week before tech—"Erin's [Dilly] sick. We want you to learn Millie today in rehearsals." I wasn't supposed to be there 'til 1:00 and they wanted me there at 10:00. I was flying down the highway, trying to get there, kind of freaking out. I get in the room and they'd just started rehearsing and I just stepped in. It was like two days of rehearsal and I would go home and cram lines, trying to learn as much as I could. That was on a Tuesday and by Thursday I got off book and learned the choreography. Freak of nature. And then on Friday they called me and offered me the part. I bawled and I freaked out. "You're making a horrible mistake!" I was in a costume fitting that day and went and had lunch with Michael Mayer and Erin Dilly. She came to rehearsal and said goodbye to everyone. I was frozen. That weekend, I didn't do anything. I just sort of thought, "Oh my god" and tried to learn my part. The whole cast really pulled together over that weekend and rallied behind me. They were so mad that—it's a major, major thing. You're firing your leading lady a week before previews? That's insanity. But the cast really pulled together. They were there for me.

I can imagine faith being shaken in the entire production.
Absolutely. So scary. I actually don't remember a lot of it.

Because you blocked it out?
I think I was just trying to get through it. I was in sheer panic mode. Overwhelmed. I was twenty-five. Really young. So green. Overeager, talented, ready to go for it but with nothing to back it up. I look back on it and I'm like I don't know *how* that happened.

That takes us back to something you said before about being fearless and not knowing any better.
Yeah. Before, I wouldn't think. Now, I think more. And maybe I'll still do it but maybe I won't. I just think a little bit more now.

In this case, there wasn't the opportunity to think. You would have gotten in your own way.
That's what saved me. I didn't have time to think. I just did it.

During the La Jolla run, did you have a moment when you felt like "I got it. I'm no longer running to catch up to it?"
I think during my second year on Broadway. I swear to God, finally I was like "All right, all right." I started gaining weight again. I can do this. But never in La Jolla. After the Tonys, maybe a little bit, but that was a bit of a blur. I struggled so much. We are our own worst enemies. And I internalize things so much, so whenever I have any type of stress or anxiety in my life, I get sick. I just didn't know how to sing eight shows a week. I sang thirteen songs or

something retarded and I just didn't know how to do it. But eventually I was able to. I learned how to do it but it took time. I did everything within my power to try to figure out how to do it.

When the show closed in La Jolla, did you know if you'd be doing it in New York?
At the end of the La Jolla run they asked me to do it in New York.

But you had a ten-month waiting period, right?
Yeah. I did two shows. I did *The Three Musketeers* in San Jose. Not good. But that show, made me fall in love with theater. All of a sudden I was like, "Oh my gosh, this is what I want to do!" It happened, in an instant when I was onstage one night.

I assumed that you had made that commitment back around the time of *Grease!*
Until that moment I was always entertaining other options.

Like what?
I don't know. Teaching. Or going back to school. That was a big priority for awhile. I took a class at Hunter College during *Les Miz*. I always felt like I had three toes in but not the whole foot. During *Three Musketeers*, I put the whole foot in and I never took it back out. I did a production of *Dorian* at Goodspeed. Then I did *South Pacific* at Pittsburgh Civic Light Opera.

So you were keeping yourself pretty busy while you were waiting. Were you working on *Millie* at the same time?
I was starting to. I had also met my ex, Christian [Borle]. We had gone to school together and we re-met during *Three Musketeers*. During that time, we started dating. So even though I was doing shows, I had all this free time before *Millie* started so we were able to get a real foundation. That was nice. We started rehearsals in January of 2002. I think I've only ever dated actors. Sadly.

Then *Millie* in New York.
Right. We had a long rehearsal. Six weeks of rehearsals, two weeks tech, four weeks of previews, and the show changed a *lot* during previews. And, of course the show changed a lot from La Jolla. New cast members. During the summer I did photo shoots and demos.

What was that like? On the one hand, there's the whole fairy tale coming true, and on the other was it terrifying?
Bawling my eyes out naked in my dressing room after the second preview.

How did the naked part happen?
Taking off my costume and then just crumpling in a heap of tears and terror. I was overwhelmed. My dresser Julian, who I met on *Millie*—we've done all of my shows together—we talk about that moment. I was so scared, and there's nothing else to do but cry.

Do you remember what you were scared of specifically?
I was scared of letting everyone down. My voice was going. I wasn't eating. I was afraid I was gonna fail and I had never felt that before. I had always been so tenacious and now I thought, "Oh my god, I'm gonna fail in a big way." If you think about my story . . . as all of this was happening, I had no concept of anything. I remember other people who were trying so desperately to help me. They were saying, "I really want you to take this in and try to

understand what is happening to you." You can't. I can *now*. I try to do that, I try to take little mental snapshots of certain times and shows that you are never going to get back. But it's so hard! Most of the time you don't want to—it's protective measures because—sometimes when shows aren't as successful, like *Little Women*, which didn't run long and didn't do well, you're heartbroken. You try to keep a protective distance because you don't want to become emotionally invested.

But you can't do a show and not commit to it, can you?
And that's one of the main reasons why I decided to do *Drowsy Chaperone* and *Young Frankenstein*. Because I couldn't handle all of the responsibility and pressures of starring in a show and I started to not like what I do. My whole life was about my voice or the fact that I was just so tired all the time.

When you are carrying a show like *Millie* or *Little Women*, do you become a nun, never going out?
Totally. I don't know how my relationship survived. That's why I wanted to do smaller roles. I wanted to remove the "starring in" thing. To make a career out of that is exhausting. You've got to open up the realm to other types of jobs you want to do. Again, I am just trying to make my own rules. I didn't want to be pigeon-holed into having to be the leading lady.

It would seem to me that most people aspire to a certain level and when you get to that point . . .
But you have to remember where I started. I started here and was immediately *here*. What about all of this middle stuff that I haven't experienced yet? I felt like I still had so much to learn. I still feel that way. And I wanted to take myself out of the theatrical limelight. Even being above the title in *Little Women*, I never wanted that. I just want to go back to the ensemble.

You remember that an hour ago you said you wanted everyone to be paying attention to you.
I know. Isn't that funny? Of course, I'm very complicated. I'm such a contradiction.

Or is it that now that you know what the grass looks like on the other side of the fence . . .
Totally! It's a combination of the two—wanting to make sure that I had a really varied career but also when people are casting a show, I want them to think of me for Frankenstein's chick.

When *Millie* opened, did you read the reviews?
I did.

And how was that for you?
I don't read them any more. I wasn't prepared for it at all. I'm a Pisces. I'm enormously idealistic and romantic, and so I sort of painted this fantasy: "I'm going to be heralded in the *New York Times* as the next best thing." And of course that wasn't what happened. So I think I was kind of, "Oh, shit, now what?" I was twenty-seven and I was reading things on the Internet and desperately trying to find validation. The day after we opened I didn't open up the blinds in my apartment. I felt so responsible, like I somehow let down the show. We got mixed reviews. We got some good reviews and we got some bad reviews and I read most of them. I remember our press representative came to my apartment and showed me the double truck ad of all the

great quotes that was going in the *New York Times* that weekend. He said, "Look, we did fine," but I remember I felt like such a failure. Isn't that awful? At the top of your game doing the biggest thing ever happening to you, and you feel like you've let everybody down? It was awful. And then, of course, all the Tony stuff came. I remember winning the Outer Critics Circle Award or something and I was shocked. I thought I was terrible. I thought people hated me. And then I won the Drama Desk. I was basically believing all the press but the community really had embraced the show. When the Tony stuff started coming out, in a way I had ruined it for myself because I was just caught up in all of the crap. So that's why I stopped reading everything. I just didn't want to ruin my experiences, good or bad. It's just been so much healthier for me.

Well, when you say you ruined it for yourself are you saying that during the whole experience of awards season you were just in a horrible place?

I just thought, "Oh, this is a fluke. I don't deserve it." Even years later I felt that way. It's what you do to yourself because we self-sabotage. I look back on it now, and I can think, "Wow." I have perspective now. But I also think that's what pushed me to keep going. I'm very resilient and so I was determined to learn and try to prove them wrong. Not consciously. I believed in myself and I believed in the show and everything, Then the Tonys happened, and it—I mean, I won't say that I was miserable. I definitely enjoyed the moment and took it all in, but . . .

So in that period of time, from the day that you read the reviews to the awards, you were going onstage every night feeling like the show was going to close and it was your fault?

Mm-hmm! It was hard. It was crippling. That show was very crippling for me and my own self-esteem, and that's something that I've worked on extensively for years.

How do you work on that?

Well, a lot of it was to stop reading reviews, to stop reading chat boards. All of that stuff was basically making me crazy.

It's so hard to resist, though.

Not so much. Not any more. I could care less. It took years, though. It's more about making my life awesome, and my work is just what I do, it's not who I am. But with *Millie*, I was all wrapped up in it, and so if I cracked onstage at night, it would ruin my day. It'd be awful. Now I just don't buy into it. I don't read it. I don't read anything. I stay away from all of it. Because frankly, it's none of my business. All I can do is just keep trying. It's different when you do a movie. You shot the movie and then the reviews come out. You don't have to go back out there and do it again and again. It just sucks—reviews. I don't want that in my head. I trust the director. I trust my peers. I trust my friends. And frankly, I can't do anything once the reviews come out. I can't do anything about it.

Even if you're not reading them, you have to know—

I'm very aware. I get a feeling. I know.

What do you remember about the Tonys?

Tony day I was really, really freaked out. We were going to do "Forget About the Boy" and I was so excited to do that. I remember right before the performance, Gregory Hines came by and tapped our desks and wished us luck. You never forget that first moment. I'd never been at Radio City before and just—the curtain goes up, and you're like, "What???" My high school drama teacher was there and it was really cool. And then winning it was crazy! And they whisk you to the Rainbow Room. I watched on the TV when the show won because I wasn't there. We had a party that night and I was out until four in the morning at Vintage, eating pizza out of a box. Then I came home and I had like thirty-five messages on my phone and one of them was Alice Ripley. I remember her message meaning a lot to me because I admired her so much. I had just moved into my new apartment [with Borle], and one of the doormen had put a sign on my door. It said, "To our newest tenant who just won the first of many Tony Awards, congratulations." We barely had any furniture and I remember just lying on the floor in my Tony dress and listening to all these messages. Then the next day we went and bought a couch because I said if I win a Tony I'm going to buy a couch. Because it wasn't clear 'til then that we were going to run. We did not get solid reviews.

Christian eventually joined you in the show.

He came in during my second year and we had already been together for awhile. It was great working opposite of each other because I respect him so much as an actor, so it didn't feel like I was working with my boyfriend, even though we were working and living together. We really didn't see each other much at work, which was kind of interesting. It was better that way. I just went and focused on my show. I'm that way at work anyway. I'm very solitary. I don't really—it's something I'm working on. I'm trying to become a little more social and stuff but generally I really try to focus.

And that's just because you think you need it in order to pull out the performance?

Yeah, I guess. I don't know. I'm a pretty solitary person in general. I have always sort of been that way. I crochet, and I draw or I read. It's a protective mechanism.

You left *Millie* to do *Little Women*.

Yeah. That one almost killed me. To be honest, I turned it down twice.

Why?

I had some friends who had played the role and I didn't—this is honestly the reason: I didn't want to take a part away from someone else. They were going to replace them anyway but it became a moral thing. I was also nervous about what to do next. And then something changed. I think they gave me an offer I couldn't refuse. I did a one-week reading of it and really fell in love with it. And I just thought, "Okay, this is going to be fun." We went out of town to Duke University and it was like three and a half hours long. But it was a really beautiful show. When they moved it to New York, they chopped it a lot. I loved working with [director] Susan Schulman. Loved [actor] Megan McGinnis. We became really close out of that. Julian, my dresser, came with me. We ran maybe five months total. It was a bear, and again, I was having vocal problems the whole time. Could not sing it. I could, but not eight times a week. And I wasn't strong enough to give limits and say, "I cannot belt E-flats eight times a week." I wanted to do *Little Women* because I thought it would be really different than *Millie* but it ended up turning out to be very similar. The character was just as headstrong, and the show—I thought, "Oh, it's a show about sisters" but it ended up becoming a show about Jo. I never wanted to be above the title. I think I will look back on it fondly. Unfortunately I still think of it as almost breaking me.

You implied that as they cut the show, you liked the show less. Knowing that you're less in love with the material—

It was hard. And the show was dying. The audiences were getting smaller and smaller and smaller and we didn't get nominated for any Tonys. I got nominated but I felt like that was

With John Hickok in *Little Women*, the show that led Foster to conclude that she needed a break from above-the-title, leading lady status. (Paul Kolnik)

such a bizarre experience to be nominated in a show that was a flop. I lost even more weight. I remember getting on the scale at one point and being like 118 pounds or something at five nine. None of my clothes would fit. It was the strangest time in my life.

What was it like going to the Tonys for a show that you feel less good about?

I had fun. I had a great dress, and the show had already closed. It was actually great because I didn't have to perform, I could just go, be pretty and sit there.

During *Little Women*, Ben Brantley wrote an article about singing in musical theater. He faulted *Wicked* for starting a trend of sing-your-face-off performances. That's what we now expect our musical theater leading women to do—

I'm anti that. Unfortunately though it's become very popular. I could care less how high you sing if you don't know what you're singing about. "Astonishing" and "Defying Gravity" are saying a certain thing, (and they're basically saying the same thing) but they are about high notes. I want to see a story being told. I think we all do ultimately. That's why when I did a solo album, I think I had only two songs where I belted. And I was nervous because I thought, "I don't want to belt but I have to give people what they want." I have a million opinions about it obviously.

You said you took *The Drowsy Chaperone* because you didn't want to carry the weight of the show.

Right. I was so excited because I thought, "Oh, my God, I want this because it's *not* the lead." It was such an ensemble. It was also more of an adult character. It was exactly the type of musical I needed to do. Careers are crazy, you know? You have to have the ups and the downs. *Drowsy* is probably one of the best things that happened to my career because I think it showed people that I could do something different and also that I could do crazy shit and surprise people. Although my body is still messed up from that jump split. But it's sustainability, it's longevity. This is all very fleeting. There's a new season every year. There's a new hot tomato. *Drowsy* felt very validating. Once *Drowsy* happened, I thought, "Maybe I might be all right." And I think I started to calm down.

Were you able to take a different kind of ownership of your career?

I did. Yeah. Definitely. *Drowsy* changed everything because after *Little Women* I was thinking "uh-oh," and then *Drowsy* happened and it was okay. Then during *Drowsy*, *Shrek* and *Young Frankenstein* happened so I realized, "OK, there's a future, and there's interest, and people want me." During *Drowsy*, I wasn't as nervous, I didn't lose any weight, I stayed healthy, I started working out. I was able to chill the fuck out. After *Millie* I was like, "Is Petland hiring, because I'm dying? Can I handle this? Can I handle the pressure? Can I handle the criticism?" Even though I didn't read the reviews, there was validation from the press from *Drowsy*, from what I heard, and so that made me feel better, too. I felt like people were starting to get me and my talent and what I had to offer.

You said *Shrek* and *Young Frankenstein* happened during that?

Yes. *Shrek* came first. When the first reading came I pursued it like crazy because I thought Fiona would be really fun. And then I got the call about *Young Frankenstein*. I remember screaming and running around in circles. There was a time when I was going to have to choose between the two because they were both scheduled to go at the same time. The two actually overlapped for four weeks. I was running on fumes for about a year. Who am I to complain about incredible opportunities, but that's why I took time off [after *Shrek*]. If someone were to have offered me something, even if it were something I couldn't turn down, I had to because I was going to end up in a mental hospital.

The experience of doing *Young Frankenstein* . . .

It was such a bummer. There was all this anticipation and hope and hype and bad press. The whole thing was just a bummer.

It was a bummer to perform in, too?

It was actually kind of fun to do. I really enjoyed doing it. And I loved my number, "Roll in the Hay." I got to yodel and be boobylicious and do something completely different. But it was a hard situation. As I said before, when we did it in Seattle, the audiences loved it. They thought it was fabulous and hilarious. We were on top of the world. We came to New York and we just had nothing on our side.

Do you think that New Yorkers were so influenced by *The Producers* that their expectations were too high?

I think so. I think it's a combination of that and our producers' hubris that fucked us. I just wish they had come in with a little more humility. It could have been handled so much better, and I think the show would have fared better. I also think we were at a disservice being in that theater because it's such a barn. But I actually think the show is so much better than it was ever given credit for. The difference between Seattle and here was shocking. I thought it would be that way with *Shrek*, and it wasn't. *Shrek* was received incredibly similarly in Seattle and New York. I felt like New York embraced it incredibly warmly. But *Young Frankenstein* was just a big, old bummer.

What was Mel Brooks like for you?

He was awesome. He's a lovely man. Unfortunately, once we opened and all the really bad press came out, we saw less and less of him and Susan as well. But I sort of understand it, too. I remember after the opening night in Seattle, we were all hanging out at this bar, and him just like holding court. He's just so full of life and energy. He's everything that you'd hope.

In *Shrek* you were not the lead, but you carried more than you did in *Drowsy* and *Young Frankenstein*. Did it feel more balanced?

Yes. Definitely. It was sort of between *Millie* and *Drowsy*. It's probably one of the favorite things I've done. I hate talking about myself, but it's interesting to sort of talk about it in this way because it's reminding me of things that are important. On *Drowsy* I started to set limits. I was like, "Can we take this down a half a step?" I don't want the show to be about losing my voice. I feel like my voice has only gotten stronger and better. And with *Shrek* and my solo cd I've been able to find a whole new, exciting way to express myself that isn't dependent on belting to the rafters.

After *Shrek* you did your first Encores!

Anyone Can Whistle! Oh, yeah. That was one of my most proud achievements. To work with Donna Murphy and Raul Esparza—the three of us got along so well and worked so well together. It was a really special production.

How did you find Sondheim to work with?

He was wonderful. I've admired him for so long, and unfortunately I become very intimidated around him. I don't know if I ever said a sentence, and I wish I could have a do-over in that regard. I just didn't want to mess up. I remember singing "There Won't Be Trumpets" three feet from his face. Very intimidating. He wrote me a card after we closed, very succinct. Two sentences. "Thank you for City Center [a birthday concert Foster performed in] and thank you for *Anyone Can Whistle*, Stephen." I took that as an opportunity to write him a gushing four-page letter, like an idiot, and he wrote back again two sentences, "Thank you for the extravagant note and again, thank you."

Doing the piece, did it feel like a departure for you in any way?

Absolutely. I think after *Shrek* I was really looking to do things that were out of my comfort zone, out of the box. I was looking to transition into more mature roles. It's safe to say that

Opening Act 2 with tap-dancing mice in *Shrek*. (Joan Marcus)

from *Millie* to *Little Women* to *Drowsy* to Inga [*Young Frankenstein*] to *Shrek*, all of those were of a certain type. I was looking to broaden and challenge myself and *Anyone Can Whistle* was the beginning of that. Then I did a play at Second Stage, *Trust*. I think both of those moves led directly to doing Reno in *Anything Goes*.

Why do you think that?

People were ready to see me as an adult. I was incredibly intimidated by playing Reno. I almost turned it down because I thought I was going to bomb majorly. Then I realized, "Maybe that's exactly why you should do it." I didn't even know how to begin to prepare for it. When we first started rehearsals, I think I had read the script once because you know how when you get scared of something, you just avoid it? You would think the opposite—that I would delve in. I don't know what I was thinking. It was all confidence.

How did you get there? Was it just playing it, or did you have a lightbulb moment?

Literally it was an overnight thing. It took a really long time to slowly convince myself that I could do it. But then one day late in previews, she was just there. It was fun to find her in my own way and to discover parts of myself in her. I never thought it would be received the way it was. I never thought I'd be nominated, let alone win, a Tony. That was not in the cards. I have never been happier in a show.

You have ardent young fans whose love of theater is influenced by what you do. Does that resonate for you at all?

Yeah! It's exciting. I've had so many people that have said, "*Millie* was my first show. It's why I moved to New York. It's why I wanted to do theater." I have those shows, too. We all have those things. Growing up, I wanted to be Lea Salonga and Patti LuPone. When I talk to these kids, I say, "I'm you. I'm just twenty years older than you." I'm letting them know that it's not this far-fetched thing. It's actually attainable. "The only thing that separates us is a bunch of years." I never thought, when I was fifteen that I could ever be starring in a Broadway show or winning a Tony Award or hanging out with Patti LuPone. Never. It was not even something I thought about. It was not even an option.

Of the women who came of age as Broadway stars when you did, you seem singularly dedicated to a career in theater.

In my mind, I have a sense that I'd love to be remembered as a Broadway performer. I think that's what I was born to do. But I have so much more to learn. I'm not done. TV and film don't bring me the same kind of joy. I love being in rehearsal for twelve hours a day. I love the camaraderie of a cast. I love performing eight shows a week. I get tired of having to think about my voice all the time but I love to sing. I love singing live. I can't imagine what else would bring me as much joy.

What do you think you still have to learn?

Every experience I've had has brought something new, whether it's how to deal with expectations, success . . . *Young Frankenstein* taught me so much about the business. I've never had an experience like that. That whole experience was fascinating. *Drowsy Chaperone*, being in a show that no one knew anything about, and how, as an actor, being part of those things affects you. I feel like I have so much to learn about how to be a better performer, too. Hopefully you never stop. Who knows what I'll be in the next ten years? You just hope you keep growing.

LAURA BENANTI

September and October 2012

LATE IN THE SECOND ACT of *Gypsy*, the character Louise, who will become Gypsy Rose Lee, is thrust in front of an audience for her first striptease. She is dressed like a glamorous sophisticate, while her face and shaking hands betray her for the amateur that she is. Harnessing that duality is not only what won Laura Benanti a Tony Award for her heartbreaking portrayal of Louise; it's the specialty that is Benanti's calling card and, in many ways, a mirror for her life.

Laura Benanti grew up in New Jersey with supportive parents (her mother was an actor and music teacher, married to a psychologist whom Benanti calls her father. Her biological father is the actor Martin Vidnovic, one of Broadway's leading baritones in the early '80s), yet she felt like an outcast. Her love of theater was so foreign to her peers that she spent her youth feeling misunderstood. In fact, she claims to have used her own childhood as a reference point for Louise's loneliness and to this day, Benanti refers to herself as "a total dork." Yet, to the outside eye, she is a beautiful, poised, radiant, confident, critically lauded woman at the peak of her powers. When she was only twenty-one, Ben Brantley, in his review of the ill-fated off-Broadway show *Time and Again*, called her "[an] actress with uncanny self-possession and professional polish, not to mention a cut-crystal soprano." So what gives? Why does this swan still see herself as a duck? Whatever the reason, it makes her a perfect match for the roles she's played, almost all of which fit squarely, like Louise, into the category of the leading lady who is just off center.

It started with her very first Broadway role at the age of seventeen, understudying and then replacing Rebecca Luker as Maria in *The Sound of Music*, one of the all-time great heroines who doesn't quite fit in. She was Cinderella in *Into the Woods*, the princess who doesn't match the image of "princess." In *The Wedding Singer*, and in *Women on the Verge of a Nervous Breakdown*, she was beautiful but also quirky and neurotic. And, of course, she was Louise.

It's an impressive resumé, made all the more impressive when one learns that Benanti spent most of her professional life in physical pain. During the run of *Into the Woods*, she fell hard during an onstage pratfall and suffered spinal injuries that plagued her for the next decade. After three surgeries, *Women on the Verge . . .* was the first show in which she performed pain-free.

We meet in Hollywood, where Benanti is shooting a series, *Go On* (which would be canceled after its first year). In person, it's easy to see why Benanti does so well with nontraditional roles. She is lovely, but not Hollywood lovely in that she is also razor sharp and quick-witted, and she likes to say what's on her mind. She realizes that in show business she might be better off if she held back a bit, but she has no interest in that. She would rather

As Candela, breaking down in *Women on the Verge of a Nervous Breakdown*. (Paul Kolnik)

Laura Benanti

The Sound of Music, Broadway, 1998
Swing! Broadway, 1999
Wonderful Town, Encores! 2000
Time and Again, off-Broadway, 2001
Into the Woods, Broadway, 2002
Nine, Broadway, 2003
A Little Night Music, Los Angeles, 2004
The Wedding Singer, Broadway, 2006
Gypsy, Encores! and Broadway, 2007 and
    2008 (Tony Award)
Women on the Verge of a Nervous
    Breakdown, Broadway, 2010
The Most Happy Fella, Encores! 2014

simply be who she is. She laughs freely and often, and will say virtually anything if she thinks it's funny. She is, in a word, free. It's an unexpected quality in a woman in her position, but it's what makes Benanti who she is and so good at what she does.

You were born in New York City to a father who was on Broadway. Did that play into your own Broadway desires?

Who knows. My therapist could answer that question, but my mom was a performer, too, and that's how they knew each other. They went to college together. They met when they were seventeen years old. And so I do think that having music in our house all the time—because my mom taught out of the house—and knowing that my father was on Broadway . . . Being backstage at *Baby*, those were some of my fondest memories of my father. I remember Liz Callaway carrying me up the stairs. So I do think part of it was, "there's this magical world, this magical place where my father lives and he performs and sings, and people clap for him." And hearing my mom teach people, hearing them go from not being able to sing to being able to sing. But more than that, I think I was just born with it. My earliest memories are singing and dancing in my room. It was always part of my consciousness. I can't remember a time when I didn't want to be on Broadway, truly.

When you talk about seeing your mom help people go from not being able to sing to being able to sing, were you aware of the difference?

My mom tells this story that when I was two years old she was teaching somebody and I was in her lap. He kept doing the scale, and I said, "No." And he kind of looked at me and she said, "Oh, I'm sorry, I'm so sorry." And he did it again, and I said, "No." And he looked at my mom like "Are you going to let her keep doing this?" And then she gave him a correction, and he did it, and I said, "Yes." It was my world from the time I entered the world.

I read that you were fascinated with Snow White.

I was obsessed with *Snow White!* Any time I would bite into an apple I would faint and let it roll out of my hand just perfectly. I knew how to do it so that my last finger slowly opened and gracefully, and the apple would roll like twice. I was four.

Would you lie there and wait to be kissed?

I would wait there for awhile. It didn't matter where. On the street. In New York. Anywhere. So my mom was like, "Well, I can't give you an apple unless you're already lying down because this is dangerous."

Did you take any kind of acting classes?

I took dance classes, but I wasn't very good. I was so much taller than everybody else, and I had big boobs, so being in that leotard was [torture]. I took some acting classes. Our rule was as long as my grades maintained, I could do one community theater production a year and the high school musical.

Was there a lot of negotiation about that kind of thing?

Yeah, because I was like, "I want an agent," and they were like, "No, you're going to be quote/unquote normal, and you're going to get good grades, and you're going to experience your creativity in a normal environment." I always was an old soul. I always seemed creepily older than I actually was. While other kids were idolizing Madonna, I was all about Rosemary Clooney and Patti LuPone, and Chita Rivera. My friends were like, "Who are you talking about?" And I was genuinely horrified that they didn't know who these people were. I always joke in my cabaret show that I was like a forty-five-year-old gay man in a little girl's body. I was and still am. I was always—I don't know, just different. And I think my mom understood I wasn't going to be cast as Annie. I was a five foot four eleven-year-old so I wasn't going to be cast as a kid because I didn't look like a kid and I didn't seem like a kid. When I was seventeen years old, they cast me as an understudy for Maria in *The Sound of Music* on Broadway. That's crazy. No one else [in school] cared about the musical but me. I remember going to all of the sports teams and flirting with the boys to get them to be in the musical.

So at seventeen, when you auditioned for *The Sound of Music*, how much professional auditioning had you done?

None. I auditioned for my high school musical against one other person who was like, "I don't even care. I don't want to be here." I don't think I even auditioned for *Man of La Mancha* or *Jane Eyre* at Paper Mill Playhouse [both of which she was in]. I auditioned for *Evita*, for The Mistress, and they said, "No. You seem too old." I was fifteen. So I only had one professional audition. I didn't even think about it 'til you asked me that question. Yeah. And I auditioned for Liesl, and they said, "You seem too mature for Liesl." And I thought they were just going to bring me in for the ensemble, but at the very last audition, after seven auditions, they had me read for Maria. So crazy.

[The director] Susan Schulman has told the story that she said to the other people at the table, "I know you're going to think I'm crazy, but we have to bring her in for Maria." What was going through your head?

I was so fearless then. I hadn't yet learned that things go wrong or that people don't root for you. I'd come from this little, tiny town where people were like, "We love you. You were amazing." And from a family that was that way, too. I came into that audition in such an open space, thinking, "Of course these people want me to be good." It felt exactly like it felt in my room.

You had no terror of the stakes being so much higher?

No. It was so weird. I had taken every other show so seriously and this was no different. I had a very clear vision at a very young age of what I wanted in my life, which was to be on Broadway, and I knew what I needed to do to get there. I had this very singular focus. It felt like the stars aligned, and in that moment, it was just like, "this is what I've been preparing for. This is what I've been waiting for." And it was fun. I remember it being fun.

How did your getting the role go over at school?

I had gotten into NYU on a scholarship. I told my dean that I got this job and asked what I should do. He was really cool. He said, "You're here for musical theater. If you don't like it, then you can come back and major in something else. But why don't you go do this and see if you like it because basically everyone here is training to do what you just did." So two weeks later, my parents moved me back home, and I commuted on the bus until I got a studio apartment by myself in New York.

At the age of eighteen?

Yeah. I don't regret any part of my life at all, but that's where I feel like maybe staying in college would have been better for my personal growth. I would have been surrounded by other kids who were messing up, making mistakes, imperfect, scared, and missing home. I went through all of those things with ten nuns in a dressing room.

Did you have the sense that you were learning other life lessons?

Those women were amazing to me. They were my sisters, and my mothers, and my friends, and they loved and supported me, and they taught me a lot. I learned a lot about professionalism. I just had to grow up. I felt oddly lonely but also really a part of things. I felt really grown-up and really infantilized. I felt really excited, and also like, "Well, this is what I wanted my whole life, so now what do I do?" I was eighteen. I was a kid. But I wouldn't change it for the world. It was one of the greatest experiences of my life.

You went on for Rebecca Luker during her two-week vacation. What do you remember about that?

I was sick right before I went on because I was so nervous. All of a sudden it became extremely real to me. My parents came to every single show. Sixteen shows. The first time I went on I remember putting my arms in the iconic Julie Andrews [pose], and I could see my arms shaking in the shadow. So I kept them on my head the entire song because I was so scared.

Did you feel like you were able to find your own characterization or were you just trying to make it through Rebecca's stuff?

Honestly, now as an understudy I would probably be much more understanding of the other performers and what they're used to, but I was like a pony who was just let out of the gate, and I was like, "this is how I'm doing it y'all." But I think it was exciting for them in a weird way. I was closer in age to the kids than I was to the grown-ups. They would sleep over at my house. We would do Easter egg hunts. We'd call it "Easter every day." Every time they slept over, we'd do Easter egg hunts and—

So you'd dye eggs no matter what time of year?

Yeah. And then a month later I found one, and I was like, "okay, now we're going to do plastic eggs with candy in them." They would sleep over and we would watch movies. It was so adorable.

Do you think that befriending those kids was reclaiming some of the childhood you missed?

One hundred percent. And I missed my little sister. She was eleven when I left home. I have such a close-knit family, and I was so lonely. There was no one my age. I was too young to drink, so I would go home by myself after the show.

And when Rebecca left, you got the role.

I have to say Rebecca taught me how to be a leading lady. She was so gracious to me, so kind, so loving. She could have been like, "Okay, little girl, back it up. You're a little too excited." She was loving and supportive. She's just a wonderful woman. She was so committed in those rehearsals, so detail-oriented, so interested, so thoughtful. She could not have been a better role model for me in that way. And also with press; I remember she had a piece in the *Times*, and I saw that it hurt her, but she had to go on and live her life.

And what's your experience with that?

Well, I've been pretty lucky in terms of reviews, but I remember Michael Riedel said that I had been fired from a play [*The Violet Hour*]. That wasn't true. I remember sitting on the bus going home to New Jersey and looking in between the seats and seeing a picture of myself. I said to this lady [whose paper it was], "Do you mind if I just see that?" And just crying on the bus home. The idea that you were allowed to write something that isn't true didn't even make sense to me.

Do you read reviews now?

I'll say that I don't, but I do.

Why do you say that you don't?

To make me sound like a better person. I mean look, I think the smart thing to do is not read them because they never help. They only hurt. When I did *Sound of Music*, somebody said I was "unaffectedly graceful," and then I was onstage, and thinking, "I'm unaffectedly . . . ," and I fell. Even the good ones make you self-conscious. But I kept reading them, which was foolish.

Why? Did it negatively impact you later?

Yeah. I think it made me more self-conscious than I need to be. You get to moments and you're thinking, "how did I do it the way that they liked it?" and you're not organic. You're not in the moment. And truly, if you believe the good ones, you have to believe the bad ones. I've gotten better about not reading them. But it's so hard not to read because now we live in a Facebook, Twitter universe where people are posting, "Fuck Ben Brantley. He doesn't know what he's talking about." And you think, "What do you mean?"

When Rebecca left *The Sound of Music*, you were asked to audition to take over the lead . . .

Yeah, I did have to audition for Richard Chamberlain. That was amazing. It's so funny—I [went straight from a reading to the audition] and it was raining and I didn't have an umbrella, so I showed up soaking wet, and I was late. Richard literally turned to them and said, "Well, she *is* Maria." Things that are adorable when you're eighteen and don't work anymore when you're older . . .

But there you are at eighteen, doing this role. Do you remember the experience of getting to own it, and live it, and also getting press?

I was excited. I was also nervous. I remember somebody interviewed me and said, "What does it feel like to have a $10 million production on your back?" I hadn't thought about it 'til then. Then I started to get some anxiety about it. But I loved it. Richard was wonderful to me. He was so loving. We had a really nice chemistry. I think I got a taste of being truly tired. Doing eight shows a week in that role when you're nineteen years old, you would think you'd have more energy, but you don't. And I think I started to realize that while this was what I'd wanted my whole life and I assumed this was the thing that was going to make the world perfect and make me completely and entirely happy, it didn't. Things don't bring you happiness. It's inside of you. I was willing and ready and mentally prepared to spend my whole life struggling and working up to that moment, and here it was so beautifully handed to me like a gift. I had feelings of, "I don't deserve this. I'm not good enough." But the overwhelming, overriding feeling was gratitude: "I cannot believe that I'm getting to do this. This is what I've always wanted to do."

And when it ended?

I got real depressed. I spent an entire week in bed. I felt like my world was over. That had been my world for a year and a half. I didn't know what to do. I didn't know if I should go back to school or if I was ever going to get another job. And then, two weeks later, those same producers and [director] Jerry Zaks brought me in for *Swing!* and I was happy again, which was an interesting lesson—realizing that I needed the business to validate me. But I loved it. So when *Swing!* started I was so excited, and it was so cool to be around all those dancers who were championship swing dancers. That was really interesting. That's also when I started getting crazy about eating.

Because of the dancers?

Yeah. Standing next to these gorgeous dancers, I was like, "I've got to get it together." Also, I was twenty and that's what you do when you're twenty. I'm starting to realize that some of the things that I sort of pathologized about myself were actually because I was a kid. I just didn't have anybody else around doing the same thing. If I was in college, everybody would [have been going through it].

You had reservations about doing *Swing!* because it was a non-book show, right?

Yeah. I was nervous that people were going to assume I was just a singer and I couldn't act. But I think the brilliant thing that Jerry Zaks did was, without a book, he made a sort of narrative and I was able to express through song. It was a cool show and the sweetest, nicest, most wonderful people.

You got your first Tony nomination at twenty.

That was crazy. I remember my mom called me super early in the morning: "Oh, my God, you got a Tony nomination." "What, Mom? No. No. The show. It must have been the show." And she was like, "I'm so sorry. Somebody called me and told me it was you. Go back to bed. Go back to bed." I went to sleep, and then my phone started ringing off the hook. I kept saying, "No, guys, no. It was the show." And then it really was me. It was so weird. It still seems crazy to me. I had just done *Wonderful Town* with Donna Murphy [at Encores!] the night before. My head was not in it [awards season] at all. It was awesome. I got to be around all of these people who I admire. I think there was a part of me that felt like I didn't deserve it or like I just couldn't believe I was there. I just wasn't processing it. All I wanted in my whole life was happening right then, and I didn't know how I felt about it. What more is there? And I think that's where I started to get into an unhealthy space of thinking I just had to keep doing more and being more, instead of letting it be blissful. Which may be my journey.

Are you saying that you still have trouble enjoying the moment and basking in it?

I've gotten a lot better about it since I've gotten older, but it's something I have to practice. I feel like I'm always looking for the thing that could potentially go wrong so that I can stop it from happening, not only for myself but for people that I love.

Were you always that person or is it learned behavior?

I think it's a little bit of both. I think some people approach life like Patti LuPone and my husband [actor Steven Pasquale] approach life: "What's next? C'mon on world. What do you got?" And I feel like I have a tendency to approach life like, "Hey, um, if you don't mind . . . " It's very skittish. That's something I've really worked on. But I feel like I'm timid in my own, personal, private time. When I'm by myself I can get really, really reflective. Fortunately I have my mother's sense of humor, and I can laugh at myself. And as I've gotten older, I'm able to be not all that serious. It's not brain surgery. I hope that I'm not coming off as some pathological weirdo, but I do think that I am a naturally brave person who's had some things in my life that made me become a tiny bit more timid. But at the end of the day, when push comes to shove, I am that person that you see. I don't really have a bullshit me, and I think, in a way, that's my problem.

Why is that a problem?

Because I do think that I need to have more of that, especially if you're in Los Angeles. There's a version of yourself that you sell so people don't get all of you, so that you have some of you left. And I feel like that's where I have gone astray in a way that's not been healthy for me. I came into it so young. I never really learned how to create that persona that would protect the person.

Maybe to become something else would actually be a disservice to what you can bring to the table.

Maybe that's true. It's in moments where I have to do bullshitty things like parties, and Hollywood-y interviews—in those moments, I see other actresses who I admire being so pulled together, and I just feel awkward and weird. So I want to get better at that. I don't even know how I got on that.

Well, let's go back to *Wonderful Town*.

That was awesome. And to work with Donna who is a consummate professional. Playing her sister was incredible. Getting to act—Eileen is this beautiful girl that everybody fawns over. That was not my experience, so I was really acting. It was so exciting for me to do that. And it was fun. I got to dance some crazy Irish jig.

Was working with someone as detail oriented as Donna ever intimidating?

No. I was just like, "teach me everything you know!"

You were obsessed with *Passion*, so how did you get past being a huge fan?

I don't know. At that point, I had done enough and met enough people that I understood "This is my job. Don't mess up. Get your head in the game." And then I would have my geek-out moments when I would get home, where I'd be like, "Oh, my God!" But also that's a credit to Donna, and to Chita, and to Patti, and to all these incredible people that I've worked with, because they are just humans. It's a credit to them that I forgot that they were my idols. It says more about them than it does about me.

For *Wonderful Town* Comden and Green were still alive and coming to rehearsals.

Yes. Which was so crazy. And it's so funny because I don't feel like anyone from my high school would even understand what that meant. It would be like if Dave Matthews showed up. I don't even know who other people like. I'm so not pop culture. They were so loving and so sweet to me and so complimentary in my work. It was just amazing.

Also during your run in *Swing!* you did the workshop of *Time and Again*.

Yeah. And then we did the production of it. They gave me a leave of absence. It was the same producers. Those were the only bad reviews I've ever gotten. One review said, "At the opening of *Time and Again* the man behind me threw up, and that says it all" or something like that. And another one was, "As I smelled the stench lofting off the stage, I realized these actors have mothers, and I pitied them." I was thinking, "Who do you pity? Do you pity my mother or do you pity me?" I'll never know. So many questions, so many questions that will never be answered!

Was that devastating?

It was really devastating, I loved the show, and I actually think it didn't get a fair shake. And I had been working on it for so long, and I loved that character, so I was really sad.

At least you had a show to go back to.

I did, but I felt like a failure. I felt like I went back with my tail between my legs. I took it personally because I really invest in my characters and I love them so so much.

Were you aware that it was not working?

No, I wasn't. I loved it. I thought it was great. Actually, when the reviews came out, all of us as a company just did the show that we loved. And that was a good lesson.

Did you recognize that what you'd been investing in hadn't lost anything because of one guy's opinion?

Or everyone's.

Did you feel a difference in the audience, too?

Yeah. That is where I learned that audiences will be led by reviews in theater. Not in TV. No one gives a crap in TV. I definitely felt like the audience had been like, "Yeah, we love this." And then literally the day after we opened, they were sitting on their hands. It's the business-y aspect of it. It's not the art.

As all of this was happening, did you find yourself learning the business and becoming slightly less wide-eyed about it?

Yeah. I think that that experience made me try to look at potential jobs and scripts a little bit more objectively.

What does that mean? You look at a script and you either like it or you don't, right?

Yeah, but I feel like I was at the stage where I was like "I'll do any musical." And then I started to look more at structure. What does and doesn't work about this; is there time to fix it?

And as you were processing things this way, who were your peers?

My parents and my sister. My boyfriend at the time was Matthew Morrison. He was such a sweetheart, and I had Michael Benjamin Washington. There were three of us. Me, and Michael, and Matthew were like a little trio. Julia Murney was a wonderful friend to me. She already had a group of friends and had gone to college and was a very well-adjusted grown-up. She sort of understood that I was a kid but living in a grown-up world, and she had a lot of empathy for that, whereas I think some people were put off by it or annoyed by it. She was really loving to me. She's a good, good, good woman.

Is there a point that you realized that you didn't have to wait tables?

Yes. I did have a lot of gratitude for that truly. I am super, overly nice to waiters to where it must have seemed weird and creepy. You know what I do? I wink. I didn't realize that I wink, and I wink. It's just a sense of, "I don't think I'm better than you. I could be you in a heartbeat, and I get that." And I do think it's true that you can judge a person's character by how they treat people who can do nothing for them.

Is thinking "I coud be you in a heartbeat" ever something that you get past?

No. I wake up a lot of times, and I'm like, "today's the day that everybody finds out that I don't know what I'm doing."

As the daughter of a psychologist you must realize that that is the voice of your demons.

Of course. I do. When I'm in a really bad place, I'll go to that extreme. Everyone goes through their hard times. I don't know what happened between being a new kid and now being thirty-three years old. I feel like I blinked and now I'm no longer a kid. And I am feeling that pressure of these being prime baby-making years and prime acting years, so what does that mean for me? How do I negotiate that? Will people want me back? Will I want to go back? I have so many more considerations than I had when I was younger.

So what do you think it means for you going forward?

I think that I have to learn to understand that some things are out of my control. I just have to allow myself to say, "I don't know what's going to happen. I'm going to do my job, and I'm going to live my life, and hope that there is something out there, a power that's greater than me, that will continue to provide for me." Other than my own performance there's very little that is within my power right now. And I just have to accept that.

So if you're thinking about a future . . .

I would like to do theater for the rest of my life. I love the fellowship and the community of theater. I love the palpable living, breathing being that is the audience. During the Twitter, Facebook, television, reality television show phase of our universe, the fact that we are communing in a beautiful theater where live people are right there in that moment, in that space and time, I think it's so important. And I want to do that forever. I would like to be part of changing the landscape for theater lovers to get theater back into our culture, and not just in a *Glee* way and not just a who-can-belt-the-loudest way, but in a truly meaningful way.

Right after *Swing!* you did a workshop of *The Royal Family* with Elaine Stritch. What was that like?

That was intense. She never called me by my name. She only called me by my character's name. I'm like deathly afraid of needles, and she has diabetes, and the first time I met her she was injecting herself, and I literally was like, "it's so nice . . . [mocks gagging]." I had to sit down. Jerry Zaks was just looking at me like, "Don't you fucking pass out. Don't you fucking pass out." But she was great to me. I think she thought I was talented so that worked well for me. Was it the easiest situation in the world? No. But it was amazing to be in the same room as her. And Carolee Carmello is just so warm and brilliant and wonderful, and talk about a voice! I feel so grateful that I got let into this club when I don't have that kind of voice. I don't have that big, belty, mixy thing. My voice is very tender, for lack of a better word. I can belt up to a certain point, but it really is legit. I can't compete with those ladies when it comes to who can belt the highest. I'm out.

It almost sounds like you are Stella Dallas peering in the window—

Yeah. I mean, I feel a part of the club, but I got let in when I was really young. Some people get in and some people don't, and it's luck. I have friends who are way more talented than me that do not have the success that I've had, and I don't know why. Luck.

Immediately following *The Royal Family* comes what would sound like a dream opportunity: *Into the Woods*.

That was an incredible experience. It was my favorite show. I was obsessed with Stephen Sondheim and I loved James Lapine. I was so excited. I was so people-pleasing at that point that when they gave me a pratfall, even though it terrified me, I was like, "I'm going to do this." I did not want to do that pratfall. But I didn't want them to be mad at me, and I didn't want them to think that I couldn't handle it. I did that pratfall for eight months. I remember the first time I did it in LA. I sat up, and I was shaking and the crew said, "she's never doing that again." That was scary for everyone. But I was saying, "I'm going to do it, I'm going to do it." So martyr-y and weird and not necessary. They would have changed it [had I said anything]. But everyone was saying, "it looks so good. It looks so funny." So I just did it. I did it all through LA, and then I did it in New York, and then little things started to happen. I broke my wrist. My body just started to break down. I started to get exhausted doing that. And one night, it just went wrong. I sat up and Kerry O'Malley was like, "Are you okay?"

Onstage, she's saying "Are you okay?"

Yeah. Because it was intense. The audience gasped. This is the point in my life where I realized that my people-pleasing literally broke my neck, and this had to stop. I had to stop doing things because I wanted people to like me. I had to protect myself because no one else was going to do it. The next day I went to a doctor who said, "You herniated three discs, but they're herniated to the side. Just don't do the show for a couple weeks, and then you can go back. Go to physical therapy. Do these exercises." So I did that, and I wasn't getting any better. I went back into the show and I was in so much pain. I couldn't even take a deep breath to sing. I slept on the floor with a towel under my neck, and I would cry hysterically. I was getting progressively worse. I would go to the doctor, and she would say, "Just keep doing your physical therapy, but you really shouldn't do the show for a couple weeks." So I'd be in and out, in and out, in and out trying to do it. And then one show I start throwing up, and I pass out. They call the ambulance, and I stay in the hospital for three days. I go back to this doctor, and she says, "You've got to leave the show. You're so swollen." So I leave. Without getting too into detail, it's handled horrifically by my producers. Really truly callous and horrible.

Well, it's been on record that they wouldn't let you talk about it.

They wouldn't let me talk about it. And when asked by the *Post*, "What's going on? Why is this woman in and out?" their response was, "We think Laura's so talented, but we wish she'd show up for work more." Meanwhile, I'm in a neck brace on my floor hysterically crying. When I got cast in *Nine*, I was still in tons of pain, and I was thinking, "I don't have to do a pratfall so maybe I'll be okay." At this point I was twenty pounds heavier, and I was not doing anything different. I was just swollen. If you look at me in the cast photos of *Nine*, I look like a completely different person. I was in rehearsals for *Nine*, doing an exercise, and I couldn't get up off the ground. I go to this different doctor that Mary Stuart Masterson recommended for me. He looks at the exact same MRI and says, "Your discs are not herniated to the side. They're herniated directly on your spinal cord. Your spinal cord is being choked. We have to do surgery on you right now. You cannot mess around with this." The next day I get surgery through the front of my neck in which they have to move my vocal cords to the side. I had to sign a piece of paper that said if I can never sing again, I'm not going to sue this doctor because this is a life-saving procedure. And three weeks later I'm onstage.

Before we talk about *Nine*, Let's go back to *Into the Woods*. Aside from the accident, how was the playing of that for you?

James was so collaborative and so supportive of me. I really feel like I got to portray her in a way I was really proud of, which made it all the sadder when I hurt myself, and I couldn't keep being her. That was really hard. I loved every minute of that show up until I couldn't do it any more, and then it was like probably the most heartbreaking thing that's ever happened to me.

Any recollections of Sondheim?

We never sat down for an hour over wine and chatted. It's never been that. I've heard through the grapevine things he said about me to other people, which are amazing, and that's always incredible to hear. But I'm still so in awe of him that I can't quite get in there because I'm just like, "Hello. I love you," and then I run away.

You turned down *Nine* multiple times before you took it. Was it because of your neck or were there other reasons?

I didn't want people to know how much I was still hurting. I was given some bad advice: to downplay it so that people didn't think there was something wrong with me. And at the point when they were offering it to me, I was still doing physical therapy and acupuncture, and I was feeling a bit better because I wasn't working. My entire day revolved around bodywork to feel better, but I still felt horrible. Eventually I thought, "If this is going to be my life," which is what this doctor had told me, "I'm going to just have to deal with this, I have to work." So I took *Nine*, which was the most glorious group of women and people I've ever worked with. That was a magical experience. I got surgery, and three weeks later I was back in rehearsal. I went back too soon, and then I missed again because I was in pain. I didn't have the strength. When you have major surgery, you're supposed to rest, not do a show on Broadway. I should have been in a neck brace for a lot longer than I was. I shouldn't have done it. I don't regret doing it because that group of women I will love like no other until the day that I die. *Nine* was very healing. But I do regret missing shows. The only time I didn't go to work is when I literally could not get out of bed. But considering what I had been through, I didn't miss a lot at all. And then who knows which came first, the chicken or the egg, but ultimately when I got the revision surgery in 2010, and the doctor said, "you never fused, and the screws that that doctor used broke your vertebrae and made you worse," maybe that wouldn't have happened if I—who knows? I don't know. Hindsight is 20/20. I can't go back and figure out what it was, but going back to work after such a difficult surgery told my body that it couldn't trust me. So my immune system no longer worked to protect me from colds and viruses and flus and stuff. I started getting sicker a lot. I was really fragile.

Your costume was designed to cover your neck, right?
Yeah. My scar.

Injury aside, the experience of doing *Nine* . . .

It was incredible. Antonio Banderas is such a generous person. I learned so much from him. I feel like that's when I started to really come into my own as an actor. In a weird way, the pain required that I be completely present, which is when the best acting happens. I loved that show. I loved that group of women. I loved Antonio. Chita Rivera became my friend, not just a lady who I always admired. And to see that you could be fallible and weak and still loved, that was huge for me with that cast. And it was so beautifully staged and directed. I just loved it.

That show is unusual in that the principals are also ensemble members.

It forces you to be egoless. We are in a business of ego, so to see all of these women who were cogs in this beautiful wheel was amazing. We were a team. We were a unit. There was never any fighting or bullshit.

Do you have a specific memory of Chita?

I would always do these characters for her, and she would laugh really hard. We would all go into her dressing room and she would just tell us stories. But my favorite memory is when I when would sing "Unusual Way" with Antonio. Eight times a week for the entire run, she would stand in the wings and listen. And every time I would walk upstage to walk up that spiral staircase, she would put her hand over her heart like, "I love you." Every single show.

You left *Nine* to do *The Violet Hour*, which you quit, but that incident brought your first experience with a lot of negative press.

Yeah. That was really hard. I was like, "I don't want to do this any more." I did a limited run of *A Little Night Music*, and that was amazing. It was one of my favorite shows ever. And then I didn't work again for a little while.

You were consciously backing away?

Yeah.

What were you thinking you wanted to do instead?

I didn't know. I thought maybe I'd write music, but I wasn't good enough at it to really do it. I was having sort of a renewed adolescence at that point, and I was dating my ex-husband who had a daughter, and I was really involved in her life. Caring for her became a really big part of my universe. And I was scared. But I missed it. And then I did *The Wedding Singer*, which probably wasn't the best thing to come back in.

Why not?

I don't know if I was the right person to play that character. I do complicated really well. I don't necessarily do simple really well. That's not where I live. But I think also the leading lady in a comedy can sometimes get pushed to the back and not dealt with because it's always more fun to direct your attention to the character-y characters. I felt like I ended up having to fight for her, which—

You mean with the director and writers?

Everyone involved were all incredibly lovely people, all of whom I'd like to work with again at some point. But I think the speed with which it needed to get together—I think they learned about the character a lot in Seattle, and I think she grew from Seattle to New York, just not enough. I should have been more vocal early on to say, "Hey, guys, let's fix this. How are we going to make her interesting?" But up until this point I had only done revivals, except for *Swing!* I still struggle with questioning if I have any right to have a voice whatsoever. I was fighting for Amy Spanger to get the 11:00 number because she was my friend, and I

During the Seattle run of *The Wedding Singer*. (Joan Marcus)

wanted that for her. What I should have been doing, because it's not fucking camp, it's show-biz, is concentrating on my own self and my own character. I wasn't doing my work in Seattle. I needed to raise my hand. I think if I had been more of a diva in Seattle, that would have helped.

So are you saying that there's a lesson in that you should be more of a diva?

I don't think diva is the right word, but I do think my only job is to fight for my character, and I learned that. It's not to be best friends with everyone. And it's not to complain behind people's backs. It's to get shit done. And I didn't start doing that for personal reasons. I was having a lot of hard issues with my now ex-husband and his daughter and her mom, and it was really, really hard, but that's my job.

You ended up missing a lot during that, too?

Yeah. My neck wasn't fixed until 2010. I wasn't fused and I had fractured vertebrae. Your body stops trying to fend off any illness.

So during that whole seven-year period—when you said you were getting colds and sick all the time, your immune system was compromised?

Yeah. And I was in constant pain. I was doing acupuncture, physical therapy, new pillows, lying on the ground, exercise, anything and everything that I could.

So all your free time was spent in pursuit of not being in pain?

Every single minute of my life was spent not being—when I think about it, it makes me very angry because my whole twenties, which is supposed to be the best time of your life, was the hardest time of my life. And I actually thought I was crazy. I would go back to this doctor, and say, "What's going on with me? Why am I not better?" and he'd say, "I don't know. And it took a new doctor looking at the MRIs to say, "There's no way your doctor didn't know you weren't fused." But there's a two-year statute of limitations in New York, so I can't sue him. I've dealt with this for so long. I want it to be done. But yeah, I missed a lot in *The Wedding Singer*. I was going through a divorce and I was in so much fucking pain. And getting so, so, so unbelievably sick. I developed an autoimmune disorder. It was just crazy. So then I thought again, "Well, I just can't do this for a living any more. I'm going to have to do something else because I physically can't handle it." So I auditioned for a television show, and I got that [*Eli Stone*]. And in between the pilot and the series being picked up I did *Gypsy* at Encores! because I thought, "Oh, it's a limited run. I'll be fine." And it was amazing. I was still hurting but hiding it. And if you ask anybody who's ever worked with me, their most vivid memory would probably be me rubbing my neck constantly, or with a ball up against the wall rubbing my neck. So I did *Gypsy* and it was the most miraculous experience I've ever had in my life. It's everything that I had ever wanted theater to be ever. It was life altering.

In what way?

I got to watch my idol work. Not be perfect, not be performance ready, but work, figure it out. And we got the benefit of Arthur Laurents's 7,000 years with that show. And the trials and tribulations of other [productions] and what worked and what didn't. And quite frankly, he walked me through a lot of my own bullshit. He got me out of my own way. I developed a lot of patterns and—

Like what?

Like showing how I'm feeling rather than being how I'm feeling. A lot of self-protective stuff in life that trickled into my performance.

Is that self-protection because you were always having to be conscious of your physicality and hold yourself protectively?

One hundred percent. It was a learned behavior. I also learned how to look like I was more fluid than I was.

How to fake it?

Yeah. So I spent a lot of years being inauthentic in my real life and onstage in order to get through my life. And I hate to be all Debbie Downer about it, but it's just the truth. It was a lot. But I should also say that interspersed in all of this pain are really wonderful moments of friendship and love and family and excitement. Even though it was hard to be onstage, it was a joy because there were times that Dr. Footlights would kick in, and I would be like, "I don't feel pain right now."

When you auditioned for *Gypsy*, did you go in thinking "That's my role?"

No. I didn't. I told my agent, Gary Gersh—God bless him—"I don't want to do a musical. I can't do it." And he said, "if I have to come drag your lifeless body to that audition, I will. You're going. You are her." They told me that day that I got it, and I was so excited.

Were you convinced then that you should be playing this role?

No. I felt like I was too old to play it. No one's going to believe these boobs on a twelve-year-old. And the first couple weeks of rehearsal, I wasn't very good because I was so busy playing young. Arthur would get really pissed at me, and I would get pissed at him. Patti [LuPone] talked to him and he came to me and said, "I'm sorry. I assumed that you would be the type of person I'd need to break down, but I know now that I need to build you up, and I'm sorry." And for him, that's huge. I cried and he hugged me, and then from then on we were inseparable. He cared so much for me. He learned my language, which I appreciate—

How do you define your language?

I am not like an athlete. I am not the person that you can say, "fucking do it," to get results. I need the language of love, care, encouragement, empathy, kindness, and intellect. And he learned to speak to me that way, which I really, really appreciated. And I learned to take it on the chin more, too. He'd be like, "just stop, just fucking say the line." And I would just say it. So I stopped trying to play young, and I just tried to get to that little kid that was still inside of me that just wanted to be loved. Because that's all Louise wanted: the love of her mother.

You certainly have the love of your parents, so where was that kid coming from?

I think a lot of it was the kid that grew up too fast in this business. And having the courage to allow myself to just be. That's what kids do. They don't put on anything. They just are. So Arthur taught me I didn't have to act young. I just had to be present. And that was an incredible gift for an actor. And Patti and Boyd [Gaines] are so generous. So all I had to do is be present and with them and then I was going to be fine.

In what ways would you say that generosity manifests?

I would have to sometimes say, "Patti, you are faced entirely upstage right now," and she would have no idea. She's not thinking about opening up to the audience, she's thinking about playing the fucking scene. She wants everyone to be as good as her. She does not want to be the best thing in the show. She wants the show to be the best it can be, and so if you are on your game and professional, that's all she wants. That spirit of generosity from the star was amazing to watch. And same with Boyd. He's such a leader and so kind and sensitive and empathetic and so smart. It was all about figuring out these relationships.

So in a show whose book is often called the best book ever written for a Broadway musical, to be approaching it from an intellectual standpoint, not above all else but . . .

It was above all else. It wasn't about the choreography and the show-stopping numbers that musicals can be. It was about the scenes. We were playing it like a play. Those relationships were incredibly important, and Arthur investigated every inch of those relationships and how to make them authentic. And that bonded us in a way that I don't think can ever un-bond us. We'll always be a family because of that.

And yet it was over really quickly.
I know. I was so sad to stop being her.

But there were murmurings about a Broadway transfer almost immediately. But you didn't think you were going to go because you had *Eli Stone*?
I went to [TV Producer] Greg Berlanti and he said, "Okay. Do it. We'll bring you out to work on it when you can. We'll figure it out." Most actors would not give up [a series]—just financially! I just knew I would never get another role like this. So then we dug into it on Broadway, and it was amazing to see Patti, after the knowledge that she gleaned from the limited engagement at City Center, come back in like she'd never played the part before. That was amazing.

Was it like you were starting again from scratch?
Yeah. We sat around the table again for a week. We really reinvestigated the moments that we didn't get to investigate enough in the three weeks that we had done it, and that was amazing. In some ways the show got an even better balance. It was an unbelievable experience. Now granted, I was still hurting a lot. I just got through it like I got through everything. I had a really good physical therapist. I would go two or three times a week. It was during the very end of that show that it finally got so debilitating. The overwhelming experience of that show was blissful, but it was hard to not be able to appreciate it completely. Finally I went to a different doctor who told me I needed another surgery.

But you were not missing during this show, so you had either learned to cope well enough in order to keep going, or your body adjusted?
Yeah. I had to take pain pills though. I'm not super proud of that. But yeah, I did whatever I had to do to not miss. And then right after that, was when I got the second surgery.

Let's talk a little bit about playing Louise. Can you cite growth or change as it was happening?
I felt like in the beginning I wasn't comfortable being Gypsy. The sexuality of her scared me. And Arthur had really wanted me to pitch my voice a lot lower in the final scene in the dressing room. That was the one piece of direction that did not serve me because I was so concentrated on creating this low sound that it sometimes took me out of the scene.

How did you get around that?
I just stopped doing it. I realized, "I'm only doing this to please Arthur." I just stopped doing it, and he was like, "Oh, yeah, that's better." But we had to get through that. Once I was able to physicalize—she had been seeking her mother's love for so long and had been ignored, and the moment that her mother throws her out onstage to strip, looking back at her are all of these adoring, smiling faces. I would look directly into the audience and I learned to open my heart to that and take it in. Somebody loves me. And all I have to do is take my clothes off. But for me, the key during that small transition point of the strip was that I had to get to anger. I had to get from "this feels amazing" to "you're all fucking idiots." Getting to her loss of innocence within the number. So to get to that place—I've tricked everybody into loving me, and I don't give a shit about them because the one person I wanted

to love me just slammed the door in my face again—to get to that anger in that scene, was the goal. I would watch "Rose's Turn" every night, and, in my imagination, Louise/Gypsy saw the whole thing and got to see her mother as a fallible creature again. That was the healing: my mom is just a fallible human being, and I am going to forgive her, but I'm never going to let her in. I intellectually understood it, but I hadn't gotten it in my muscles and my bones until a little bit later.

And you could feel the difference?

I could feel a difference entirely. It's like anything; once you release it, it comes to you. Realizing that I didn't have to show the audience I was mad or show her that I was mad . . . If I let the anger build in the strip, then it was there like a well. But if I tried to keep loving the audience in that strip, then it wasn't there for me. And when I was in the gold dress, even though I was winking at them and flirting with them, I hated them. Naturally as actors and as people, we all want to be liked. [I had to] not fear that the audience might like Louise better [than Gypsy]. So did Louise. But there has to be an innocence that's lost in a life like that. The greatest compliment ever given me was by Gypsy's son. He said, "I have seen this show countless times. It was the first time where I felt like, 'oh, my God, I'm watching my mother.'" I was still in the dress and wig, so it must have been really trippy for him. I know it was for me. I hugged him and we both were crying. And he said, "I wish my mom could have seen you. I think she would have been really happy with what you did."

Arthur Laurents was known to be a monster, but everything about this production sounds like he was in love with you guys, and that you were blessedly spared that side of him.

I think in losing his partner, he realized that the most important thing in life is love, and so I think he was making a conscious effort to be a better person. I think this was a love letter to Tom, and so he infused every aspect of it with love. He behaved like Tom was watching.

During that run you won a Tony.

Yay! That was incredible. I'll never forget that moment. That's all I'd ever wanted my entire life.

So what's it feel like to get that thing that's all you ever wanted in your entire life?

Pretty awesome. It felt pretty awesome. It felt like I had grown up. I remember looking for my family after I won at every single commercial break. My husband was like, "Sweetie, you have to sit down. You look like a maniac." I would run up and down the aisles searching for them. I wanted to hug them. I remember Patti's unbelievable performance. I was in the pressroom when Boyd won, and that was incredible. Then Tuesday, when I came out, the audience applauded. I very rarely ever got entrance applause and I just started crying. And then I was like, "pull it together, you got a show to do, bitch."

Between *Gypsy* and *Women on the Verge* you had the surgery?

I did two plays and then I got spinal surgery. They went in through the back. I showed you my scar, right? [She shows her scar]. It's not bad. It was like four months of rehab because they have to cut all these muscles. I lived at home because my husband was doing *Rescue Me* so he couldn't be with me. But I had to have somebody bring me to the bathroom and bathe me. My mom was taking care of me all day long and my husband would do the night shift after shooting. And then [director] Bart Sher called. I was still in a neck brace. He said, "I want you to play this model in *Women on the Verge of a Nervous Breakdown*." He sent me the song, and I

With Patti LuPone and Boyd Gaines in *Gypsy*, the professional experience Benanti credits with teaching her more than any other to date. (Paul Kolnik)

was in love with it. My doctor gave me permission to do it. It was the first rehearsal period since *Into the Woods* that I wasn't in pain. And Lincoln Center was so generous in terms of allowing me to go to physical therapy three times a week. It was awesome to be with Patti again. And Mary Beth Peil. She told me the single, most important thing that I know in my life, which is the minute that you meet someone, they show you exactly who they are and what they're going to do to you. We just choose whether or not to believe it. I'm obsessed with that woman. I want to bow every time I see her. She's a queen. I loved that experience. I know it was a mixed bag, but—

Candela was a great role, though.

She's awesome. I worked hard on her. I was given one of the most brilliant songs I've ever had the great pleasure to sing, but also Patti and I both worked our asses off to create those characters. You've got to work hard. And that's what I didn't do in *The Wedding Singer* until it was too late. Patti taught me how to do that in a very politically correct way.

Barbara Cook told me that she can never be objective about what she's doing because she can't see it. So how do you know whether or not what you're doing is working?

You know what rings true and what doesn't. You know that when you're standing there going, "what the fuck am I doing right now?" you don't have an action to play. If it happens over and over and over again, and you can't figure it out for yourself, then it's probably something that needs to be changed. And Bart Sher is so collaborative. I loved that experience— probably because I wasn't hurting, and I got to be funny. I was really sad that it went away so quickly. We should have gone out of town. I feel like the piece didn't get served in the way that it could have because of that.

After you won your Tony, you were even more in demand for TV work.

Yeah. But it's weird. I feel like I'm constantly humbled because in LA, it doesn't really matter. Some people care that you have a Tony Award, some people don't know what it is. And I am aware that I've taken myself to television a lot, and I wonder how that will affect my going back into theater.

Well, then why do you do it?

Money. I want to make enough money so that I can do theater for the rest of my life, but it is becoming more and more prohibitive to be an actor on the stage, and I don't want to have to do some bullshit theme park musical. I want to do good work. I did not-for-profit theater for two years because my husband was on television. If I want to work at Lincoln Center or if I want to work at Roundabout, then I will get paid as much as I made in the chorus of *The Sound of Music* when I was eighteen years old. And I want to have a family. I want to make enough money so that I can do quality work for the rest of my life onstage. And I do find the TV work gratifying. It's very different. You cannot tell a lie because that camera is right there. But I miss doing theater, and I do get nervous sometimes that people are going to be like, "Fuck you. You went to LA." I would love to have a career like Patti's. I'll never be Patti LuPone, but when I look at careers like Patti's or Angela Lansbury's or these women who will continue to do theater for the rest of their lives with integrity and grace, that's what I want to do. And they do concerts, and they do TV, and they do film, but theater is their home, and that's what I want for myself.

LACHANZE

November 2014

"I LIKE IT WARM AND MOIST," says LaChanze of her dressing room at the Richard Rodgers Theatre where she is appearing in *If/Then*. It is both. Humid and balmy. Add the aquamarine walls, the brightly patterned curtain that separates the bathroom area, and LaChanze's bare feet, and it's positively evocative of the Caribbean, or the set of her breakout Broadway show, *Once on This Island*, the 1990 retelling of *The Little Mermaid* in which LaChanze first lit up the stage with her mile-wide smile, her soaring voice, and a burst of energy that became her signature. It was a game-changer, not only for her but for the composers Lynn Ahrens and Stephen Flaherty and the director/choreographer Graciela Daniele, all of whom would collaborate again on *Ragtime* and *Dessa Rose*. *Dessa Rose*, though, is an anomaly on the LaChanze resume; it is the only show she's done that doesn't trade on her ebullience. There is a light, a joy, an ageless buoyancy that LaChanze brings to virtually every role. It's what made her such a memorable Marta in the Roundabout's revival of *Company*, it's what broke hearts when it was snuffed out in *Ragtime*, it's what balances the confused angst of Idina Menzel's character in *If/Then*, and it was all but guaranteed in abundance by the very title of her off-Broadway outing *The Bubbly Black Girl Sheds Her Chameleon Skin*. But it was in *The Color Purple*, where, as the abused Celie, she had to douse that light and slowly reignite it nightly, parsing her natural presence in calibrated doses as the character takes ownership of herself, that LaChanze proved her greatness, taking home the 2006 Tony Award for Best Actress in a Musical.

Given her infectious energy, it would be easy to assume that LaChanze has led a charmed life. She hasn't. Born Rhonda Sapp in St. Augustine, Florida, she moved to Connecticut with her mother as a small child when her parents divorced. And in 2001, when she was pregnant with her second child, her husband, a trader at Cantor Fitzgerald, was killed in the World Trade Center attacks. She married again but divorced a few years later after what she characterizes as "a horrible marriage." Hers is not a life without darkness. But darkness isn't where she lives or chooses to linger.

The cozy dressing room at the Rodgers also features some narrow, brightly colored shelves, which are overflowing with candies and cookies displayed in tall glass jars, like in an old-fashioned British sweet shoppe. Also visibly prominent is one book: a copy of the hardcover edition of *Nothing Like a Dame*, in which I had wanted to include LaChanze. When I first contacted her, however, she was still hunkered down after an exhausting run in *The Color Purple* and needed time away from all things Broadway. It was therefore especially gratifying to have the opportunity to sit down with her in 2014, in the midst of *If/Then*'s run and her eagerly anticipated return to the stage.

In her Tony Award–winning role as Celie in *The Color Purple*. (Paul Kolnik)

When did you start performing?

My mother had me in dancing school when I was six, but I didn't know I wanted to do this professionally until I was a teenager.

What made you decide to pursue it?

It was the only thing I wanted to do—performing. But I had only trained in dance. When I got to New York I realized that dance was not the only thing I wanted to do.

LaChanze

Uptown . . . It's Hot! Broadway, 1986
Dreamgirls, National Tour and Broadway, 1986
Once on This Island, Broadway, 1990
Out of This World, Encores! 1995
Company, Broadway, 1995
Ragtime, Los Angeles and Broadway, 1997
The Bubbly Black Girl Sheds Her Chameleon Skin, off-Broadway, 2000
Baby, Milburn, NJ, 2004
Dessa Rose, off-Broadway, 2005
The Color Purple, Broadway, 2005 (Tony Award)
The Wiz, Encores! 2009
If/Then, Broadway, 2014

You did musicals in high school.

Yeah, I was the star of the shows in high school. That was fun. I went to Morgan State University, a small university in Baltimore, for two years. I was a theater major there. But it wasn't enough for me, so I transferred to University of the Arts in Philadelphia and was a theater/dance major.

So when did you discover your voice?

I knew [I could sing] when I was a kid. But I wasn't trained professionally.

Were you singing incorrectly?

Probably. I didn't know I was ruining my voice but I thought, "If I am gonna be doing this, I better get some training under my belt." I didn't start training until the summer before I got *Once on This Island.* I was raw.

At that point you had already been on Broadway.

I had already done *Uptown . . . It's Hot!* and been on the road with *Dreamgirls* for three years, but I wasn't trained. A girlfriend, Lola Knox, an incredible singer/dancer, said, "I have this great vocal coach. You should take a lesson with him." Mark Truitt. I loved him. He was doing things with my voice that I didn't know I could do. He taught me that I have gold in my voice. After I booked *Once on This Island* we had a break for the summer [before rehearsals started]. I came back after training with him, and they had to raise all my keys. I'll never forget that. Mark Truitt is the reason I have the voice I do today.

How did you get to New York?

Uptown . . . It's Hot! came to Broadway. I was in college, going into my senior year, and I got this job for the summer at the Tropicana in Atlantic City, this late show. 11:00. The music of African American culture from the 1920s on. Maurice Hines was the choreographer and lead. I was twenty. I thought I would be going back to school but the show went on tour and to Broadway. I didn't go back to college after that.

So you are doing this show and suddenly they offer you your Equity card and a tour/Broadway contract?

And it closed [on Broadway] in four days. Horrible reviews. I was so young. It was really exciting.

And then it wasn't all of a sudden.

And there I was without anywhere to go. I had taken a year off from school and had planned to go back in the fall. It was February. And I didn't want to go home to my mother's and move into my old bedroom. I felt like a failure. I wanted to stay in New York and be a part of things. So I slept on my ex-boyfriend's aunt's couch. But in less than a month I had booked the international tour of *Dreamgirls.* I was gone for almost three years. I came back to New York with the show in 1988, and that's when it all started.

Did you get to meet Michael Bennett?

I auditioned for him and Michael Peters. I remember them needing me to be taller than I am. They said minimum height was 5' 5" [to understudy the role of Deena] and I am like 5' 4" on a good day. So I put all these shoulder pads on and wore my hair up in a topknot. They knew what I was doing. They were laughing at me. But after I sang, they knew they wanted me. They made me the Deena and Michelle cover. The tour was already going on. I met them in D.C. That was an experience for me. In *Uptown*, we were all so young and so green, we were all so excited to be a part of what was happening, and everybody was nice. I got to *Dreamgirls* and everybody was mean and nasty! There were all these affairs going on in the company. It was awful. My boyfriend at the time was in the pit, so he and I hung out. But everyone else was so bitter and competitive.

You have been in enough casts to have seen that dynamic. Where do you think that was coming from?

By the time I [joined the tour] the personality of the company was already established. And we were on the road, which is a very different kind of thing. They had already established their bonds, their relationships. My boyfriend had come in like a month before me. He was the youngest guy in the pit and I was the youngest woman on the stage. We kind of connected because we hadn't been part of whatever had been happening. But whenever I tried to be a part of something, I remember people being so nasty. I said to my mother, "If this is what the business is made of, I don't want to be a part of it. I am going to go back to school." But when I got back to New York, I started booking things outside of the show. I booked a recurring role on *The Cosby Show*, I booked all these commercials. I was making all of this money outside of the show. I was making my own relationships.

So when you came to New York, you suddenly discovered the rest of the Broadway community?

Yes, that's exactly what happened. When I got back [from the *Dreamgirls* tour] I had lost all of this weight. I was in the 90s. My mother thought I was sick. I was just very unhappy. The women in the show were just horrible to me. People used to make fun of the way that I sang and danced. There were horrible women in that cast. They would laugh in my face, talk about me. I didn't know how to deal with this level of bitchiness. I would say, "Why are you so mean to me?" They would laugh. They always assumed that I was pretending to be nice or something. One woman said to me, "You know what your problem is? You're too ambitious." Three of those women have since written me apology letters. Because my star started to rise.

Lillias White was in that company.

Lillias was an ANGEL. Lillias was NEVER mean. Lillias, to this day, is one of my closest friends. Class act from the beginning. In fact, she helped me deal with them. I was also close with a couple of guys. But NONE of the other women.

And you would work with Lillias again in your very next show, *Once on This Island*.

I ended up going to Europe and singing and dancing in Monte Carlo for a year. Then, when I got back I auditioned for this little show out of *Backstage* called *Once on This Island*. I had five auditions. At my final audition, it was with all of the women who were up for the role at a huge dance session. They called us all in. I remember one of those women who were mean to me in *Dreamgirls* at the time thought she was going to get the part. I was at the back, but she was up front and all over the place; being loud and laughing with [director] Graciela Daniele and joking with [composers] Lynn Ahrens and Stephen Flaherty, and being like, "This is my job, this is my job." I wasn't really attached to it at all. At that time, I wasn't working that hard for it.

You had already put in four previous auditions.
But I was never a cutthroat woman. I was just doing what I had to do, doing the best I could. I left the audition and about two days later I got the call that I got the part. I was very excited. I was working at the time as a telemarketer somewhere and I called my service. They told me and I remember screaming. So I am home working on the music, learning it, and I get a call from this woman who had been acting like she was gonna get the job. She said, "I haven't heard anything from them yet and I KNOW I got the part. They practically gave it to me at the audition." She was just talking, talking, talking, talking, talking. And when she finally stopped talking, she said, "Wait a minute, what are you listening to?" And I said, "The music to the show." "Why are you listening to that?" And I said, "Because I got the part." And she said, "Well you better turn it out." And hung up.

Did you speak to her again?
She was cast as my understudy. She wrote me an apology letter.

Sometime between *Dreamgirls* and *Once on This Island*, you changed your name.
Yep. Actually it was before that. I stopped wanting to use "Rhonda" as soon as I left high school. I never liked it. I thought it was an average name for an average person, and I never felt average. I loved LaChanze, which is my grandmother's name. It's been passed down in my family. There are four LaChanzes in my family.

It's Creole?
Yeah, but we're not. But she was raised in Louisiana. It means "one who is charming."

And what made you lose your last name, Sapp?
Are you joking?

Sapp is not awful…
Sapp is not awful?

As a twenty-something deciding to operate without a last name is unusual.
Sapp?

Well, you could have changed it to something else.
There was nothing to change it to. I didn't want to create a name, and Sapp? Sapp was just wide open for jokes. Sapp sucked. I just saw so many headlines with that that were not favorable.

That says something right there: at twenty you were envisioning headlines.
I knew that I wanted to be on Broadway for a very long time. I knew that I wanted to be a performer. I knew where I wanted to live. I knew how I wanted to live. I just had this vision.

Well, *Once on This Island* kicked that off for you. At the beginning, the show was just going to play for a couple of months at Playwrights Horizons. Could you tell that it was something special?

I just knew I liked it and it was fun, but we had no idea! A show about a West Indian girl who fell in love with a guy from the wrong side of the tracks? It didn't have any money behind it. It was at Playwrights Horizons when Playwrights had one teeny theater with no stage left exit. But it really introduced Lynn and Stephen. They had only done *Lucky Stiff* before that.

That show really established Graciela Daniele as a director, too.
It sure did. It put us all on the map a little bit.

Riding that wave, being the leader of that company, what was that like?
I didn't really understand what people expected of the lead of a show. We had favored nations deals as a cast. It was an ensemble. Even my Tony nomination was for featured actress [as opposed to leading]. Which was weird to me. But it was an ensemble piece. So that's how I treated it. We had a company bow, not individual bows. I never thought of being separate from everyone else. I didn't realize that I had gotten any kind of individual fame until I left the show and people started treating me differently.

What kind of people?
Casting Directors. Agents. I started getting calls for things. I was asked if I would move to LA. Norman Lear did this whole [courtship] with me. People were starting to develop things for me. Not knowing enough about the business, I just went along with everything. I just kept going. But I never wanted to leave New York. I lived on 44th Street in a little walk-up studio. I would walk over to the theater, do my show, and walk home.

What do you remember about rehearsing that show?
I remember Graciela and I had a biiiiig fight. Oh my God! She quit for three days! I had like twelve songs to learn and dance numbers and [I was feeling the pressure]. One of the actresses came to work one day crying about her childhood and making it all about her. Graciela made us all sit down in a circle and listen to this woman do a "poor me" party. I remember Grazi saying, "Anyone have anything they want to say?" And I said, "I do. We don't have time for this. I have twelve songs to learn and I do not have time to listen to her complain about her childhood. I have got to get to work." And she said, "Well, Miss Diva, if you think you are the lead of this show, I quit." And she walked out. I felt awful. We didn't have rehearsal for three days. They kept saying, "LaChanze, you have to apologize," and I said, "Of course I will apologize but this seems extreme." Years later Grazi and I worked together again and again and again. Turns out what she did was go across the street and have a drink, and she told Lynn and Stephen that you have to do this because when you have a diva on the rise you have to let her know who the real person in charge is.

So this was all a strategic move for her?
It was all a strategic move. She was trying to put me in my place. But it completely wrecked me. And she did put me right in my place. I was like, "Okay! We'll do whatever you want. Let's just get back to work." I felt the pressure.

Donna McKechnie told me that when *A Chorus Line* moved from off-Broadway to Broadway, it was really hard for that company to stay level-headed and cohesive. Was that a challenge for your cast?
I know that you would imagine that it was, but I have to say it wasn't. This show was so unusual in that it was so small. We were the little show that could. People thought that we were

just going to go away. "Oh, there's that sweet little black show over there directed by that Argentinean woman." No one knew that we had that much fan support and we were loved. To this day it's still a cult favorite.

It was so simple, so theatrical. It came on the heels of spectacles like *Miss Saigon* and *Phantom*. It was just people on a bare stage—

People on the stage, yep. It didn't cost producers any money for that show. It was a magical experience for all of us involved. And we're all still very close. The cast of that show, if we see each other, we just bawl because we loved each other so much. We really bonded. There wasn't one person, other than this woman who was let go, that created a problem or that was a diva or anything.

How did you decide it was time to leave?

My agents at the time kept telling me that no self-respecting actor/lead of a show stays on after a year, that she leaves. And I thought, "Well, I don't have another job to go to so why would I leave?' And they were like, "That's just what you have to do. It's what everyone expects you to do after a year." They basically made me put my notice in. I didn't have anywhere else to go. Today I know better, but at that time I didn't know. So I put my notice in when my year contract was up, and for a few months I kind of sat around thinking, "Why did I do that?" But then I booked the movie *Leap of Faith* with Steve Martin, and then I did a regional production of *Jesus Christ Superstar*. I had so much fun doing that. But that's why I left the show. Isn't that crazy? It was so weird. I didn't know. I didn't know.

You got Tony nominated, though.

That was amazing. Bob Mackie dressed me. It was like nothing else. The most exciting experience. Everyone kept telling me, "Oh, you're going to win, you're going to win, you're going to win." I wasn't sure about that, and when I didn't win, I had to go perform like the next moment. Everyone [in my cast] was just looking at me. They were so upset. We were in the wings getting ready to go on and I was like, "Guys, we've got to pull it together! We've got to get out there and perform!" I really didn't feel badly until the party was over and everyone left. I had rented a suite at the Empire Hotel and it was just me in this huge suite, and that's when I finally just felt sad enough to cry. But I had to get alone and do it.

Did you have to work survival jobs at all?

I worked at a cemetery. It was my summer job. It was telemarketing at a cemetery.

To sell graves?

Sell cemetery plots. I called these elderly people and told them that they had just been awarded a free cemetery plot. Now, this was the catch: We would give them a free cemetery plot if they bought one—it was like buy one, get one free.

Oh, my God.

Oh, my God is right. The slogan was "We're the Last Ones to Let You Down." It was a great job. I loved it. We would laugh so hard. It was a bunch of kids. We would just drink beer and sell cemetery plots. [But that was before I got to New York.] Once I got to the city, I worked at the restaurant Jezebel in the coat check. I would rehearse *Once on This Island* in the day and go to Jezebel at night. That was my last survival job.

So during *Once on This Island*, did you feel like, "Okay, I know now that I am going to be making my living at this, and I don't have to worry about where the money's going to be coming from?"

Weirdly, I never really worried about where money was coming from. I'm one of those kinds of people who just expect it to come, and when it doesn't come, then I figure it out. I don't know why that is. I've always been that way. If I need to get a job, I'll get a job. And if I can't afford something, I won't buy it. If I can afford it, then I spend like crazy. I'm that, too, at the other end of the spectrum. I don't worry about work like that, but there was a time when I was in *Once on This Island* when I had a validation moment. I questioned for a long time if this was the right thing that I was supposed to be doing. My dad told me that if my creative tree did not bear fruit, I would have to go back to school and get a degree. And the only thing I wanted to study was law so I would have to go back and get a law degree. I kept working but I still kept thinking, "Oh, God, I've got to keep my eye at Brown or somewhere. Yale." My mind was always thinking that way.

So what made that change?

The deciding factor was—and I know this is crazy because I don't always believe in reviews—but Frank Rich gave me such an amazing review in the *New York Times*. [He said, among other things, "The most golden throats and ethereal presences belong to LaChanze and Nikki Rene."] Even though actors like to say we don't pay attention to reviews, that's bullshit. Everyone pays attention to reviews. Everyone reads them even if they say they don't. Everyone listens. They pay attention. And he gave us a rave review, and more specifically, he said these things about me that were so—no one had ever said anything like that about me. And it was in the *New York Times*! So I felt that if I can get a review in the *New York Times* from Frank Rich as a twenty-something, I'm supposed to be doing this.

After *Once on This Island*, your next Broadway show was *Company*.

Was it *Company*? Yes, it was! But prior to that, I did [the Disney animated movie] *Hercules*. That was huge. We recorded at Sony and Alan Menken was there conducting the whole time, and he was directing us every moment. There was never a moment that he wasn't with us. We even recorded some of it at his house in Connecticut. That was a great time. I sang so high on that, I couldn't believe it. Even now fans come to see me and they're like, "Oh, my God, you were in *Hercules*!" These kids—they're so intense.

Do your kids get excited about it?

Not so much. They totally don't care. It only matters to them when their friends are interested. Then they're like, "Yeah, yeah, that was our mom."

What can you tell me about working with Alan Menken and David Zippel?

David is just the warmest, sweetest guy ever. And Alan was just so great and so smart. They are so talented, but so unassuming. So down to earth.

I should also have asked you about working with Stephen Flaherty and Lynn Ahrens.

Now, that was a wonderful experience in my life. I have so much respect for them. To me, they can write anything. They are just so talented. I would do anything for them. When we were doing *Once on This Island*, we were all so young. They were very fresh. I was fresh. They were writing this incredible music, but they were also open and eager to make it work for everyone.

There's nothing that they can ask me that I won't do. I've worked with them so much. Even outside of shows, I've done concerts with them and filming other things. They know my voice. They know my acting style. They know how I am on stage. I've grown with them through the years. And we're in a friendship as well. I feel very grateful for the relationship with them. I really am.

Back to *Company*. Working with Sondheim and [director] Scott Ellis...

Auditioning for Stephen Sondheim, I was so nervous that I sang *Another Hundred People* seated, sitting on my hands because I didn't want him to see my hands shaking. The entire song is fast and wordy and high. And I just sat there and sat there. And then, at the end, I started to get my courage so I stood up and I sang it long and loud and just belted that thing out, and they just kept playing and playing it. After I finished Stephen Sondheim stood up and applauded like this [with his hands above his head]. That's a memory forever and ever and ever. At that point, I was like, "I don't care if they don't cast me, because Stephen Sondheim— I just got a standing ovation with him applauding over his head for me." I really loved doing that show. I loved working with Jane Krakowski and Charlotte d'Amboise. It was a really strong group of actors. Scott Ellis directed and Rob Marshall choreographed, so we had this powerful creative team.

They were at the very beginning of their careers. What do you remember about them?

Rob Marshall was a lot of fun. Ellis was—he was efficient.

That can be good, but it's hard to get a performance out of efficiency, and especially something that's as nuanced and emotional as *Company*.

He wasn't that kind of director. He wasn't touchy-feely. He wasn't one of those directors that let you explore the emotion of the character or gave you the space to indulge or talk to him about what was happening. He was like, "Stand here because this is where I want you to stand. Do this because that's what I think it should be." He was just...efficient. Yeah.

You had worked with Graciela...

Grazie was very gentle. She worked from an emotional place, and if it didn't make sense emotionally, then it didn't make sense. And Rob Marshall was about "showtime!" He loved movement, he understood it. It wasn't just telling the story, it was for dancing. That was the purpose of dancing: for dancing. To show you how cute and fabulous it looked, you know? Which is another style that very much has its place in the theater.

Both of them, and Scott Ellis are known to be very kind to actors. Unlike an earlier generation who seemed to think actors needed to be belittled.

I haven't worked with a director who would yell at actors. Michael Greif is intense, but he never raises his voice to the actors. He raises his voice at the crew!

After you finished *Company*, *Ragtime*.

Ragtime was interesting because I was cast as Sarah before Audra was, but [producer] Garth Drabinsky didn't want me. He wanted Audra to do it in Toronto. Stephen fought for me and they finally asked me to go to Toronto for a year, but for like no money. [Drabinsky] offered me less than what I was making in *Once on This Island* on a favored nations contract. I was like, "I'm not working for that." But then they offered the LA Company for double the amount.

And I didn't care because at the time I wanted to go to LA. [Audra did] the Toronto company. She really wanted the job. She petitioned for it. There was a little while there that I felt like all I did was complete with Audra McDonald.

Were you guys friendly then?

No. We were not friendly then. We became friendly, but we were not friendly. I didn't even know her really. I knew who she was. I went to see her when she was in *Carousel* and I thought she was great. But I thought she was so different from me so I didn't think anything of it. But they always compared us, and it drove me crazy.

That is bizarre because there's nothing similar about you except that you are both black women in musical theater. Although one thing that you do have in common is that you've both had the opportunity to play a number of roles that are not written for black women, and that's not true for many other black actresses. Was Kate [LaChanze's role in *If/Then*] written to be a black woman?

No. In fact, Jen Colella [who plays opposite LaChanze] says that Kate was modeled after her. She didn't hesitate to tell me that when I first met her, too. This character was written because Jen Colella and [creators] Tom Kitt and Brian Yorkey are friends. They wrote this character based on her. But she played it, [in workshop] from what I hear, a little bit more like the character of Lucas: wisecracking, kind of edgy. So [the characters of] Elizabeth's friends weren't very different in the way that they were being played. I came in and you got to see this character's hope and light and levity. I'm told they really wanted to balance out the energy that was coming from the three leads, and that's why they went with someone like me.

So Kate was not originally black, and you've had other roles—*Baby* at Paper Mill, *Company*... As you're playing these roles that were not written for black women, does that feel like you're helping break down boundaries at all? Are you conscious of it in any way other than "I'm just doing my work?"

Of course. I mean I think about it. I get to just play a woman. Race doesn't come up. So as an audience member, you may think, "Oh, this is interesting that she's black." But you may not think about that. You're able to just get into this character.

It doesn't happen often enough. Although Brian Stokes Mitchell has played several roles not specifically written for black men. I hate to ask this, but do you think it's because he has lighter skin?

While I love Stokes like a brother, he played Coalhouse in *Ragtime* and the thing about Coalhouse Walker is that he was jet black. We all felt like we didn't know why they would cast Stokes as Coalhouse originally. We all love him, we love his work, but it is a detail that we can't overlook. As darker-skinned African American actors, oftentimes we are cast as people like Celie [in *The Color Purple*] or Dessa [in *Dessa Rose*], and sometimes certain types of roles go to lighter-skinned people. I feel two ways about this because if I look at my career, I can't necessarily—I have had a little bit more of a balance. I can say that there have been times in my life where I've wondered if certain things aren't happening for me because of the fact that I'm a dark-skinned actor. But then at the same time, I play roles like this [in *If/Then*], and I do things like *Company*. In theater oftentimes it's about what you can do, not necessarily what you—this is what I bring, this is what I have. If you don't see the value in it, then I'm not supposed to be in your play.

Actually I think the thing that you bring has very little to do with black. I think your specialty is effervescence. There is a light. In *Once on This Island* Ti Moune is the light. And in *If/Then*, Kate is the light. It's pure joy.

How sweet.

That's what you bring to the table in everything. Do you perceive that about yourself?

Well, I've heard that said about me a lot. In life generally I am an optimist. I tend to be more of the glass half-full kind of person, and I choose to be more of a supportive, confident person. Life is too short. I've had some horrible things happen to me in my life, really traumatic experiences, and I feel like if I walk around attached to that, then I won't be able to lift off and give and do and be a part of this amazing industry, having roles that do something and affect people. I think that it's an actor's responsibility to show the humanity of characters.

You choose it.

I choose to bring something positive to what I'm doing on stage as well as in life. I just choose it. It's something that I think is tangible. It's human. People respond. They like it. But I also think vulnerability is important, so I like to be very open. I like to be as honest as possible, and that's just the way I live my life. So that probably comes out in my work. I have friends in my life who are just so negative about everything, and I can't even deal with those people. I limit my time with them. I choose joy. I choose joy.

Let's get back to your timeline: What was it like doing *Ragtime* in L.A.?

It was weird.

Why?

Because it was theater in LA. After the show, there would be nothing to do. It would be a ghost town. I didn't particularly like living in L.A. I felt very lonely out there.

What about the experience of doing the show?

I loved doing the show out there. I loved working with John Rubinstein. Oh, my God how much do I love John Rubinstein? And Judy Kaye. And Stokes, and I just had such a great time out there working on the show and meeting my husband. So the experience out there was wonderful. There were times when I was a little bored because I get bored if I'm not doing a lot on stage. I just do. I want to be out there. I want to be doing something. I don't want to just pop in and out. I'm getting bored in *If/Then*. I mean, I love it. I'm having fun. But it's a little limiting for me. I want to sing more. And in the workshop, I did. When we got to Broadway and so much of it had been cut out I was so disappointed. And in *Ragtime* I wanted to do more but I loved the job. I loved working with the people I got to meet.

And then what was it like to take it over here in New York?

I was just so happy to be working in New York. I didn't realize that there was this stigma in replacing an actor on Broadway. I didn't know that. I just didn't think that it was an issue, but—

For whom was it an issue?

My agents and the people around me. People in my professional circle that were on my team really took issue with me replacing. They wanted me to just let that go altogether and start doing another show. But I liked working on the show, and it brought me back to New York in a job that I enjoyed. I was gainfully employed, and I was about to have a baby, and I just wanted to work in New York. I had been gone a year and a half so I didn't know what the vibe was. No one had seen me on stage in New York in a while so I needed to build that audience back up and get my face out there more.

And do you feel like that's what happened?
Definitely. I got back in the circle of things rather quickly.

So you left *Ragtime* to have a baby? Were you showing?
I was. It was ridiculous. Even though I had that costume [with the high waist]. They just kept raising it up. But finally I stopped and I had my baby. And I went back to work right after she was born.

Right after?
Three weeks after. In *The Bubbly Black Girl Sheds Her Chameleon Skin*. I did the workshop of *Bubbly* after leaving *Ragtime* seven months pregnant. [Producer] Ira Weitzman said, "LaChanze, you're the only person I can see doing this," and I was seven months pregnant. And so I did the workshop and I figured they would produce it with someone else. They already had it scheduled in the season. But then Ira called me one day and said, "LaChanze, we really can't do this without you." I said, "Ira, I'm about to have a baby." I hadn't had a baby yet so I didn't know what that meant. He said, "What if we move the play to the end of the season? How much time do you think you would need after you have the baby to come back to work?" And I said, " Probably like three weeks."

It didn't occur to you to ask anybody?
Nope. So they started rehearsals. Everything was scheduled around me coming back with my baby.

Were you nursing?
I was nursing. I had had a C-section. I was such a mess, and there I was in this rehearsal hall three weeks to the day after giving birth with my little three-week-old tiny little baby and my nanny. We were working on the scene where I had to straddle a twin bed and my hips hadn't even gelled back together yet. I remember feeling that pain, and I remember crying, "Oh, my God!" On break I would just go in the back and cry and cry. "Why did I do this, why did I do this?" My nipple pads were soaked and I was leaking all over the stage. It was horrible. But I snapped back! I had giant breasts, a flat stomach, but I did it. I don't know how I did it. It was crazy. Two months after having a baby I started performing on stage. It was so stupid. It was just stupid. I would never recommend that to anybody.

I understand that the physical challenges of doing it with a newborn, but was it harder for you as a mother later, once they got older and needed more attention?
Yes, it was harder because I felt like I was missing stuff. When Celia was a baby, her dad was there, no matter what was going on. His hours were 6:00 a.m. to 3:00 in the afternoon so he would come home from work and take over. He loved his baby girl. He was a great, great dad. He would always bring clients to the theater. All of his clients saw me in whatever I did. He was so proud of me. He brought me flowers every Friday. And he was always there at night for our daughter. I could relax knowing that he was there, but when he passed away, and I was pregnant with our other daughter, that's when I started to develop real separation issues,

having a hard time being away from them. But that was all because of how he died. I was experiencing this whole PTSD period with my children, and that's how it manifested itself. I was just afraid to be without them. No matter where I went, I wanted my children with me.

You didn't work for a while. Because you just needed to be with them?

Yeah. I was nervous about leaving them. I was scared something was going to happen to me or to them.

How did you get through that?

I just decided, "I'm not going to work anymore. I'm just not going to work."

And you didn't have to? The money was there?

No, I didn't have to. My husband was a trader on Wall Street so we were okay. But then Eve Ensler called me. I didn't know her from Adam. I knew who she was. I knew she had that play, *The Vagina Monologues*. She called me up when Zaya was five weeks old and she said, "How are you?" Everyone in the theater knew what had happened. She said, "Listen, I want to see if you'd be interesting in coming to do a few weeks at *The Vagina Monologues*. It's the easiest thing in the world. You can sit on a stool. You read. You don't have to memorize lines. You have one week of rehearsal, and you do it for three weeks. I would love to have you come do my play." This was a personal invitation from a woman I highly respected, and she did make it easy for me. I had decided that I wasn't going to ever leave my children, but something about this conversation... We were crying. And she got me to agree to do it. It really was the catalyst for me to continue in this business. I remembered why I was there on stage. I remembered that I had talent. Because all of that had been blocked out. It was gone. One of the things that the therapist said later on is that women [after a trauma] put themselves away. They don't deal with themselves at all, they just immediately focus on their children. And I did the same thing. But Eve got me to reengage in theater and that's how I eased back into my career. I credit that to Eve Ensler.

So after *The Vagina Monologues*, you were ready to take on *Dessa Rose*.

I went to New Zealand first and shot a miniseries with Rachel York [her co-star in *Dessa Rose*]. That's when we first met each other. It was called *Lucy*. She played Lucy and I played her maid. Go figure. [In *Dessa Rose*, LaChanze's character pretends to be York's character's maid.] Then we came back and did *Dessa Rose*. But they had been talking to me about *Dessa* for a long time. *Dessa* was one of those projects that they had been working on for a couple years. I knew about *Dessa* before Calvin passed away. When it actually happened I was ready for it. I had decided to leave the business but because of Eve Ensler, I decided, "okay."

Did you see the character of Dessa as a change for you?

Yes, definitely. It was the first time for me that I got to engage anger and rage. No one had really seen me like that before. But I really needed to unleash some anger and rage at that point!

Was it therapeutic in that way?

I guess it was at times because I really wanted—I wanted to be angry. I wanted to have a reason to be angry at somebody, at some thing. That's one great thing about being an actor: you get to use your emotions. You get to go for it and nobody can say anything to you because you're on stage. [With slavery] there's a fair amount of communal angst that we as black people

The one dark role in the LaChanze canon: the murderous title role in *Dessa Rose*. (Joan Marcus)

carry from that shit, so there was a chance for me to address that in a way. It was a good therapeutic moment for me, outside of my own personal life, but as an African American female
living today. Lynn and Stephen and Grazie gave me the opportunity to engage rage. They
wanted that from me. Grazie used to always tell me to do that, even in *Once on This Island*.

She felt that I covered that side up, that I didn't have the courage to go there. In *Once,* she used to tell me I wasn't tapping into the scene where I was supposed to stab Daniel. She said, "You're too nice here. I need to see that you can stab him." For a long time that was the hardest part of the show for me, getting enraged. But when I got to *Dessa*...

You were ready for it.

I was ready for it. I was older. I had a few things happen to me, so I was ready to engage in some rage. That's when the roles started getting darker for me. Even outside of the theater. I played a crack addict in prison. And people really started seeing that in me. But Grazie wanted me to find that color because she thought that it would give so much dimension to my work, and it really did. I wanted meatier roles. I wanted some of those Viola Davis kind of roles. I wanted to go there. That is how Celie [in *The Color Purple*] came up. I saw [that it was casting] and I was like, "I want to do this."

Do you think that the darkness you were able to access for *Dessa Rose* helped people envision you as Celie?

Celie was not dark to me. Celie was wounded. So it's a very different place to go, you know? I identified with her from the standpoint of someone wanting something so badly, but being limited because of her own thoughts of herself. Celie is profoundly human. Anyone can relate to Celie: black, white, old, young, male, female. Anyone can relate to that kind of desperate human need for love, and that's all she wanted. But she was so wounded that she believed so little of herself. I identified right away with the simplicity of it. It was rich with possibilities. I completely understood her right away. [She] wasn't necessarily about anger. It was more extreme vulnerability and hurt.

How did you end up in that show? You told me that you had to audition for it, which surprised me?

Yeah, I sure did. I went to the audition like everybody else.

You told me that when you were in *Once on This Island* you did not experience the pressure of leading a company because you were treated as an ensemble member. In this case you were very clearly the lead.

I've got to be honest with you; it was so much work! I had small children at home. I was so busy trying to make sure that I got everything done and that I did it well, the pressure of the show I didn't feel as much.

When you are working on a character like Celie, is it hard to leave the feelings at the theater? Do you end up carrying the emotions home with you?

Yeah, definitely. I took it home too much. I would feel so drained. I remember getting to the end of my contract—I had been with the show for three years—and everyone was saying, "Oh, you're going to extend, you're going to extend." The last thing I wanted to do was extend on that show because it was so physically and emotionally draining. I remember wanting to go have a drink after the show [nightly]. I needed to change my mood. It was just so heavy. It was a huge journey. I lived a life in that show. [The character] started at sixteen and went all the way up to a sixty-five-year-old woman. And the play was so heavy—getting beaten and raped every night. And to do it well, I had to be in every single moment and commit. It was a lot for me. I was very glad when it was over.

And then on top of all of that, there was all of the work you had to do to promote the show.

And there was so much of that. All the talk shows, the morning shows, the press. I had hired my own individual press agent. The producer had one idea of how the play should be marketed, and I had another idea of how I should be marketed.

What made you decide to do that for yourself at that stage of your career?

He was not selling LaChanze starring in *The Color Purple*. He was selling Oprah Winfrey's *The Color Purple*. And that's fine. He can do that. It was his play. But I felt with this role, I wanted people to see me as a leading lady from that point on, not as someone who could go back and do roles that weren't as important anymore. I wanted to make sure that I stood out. I didn't want to be in the ensemble of a piece again. I'd learned my lesson from that with *Once on This Island* so I did what any businesswoman would do in this business: I promoted myself. It's an investment. It's not cheap either.

If you're trying to promote yourself but you're also feeling exhausted by all of the press and publicity that you have to do, does it become a double-edged thing?

Well, yes and no. The individual promotion that I was doing was fun. I got to meet great people, go to events. But a lot of time the producers wanted to make it about the three women in *The Color Purple*. I remember the other actresses were hugely upset with me because they thought that while the producers told us that he was going to market all three of us, he was marketing me. And I was like, "No, I'm marketing myself." They didn't like that.

Did that make it tricky backstage?

It did to a point. But what can you do about that? It's a business. I'm not going to not do what's best for my profession, my career, because of how you feel. You have the choice to do that for your career as well. Another perfect example is with *If/Then*. I did not do my own individual self-promotion, and the producer didn't promote me in the show. He promoted Idina Menzel. That is not how it was presented to me originally. But I'm fine. I knew what I wanted to get out of it, which was to be seen as a modern woman.

Now that you mention it, you've never done a contemporary woman on Broadway until now.

Not until now. Exactly. And that's why I picked this role, a supporting part, because I wanted to play a contemporary woman.

Let's go back to *The Color Purple* for a minute. What was it like having Oprah come on as a producer?

It's Oprah! I remember the day she walked into rehearsal. People jumped up and down and screamed because she was Oprah. And we were so proud to be in a show that Oprah was producing. It was really incredible. All of a sudden the world starts watching, you know? And then we went to do her show out in Chicago. That took us to another level.

Were you star-struck at all?

I wasn't star-struck with Oprah because she's not like that. It wasn't like being in the room with Angelina Jolie. She's warm, and inviting, and kind, and generous, and personable. If you were star-struck when you first saw her, in the first few minutes you lost all of that.

Was she also collaborative on the show?

No, she was not involved in the creative process at all.

You were Tony nominated again, this time as a leading actor. Was the experience different for you?

When I was nominated for *Once on This Island*, I was so excited to be invited to the party. You know what I mean? I was young, and it was all so exciting, and new, and fabulous, and amazing. It's what a young actor would want more than anything. By the time I was nominated with *The Color Purple*, it was more like work. It was going to all the events, meeting with all the people, deciding who's going to dress me, and what jewelry. It was just another level up. It was fun, I enjoyed myself, but I also remember thinking, "Boy, I'll be glad when this part of it is over so I can relax." It's a lot of work to be a glamorous actress on Broadway! I didn't think I was going to win, that's for sure. You know who was in my category? Patti LuPone, Sutton Foster, Kelli O'Hara, and Chita Rivera!

So when you did win it...

It was amazing. I didn't thank my producer or my director, and they never let me forget that. I was so excited and happy that this amazing piece was acknowledged. [The film] didn't win an Oscar. It didn't win anything. The book won the Pulitzer. But it didn't win an Oscar, and we hadn't won any Tonys up to that point. I was with my husband at the time. We're divorced now, by the way. I didn't thank him either. But it was an amazing night because all of my family was there. Oprah came to my party. That night, John Ritter came up to me and said, "Do you know who you remind me of?" And I said, "Who?" And he said, "No one." I'll never forget that.

Did winning a Tony Award change your career?

Yes. If you think about tiers, actors in theater, we're on the second tier. We don't have the prestige or the celebrity of movie actors. They are on the A tier. We're on the B tier. I've been at the top of the B tier for a long time, and then when I won the Tony, I was bumped into the bottom of the A tier. I'm at the bottom of it but I'm in the A tier now!

You told me that after *Color Purple* you needed time off?

Yeah, I did. I took about three years off. I needed a break. That play really took a lot of me. And then there wasn't really anything that came my way that I thought was interesting enough to do right after *The Color Purple*. I really wanted to do a great TV role, and that just didn't happen. You're given a Tony for a role like Celie, the next thing has got to be pretty powerful. Nothing was coming my way that I liked.

Did you feel that they should have been knocking down your door and weren't?

It was weird. Right? I didn't get it. My press agent didn't get it. Even my manager was like, "I don't understand this. " It was quiet for a while, and I don't know why. It's like you do this big, amazing thing, and after that they don't know what to do with you. And I'm not the only one who experienced that. A couple of actress friends of mine who were Tony Award–winning actresses had that experience. Idina won for *Wicked*, and she didn't do theater for ten years. We talked about that and how it really does feel like you have the audience, you have the fans, you have the acknowledgment, but then the next offer that comes your way—they're scared. They don't know where to put you.

With Jen Colella in her first contemporary role in *If/Then*. (Joan Marcus)

Do you feel the desire to try to find something and develop it?

Well, that's what's happening next for me. I'm sitting down with producers now, talking about developing something for me next so that I don't have so much time before my next thing on Broadway. I'm looking at stories. I'm looking at women. I'm looking at ideas. I can't leave it all up to someone else.

We already touched a lot on *If/Then*, but is there anything else you want to share about it?

In theater, because we spend so much time with the people we are working with, the cast becomes part of your life. [Other] people have their private lives and their work lives—for actors it can meld together. We are exposing ourselves onstage everyday, and then backstage you are already wide open and ready to express yourself. You share different things. With this particular group of actors, I have a connection with every single one of them. They are so cool. Maybe because there are only sixteen of us. We bonded like I have not bonded with any other company except the cast of *Once on This Island*. I have worked on a lot of shows and made some good friendships, but this show has left an impression on me from the top down. We bonded in a way that I will never forget. There is no bad seed. It's a sane group! It's such a re-freshing experience. I am playing a lesbian and everyone keeps asking what it's like to play a lesbian. I don't know. All I can tell you is I am playing a woman who is in love. I know how to play love. I don't know what it's like to be sexually attracted to another woman, but I do know what it's like to be in love. I love coming to work every day.

What can you tell me about Idina?

I admire her for being so open all the time. Everywhere. She is not the type of actor who is one way onstage and another way offstage. She is who she is everywhere, and it's refreshing to see that. She is a really open and generous person onstage. If someone goes off book, she will crack up in your face onstage and not apologize for it. She is a real human being and really smart. She doesn't go in for gossip and drama and all of that and neither do I, so I appreciate that. There's no time for that. We're not curing cancer in the theater. We are actors. We are portraying behavior on stage. And while it takes a skill set to do that, we're not saving lives. We're teaching people how to feel. I am so honored that this is what I get to do. It's a blessing. I am so grateful to God. Being a creative being and being able to tap into that creativity is a blessing. Every night it's something different and I appreciate it.

I have noticed that you usually get to the theater right at half hour. Is that specific to this show, or do you always arrive just before show time?

I am one of those 7:25 ladies. I hate being at the theater super early. There is something about walking on stage fresh. I don't like to be there early, thinking about the show because I get in my head too much. I start analyzing. I am better and more honest when I am less prepared. I know that sounds weird. But I already went through rehearsal, I've already memorized the lines, I have already investigated the emotions I need to. So the work is done. The homework and all the preparation is already in me. When I get to theater, I don't need to do the work again. I need to get onstage and live it. I don't need to live it in my dressing room for an hour. I like to get there and catch the wave and go. I even hate too much time between shows. I wish there was less time [between the matinee and evening shows]. That's just me, though. It creates problems with people.

How so?

Some people think I am being anti-social. It's just my process. A lot of people come to the theater and like to hang out. That's wonderful but not before the show as far as I am concerned. After the show? I am all for it.

Is there a role you are dying to play?

I would like someone to create a musical about the life of Diana Ross. The woman from the projects who became what she became. I would like to do her journey. Her career spans five decades. No one touches Diana Ross because she's alive and because she's such a fucking diva. She doesn't want anyone touching her shit. I get it. She doesn't want to be considered a legend [from the past.] But her life and story are fascinating to me. And I would love to play Evita. I would kill that.

Vocally I could see that, but it's so against type.

That's why I want to do it!

Acknowledgments

TO SAY IT TOOK A village to get this book together is a cliché. It also happens to be true. The numbers of people who helped me, over the very long process that led to what you hold in your hands, is staggering, and I am so very appreciative.

Jennifer Keller hatched the idea for this book with me over lunch one day on 57th Street. She has always been my conscience, my sounding board, my proofreader, and my confidant. I have said before that without her, I'd be sucking my thumb in a corner somewhere. Still true.

Tom Viola and Frank Conway at Broadway Cares/Equity Fights AIDS embraced the idea for this book immediately and were supportive and helpful throughout the journey.

There are a number of dear friends whose support included, but was not limited to, helping me find an appropriate agent and publisher, and/or get access to the more elusive women in this book. They are a loving and supportive bunch: Pam Bernstein, Elizabeth Bauman, Ben Baur, Scott Cameron, John Carroll, Danielle Chambers, Richard Cohen, Mara Davi Gaines, Frank DeCaro, Jeffrey Dersh, Jeffrey Epstein, Barrett Foa, Charlie Finlay, Mary Francis, Sue Goodman, Deidre Goodwin, Chad Hodge, Barry Hoff, Cheryl Keller, Tom Kirdahy, Korbin Krauss, Harry Kullijian, Jeffrey Landman, Wendy Lefkon, Tom Leonardis, Norm Lewis, Judith Light, Tom Lowe, Kevin McClain, James Morgan, Julia Murney, Justin Peebles, Michael Paternostro, Billy Porter, Grahame Pratt, Joe Quenqua, Anthony Rapp, Marc Shaiman, Mark Shenton, Michael Sinatra, Timothy Slope, Billy Stritch, John Tartaglia, Michael Urie, Bruce Vilanch, Frank Vlastnik, Ken Werther, Justin Michael Wilcox, Gilles Wheeler, John Lloyd Young, George Youngdahl, and David Zippel.

There is also a group of people who work with the women in this book as assistants, publicists, managers, or friends who were charged with handling the onslaught of communications from me. My hat is off to Rosie Bentinck, Harlan Boll, Cathy Brighenti, Robert Callely, Jill C. Frese, Jill Fritzo, Nick Fiveash, Lisa Goldberg, Judy Katz, Michele Kole, Travis Milliken, Michele Paape, Heather Reynolds, Philip Rinaldi, Daniele Thomas, Julie Trussell, and Erica Tuchman.

Then there are the people other than me who worked on the book. Ken Wright at Writer's House was one of the first believers in this project and he invaluably helped me shape the proposal that ultimately sold the book.

I couldn't ask for a better agent/cheerleader than Rob McQuilkin, at Lippincott Massie McQuilkin. Thanks, too, to Christina Shideler for her assistance.

Norman Hirschy and his wonderful team at Oxford University Press convinced me with their enthusiasm that Oxford was the home for this book. I am deeply grateful for their wisdom, their work, and their faith.

Melinda Berk, you listened to every annoying story, you read every one of these pages, suffering through my typos and ego. You gave me perspective. And sometimes you even transcribed for me. Your support throughout was absolute and I am forever indebted.

Thank you Elaine Paige for graciously contributing the book's foreword.

And, of course, thank you to all of the women in these pages, who spent hours and hours talking to me. I thank them for the generosity of their time, their stories, and sometimes even their food.

Finally, my parents. It was they who first took me to the theater at age five and it was they who knew that at eleven, I NEEDED to see Ethel Merman in concert. My sisters joined them in tolerating my cast albums blaring through the house, and the four of them have always believed in me, even when I had my own doubts on the topic. My thanks and love to my parents, Ann and Donald Shapiro, my sisters, Rona Shapiro and Emma Morgan. Later they were joined by the family that loves me even though they don't have to: Arlene Shapiro, David Franklin, Paul Ehrlich, and my amazing nieces Noa and Hallel Shapiro-Franklin, who still go the theater wide-eyed.

David Wolf, I am sorry you missed this. You really would have liked it.

Index

Note: Numbers in **boldface** type indicate pages with illustrations.

CPSIA information can be obtained
at www.ICGtesting.com
Printed in the USA
BVHW011250310722
643171BV00006B/9